ACADEMIC FREEDOM
IN THE WIRED WORLD

ACADEMIC FREEDOM IN THE WIRED WORLD

POLITICAL EXTREMISM, CORPORATE POWER, AND THE UNIVERSITY

ROBERT O'NEIL

Viva Books

New Delhi | Mumbai | Chennai | Kolkata | Bangalore | Hyderabad | Kochi | Guwahati

First Indian Edition 2010

VIVA BOOKS PRIVATE LIMITED

- 4737/23 Ansari Road, Daryaganj, New Delhi 110 002
  E-mail: vivadelhi@vivagroupindia.net, Tel. 42242200
- Plot No. 76, Service Industries, Shirvane, Sector 1, Nerul, Navi Mumbai 400 706
  E-mail: vivamumbai@vivagroupindia.net, Tel. 27721273, 27721274
- Jamals Fazal Chambers, 26 Greams Road, Chennai 600 006
  E-mail: vivachennai@vivagroupindia.net, Tel. 28290304, 28294241
- B-103, Jindal Towers, 21/1A/3 Darga Road, Kolkata 700 017
  E-mail: vivakolkata@vivagroupindia.net, Tel. 22836381, 22816713
- 7, Sovereign Park Apartments, 56-58, K. R. Road, Basavanagudi, Bangalore 560 004
  E-mail: vivabangalore@vivagroupindia.net, Tel. 26607409, 26607410
- 101-102 Mughal Marc Aptt., 3-4-637 to 641, Narayanguda, Hyderabad 500 029
  E-mail: vivahyderabad@vivagroupindia.net, Tel. 27564481, 27564482
- First Floor, Beevi Towers, SRM Road, Kaloor, Kochi 682 018, Kerala
  E-mail: vivakochi@vivagroupindia.net, Tel: 0484-2403055, 2403056
- 232, GNB Road, Beside UCO Bank, Silpukhuri, Guwahati 781 003
  E-mail: vivaguwahati@vivagroupindia.net, Tel: 0361-2666386

Published by arrangement with

Harvard University Press
79, Garden Street, Cambridge
Massachussetts 02138-1499
USA

ISBN 978-81-309-1256-1

Published by Vinod Vasishtha for Viva Books Private Limited, 4737/23, Ansari Road, New Delhi - 110 002. Printed and bound by Anand Sons, Delhi - 110 092.

Contents

Acknowledgments

My introduction to academic freedom occurred soon after I began teaching law at the University of California-Berkeley in the early 1960s. Although during a half century as a professor, I have never been the target of any threat to my own free inquiry or expression, I have observed such threats directed at numerous colleagues. Initially as an active member of the American Association of University Professors (serving on two occasions as the organization's General Counsel) and, in the late 1960s, chairing the Academic Freedom Committee of the UC-Berkeley Academic Senate, I discovered three elusive truths that have helped materially to shape this book: First, that most university professors are relatively indifferent to academic freedom threats, which they typically view as someone else's problem; second, that the defense and survival of academic freedom depends most upon the commitment of those faculty members who are least likely to need its protection for their own careers; and third, that academic freedom is most severely tested by outspoken colleagues with whom most mainstream scholars would not normally or willingly associate. All of that makes academic freedom a curious concept, not easily defined and poorly understood beyond (and even within) the collegiate community. Yet there seemed much that ought to be said on this subject, especially by someone who had spent roughly equal periods as a professor and as a university president, chancellor, and provost.

Many friends and colleagues have substantially aided this project. My mentors in the AAUP deserve recognition and appreciation—my senior California colleague Sanford Kadish, who as association president designated me general counsel; long-time staff counsel Herman Orentlicher; and for the past four decades associate general secretary Jordan Kurland—have been exceptionally wise and patient teachers in this field. Many academic colleagues have graciously shared insight and wisdom—notably Walter Metzger, Ralph Brown, William Van Alstyne, Alison Bernstein, David Rabban, Robert Gorman, Matthew Finkin, Joan Wallach Scott,

Michael Olivas, Peggie Hollingsworth, Peter Byrne, and Donald Downs to mention but a few. Among AAUP staff colleagues, I owe a special debt to Ann Franke, Jonathan Alger, Donna Euben, Ann Springer, and Rachel Levinson for enabling me to help shape academic freedom safeguards in the courts, and to Jonathan Knight, Robert Kreiser, and Anita Levy (as Committee A stalwarts) for their guidance and wisdom in the handling of invariably challenging academic freedom cases.

The vital research that made this book possible reflects the commitment of a creative and conscientious group of University of Virginia law students, notably Brandon Butler, Brian Tiemann, and John Anderson. Rebecca Schoff, who joined the project near its conclusion, merits special appreciation and commendation for her scrutiny (both meticulous and perceptive) of the entire manuscript and page proofs, as well as invaluable preparation of the index. Amy McClung, the administrator of the Thomas Jefferson Center, read (and improved) the entire text in several formats, as well as ensuring both its accuracy and its electronic mobility. The Center's program could not have flourished during the director's distraction without the constant guidance and imaginative collaboration of associate director Josh Wheeler.

Finally, this book benefits from the editorial guidance and insight of two people who deserve special recognition. Elizabeth Knoll of the Harvard University Press not only sensed the potential for a new and different approach to academic freedom, but also shaped the task boldly and imaginatively. Realizing that potential was the singular contribution of my wife, Karen Elson O'Neil, a seasoned English teacher and college counselor who appreciated far better than I what could be accomplished by such a study. As she has done with every writing project these last forty years, Karen kept me on the proper course, as well as shared in the nurture of our four children and seven grandchildren.

Karen comes honestly by her appreciation of academic freedom, for it is to her father, Alex Elson, this book is appropriately dedicated. During the darkest days of the McCarthy era, he volunteered his time and counsel as a practicing attorney to the defense of more than a hundred University of Chicago, Northwestern, and other Chicago-area faculty members and professionals who had become suspect because of their political views or affiliations or writings. That he did at great personal risk, long before the protection of academic freedom became fashionable and widely accepted.

1

Discovering Academic Freedom

In late January 2006, Northwestern University engineering professor Arthur Butz publicly endorsed the views of Iranian president Mahmoud Ahmadinejad, who had termed the Holocaust a "myth." "I congratulate him [Ahmadinejad] on becoming the first head of state to speak out clearly on these issues," announced Butz, adding his "regret that it was not a Western head of state." Professor Butz is no stranger to controversy on the subject of the Holocaust. The publication in 1976 of his book, *The Hoax of the Twentieth Century,* established his reputation as the most outspoken Holocaust denier among American university faculties. Two decades later, the same views appeared on the engineering professor's Northwestern University webpage, reopening old wounds and reviving intense controversy. Public expression of support for Ahmadinejad's statements might thus have been anticipated, although few in Evanston or elsewhere were fully prepared to hear such shocking views from an American academic.[1]

The response was immediate and intense. The executive director of the Holocaust Foundation of Illinois declared that "Butz's most recent invective demonstrates the power of hate to rally extremists, anti-Semites and Holocaust deniers out from under their rocks throughout the world." Benjamin Sommer, a Northwestern religion professor and director of the university's Crown Family Center for Jewish Studies, observed that Butz's latest outburst could be even more damaging than his earlier statements because he was now endorsing the views of an avowedly anti-Semitic world leader, who had earlier called for the destruction of Israel. "There's a need this time to say something to the students and the larger community," insisted Sommer, "to make clear what the faculty tend to regard as self-evident, that of course, we think this person's an outrageous fool." Several hundred Northwestern students promptly signed a petition that called upon the administration to take action and to prevent Butz from causing future embarrassment.[2]

Faculty condemnation followed soon thereafter. A group of Butz's immediate engineering colleagues were so concerned that "he's tarnishing the reputation of our department," they felt moved to convey their condemnation through a letter to the *Chicago Tribune*. The letter concluded with an unequivocal rebuke: "We repudiate Butz [and] we wish that he would leave our department and our university and stop trading on our reputation for academic excellence." The letter amplified the basis for this harsh view. "His words and deeds in this regard are an extreme embarrassment to our department and to Northwestern," wrote Butz's closest faculty peers, adding that their colleague's "Holocaust denial is an affront to our humanity and our standards as scholars, and hence mandates our censure."[3]

The response of Northwestern's administration, though predictable, was noteworthy. President Henry Bienen began his e-mail to the university community by noting that Butz's latest statement reflected solely the errant professor's personal views, adding that "his reprehensible opinions on this issue are an embarrassment to Northwestern." But the official announcement did not stop there. President Bienen continued: "We cannot take action based on the content of what Butz says regarding the Holocaust—however odious it may be—without undermining the vital principle of intellectual freedom that all academic institutions serve to protect." This latest defense of Butz's right to make outrageous statements while remaining a Northwestern professor was wholly consistent with the university's official posture over the past three decades, ever since publication of the infamous book established its author as an ardent Holocaust denier.[4]

The Northwestern administration was not alone in taking such a bold position in Butz's defense. That very evening the incident was featured on the Fox News show *The O'Reilly Factor*. Host Bill O'Reilly, a seemingly unlikely champion of free expression, interviewed Emory University professor Deborah Lipstadt, a distinguished Holocaust scholar and persistent critic of Butz and other Holocaust deniers. When asked what institutional response she would deem most appropriate, Professor Lipstadt suggested that "the guy shouldn't be allowed in the classroom. . . . [And he] shouldn't be near the students." O'Reilly seemed troubled by this approach and asked his guest, "Wouldn't that be a violation of some kind of academic freedom?" After eliciting a brief negative response, O'Reilly insisted that any such disposition would be "punishing him." The basis for that view, in O'Reilly's words, bears attention: "You [Lipstadt] teach at a university and you know what the university is. That it's a place where all views, even abhorrent views, are tolerated for the sake of freedom of expression. You don't want to inhibit anybody."[5]

Northwestern's president and Fox News' talk-show host made essentially the same point; indeed, O'Reilly's statement of this basic precept may even have been slightly more forceful. Clearly the protection that Professor Butz has received over three decades would not be afforded to anyone other than a university professor—not to a business executive, not to a government official, not even to a university professional employee holding a nonfaculty position. The central question posed by this and many other incidents involving outspoken scholars is: why are university teachers treated so differently and what are the dimensions and implications of that difference?

The starting point for understanding the rationale for academic freedom is the special nature of a university as a singular institution. On the very issue of tolerating Holocaust deniers, former Cornell University president Frank Rhodes explained recently that "free and open debate on a wide range of issues, however outrageous or offensive some of them may be, lies at the heart of a university community."[6] Mary Burgan, distinguished professor of English at Indiana University and for a decade general secretary of the American Association of University Professors, explained it in this way: "The University is a place for going to the source of ideas that threaten us—for finding causes, explaining problems, and seeking out solutions based on knowledge."[7] Columbia University president (formerly president of the University of Michigan) Lee Bollinger, who is no stranger to campus controversy, has recently insisted that "the health and vigor of universities depend upon our fidelity to the unique responsibilities of our profession. Many people say that the primary purpose of a university is to preserve and advance our understanding of life, the world and the universe. They say that it is to discover truth, to transmit as much of human understanding as we can from one generation to the next and add as much new knowledge as we can to the store of human knowledge." To these attributes Bollinger would add one more of his own: "Universities are also charged with nurturing a distinctive intellectual character—what I would call a scholarly temperament."[8]

Such defenses of an open and tolerant university are not confined to professors and administrators. Writing in the summer of 2006 about several recent faculty outbursts, including the latest Butz incident, *Chicago Tribune* columnist Steve Chapman conceded that some students and families might "think their [tuition] money is being misused when it goes into the pockets of instructors like these." His response, however, went far beyond the immediate controversies: "Their dollars are really going to a broader and entirely worthy purpose, namely open inquiry in the pursuit of truth. [Such outspoken professors] have reached crazy and offensive conclusions, but just as bad movies can heighten our appreciation for good ones, their errors can sharpen our perception of the truth." Chapman closed his column with a largely pragmatic premise in support of such tolerance: "[S]ilencing them doesn't refute their arguments. You can't refute an argument without first hearing it. To remove them from teaching is to lend credence by suggesting we're afraid they may change minds. In fact, the best antidote to error is unbridled, vigorous and searching debate. When that sort of debate occurs, the truth has nothing to fear."[9]

While much more could be said about the essential nature of a university, such statements identify the distinctive character of the one and only institution in American society that is unambiguously committed to the quest for truth and the advancement of knowledge and within which no avenue to those ends may be closed, blocked, or declared to be "off limits." Such recognition does not, however, automatically make the case for protecting academic freedom in general. Indeed, it only invites a further set of even harder questions: Why, for example, within a university, are its professors the only employees who are fully insulated from sanctions for public expression of abhorrent views? And why do we insist that a professor like Arthur Butz enjoy total immunity for the persistent public proclamation of demonstrably false—and deeply injurious—opinions about world history?

Indeed, as eminent a scholar as Emory's Deborah Lipstadt (the Holocaust expert to whom Fox News turned for the Butz segment) fully supports academic freedom, but she questions whether it properly extends this far. In her judgment, which is widely shared by thoughtful observers within and beyond the academic world, Holocaust denial simply cannot be accepted as a "view" or "viewpoint" for which tolerance is warranted, much less compelled. There is more to the argument, and it merits close scrutiny. Professor Lipstadt recalls that in the early 1990s the Organization of American Historians (OAH) was riven by discord over whether to publish a call for papers from a journal that featured "revisionist" views on topics such as the Holocaust. She considered the OAH decision to carry the notice—premised upon the organization's "commitments to freedom of expression and historical truth"—wrong at the time and still does. She found naïve the suggestion that OAH should "pressure" the maverick journal to abide by international standards of scholarship, including peer review. "Engaging them in reasoned discussion," she insisted, "would be the equivalent of engaging a Ku Klux Klan wizard in a balanced discussion of African Americans' place in society."[10]

Returning to the current controversy over Nazi atrocities, Lipstadt and those who share her views emphasize not only that Holocaust denial is demonstrably false and severely damaging to the psychological well-being of millions of Americans, but also that protecting it sets a dangerous precedent. Such tolerance, she argues, "suggests that if correctly cast and properly camouflaged, a wide range of attacks on truth and history have a good chance of finding a foothold among coming generations." Thus the issue is clearly joined in ways that demand a more probing response than the ipse dixit that most champions of academic freedom usually offer.

The countervailing case for tolerating such bizarre views as Holocaust denial rests partly, though only partly, on the unique role of a university as the one institution in our society that can afford to admit an infinite range of views—indeed, it cannot afford *not* to be open and accessible to all opinions. There is also a nagging doubt about the "certainty" on which the exclusionary case rests. Every person of any intelligence knows that Holocaust denial is irresponsible nonsense, readily refutable by abundant facts and figures. Yet Galileo's detractors were equally sure that his unorthodox view of the solar system was both demonstrably false and dangerous and had to be suppressed for the best interests of civilized society. Granting that the analogy between Galileo and Butz is imperfect, lessons learned from the time of Galileo counsel us today to let Butz have his say, however outrageous and opprobrious his views may seem.

Two practical considerations militate in the same direction. The chairman of Northwestern's German Department, Professor Peter Hayes, urged his colleagues not to "overreact" to the latest tirade, noting that Butz "loves the attention [since] this is how he publicizes his crazy views, and we should just treat them with the contempt they deserve."[11] Equally pragmatic, a Northwestern undergraduate who had drafted an anti-Butz petition, conceded no formal sanction would comport with the institutional commitment to academic freedom. Instead, she urged, "there's much that can be done in terms of taking moral and ethical stands against this lie," adding that "we need to prove him wrong through long-lasting education and awareness."[12] She might have added that those who would drive Butz underground would, perforce, moot the prospect of any such educational process.

The case for less than total tolerance of professorial perversity has another, in some ways even more troubling, asymmetry. The central premise of a university's openness to all ideas and opinions rests largely on its commitment to seek the truth and advance knowledge. Accordingly, even some articulate defenders of academic freedom would confine its scope to statements uttered or published within the speaker's area of expertise. That concept would probably leave a Holocaust-denying electrical engineer out in the cold. Even Professor Butz's strongest defenders (and there are more than a handful) would concede that his widely publicized Holocaust denial does little if anything to advance our understanding of history or knowledge of events that occurred in the 1930s. The subject matter is quite remote from his areas of expertise in electrical engineering, and he does not invoke serious scholarship or inquiry on the topic. Thus it becomes almost impossible to frame the case for Holocaust denial by someone like Butz in terms of the "advancing truth and knowledge" rationale for academic freedom. Once again, however, the exception may severely test the rule, but it does not necessarily invalidate it. The grounds on which we might deny protection to someone as remote from the subject of discussion as Butz may apply clearly and easily to his case but with less ease or certainty in cases where the dissonance between opinion and expertise is less pronounced. The Galileo problem is with us once again and gives us pause here as well.

What, then, if Professor Butz's academic discipline were in fact modern European history? Superficially, the case for protection might seem stronger. Indeed, some critics, such as Professor Lipstadt, seem to assume that protecting the actual Arthur Butz would require at least comparable treatment of a Holocaust denier whose heresy arises within his field of expertise. Ironically, the consensus of the academic freedom community is precisely the opposite. The American Association of University Professors, whose policies provide the gold standard for such matters, has long posited that even tenured professors may be dismissed when they have demonstrated a clear lack of "fitness . . . in their professional capacities as teachers or researchers."[13] This focus on fitness becomes crucial to understanding what academic freedom does not protect.

Although scholars in most fields might alienate colleagues and forfeit friends by going about publicly proclaiming that the earth's surface is really flat, loss of university employment could not follow. But suppose the flat-earth advocate is a geologist or geographer. Now the university would presumably charge such a person with demonstrated "lack of fitness," because knowledge of the actual contours of the earth's surface is crucial to competence in the scholar's field. Such charges would need to be proved before a panel of faculty peers, to be sure, but that would not be difficult. At this point, academic freedom, quite appropriately, turns out to protect less than freedom of speech under the First Amendment, since the flat-earth geologist or geographer would be fully protected against any nonuniversity sanctions.

A Holocaust-denying modern European historian would and should be treated in the same way. Insisting that the Holocaust never happened—that 6 million Jews committed suicide or were victims of some mysterious epidemic—simply cannot be reconciled with the degree of fitness or competence one must bring to the study of European history. Where the inaccuracy of such a statement may be documented with certainty, and where the advancement of knowledge in a particular field depends on accuracy and fidelity, such a judgment may and would be made within the academic community.

Such a resolution of this hypothetical case is in fact quite consistent with Northwestern's treatment of the real Professor Butz. Since the issue first arose in 1976, the university has imposed only two conditions for his continued membership on the faculty: one, that Butz continue to meet the general expectations for teaching and research in electrical engineering; and two, that he never impose his views on students and, most especially, never mention them in his classes. Both conditions seem to have been scrupulously observed.

Ironically, the only person at Northwestern ever charged with crossing the forbidden line was an adjunct instructor in engineering, Sheldon Epstein, who made Holocaust-affirming materials available to his students. The relationship between that subject and the engineering course to which Epstein was assigned as an adjunct seemed tenuous at best, and Epstein's appointment was not renewed. When a reporter asked why Butz continued to be protected, the dean replied that Butz had never mentioned the Holocaust in class; "if he did," the dean cautioned, "we would consider it grounds for bringing him up on charges for dismissal from the faculty."[14]

Pressing the "unfitness" concept too far may be risky, however. One is tempted to assimilate to the flat-earth geologist a Creationist who teaches biology while espousing the Biblical view of life's origins. On that issue, academic freedom experts are understandably divided. The explanation of the origins of human life offered in the Book of Genesis may seem as "demonstrably false" as the flat-earth position or Holocaust denial. Accordingly, many would argue that the creationist should suffer a similar fate. On the other hand, the Darwinian view is labeled a "theory," in which there are still elements not all of which have been established with the certainty that we know the earth's curvature. Moreover, there are variants such as "Intelligent Design" that claim to eschew Biblical inspiration and invoke semi-scientific premises. Thus the case for caution acquires a somewhat greater force than in the clearest and most egregious of the "unfitness" cases.

This discussion brings us back once again to the real Arthur Butz. One has the uneasy feeling that he has been protected in part because what he says about the Holocaust really doesn't matter—that having no expertise in the subject matter makes his absurd claims dismissible in ways that similar views from an expert would not be. That is indeed the distinction that the doctrine of academic freedom recognizes, though the reasoning is slightly different. It is not so much that the academic community tolerates incompetence among nonexperts as that the expectations for those who are expert are exceptionally high, and do not impose comparable responsibilities on those from remote disciplines. Wholly consistent is Northwestern's expectation that Butz continue to perform adequately his day-job as a teacher and researcher in electrical engineering. That obligation includes confining his classes to the assigned subject matter, and most especially keeping any Holocaust discussion out of those classes. The university may well find his "reprehensible" opinions—as President Bienen has recently reaffirmed—an "embarrassment to Northwestern." But such embarrassment is tolerated as the price of keeping the university open to a broad and diverse array of views, some of which may be even worse than "embarrassing" but are tolerated nonetheless.

One basic issue that has been deferred, but must now be addressed, is the scope of whatever freedom merits protection. Definitions prove surprisingly elusive. The basic policy of the American Association of University Professors, its "1940 Statement of Principles on Academic Freedom and Tenure," declares that a university teacher is entitled to three things: "full freedom in research and in the publication of the results . . . freedom in the classroom in discussing his subject . . . and when he speaks and writes as a citizen [freedom] from institutional censorship or discipline."

Each of the freedoms is qualified in important respects; freedom in research is "subject to the adequate performance of his other duties;" freedom in the classroom does not include "introduc[ing] into his teaching controversial matter which has no relation to his subject;" and freedom to speak as a citizen recognizes that a professor "should at all times be accurate, should exercise appropriate restraint, should show respect for the opinions of others, and should make every effort to indicate that he is not an institutional spokesman."[15]

Such an enumeration of the elements of academic freedom at once raises serious questions of scope and application. Freedom in the classroom and in the publication of research seems beyond question, although in practice even safeguards in these arenas have occasionally proved problematic, as we shall discover. The sticking point is the third element of the AAUP policy—the professor's right to speak as a citizen without institutional constraint or sanction. Even so staunch a defender of academic freedom as Professor William Van Alstyne of the College of William and Mary has long been troubled by the ready assimilation of academic speech and extracurricular political expression. For him, and for others who take a more limited view on this issue, as a colleague recently summarized his position, "one cannot . . . abstract a liberty for utterance unrelated to vocation from a doctrine grounded in the need to protect vocational utterance." Indeed, Van Alstyne adds, the core value of academic freedom as a vital safeguard for controversial research and teaching risks dilution by being overextended to situations where it does not really belong.[16]

The same point was made rather differently, though consistently, by longtime Boston University president John Silber (shortly before he assumed that post) in justifying the denial of reappointment to a nontenured philosopher at the University of Texas who had made seriously false statements in the course of a speech from the steps of the state capitol. Such deliberate falsehoods, in Silber's view, were "a clear case of poisoning the well in the marketplace of ideas and a gross betrayal of academic freedom through gross academic irresponsibility." Academic freedom did not encompass such expression, Silber insisted, because "the academic neither needs nor deserves greater protection for his political freedom than that afforded the ordinary citizen."[17]

Suffice it to say at this point that even those who have carefully studied and defended academic freedom may agree on the rationale but may also differ substantially when it comes to the definition and scope of this concept. The divergence of views on the issue of extramural utterances, such as letters to a newspaper or magazine, radio and television appearances, and now Internet postings or e-mail messages, is both fascinating and troubling. One might observe that, even going back a century to a time before academic freedom was generally recognized, it was just such extracurricular expressions of unpopular or unorthodox views that often got controversial scholars into trouble. Yet it is important to note that not every proponent of academic freedom would agree that someone like Professor Butz should be protected when he speaks and writes outside his discipline, off campus, and in media that clearly are not scholarly journals. Later chapters revisit this paradoxical issue.

One further question has been deferred but should now be addressed: Granting that broad tolerance of abhorrent views is vital for a university—in contrast to all other institutions in our society—what's so special about professors? Many other university employees are unquestionably engaged in the quest for truth and the advancement of knowledge, but they lack comparable protection. Members of the professional library staff, some student personnel officers, and a host of laboratory scientists who hold no professorial rank all engage in the core mission of the university and are potentially at risk for the expression of unpopular views, publication of controversial research results, or otherwise crossing or offending the dominant mores of society. Conversely, most people who hold professorial rank seldom if ever engender or invite controversy and thus arguably would be as secure as they need to be without any protections along the lines of academic freedom. Thus a case could be made that the safeguards of academic freedom should be reserved for the relatively few members of the academic community who truly need it, regardless of the rank or title they hold.

Appealing though such a restructuring might seem, practical and even principled objections abound. For one, such protection needs to be established before the fact, in ways that are "available to those who discover they need it" approach could not possibly satisfy, if it is to embolden those who press the frontiers of knowledge and understanding. Should the scope of such protection be tied to the subject matter a person studies rather than to a scholar's rank or position, there would be intolerable and unpredictable variations in a system that urgently needs stability and certainty to serve its essential purpose. Finally, it is overwhelmingly professors who engage in and publish the results of research that is likely to evoke displeasure from trustees, donors, legislators, and others who could demand their silence or removal if they lacked such protection. The relatively few nonprofessorial professionals who may be at comparable risk can be and often are shielded against reprisal even without such formal safeguards as faculty tenure. Thus the current link between the protection that academic freedom affords and the risks against which it guards is both logical and defensible, if only because professors' assigned tasks within the academy are invariably the most provocative.

Finally, there is a unique nexus between the professor's calling and the search for truth. The late James O. Freedman, president of the University of Iowa, Dartmouth College, and the American Academy of Arts and Sciences, wrote poignantly of the costs of being a university professor and juxtaposed them with the undoubted benefits of living a scholar's life. First among those costs, he noted, "is the continuous struggle to learn afresh what remains fundamental about a discipline that is always evolving, while bringing that language to life in the minds of new students." Perhaps the greatest of such costs, as Freedman saw them, "is the responsibility to create new knowledge, whether in the library, the laboratory, or the studio. . . . When a professor confronts the emptiness of the unwritten page, the silence of the laboratory instrument, the blankness of the computer screen, all certainties evaporate."[18] So the special treatment of professors, not only among professionals in the larger society but even among university professionals, reflects the ultimate dependence of society upon their creativity and their willingness to take risks in exercising that creativity.

There remains in this early analysis another, even more basic, paradox: If academic freedom literally protects the "freedom of the academy," how does it end up safeguarding individual members of the academy from adverse institutional judgments? Granting that Northwestern University and especially its faculty should have the final say about Professor Butz's professional position—free from the Illinois legislature and governor, the city council of Evanston, the alumni association, major donors, and a host of others who might wish to intrude—what if the faculty of electrical engineering to a person concluded that their errant colleague must be removed? Were the university then to bring dismissal charges on that basis, does it still make sense to protect Professor Butz on the ground that (as President Bienen has consistently said) "we cannot take action based on the content of what Butz says . . ., without undermining the vital principle of intellectual freedom"?

Acclaimed experts on academic freedom are curiously divided on that issue. Many agree completely with President Bienen, refusing to permit such action even when the actors are the very entities that academic freedom in large measure protects. Others, with equal conviction, insist that where institutional and individual interests diverge, the role of academic freedom is to protect the former. Georgetown's Professor Peter Byrne, for example, argues that "protection of institutional autonomy is the appropriate concern of constitutional academic freedom," so that "faculty should not be able legally to challenge good faith, internal personnel decisions as violations of academic freedom."[19] By that theory, academic freedom does indeed safeguard the "freedom of the academy" but does not necessarily protect every errant member of that community from adverse judgments by the institution. Nor does such analysis offer any guidance on an issue considered at length in Chapter 8—what happens when the academic freedom of professors seems to infringe or curtail the freedoms of students to learn, or to speak, or to worship freely? We return at much greater length to these perplexing questions in later chapters. Suffice it to say that President Bienen's view represents the conventional wisdom of the early twenty-first century.

Conditions have not always been nearly so protective of the outspoken professor as they are today. Indeed, a striking feature of the doctrine of academic freedom is the recency of its emergence. A century ago and even less, such safeguards were uncertain and varied widely. If one goes back to the previous century, the situation for academics was even less comfortable. Professor Byrne, who has extensively studied academic freedom and its roots, has observed that "in the old-time college, prior to the Civil War, the concept of academic freedom was literally inconceivable." The reason for such a condition was not hard to find; even the major state universities of the early nineteenth century, let alone the major private colleges, had as their goal (in Byrne's account) "to train young men in religious piety and mental discipline as a preparation for the clergy and other gentlemanly professions, such as law and medicine."[20]

The University of Virginia, opened in 1826, was the first truly secular institution of higher learning—a unique attribute of which its founder, Thomas Jefferson, was constantly reminded by critics who attacked him mercilessly for creating a "Godless institution." His commitment was not only to keep church and state separate but also to establish a university "based on the illimitable freedom of the human mind . . . for here we are not afraid to follow the truth wherever it may lead, nor to tolerate any error so long as reason is left free to combat it." Yet even in Charlottesville, academic freedom as we know it today was not fully guaranteed; it was Jefferson himself who (if left to his own counsel) would almost certainly have barred the study in government classes of *The Federalist.* "It is our duty," he wrote to fellow members of the charter governing board, "to guard against such principles being disseminated among our youth, and the diffusion of that poison, by a previous prescription of the texts to be followed in their discourses." As on many other occasions, James Madison's wiser counsel prevailed, and (with certain cautions) *The Federalist* and other texts uncongenial to early Republicans were allowed to be taught at Mr. Jefferson's university.[21]

A half century later, the closing years of the nineteenth century brought early recognition that a learning environment required broad latitude for the scope of inquiry. Many of the formerly sectarian institutions had by now reduced their dependence on religious bodies, and they were thus freer not only to pursue a broader range of subjects, but also to approach them in a less inhibited fashion than had their predecessors. Professor Byrne describes this process as "a movement from a paradigm of fixed values vouchsafed by religious faiths to one of relative truths continuously revised by scientific endeavor." Thus in the post–Civil War period, "universities became secular; religion was usually retained only as a polite ornament."[22]

Such profound structural changes did not, however, automatically ensure greater latitude for professors who expressed controversial views. The only meaningful protection for outspoken scholars remained little more than the wholly voluntary commitment of benign or enlightened governing boards. Gradually, faculties began to assert their collective interests in support of such freedom, inspired largely by the example of the major German universities, which by now had accorded their professors substantial leeway in scholarship and publication. Perhaps the earliest recognition of such a change occurred at the University of Wisconsin in the early 1890s. The university's board of regents startled the academic world by refusing (as some powerful people had demanded) to dismiss economist Richard Ely because of his strongly pro-labor and pro-strike views. In a major report on the case, the regents declared that their firm commitment to academic freedom was the university's central mission.

Two crucial sentences from the report have echoed through the century-plus since its release: "We cannot for a moment believe this knowledge has reached its final goal, or that the present condition of society is perfect. . . . Whatever may be the limitations which trammel inquiry elsewhere we believe the great state university of Wisconsin should ever encourage that continual sifting and winnowing by which alone truth can be found." The latter declaration is permanently inscribed on a bronze plaque in front of Bascom

Hall, the administration building of the Madison campus, as a durable reminder of the role of academic freedom in the life of at least one great state university.

These principles faced an early test a decade and a half later when some more conservative regents attacked sociology professor Edward A. Ross for his association on campus with the renowned anarchist Emma Goldman and free-love advocate Peter Sercombe. Ross had earlier been dismissed by the fledgling Stanford University, at the insistence of one trustee whose industrialist friends and colleagues had been deeply offended by Ross's unorthodox advocacy of populist economic principles. He then found refuge in Madison, where a different set of concerns confronted him and set in motion another wave of threats. But after Wisconsin faculty and students had rallied to Ross's defense, President Charles Van Hise refused to take any action against him. It was after this encounter that the graduating class commissioned the bronze plaque with the "sifting and winnowing" statement. Initially an embarrassed board of regents refused to accept the plaque, apparently still smarting from the Ross episode, but a few years later the board relented and gave the academic-freedom pledge a position of unmatched prominence and visibility in front of the administration building, which it still enjoys.[23]

The Wisconsin approach still represented much more the exception than the rule. It would be some time before such values were anywhere near universally accepted. Powerful trustees and donors found increasingly uncongenial the publicly expressed views of professors in the newly emerging social sciences and not infrequently sought to silence—or at least banish—such heresies. During and soon after World War I, conditions even on the seemingly safest of campuses were unpredictable. When in 1915 the University of Pennsylvania dismissed nonrevolutionary Marxist professor Scott Nearing from the faculty of the Wharton School because his published views angered many trustees, not only was there modest protest, but Nearing became essentially an academic pariah until the University of Toledo showed compassion and took him in. Other outspoken social scientists faced similar threats, ending either in dismissal or resignation, at quite reputable institutions.

However, in the same year as the Nearing dismissal, Harvard president A. Lawrence Lowell refused to remove a controversial professor because of his pro-German utterances and thereby risked forfeiture of a major gift. Lowell's defense of his bold step was quite pragmatic; the university that condemned one professor's public utterances, he explained, thereby implied its acceptance—if not its endorsement—of every other faculty member's statements. This practical notion of institutional neutrality would prove helpful to the burgeoning effort to safeguard academic freedom. Much of this evolution involved the embryonic American Association of University Professors, the role of which is described in the next chapter. For the moment, it should suffice to note that the universal acceptance of academic freedom, by private as well as state universities, is a surprisingly recent phenomenon.[24] It is also a surprisingly fragile concept, as we are reminded by recalling the dismissal on ideological grounds of nearly a hundred tenured or tenure-track faculty during the McCarthy era. The process of protecting academic freedom is in every sense a work in progress.

Even though no single date can be identified as the moment at which academic freedom could be said to be secure—if that has ever been the case—the second half of the twentieth century did see a steady and impressive growth in the number of institutions that could assure prospective faculty members that they would be protected in their teaching, research, and extramural utterances. Even the relatively few institutions (e.g., Hampshire College in western Massachusetts) that have never offered tenure to their faculties have been scrupulous in their commitment to protecting academic freedom by other means. (Later chapters probe more deeply the nexus between academic freedom and tenure.)

The emergence of what today seems a nearly universal acceptance of academic freedom for university professors reflects myriad factors within and far beyond higher education. This process has involved numerous organizations, perhaps most notably but by no means solely the American Association of University Professors. Other faculty groups, such as the National Education Association and the American Federation of Teachers, have played significant parts, as have the major presidential groups, such as the American Council on Education, the Association of American Universities, and especially the American Association of Colleges and Universities. Their respective contributions need now to be probed more deeply, as preludes to better understanding the disposition of a case such as that of Professor Butz. That appraisal is the focus of the following chapter.

2

Protecting Academic Freedom

In the mid-1990s, Brigham Young University was eager to establish on its campus a Phi Beta Kappa chapter as part of its quest for major university status. An application had been filed with the national scholarly society and was awaiting review. At its 1998 annual meeting, however, the American Association of University Professors (AAUP) voted to censure the BYU administration because of the way it had treated several of its professors who were members of the Church of Latter-day Saints, with which the university had close ties. The Phi Beta Kappa application was already in trouble because of a BYU policy that demanded recognition of the primacy of Christianity, without which "any education is inadequate." The national scholarly society has long taken respect for academic freedom into account in recognizing new chapters; Secretary Douglas Foard explained that "what Phi Beta Kappa is about is the quest of excellence and open-ended inquiry." Thus the AAUP censure vote effectively sealed the fate of BYU's quest for a Phi Beta Kappa chapter for no reason other than (in Foard's words) its "limitation on academic freedom."[1] The elite national honor society has long refused to admit to membership any institution that has been placed on the AAUP's censure list—one of several grave consequences of incurring the condemnation of the faculty organization and its investigative process.

Other repercussions may also follow. Faculty recruitment would almost certainly face new obstacles, since learned societies such as the Modern Language Association and the American Historical Association keep members apprised of the AAUP's censure list and suggest that those considering academic appointments should at least be conscious of such collegial condemnation. Accrediting groups, both regional and specialized, do take academic freedom into account, and in extreme circumstances, the renewal of accreditation has been qualified or tempered as a result of severe transgressions, whether or not actual censure was imposed. Brigham Young officials thus learned a lesson that has been replicated many times across the American academic landscape—that threats to academic freedom grave enough to merit AAUP's ultimate sanction are not lightly overlooked, nor are they solely of concern to the organization that makes such a judgment.[2]

The focus of this chapter is the means by which academic freedom has been and is protected. In large measure, such protection derives from contractual commitments that are made by institutions of higher learning at the time of initial faculty appointments and, even more clearly, when a professor is granted tenure. Yet if the only consequence of terminating a faculty appointment were the risk of incurring possible liability in a civil suit for damages based on a breach of contract, the deterrent to such adverse actions would be modest to nonexistent. Such potential liability might be treated, at least by the cynical or venal among academic administrators, as simply a cost of doing business. If the value, financial and otherwise, of getting an obnoxious or contentious professor off the roster and banished from the campus clearly exceeded the potential damages in a lawsuit or settlement, and that were the sole hazard of taking such action, the temptation to terminate the troublemaker would be powerful indeed. Thus, to make academic freedom effective, there must be some deterrent substantially stronger than the prospect of fiscal liability.

Such protection occurs in several interdependent forms. At the core, there is the collective commitment of the American academic community—virtually all learned and professional societies, most governing boards and administrators quite as much as professors—that protecting academic freedom demands a high tolerance for unorthodox and even bizarre or aberrant views. As noted in the previous chapter, such tolerance was not always the case. Indeed as recently as the early twentieth century, universities felt themselves largely free to impose sanctions on faculty who espoused what those in power deemed heretical views—and those professors who were dismissed or removed for their views had little or no recourse. The process of change began soon after the first decade of the century and has continued unabated ever since.

There are several major sources of protection, which we should appraise in order, beginning with faculty organizations, then turning to other academic concerned groups and contractual safeguards (including, of course, faculty unions and collective bargaining), and finally returning to the collective conscience of the academic community. As we review this rather complex terrain, it is important to caution that the American Association of University Professors—though a major player—is hardly the only game in town. We begin with AAUP simply because of its dominance of the field, but in so doing we must recognize that it represents only a modest fraction of the professoriate and that many champions of academic freedom find equal or greater support from other organizations, accompanied by misgivings in some quarters about the primacy of AAUP.

In 1915, a group of scholars, led by philosopher John Dewey, came together to draft a declaration in support of academic freedom. That year, the fledgling American Association of University Professors issued its "Declaration of Principles." That document, some twenty pages in length, canvassed a broad range of issues. Professor Walter Metzger of Columbia University, the nation's preeminent scholar of the history of academic freedom, has described the declaration in this way: "Utilitarian in temper and conviction, the theorists of 1915 did not view the expressional freedoms of academics as a bundle of rights. . . . They regarded them as corollaries of the contemporary public need for universities that would increase the sum of human knowledge and furnish experts for public service—new functions that had been added to the time-honored one of qualifying students for degrees."[3]

The drafters of the AAUP declaration, in explaining the necessity for such protection, characterized the emerging American university as an "intellectual experiment station, where new ideas may germinate and where their fruit, though still distasteful to the community as a whole, may be allowed to ripen until finally, perchance, it may become part of the accepted intellectual food of this nation and the world." Such a fragile institution must, the declaration continued, be prepared to tolerate a wide range of views, including those that might be unwelcome or even anathema to most members of the larger community. It must also tolerate the continued presence on its faculty of those scholars who expressed such views—if only because, like Galileo's hypothesis, today's folly may turn out to be tomorrow's wisdom. Thus institutions that sought to repress or silence such views and those who expressed them had forfeited the right to continuing respect in the academic community. Accordingly, concluded the declaration, any institution of higher learning "which lays restrictions on the intellectual freedom of its professors proclaims itself a proprietary institution, and should be so described whenever it makes a general application for funds and the public should be advised that the institution has no claim whatever to general support or regard."[4] The acceptance of these views was far from universal, even in polite and presumably sympathetic company. The *New York Times* editorialized about the issuance of the declaration and its newly proclaimed principles: " 'Academic freedom,' that is, the inalienable right of every college instructor to make a fool of himself and his college by . . . intemperate, sensational prattle about every subject under the heaven . . . and still keep on the payroll or be reft therefrom only by elaborate process, is cried to the winds by the organized dons."[5] Whatever might be said of the *Times'* dismissive view of the "intemperate" college instructor, the editorial's reference to "elaborate process" was not entirely unfair. A major element of the declaration was its recognition of the necessity for a formal procedure to terminate any continuing academic appointment. Coupled with the abstract protection of academic freedom was the concept of faculty tenure; Professor Metzger termed it "a new working plan, a series of concrete proposals concerning the acquisition and disposition of tenure citizenship that, when broadly refined and adopted, would represent a very great reform."[6]

By the close of the second decade of the twentieth century and the end of World War I, three vital elements of faculty security were in place. There was in the AAUP declaration a forceful statement of basic principles of academic freedom. There was also the nucleus of a system of tenure, in terms both of the concept of "indefinite appointment" or "appointment without term"—both implying a long duration if not permanence—and of elaborate and highly protective procedures that must be followed in the event that an institution chose to remove a professor. It soon became apparent that such safeguards would not suffice if they were limited to those professors who had already been granted formal tenure; thus AAUP policy has always treated the termination of a continuing faculty appointment before its stated expiration as a breach that is procedurally identical to the dismissal of a tenured professor.

Finally among the elements in place by the 1920s, there was an organization, created by and for the benefit of university faculty, committed not only to announcing protective principles but also to securing their adoption and to monitoring their observance. The latter task involved what has become, and remains to this day, a core component of AAUP's program as a defender of academic freedom and a source of consistent standards to judge violations—formally investigating and reporting on breaches of academic freedom and in extreme cases, imposing censure on an administration that has departed egregiously from the stated norms.

The next major step toward the acceptance of academic freedom was a shorter statement, adopted in 1925 by a conference convened by the

American Council on Education. The new version was immediately endorsed by the Association of American Colleges (at that time an organization composed chiefly of liberal arts colleges), and it paved the way for the development of a modified "Statement of Principles" issued in 1940. That statement has now been endorsed by virtually every learned society or academic disciplinary organization, now numbering over 170. Far more significant has been the eventual adherence of every major college and university, typically through formal action by its governing board and enshrined in faculty handbooks in a manner that represents a binding legal commitment to the faculty of each institution.

The 1940 statement opens with a declaration, deceptively simple in its brevity, that university professors are entitled to academic freedom in three core dimensions: "freedom in research and in publication of the results . . . freedom in the classroom in discussing their subject . . . and when they speak or write as citizens, [and freedom from] institutional censorship or discipline."[7] Each of the stated freedoms is immediately accompanied by important qualifications. With regard to research, the statement cautions that "research for pecuniary return should be based upon an understanding with the authorities of the institution." In the classroom, college teachers "should be careful not to introduce . . . controversial matter which has no relation to their subject." Finally, teachers who speak as citizens "should at all times be accurate, should exercise appropriate restraint, should show respect for the opinions of others, and should make every effort to indicate that they are not speaking for the institution."

The balance of the 1940 statement defines the vital elements of tenure, including the need for a clear declaration of the terms and conditions of every academic appointment, a finite probationary period during which the probationer fully enjoys academic freedom, and rigorous procedures for assessing charges that might lead to termination for "cause." (By implication, the safeguards for the nonrenewal of a probationary appointment are far less rigorous, though a separate policy issued in 1970 strongly urged some protections at such a critical stage in a faculty career.) A later and more detailed implementing statement also envisions that even tenured and continuing faculty appointments may be terminated for reasons other than cause—for example, for "financial exigency," though only when such dire conditions are "demonstrably bona fide."

Tenured faculty may also be terminated as a result of the good-faith discontinuance of a program or department, though only when such action is "based essentially upon educational considerations, as determined primarily by the faculty." Finally, a physical or mental disability may warrant termination, though only with "convincing medical evidence that the faculty member, even with reasonable accommodation, is no longer able to perform the essential duties of the position."

The welter of AAUP policies that define and protect academic freedom appear in a document commonly known as the "Redbook," periodically updated and augmented by new pronouncements. The current version contains a host of statements about faculty rights and responsibilities in such varied areas as artistic endeavor, research, electronic communications, personnel files, and harassment, along with the less fully protected interests of part-time and nontenure-track faculty. There are also statements about ideals of university governance, collective bargaining relations (since AAUP now represents and negotiates on behalf of a substantial number of unionized faculties), student rights, and accreditation, among many others matters of potential interest to the academic community.

What today assures the protection of academic freedom for university professors is the nearly universal adoption of the tenure system by American colleges and universities. Yet AAUP has never mandated such adherence and recognizes that an institution could adequately protect the interests of its faculty without offering tenure. The paradigm case is that of Hampshire College, a distinguished liberal arts institution in western Massachusetts founded in the 1960s. Hampshire offers faculty who meet its initial expectations contracts of five years in length.[8] These contracts may or may not be renewed; most in fact are renewed, although an occasional Hampshire professor has been denied a new contract well after a seven-year period, which is the maximum probationary term allowed to tenure-track institutions.

Of institutions like Hampshire and the few others that respect and protect academic freedom but do not award tenure, AAUP insists only that they scrupulously follow their own rules and that a nonrenewal (whether at five or twenty-five years) not be based upon activity or expression that academic freedom protects. To this day, Hampshire has never been the target of a formal AAUP investigation, much less a censure vote. Several other colleges that also opened in the 1960s without tenure—notably Washington's Evergreen State and the University of Texas Permian Basin campus—later modified their faculty personnel policies in ways that effectively provide tenure. St. Francis University in Joliet, Illinois, having long ago abolished tenure for its faculty, reinstated a traditional tenure system late in 2005 under the leadership of a new president. The Virginia Community College

System, within which faculty tenure was once abolished by action of the Virginia General Assembly, has managed over the years to achieve a de facto system of protection, affording to those who teach in the state's two-year colleges a substantial equivalent of the de jure tenure that could never be reestablished.

It would be comforting to report that such nearly universal adherence to AAUP principles has throughout the past century or so assured the primacy of academic freedom. Such a report would, however, be sadly naïve, even in relatively recent times. During the McCarthy era of the 1950s, at least a hundred tenured or continuing professors at American colleges and universities were dismissed, mainly for suspect political affiliations or even for refusing to expose or accuse colleagues when asked to do so by legislative committees. In her comprehensive study of this dreadful period, *No Ivory Tower*, Yeshiva University historian Ellen Schrecker has documented the plight of these professors and the shameful conduct of many of the nation's most eminent universities—Michigan, Washington, Harvard, and many others that today would be seen as bastions of academic freedom.[9] Although the AAUP was not totally ineffective during the McCarthy period, even its champions would concede that the association's response was too little and too late.[10] Other groups, such as the American Civil Liberties Union, were also unable to turn the tide or offer effective resistance to it in those dark days. There were investigations of the most egregious cases, and even a handful of censure actions, but little practical deterrence to the wave of repression that swept the country in the 1950s, sparing few college campuses in the process.

Where faculty interests fared relatively better, it was more because of courageous and/or creative university presidents than the actions or statements of faculty organizations. Indiana's longtime president Herman Wells managed to avoid any sanction against any member of his faculty (including some whose politics might have invited suspicion) through a bold and imaginative stroke. The state legislature's investigative committee members were invited to come to Bloomington and spend as much time as they wished, but only with academic deans and senior administrators, who were accountable for their professorial colleagues. After many days of fruitless meetings with deans and vice presidents, a frustrated and disgruntled delegation eventually returned, empty-handed, to Indianapolis. Through this remarkably creative maneuver, the Indiana University faculty members were spared the horrors of their colleagues in Ann Arbor and elsewhere.

Even where public investigations or formal charges of disloyalty or subversion did not ruin faculty careers, risks of another type accompanied the McCarthy vendetta. Many states required all their employees, including university professors, to sign an oath that typically disclaimed membership in any organization that "advocates the violent overthrow of the government." Those who refused to sign, whatever their reason, not only were barred from employment but might also find themselves on lists of "suspect" or "disloyal" persons. Although obviously aimed at active members of the Communist Party, the loose language and imprecise terms of such oaths could reach far more broadly. Most troubling was the dilemma that a conscientious scholar might feel when faced with such a demand, believing him- or herself to be a loyal American, but uncertain whether some bureaucrat or hostile lawmaker might deem an innocent affiliation decades earlier to fall under the ban. Thus many indisputably loyal state university professors, especially in California where the oath was vigorously enforced, simply declined to sign and thus forfeited their teaching positions. Eventually the Supreme Court struck down all such disclaimer-type oaths, not only as applied to university professors but (on broad free speech grounds) for all state employees. Yet grave and irreversible damage had been done during the decade that loyalty oaths were alive and well; many conscientious government workers who had nothing to hide felt they could not make the required declaration and thus lost careers as well as jobs.

Less visible as a catalyst for the protection of academic freedom has been the role of students who have occasionally come to the support or defense of an embattled professor. In the late 1940s, suspected liberals on the University of Chicago's faculty were targeted by conservative business groups and were the object of formal investigation by a committee of the Illinois legislature. President Robert Maynard Hutchins and the University of Chicago Board of Trustees staunchly defended the faculty and insisted upon respect for the autonomy of a private institution. As the hearings drew to a close, the committee received a petition signed by three thousand University of Chicago students. These students wished to convey their belief that "the position of our University, which encourages and maintains the free examination of all ideas, is the strongest possible safeguard against indoctrination." Confident that "this policy of academic freedom for both students and teachers is the best preparation for effective citizenship in the American tradition," the petitioners hoped that the outside world would join them in supporting the university in its plea for autonomy. The committee's chairman immediately demanded to "know something about the signers, of the type of students" they were. But little came of such pique, and the investigation soon collapsed.[11] On this as on several other occasions, students may have been able to advance the cause of academic freedom more effectively than could their more directly interested professors. Such statements also provide a critical reminder that academic freedom and tenure, by protecting the learning process from external pressures, serve not only the interests of those who teach but quite as much of those who learn from them.

A half century has passed since the McCarthy era, and some skeptics occasionally suggest that academic freedom no longer needs such rigorous protection, or at least that in more rational times its safeguards are at best peripheral. Actual experience in the twenty-first century suggests otherwise. On any given business day, the AAUP office that deals with academic freedom and tenure matters receives an average of three calls, e-mails, or other messages from faculty members who are concerned enough about a potential threat to seek help from the association. Although many such concerns prove groundless, or can be readily resolved through further inquiry, typically eight or ten each year lead to formal investigations—a step that is authorized only after protracted discussions, negotiations, and even threats on behalf of a beleaguered professor fail to bring about redress. At least a few such inquiries result in censure for a wayward or callous administration—the professoriate's ultimate sanction. Thus it would be quite inaccurate to suggest the need for such safeguards and declarations died with Senator McCarthy.

There is a quite different way to define the current role of formal protection for academic freedom and tenure. Consider the experience of three highly visible and public figures in the mid-1990s. When Professor Lani Guinier was denied an appointment (which President Bill Clinton had promised) as assistant U.S. attorney general, after objections were raised about comments she had made in law review articles about voting rights of minorities—congressional critics dubbed her "the quota queen"—she was able to return to her tenured professorship at the University of Pennsylvania.[12] From there she shortly moved to an equally secure faculty chair at Harvard, from which she has been free to challenge complacent assumptions about voting patterns and the effect on minorities of redistricting.

When Professor Joycelyn Elders was dismissed as surgeon general of the United States because President Clinton responded to criticism of her public comments about teen sex education and masturbation, she returned promptly and safely to her tenured professorship of medicine at the University of Arkansas. From that more secure post, a 2006 *Washington Post* article notes, she "has never stopped preaching her gospel of public health—reducing sexually transmitted diseases and teenage pregnancy and improving health care for poor people, women and minorities."[13] Indicating that such encounters reflect no political bias, one might recall the experience of history professor Christina Jeffrey. Then House Speaker Newt Gingrich appointed Jeffrey, a fellow conservative Georgian, to the post of House historian, and she prepared to move her family to Washington. It then came to light that, as a reviewer of applications for National Endowment for the Humanities funding of high school summer institutes, Professor Jeffrey had (in a marginal notation) questioned whether a particular proposal for Holocaust study accurately reflected the Nazi perspective. That news was enough for Speaker Gingrich to summarily terminate Jeffrey's appointment. Happily, she was able to return at once to her faculty position at Kennesaw State University in Georgia, where she has continued to teach and study history—and is free to raise whatever questions she believes are warranted about scholarly treatment of the Holocaust.[14]

These three cases, which stand out among many recent encounters, suggest the continuing vitality of academic freedom in later times. When subjected to intense political controversy in Washington, each of these scholars could and did return to a secure academic position—from which to speak out freely on matters as vital as voter rights, teen health, and European history. Such experiences do not argue that federal appointees such as these three professors should enjoy academic freedom in their government posts, but rather they demonstrate that the nation is the direct and substantial beneficiary of a system that does protect the expression of their views from an academic perspective. While certain controversial and unwelcome views were deemed unacceptable in the top circles of national government, they remained wholly acceptable on the university campus. In fact, the views advanced by all three of these highly visible victims of official displeasure deserved to be publicized—if only to invite contrasting opinions as part of the ongoing debate about racial disparity in voting districts, sex among teenagers, and balance in twentieth-century European history.

It now becomes important to determine just what academic freedom does protect, including what it does not protect. We noted earlier that even a tenured professor may be dismissed for cause. Although AAUP statements wisely avoid defining that essential term, a kind of "academic common law" has emerged to shape its meaning. Even the staunchest defenders of academic freedom would recognize, for example, that flagrant acts of plagiarism would constitute the requisite cause, even though they might fall well short of the degree of misappropriation of someone else's intellectual property that would violate federal copyright laws. Inexcusable dereliction of assigned duties may warrant termination—not only failing or refusing to teach assigned courses or advise students but also total abdication of such nonteaching tasks as attending departmental meetings, serving on vital committees, and participating in other ways in the essential tasks of a university. Persistent harassment, abuse, or exploitation of a student, especially within the professor-student relationship, would also rise or fall to the level of potentially dismissible conduct—subject, of course, in any such case to clear and convincing proof at a hearing where the administration bears the burden of proof before a committee of faculty peers, where the accused professor may bring an attorney, and where an adverse judgment is ultimately reviewable by the governing board. Indeed, even purely verbal harassment in the college classroom is recognized as potentially unprotected expression if (in the words of the relevant AAUP policy) it is "persistent, pervasive, [and] not germane to the subject matter" and if it "substantially impairs the academic or work opportunity of students, colleagues or co-workers."[15] Such transgressions are merely illustrative—both of the types of offenses that may forfeit even a tenured appointment and of the inherent difficulty of cataloging or shaping into a universal standard a broad array of unacceptable professorial actions.

Although the AAUP has never defined "cause," its policy does offer one useful guideline: "Adequate cause for dismissal will be related, directly and substantially, to the fitness of faculty members in their professional capacities as teachers or researchers." This brief reference adds that dismissal may not be used "to restrain faculty members in their exercise of academic freedom or other rights of American citizens."[16] The focus on "fitness" turns out to be surprisingly helpful, both in terms of what it protects and what it does not protect. As noted in the previous chapter, professors in most academic disciplines are free to proclaim their belief that the earth's surface is flat. But of geologists and geographers, the academic profession expects much more and would almost certainly deem a flat-earth proponent to be "unfit" for continued teaching and scholarship.

A similar judgment would probably (as also noted in the previous chapter) end the academic career of a modern European historian who persisted in public denial of the Holocaust—even though Professor Arthur Butz remains free to proclaim such heretical views as long as he keeps them out of his classroom and adequately performs his assigned duties in electrical engineering. Or consider a case that has nothing to do with speech but much to do with fitness. Many university professors have been convicted of driving while under the influence of alcohol, though no university (save perhaps a deeply religious institution that bans any use of alcohol) would consider such a misdeed to be job threatening. But suppose the professor so charged happens to be the one person in the state who bears total responsibility for the certification and monitoring of driver education and safety teachers. Might not the notion of fitness warrant bringing dismissal charges even for a single DUI conviction of a faculty member who bears so special and sensitive a responsibility?

Even closer to the surface has been a recent pair of controversies that some observers might analogize to the cases of the flat-earth geologist and the Holocaust-denying European historian. Soon after the terrorist attacks of September 11, University of Colorado ethnic studies professor Ward Churchill posted on an obscure website an essay which all but implied that the victims in the World Trade Center deserved their horrible fate. Suggesting that those in the financial services field who labored in the twin towers to gather data and apply investment formulas were somehow complicit in the attacks, Churchill's essay described them as "Little Eichmanns." Churchill also wrote that the hijackers "were not cowards" because they had "manifested the courage of their convictions."

When the content of this essay surfaced several years later, on the eve of Churchill's scheduled lecture at Hamilton College, Colorado's governor demanded his immediate resignation. Churchill did promptly relinquish the chairmanship of the Ethnic Studies Department, but held firm in his tenured faculty role. The administration and the University of Colorado Board of Regents appreciated that summary action would not be appropriate and instead launched an investigation of the essay and Churchill's other published writings. The initial result of that inquiry was to clear him of charges that might have warranted his dismissal, because even his most provocative statements fell within a public employee's protected freedom of speech. Curiously, the administration conducting that inquiry was not charged to—and therefore did not—consider any possible questions about Professor Churchill's fitness beyond the First Amendment standard. (Many months after this initial judgment, a probing analysis of Churchill's research activity found substantial evidence of misconduct and, on that basis, recommended major sanctions, possibly including his dismissal from the Colorado faculty. But that inquiry was totally separate from the original focus on his controversial public statements).[17]

About the same time, a strikingly parallel incident occurred in a neighboring state. Paul Mirecki, chairman of the Department of Religious Studies at the University of Kansas, proposed to offer a new course to be entitled "Special Topics in Religion, Intelligent Design, Creationism and Other Religious Mythologies." Such a title was inevitably provocative in the only state whose board of education had recently downgraded the teaching of evolution. Meanwhile, it became known that Mirecki had sent an e-mail to what he mistakenly believed was a private discussion group in which he referred to conservative Christians as "fundies" and declared that the proposed new course would be "a nice slap in their big fat face." Anti-Catholic comments were soon discovered among his other online comments. The Kansas administration promptly offered a public disclaimer, characterizing Mirecki's views as "repugnant and vile" but defending his academic freedom and free speech as a tenured professor. Mirecki soon announced that he had abandoned plans for the new course and would step down as department chair. That seemed to end the controversy, and the academic year ended without further controversy in Kansas.[18]

Curiously, in neither of these two incidents does it appear that any consideration was given to the potential relationship between the outspoken professor's statements and the question of fitness under the AAUP standard. Superficially, it might appear that no issue of fitness would arise in such a case; neither resembles the proverbial (and clearly vulnerable) flat-earth geologist or geographer or the Holocaust-denying modern European historian. Yet a closer look suggests that potential concerns about fitness or competence might merit some consideration in both cases. Arguably, an ethnic studies scholar such as Professor Churchill is substantially less free to characterize terrorist victims as "Little Eichmanns" and a religious studies expert such as Professor Mirecki is less free to call conservative Christians "fundies" than a colleague in a more remote discipline such as chemistry or philosophy would be. Yet these transgressions seem profoundly different from those of the flat-earth geographer or the Holocaust-denying historian. A single ill-considered and offensive outburst, however adversely it may reflect on the speaker's judgment, falls far short of the persistent pattern of public statements that may evidence a lack of "fitness in [a professor's] professional capacity as [a teacher or researcher.]" Only if Churchill had continued visibly to disparage the World Trade Center victims on ethnic grounds, or Mirecki had persisted in demeaning conservative Christians, could an issue of fitness reasonably have been raised. Otherwise, academic freedom must be viewed as protecting even such extreme statements, deeply troubling though they may be and however damaging to the image and reputation of the academic profession.

Both the Churchill and Mirecki cases do pose a quite separate issue, on which principles of academic freedom offer far less guidance. Both professors also held administrative posts as department chairs, in addition to their tenured teaching positions, at the time of their respective offending statements. Because both resigned their chairmanships very soon after controversy erupted, any concern about their administrative status quickly became moot, to the apparent relief of senior administrators at both institutions. The Colorado report did observe, however, that had Churchill not relinquished the chairmanship, the "outrage" generated by his essay "most likely would have warranted his removal"[19] from his administrative post. The same issue might well have arisen in Mirecki's case had he not also relinquished the chairmanship with comparable alacrity.

What little guidance may be found on this issue suggests that some comparable protection extends to an academic administrator, who typically serves at the pleasure of the governing board though usually for a stated term of office. AAUP policy makes clear that a department chair or dean, even tenured as a professor, however, cannot claim in the administrative post a level of protection comparable to faculty tenure. When a department chair or dean speaks within his or her field of expertise, the risk that such statements may be attributed to the institution seems far greater than when the speaker is an ordinary professor with no administrative rank or title. Moreover, the latitude that a scholar enjoys to provoke controversy or inflict offense, within or beyond his or her discipline, does not comparably immunize an academic administrator against reprisal with regard to the nonteaching position. The classic recent case is that of Harvard University's former president, Lawrence Summers. A brilliant economist, he achieved tenure at Harvard at an uncommonly early age. As secretary of the treasury at the close of the Clinton administration, he displayed great administrative skill. The premature end of his presidential term, in the summer of 2006, reflected many unfortunate and ill-timed forces. Yet undoubtedly pivotal to the debacle was President Summers' suggestion, at a scholarly conference of economists, that the underrepresentation of women in fields such as his might to some degree reflect gender-based genetic differences.

Publicity about this highly volatile statement quickly drew outrage and dismay from many quarters, and it accelerated a process that eventually made untenable his continued leadership of Harvard. What the central figure of this drama seems never to have fully appreciated is that the academic freedom enjoyed by *Professor* Summers (who could express with complete impunity his views on gender and technical skills) may not protect *President* Summers in making the same assertions. Just as the Pope, no matter how learned and eminent a theologian, may never speak other than ex cathedra—as the current pontiff, Pope Benedict XVI, discovered to his dismay while speaking about Islamic values in Regensburg—so the president of Harvard University may never speak or write other than ex officio, whatever eminence he may enjoy in his chosen academic field and whatever latitude he could claim if he were only a professor.

There seems to be only one court case offering much guidance on these issues, but its teaching is broadly consistent with the analysis suggested here. The case involved City College of New York Afro-American studies Chair Leonard Jeffries[20] (discussed extensively in Chapter 3) and offered limited guidance because of procedural vagaries, but the court ruling (initially in Jeffries' favor) did suggest that academic administrators enjoy at least a limited degree of academic freedom, though perhaps no broader than a citizen's freedom of speech within the First Amendment. Suffice it to say that both Colorado and Kansas administrators were mercifully spared this even more daunting challenge by the early preemptive actions taken by their outspoken colleagues. The larger issue remains for another day.

Any discussion of how academic freedom is defined and protected would be quite incomplete without discussion of church-affiliated institutions. The policies governing them are, as one would expect, quite different, even though actual practice may vary less than might be expected. Even major research universities, such as Georgetown, Notre Dame, Baylor, and Brigham Young may have quite different expectations of their faculties than do their secular peers. From the outset, AAUP has recognized that such differences exist within the academic community and should be respected. The 1940 statement thus contained a "limitations clause," declaring that "limitations of academic freedom because of religious or other aims of the institution should be clearly stated in writing at the time of the appointment." A 1970 interpretation observed, rather cryptically: "Most church-related institutions no longer need or desire the departure from the principle of academic freedom implied in the 1940 Statement and we do not now condone such a departure."[21] In the late 1980s, the AAUP's Committee on Academic Freedom and Tenure seriously considered, but ultimately rejected, a subcommittee proposal for the abandonment of the limitations clause. The full committee resolved, again somewhat ambiguously, that "the invocation of that [limitations] clause does not relieve the institution of its obligation to afford academic freedom as called for in the 1940 Statement." The committee's then chairman sought to clarify this language, noting that it "begs the question of what obligations a church-related institution has to afford academic freedom," adding that this issue "will apparently continue to vex us."[22]

Vexing indeed, that issue has remained for the AAUP and for others who define and protect academic freedom. On some occasions, religious institutions have been treated rather differently and have been permitted to impose conditions on faculty activity and expression that would not pass muster at secular campuses. Thus Gonzaga University, a Jesuit institution, was given a clean bill of academic health even though its handbook reserved the right to dismiss nontenured faculty for "inculcation of viewpoints which contradict explicit principles of Catholic faith and morals." However, a disproportionate number of targets of AAUP censure have been church-related institutions—although in each case the focus of the sanction has been a failure to specify adequately at the time of the initial appointment the administration's expectations of a faculty member whose noncompliant speech or activity brought about the investigation. Rather recently, Nyack College, an Evangelical Christian institution in New York's mid-Hudson region, was placed on the censure list after it denied reappointment to a faculty member after she had made in class several negative comments about the Christian Coalition and had displayed on her briefcase a "Support Gay Rights" button. She was also active in the ACLU and other off-campus liberal causes. The applicable policies declared only that Nyack faculty members were assured academic freedom "as long as they remain within the accepted confessional basis of the institution and the Christian and Missionary Alliance [with which the College was affiliated]." [23] The AAUP investigation and the resulting report faulted the college in part because it denied to the probationary professor important procedural rights, though equally because its policies failed sufficiently and precisely to apprise a junior teacher of activities and expression the college deemed unacceptable and thus unprotected by its principles of academic freedom.

About the same time, the AAUP addressed an even more difficult situation at BYU, the flagship institution of the Mormon or Latter-day Saints (LDS) faith. The inquiry concerned only the treatment of faculty who were members of the LDS church; no issues had ever arisen about the status of non-Mormon faculty. Of special concern was the case of an otherwise promising English professor, whose off-campus activity and statements, including several publications, were "perceived as harmful to the tenets held by the Church and the university." The inquiry also noted with concern the experience of at least one BYU professor who had suffered because of what the administration viewed as insufficient involvement in the church, including imperfect attendance at LDS services, a dereliction that led to his being reported as less than "temple worthy." Here again, the AAUP report and the resulting censure took care to stress that BYU's transgression lay not in the content or substance of its expectations for its faculty but more narrowly in the clarity and precision with which the faculty had been made aware of those standards at the time of their initial appointment. The censure resolution declared that BYU's stated limitations "provide inadequate guidance to faculty members and give excessive discretion to the administration."[24] Thus the limitations clause, while obviously disfavored in AAUP circles, remains in the Redbook and is formally observed in all cases that involve apparent academic freedom violations at church-related institutions.

As noted at the start of this discussion, AAUP may be the major player, but it is by no means the only game in town—and in the view of some academic freedom champions may even miss some of the gravest threats to academic freedom. Two other faculty organizations—the National Education Association and the American Federation of Teachers—have long held a strong commitment to academic freedom and are ready to aid and defend their members who are threatened with dismissal or a lesser sanction, most often when such action violates a collective bargaining agreement. Several other organizations of a quite different type (and political outlook) that merit recognition in this regard are the American Council of Trustees and Alumni and the Foundation for Individual Rights in Education (FIRE), which in quite different ways (and with different perspectives) target threats against and intrusions upon academic freedom. As University of Pennsylvania history professor Alan Kors and Boston attorney Harvey Silverglate eloquently document in their book, *The Shadow*

University: The Betrayal of Liberty on America's Campuses, seemingly benign forces (often from what would be deemed liberal sources) have at times sought to impose an orthodoxy on campus speech and even thought.[25] The adoption by several hundred institutions (including some of the most liberal universities) of restrictive speech codes may provide the most glaring example, but surely it is not the only one. The fact that every such speech code ever challenged in court has been found unconstitutional may suggest how unwise and ill-fated this quest for campus civility and collegiality has been. Indeed, apart from the constitutional flaws, speech codes have never been shown to be at all effective in mitigating racist, sexist, homophobic, or anti-Semitic attitudes on campus—and may in fact sometimes have been counterproductive simply by driving such hateful views underground while magnifying the animus of those who hold them. Meanwhile, the mere adoption of such rules may have created false expectations among those groups that sought protection through greater civility but whose hopes seldom materialize and surely are not well served by bans on unwelcome expression. Most basically, such rules are inimical to the very nature of a university, as that institution where most clearly all ideas should be tolerated and no view—however hateful or spiteful—should be deemed unacceptable.[26] Mercifully, many such codes have been repealed—often in direct response to adverse court rulings—though not before having created much mischief, as Kors and Silverglate and FIRE as a vigilant organization have so forcefully documented. And the penchant for restricting campus speech dies hard, despite the legal pitfalls and counterclaims; University of Maryland Judicial Programs Director Gary Pavela notes that "continued adherence to speech codes is by now predictable, but remains puzzling."[27]

Such speech codes have been directed mainly at students, which has been concern enough for defenders of campus expression. In some ways even more troubling are the occasional efforts to muzzle university facilities from conveying unwelcome messages. University of Illinois professors were directed not to communicate with prospective athletic recruits at the Urbana-Champaign campus about the troubled status of Chief Illiniwek, the embattled Native American symbol of the athletic program. A faculty group challenged the ban in federal court on free speech and academic freedom grounds and prevailed against the university, even though no professor was actually sanctioned. University of Wisconsin political science professor Donald Downs has written at length and with much feeling about comparable forces that threatened faculty expression at his own institution and resulted in the formation of a new group, the Committee for Academic Freedom and Rights (CFAR), which would emerge as a champion of academic freedom. Professor Downs's recent book, *Restoring Free Speech and Liberty on Campus,* vividly recounts both the experiences on the Madison campus that led to the creation of CFAR and the risks of policies and programs that may be rooted in well-intentioned concerns for civility and equality.[28]

Finally, there has been mounting concern in some quarters over academic freedom dimensions of the college curriculum—notably directed at pressures for greater emphasis on newer fields such as ethnic and women's studies, with a perceived de-emphasis on what are sometimes characterized as "dead white males." The American Council of Trustees and Alumni (ACTA) has made such issues a special concern, insisting on "integrity" in the curricular process, and resisting what it perceives as capitulation to forces of "political correctness." Although AAUP and ACTA differ significantly on many issues, both of end and means, they share a common commitment to what each believes is the core of academic freedom. There is a more than plausible argument that the cause of academic freedom needs all the help it can get and merits support from both ends of the political spectrum as well as from the center. ACTA indisputably provides such support from the right.

Beyond defining academic freedom and its scope, and taking stock of its defenders, important questions remain about the process by which such freedom is protected in practice. Academic freedom principles are, for the most part, effective because virtually all institutions of higher learning have adopted those principles and apply them scrupulously. Equally important, the collective academic community stands ready to condemn flagrant departures from those precepts. There are, however, other levels of protection that deserve recognition because they are important—indeed, increasingly important—components of the process. Occasionally a collective bargaining agreement between a university and its faculty (or a group representing that faculty) will contain explicit academic freedom protections—much more often procedural than substantive—to which a mistreated faculty member may resort. Indeed, many such agreements negotiated by AAUP chapters simply incorporate basic Redbook principles verbatim into the text of the contract, thus making them binding in a directly contractual sense, as much upon a private as a public university.

Moreover, as the value of including such provisions suggests, the courts are another important avenue of recourse. Occasionally an aggrieved professor may be able to show that a contractual guarantee has been breached—that, for example, a right to a hearing or an appeal that was expressly guaranteed in the faculty handbook has been denied or rendered meaningless. For public institutions that violate the free speech of faculty members, recourse to the courts may be available for the vindication of constitutional rights, as Chapter 3 develops. Yet such recourse is seldom available for those who teach in independent or private colleges and universities, and it does always protect professors on public campuses. Thus there remains the critical alternative of peer judgment, which lies at the heart of the AAUP's censure process.

In 1931, when the organization was barely fifteen-years old, the AAUP began conducting detailed investigations of institutions at which grave breaches of academic freedom had been charged and informally verified. Such inquiries are authorized by the association's general secretary or chief executive officer and are undertaken only after exhaustive discussions and negotiations with senior campus officials have either failed or efforts have been repeatedly rebuffed. If the personnel matter that occasioned the inquiry has already led to litigation, the institution may refuse to discuss its substance with outsiders and might warn of its unwillingness to cooperate in the event of a campus visit. Such recalcitrance on the administration's part may well reflect sound legal advice, but it cannot be allowed to thwart the investigative process. Rather, that process may go forward without the administration's participation, relying instead on sources not constrained by the pending (and quite possibly protracted) litigation.

Typically an investigating committee of two or three professors from other institutions will spend several days on the campus where the issue arose—talking not only with the complainant but also (if possible) with relevant members of the administration and with others (faculty senate officers, for example) whose views may amplify or enlighten the inquiry. Following the campus visit, a report is prepared and, after initial internal review, is sent to the complainant and to the administration for factual appraisal. Publication of the verified report follows, and at the next meeting thereafter of the Committee on Academic Freedom and Tenure consideration is given to possible action, including a vote of censure.

If at any time during this process the administration wishes to make amends, adverse action may well be forestalled, although more than simply a change of heart is required. Not only must the catalytic personnel action typically be reversed, with some tangible recognition in the form of back pay and the like; also, usually there must be an amelioration of the policies that created the initial problem. Not infrequently, the threat of either publication of a critical report or of a vote of censure may cause institutions to become highly creative in making amends. If, however, the parties remain on a collision course, the committee may recommend censure and, if the association's council and its annual meeting concur, censure may be imposed—invariably upon the administration rather than (save for one exceptional situation) upon the governing board, even where complicity may have been shared. Once censure has been voted, the AAUP corresponds at least annually with the administration, seeking grounds for removal (which, like the initial censure, must be voted upon by several levels within the association.)

The eternal question in academic circles is whether censure is effective—whether it serves as a deterrent or has any other adverse effect. The president of one recently censured institution, rejecting a suggestion of infamy, remarked that "AAUP is out of the mainstream of modern American thought." Another censured president declared the association's condemnatory action to be "meaningless," coming as it did from "a very old-fashioned group that is still dealing with a 1940 book of rules."[29] There have even been times when censure was viewed as almost a badge of honor in some administrative circles, as when three of Oklahoma's four regional state colleges were already on the AAUP's blacklist, and the president of the fourth only half facetiously remarked that he would welcome an opportunity to join his colleagues in that dubious company.

There are, however, other indications that censure as a sanction is alive, well, and still feared. When a new president assumed office at Central Arkansas University in 2003, one of his first concerns was to address the fact that the institution was on the censure list. "I personally believe," he told a reporter, "that there is a national stigma that is associated with being on the censure list." And, with special concern about how prospective recruits would view that "stigma," he added: "Any prudent faculty member applying at a university is going to ask why." The new administration went right to work on the problem, revised the faculty handbook to remove the offending policies, made the requisite redress to the mistreated person, and relished the AAUP's action in removing censure at the next annual meeting. A strikingly similar scenario occurred at New York University when a new president, formerly the law school's dean, assumed the presidency in 2002. Among his first commitments was to seek the removal of censure; the measures necessary to achieve such redemption were among his first official acts. Indeed, as such experiences attest, one of the clearest indicia of the effectiveness of censure is the lengths to which many—though clearly not all—censured administrations will go to remove that stigma.

Even more telling, though obviously less visible, are the extraordinary efforts an administration threatened with censure may undertake to avoid the threatened sanction. Among vivid memories of Committee A members from the early 1970s was a special meeting, arranged on the eve of an imminent censure vote at the request of the president of the accused research university, who invoked the full authority not only of his institution and its board but also of his own prior role as the state supreme court's chief justice. University attorneys accompanied the president and repeatedly threatened to sue if censure were imposed. The committee was undeterred because the accuracy and integrity of the accusing report were not seriously challenged. Censure was voted the next day, and within two years the university had made redress and brought the applicable personnel policies into full compliance. Thus the best advice to those who face the occasional disparagement of censure that floats through administrative circles is to ask the president who's been there. Moreover nontrivial collateral consequences were noted at the outset of this chapter—BYU's quest for a Phi Beta Kappa chapter that foundered on academic freedom shoals and the readiness of many scholarly and learned societies to apprise their members of the current list of censured administrations.

The effects of censure may emerge through other channels as well. During a senior academic administrative search, any candidate's past involvement in activity that led to censure is certain to come to the attention of faculty members on a screening or advisory committee; more than one virtually certain prospect for a presidential or other high academic post has found such a taint to be disabling in the final selection. Some accrediting associations take special note both generally of the condition of academic freedom and specifically of any mistreatment of faculty that may have warranted placing any of its member institutions on the censure list. Thus despite occasionally disparaging comments from censured administrators—who could hardly be deemed objective—there is ample evidence that censure is taken very seriously by most of the academic community. Nonetheless, there will always be those academic outlaws who view the prospect of censure with a certain bravado and may even invite the adverse judgment that censure entails.

Implicit in much of this discussion is the vital link between academic freedom and tenure, which now deserves closer scrutiny. Tenure typically involves a contractual commitment to a professor who has survived rigorous reviews during the probationary period and is awarded what many institutions describe as "appointment without term."[30] Regardless of AAUP policy, the institution's own bylaws or regulations typically provide that such an appointment may be terminated only for exceptional reasons, such as cause or incapacitating disability or financial exigency. Due process prior to removal from the faculty is usually guaranteed, as much by private as by public institutions, though in the case of state universities the general law may augment what institutional rules ensure. Thus the importance of tenure to the protection of a tenured professor's academic freedom is central and critical. What is less clear is what policies and principles safeguard the academic freedom of others in the teaching profession.

As noted earlier, academic freedom may be secure even without tenure in at least two situations. One, of course, is the rare case of the institution, such as Hampshire College, that has never adopted a tenure system but prides itself on protecting the academic freedom of its faculty as fully as do the overwhelming majority of its peer institutions that do confer tenure. The much broader area of overlap involves junior faculty who have not yet achieved tenure but are on a recognized "track" toward that goal. During the probationary period, academic freedom is protected in two distinct ways. The termination of a term appointment before its expiration is treated under AAUP policy identically with the dismissal of an already tenured teacher—requiring proof of cause or some other permissible basis for such drastic action and the full panoply of procedural safeguards to which a tenured professor is entitled. Moreover, although the nonrenewal of such a probationary appointment may reflect considerations that fall far short of grounds for dismissal, relevant policies make clear that such action may not be based either on expression or activity that academic freedom protects or on unlawful discrimination. (The nonrenewed probationer may also seek redress on the basis of allegedly "inadequate consideration," but such a claim does not typically implicate academic freedom concerns.)

Such safeguards leave largely unprotected a substantial and steadily growing portion of the college teaching profession—those who serve on part-time or even full-time nontenure-track appointments and whose employment is typically renewed (or not) on an annual basis. Recent national data suggest that part-time faculty account for at least 40 percent of academic appointments, whereas nontenure-track full-time faculty total another 20 percent of college teaching personnel. The use of such appointments obviously offers to institutions the advantage of flexibility in dealing with unpredictable changes in state funding for higher education and shifting student enrollment patterns and choice of academic majors. Yet the status of academic freedom among such "contingent" faculty, as they have come to be described, remains murky.

Because the decision not to extend or renew such an appointment is usually accompanied by no stated reason, a lecturer or instructor who believes that he or she has earned disfavor for having criticized the administration or having spoken out on some other topic may be unable to demonstrate such a link. Even in a case where teaching evaluations and other vital signs may have been consistently positive, establishing that renewal would have occurred but for one angry letter to the campus newspaper is a daunting task. Although as a practical matter contingent faculty are far less likely than their tenured and tenure-track colleagues to evoke the wrath of legislatures, governing boards, alumni, and others, such incidents are not unknown and simply indicate a possible gap in the academic freedom safety net.

The other potential source of protection for academic freedom is collective bargaining. An impressive portion of public college and university facilities are members of bargaining units and are represented by one of several national groups—AAUP, the National Education Association, and the American Federation of Teachers—or occasionally by a local group such as a faculty senate that has been recognized for this purpose, usually by a public employee relations board or labor agency. Few members of private university faculties are unionized, since the National Labor Relations Board (which would need to certify an election on a private campus) declared in the late 1970s that most full-time professors at major universities are essentially "managers" and thus do not comprise an appropriate sector for collective bargaining. Although the National Labor Relations Board has taken a different view with respect to graduate teaching assistants at private universities, the faculty policy announced in a case that involved Yeshiva University remains largely unchanged.[31] Although a few private institutions have voluntarily recognized ad hoc arrangements through which to negotiate with their faculties on an organized basis, unionization exists almost exclusively in the public sector.

The relationship between academic freedom and collective bargaining is not easily generalized. Many agreements between faculty groups and colleges or universities contain admirably detailed and thorough commitments to academic freedom—tracking, in some cases, the relevant sections of the AAUP Redbook. Once included in a union agreement, of course, those provisions gain added stature and are legally enforceable through an additional channel, often by an arbitrator or other contractually prescribed dispute-resolution mechanism. Yet the intense pressures of collective bargaining may result in compromises and trade-offs that could undermine principles of academic freedom. On at least two occasions, the AAUP has faced the acutely uncomfortable prospect of censuring an administration for personnel actions taken in accordance with a bargaining agreement that had been negotiated with one of the association's own local chapters. The administration, not surprisingly, resisted threatened censure—noting its acceptance of terms and conditions of employment that were not only submitted by the AAUP chapter as part of the bargaining process but also had been negotiated in return for tangible faculty benefits, such as higher salaries. Such seemingly persuasive extenuation was, however, ultimately of no avail. In both instances the AAUP voted censure, disregarding the source of the offending policy within its own unionized chapter at the bargaining table.[32] The association reaffirmed that its core principles of academic freedom are transcendent and immutable, binding quite as much on its own chapters and on administrators who bargain with those chapters as upon any other sectors of American higher education.

Such novel experiences should not suggest that collective bargaining and academic freedom are inherently at odds or that acceptance of the former jeopardizes the latter. Most faculty agreements are significantly protective of faculty rights and interests, intangible as well as tangible. Yet certain tensions are inevitable, and they must be closely monitored. The particular source of an academic freedom violation matters little to the process by which it is protected—whether it is the governor, or the legislature, or the governing board, or an administration's accession to demands from an AAUP local chapter in the bargaining process.

The final topic that merits attention here is the larger arena within which academic freedom principles have found favor. Although Chapter 3 is devoted entirely to the closely related topic of academic freedom in the courts, we envision here a narrower nexus between policy and law—specific evidence of judicial acceptance and adoption of stated principles of academic freedom, notably those that have been articulated and endorsed by the AAUP. Illustratively, when the U.S. Supreme Court sought to differentiate between church-related secondary and postsecondary education, the justices noted approvingly that each of the religiously affiliated colleges in the case "subscribes to, and abides by the 1940 [AAUP] Statement."[33] A later ruling of the Minnesota Supreme Court sustained a program of tax-exempt revenue bonds that included church-related colleges in part because "the respondent colleges all follow the 1940 Statement."[34] The federal appeals court for the Fourth Circuit, ruling on a personnel dispute between a faculty member and a Maryland private college, observed: "Probably because it was formulated by both administrators and professors, all of the secondary authorities seem to agree it [the AAUP 1940 statement] is the 'most widely accepted academic definition of tenure.'"[35] Across the country, the U.S. Court of Appeals for the Ninth Circuit observed that a university's regulation on adequate cause for the dismissal of a tenured professor would not be subject to constitutional challenge as vague or overbroad if it had been construed by the governing board consistently with AAUP interpretation and application of the 1940 statement.[36] In myriad other situations, relevant and potentially applicable AAUP policies have offered welcome guidance and direction to federal and state courts seeking authoritative views from the academic community. Although no such references accord to the 1940 statement or any other AAUP policies the force of law—nor, for that matter, would any private organization necessarily wish such an imprimatur—they do indicate endorsement and approval from the most authoritative source.

3

The Constitution and the Courts

In early February 2005, Hamilton College in upstate New York awaited a lecture by University of Colorado ethnic studies professor Ward Churchill. On the eve of his visit, public attention suddenly turned to an essay that Churchill had written soon after the terrorist attacks of September 11, 2001. In that essay, which had languished in the interim on an obscure website, the hijackers were lauded as "heroes" whereas the victims of the attacks were disparaged as "little Eichmanns." The essay even implied that some among the World Trade Center casualties may have deserved their terrible fate. Revelation of Churchill's views evoked outrage and indignation on the Hamilton campus and far beyond. After several days of uncertainty, and an initial hope to maintain its planned commitment, Hamilton canceled the lecture, fearing for the safety of its students and faculty as well as that of a now highly controversial visitor.

Meanwhile, the controversy reached Churchill's home base in Colorado. Although Churchill held tenure at the Boulder campus, conservative governor Bill Owens demanded his resignation after learning of the explosive statements in his essay. Groups of students circulated petitions to the same effect. The University of Colorado Board of Regents called an emergency meeting for the end of the week, thus fueling speculation that Churchill might be summarily dismissed. But the day before the meeting, the two most recently elected board members stepped forward to combat such rumors. Regent Michael Carrigan, a Denver lawyer, said he was "personally disgusted" by Churchill's essay but insisted that "the law requires a process to fire a professor." Were the board to ignore the safeguards that protect even the most dissonant of its faculty, it would "face substantial legal liability." Other regents shared Carrigan's caution, and the board opted instead for a thorough investigation by the university's academic administration, thus relegating the controversy to an orderly campus channel for the ensuing months.

Even under intense pressure for immediate action, the Colorado regents had clearly recognized that established legal safeguards constrain any reprisal against an outspoken professor. Those safeguards contained two distinct elements—a high tolerance for even outrageous and deeply offensive speech by university faculty members and a rigorous set of procedural standards by which to judge even the most blatant of professorial misconduct. Circumstances that might warrant the summary dismissal of almost any other outspoken state employee simply do not apply in the same way when the speaker is a university professor.[1] It is those legal safeguards, and the tortuous path by which they have emerged through the courts, that are the focus of this chapter. At the outset, however, it is essential to caution that legal protection for academic freedom, as defined by the courts, is not in all respects coextensive with principles espoused by the academic community. Various nonjudicial forces have contributed powerfully to recognition of academic freedom. Indeed, there are times when one set of safeguards is more protective than another, whereas the corresponding coverage may at other times be less extensive. Though complementary, they are not identical or even at all times parallel. Here we focus on what the courts have ruled, and we examine elsewhere the nonjudicial safeguards.

What may be most striking about the body of law that protects academic freedom is the recency of its emergence.[2] When the Tennessee Supreme Court decided in 1927 the infamous case against high school teacher John Scopes, who had been charged with teaching "any theory that denie[d] the story of the divine creation of man as taught in the Bible," the legal answer seemed easy. Although the law in question applied to all teachers, including those who offered graduate courses at the University of Tennessee, such a constraint seemed to the state court "a valid exercise of the state's power to specify the curriculum in its public schools." That was the end of the case, and at least temporarily of Scopes's teaching career.[3]

Four decades later, when a nearly identical issue arose in Arkansas, one would surely have expected a more enlightened response. The applicable Arkansas law, which had been enacted just after the *Scopes* decision, forbade anyone employed by the state to teach that "mankind ascended or descended from a lower order of animals." Like its Tennessee counterpart, this law applied as fully to graduate faculty at the University of Arkansas as to elementary public school teachers. Yet as far as the Arkansas courts were concerned, little if anything had changed between the 1920s and the 1960s.

A group of Arkansas teachers brought suit in state court, claiming that such a curb on their freedom to instruct students violated several federal constitutional rights. For the Arkansas Supreme Court, the *Scopes* case had settled the matter; such a constraint on teachers was simply an exercise of state authority to shape the curriculum "in its public schools."[4] The U.S. Supreme Court agreed to review the case and eventually came to a starkly different conclusion, ruling that such a ban was patently unconstitutional. Though the high Court mentioned principles of academic freedom, its ruling relied primarily on the First Amendment's mandate for the separation of church and state in teaching about the origins of human life.

What seems striking is that, as late as 1967, the highest court of any state could so casually uphold a blanket prohibition on the teaching of scientific principles so firmly established as the Darwinian theory of evolution. Arkansas was surely not alone in acknowledging virtually no change during the four ensuing decades, and had the later case arisen in a good many other states the result would have been no more favorable to a teacher's legal rights. The emergence of firm legal protection for academic freedom is a surprisingly recent phenomenon.

The curiously belated judicial recognition of such principles also reflects the complexity of those principles and of the process by which they have been established. Several distinctions are critical as we review this striking metamorphosis. First, we focus here almost exclusively on the interests of faculty; students have also received some comparable protection, which will be considered elsewhere. Second, however, college teachers need not be tenured—nor need they even hold the title "professor"—in order to invoke legal safeguards for their academic freedom. Third, most protections that the Constitution affords to academic freedom reach only those who teach in public or state-supported institutions—although that category covers well over three-quarters of all postsecondary teachers. Those who teach in private or independent institutions are not without legal protection, mainly from what we discuss in a later chapter as "academic common law" or institutional policy, but, unlike their colleagues in the public sector, they may seldom seek legal safeguards in the courts. Fourth, our focus here is on threats to and attacks against academic freedom that originate beyond or outside the college community; a later chapter addresses the quite different problem of pressures and forces within the academic world. The sources of such external threats are many and varied—state laws that mandate pledges of loyalty or compel disclosure of sensitive information, legislative investigations, subpoenas and other forms of judicial intrusion, local regulation of campus political activity or research, criminal prosecution of members of the academic community, and a host of others. Yet even when the range of such threats is narrowed to those that are most severe and intrusive, the scope of such an inquiry remains ample.

Finally, the complexity of this subject must be noted. Speaking as we do of legal protection for academic freedom implies that a single discrete body of law exists for that purpose. In fact, the safeguards that courts have recognized for faculty activity and expression come from myriad areas of the law. There are, to be sure, important court rulings that rely upon academic freedom as a distinct interest. But much of the law that effectively protects the interests of university faculties derives from nonacademic settings—speech rights of public employees, freedom of association, procedural due process, constraints on legislative and other official inquiries, collective bargaining, and more broadly the doctrine of "unconstitutional conditions." We first review the evolution of explicit legal protection for what is termed "academic freedom," and then we turn to these complementary developments.

It would not be quite fair to say that judicial recognition of academic freedom has occurred only in the past half century, although it is true that as late as 1952 the U.S. Supreme Court was still sometimes callously indifferent to faculty claims of expressive freedom. One much earlier antecedent deserves brief mention. The first Justice John Marshall Harlan, viewed as a maverick in his time, vigorously dissented from an 1892 judgment that upheld Kentucky's power to enforce racial segregation in private higher education. The case involved Berea College, a pioneer in racially mixed admissions.

Though the majority made short shrift of the college's constitutional challenge to such a law, Justice Harlan saw the Kentucky statute very differently. He called such a mandate "an arbitrary invasion of the rights of liberty and property guaranteed by [the national Constitution against state action]." In a remarkably prescient opinion, Harlan continued: "The capacity to impart instruction to others is given by the Almighty for beneficent purposes, and its use may not be forbidden or interfered with by Government—certainly not, unless such instruction is, in its nature, harmful to the public morals or imperils the public safety."[5] No other justice joined this opinion at the time, nor did any of Harlan's like-minded successors on the Supreme Court ever invoke his words in defense of academic freedom.

It would, in fact, require no less than forty-four years (1908–1952) for principles of academic freedom to receive their first modern judicial recognition. The 1952 case involved New York's ban on the employment by government of any person who espoused the use of violence to alter the form of government or who belonged to any of a long list of suspected subversive organizations. Although the Supreme Court's majority upheld the law, rejecting constitutional claims pressed by affected faculty members, Justices Hugo Black and William O. Douglas sharply dissented.

With specific reference to a teacher who was among several plaintiffs challenging the employment ban, Black and Douglas expressly invoked academic freedom for the first time. On three occasions during their dissent, they argued that when such a law as New York's anti-Communist ban creates fear and apprehension among public school teachers and professors, "there can be no real academic freedom in the environment" and later charged that such a "system of spying and surveillance" as New York had created "cannot go hand in hand with academic freedom."[6]

A few months later, Justice Felix Frankfurter (who, like Justice Douglas, had been a university professor before joining the Court) added his support for this still-embryonic concept. The case was the first of many that would challenge a broad disclaimer-type loyalty oath required of government employees, including public school teachers and state university professors. A majority of the justices rather indifferently upheld the power of a state to impose such a test as a condition of public employment, summarily rejecting free speech and due process arguments that the challengers had posed.

Justice Frankfurter now joined Justices Black and Douglas in dissent, but he also wrote separately.[7] While noting that the Fourteenth Amendment's guarantee of due process protects all citizens, Frankfurter argued that those who labored in the academic community presented a special claim: "[I]n view of the nature of the teacher's relation to the effective exercise of the rights which are safeguarded by the Bill of Rights . . . inhibition of freedom of thought, and of action upon thought, in the case of teachers brings the safeguards of those amendments vividly into operation. Such unwarranted inhibition upon the free spirit of teachers [also] . . . has an unmistakable tendency to chill that free play of the spirit which all teachers ought especially to cultivate and practice." The opinion then added Justice Frankfurter's fervent belief that "the functions of educational institutions in our national life and the conditions under which they alone can adequately perform them are at the basis of these limitations upon State and National Power." His reliance on "these limitations" seemed cryptic at the time, and still begs explanation, though the reference must have been to the special needs and conditions of the academic community that he had described earlier in the opinion—needs and conditions with which he was of course familiar from his many years as a Harvard Law School professor.

Another five years would pass before a majority of the justices were ready to embrace academic freedom as a protective concept. The case that achieved this critical step in 1957 seemed an unlikely vehicle for so momentous a metamorphosis; at issue were demands by New Hampshire's rogue attorney general for detailed notes of lectures that had been delivered at the University of New Hampshire by a visiting scholar named Paul Sweezy, whose political views were decidedly left of center. The majority's rebuff to Attorney General Louis Wyman's demand for the lecture notes rested on rather narrow grounds—specifically, absence of any evidence that the state legislature ever meant to authorize such a probe, leading the Court to reject the asserted basis for holding the visiting scholar in contempt for refusing to respond.

Chief Justice Earl Warren, writing for the majority, underscored the uniquely sensitive setting in which the case arose Beyond the general concern for a citizen's free speech rights, "we believe t at there unquestionably was an invasion of [Sweezy's] liberties in t e area of academic freedom and political expression." The context was critical: "The essentiality of freedom in the community of American universities is almost self-evident . . . Teachers and students must always remain free to inquire, to study and to evaluate, to gain new maturity and understanding; otherwise our civilization will stagnate and die."[8] Thus for the first time, academic freedom emerged in the *Sweezy* case as a component of a majority opinion, albeit not the rationale for a judgment that reflected a narrower and more clearly procedural basis.

Academic freedom was, however, even more central to Justice Frankfurter, who would have premised the judgment in Sweezy's favor (in which he joined) solely on that ground. His long and eloquent concurring opinion amplified substantially thoughts he had initially expressed in the loyalty oath case. Of paramount importance was Frankfurter's concern about the grave harm that could result from "governmental intrusion into the intellectual life of a university . . . [given] . . . the dependence of a free society on free universities." Moreover, "it matters little whether such intervention occurs avowedly or through action that inevitably tends to check the ardor and fearlessness of scholars." Thus "political power must abstain from intrusion into this activity of [academic] freedom . . . except for reasons that are exigent and obviously compelling."[9] The latter standard, significantly, was far more rigorous than the test that would have applied at this time to a government demand for testimony by a recalcitrant witness from a nonacademic setting.

The years since 1957 have brought a nearly linear progression in the evolution of judicially recognized academic freedom safeguards. During the post-*Sweezy* decade, the Supreme Court stuck down a series of disclaimer-type loyalty oaths exacted of prospective government workers, most notably in cases that specifically involved professors at state universities in Florida, Washington, New York, and Maryland. Most significant to this day for its forceful recognition of academic freedom was Justice William J. Brennan's eloquent opinion in the case that invalidated the very New York state loyalty oath that the Court sustained in 1952 over the dissents of Justices Black and Douglas.[10] The case, led by Harry Keyishian, had been brought by five State University of New York professors who were now ready to challenge the oath requirement. The pivotal passage bears quotation in full: "[A]cademic freedom . . . is of transcendent value to all of us and not merely to the teachers concerned. That freedom is therefore a special concern of the First Amendment, which does not tolerate laws that cast a pall of orthodoxy over the classroom. . . . The classroom is peculiarly the "marketplace of ideas." The Nation's future depends upon leaders trained through wide exposure to that robust exchange of ideas which discovers truth "out of a multitude of tongues, [rather] than through any kind of authoritative selection."[11]

Several features of Justice Brennan's opinion are arresting and merit recognition for what probably to this day represent the Supreme Court's clearest exposition of academic freedom principles. The focus was not simply—or even primarily—on legal protection of freedom for those who teach. The impact upon students of intrusive inquiries and constraints was of at least equal importance for Justice Brennan and his colleagues. Also crucial was the explicit absorption of academic freedom within the array of First Amendment freedoms that a state university professor may claim; beyond the full range of free speech interests that any citizen may invoke, a college teacher enjoys a special level of protection simply because of his or her calling.

Moreover, Justice Brennan's *Keyishian* opinion amply developed the rationale for that special solicitude, emphasizing the necessity to a democratic society of untrammeled scholarship and inquiry within the academic community, with a clarity and conviction not found in most earlier opinions that recognized professorial freedoms. Thus, as Professor William Van Alstyne has observed, "*Keyishian* marks an important right of passage. What *New York Times v. Sullivan* [recognizing a news-media privilege in libel suits brought by public officials] had meant in respect to journalism in the United States . . . *Keyishian* forcefully represents in respect to academic freedom."[12]

Had the process stopped there in 1967, the academic freedom of state college and university professors would today be solidly protected. It was, however, unlikely that the evolution of so vigorous and vital a doctrine would have faltered, and indeed it did not. Before long, academic freedom would receive the Supreme Court's solicitude in several other facets of higher education. In a curious irony, one of those areas was the very aspect of academic life to which the elder Justice Harlan had addressed his 1892 dissent in the *Berea College* case—taking account of applicants' race in order to enhance their prospects for admission.

During the 1960s, American higher education began to realize—and sought to redress—the appalling underrepresentation of racial and ethnic minorities at the nation's most selective institutions. Preferential consideration of race in the admissions process was bound to end up in court, and so it did by the late 1960s. The first case, involving the University of Washington's law school, reached the Supreme Court, but it was dismissed as moot before judgment when it became clear that a ruling either way would not affect the status of a student challenger who was about to graduate. Several years later, a similar challenge by a rejected applicant named Bakke to the inclusive use of race by the University of California–Davis Medical School entered the state courts and survived to a final U.S. Supreme Court ruling on the merits. The justices were sharply split; four would generally permit the preferential use of race in selective admissions, whereas four others saw such a preference as violative of the equal protection clause.[13]

That left Justice Lewis Powell as the critical tiebreaker. His opinion thus announced a judgment for the entire Court, though it reflected views that were uniquely his—on one hand, permitting the inclusive use of race under special conditions that individualized the admission process but, on the other hand, flatly forbidding cruder preferential measures such as racial quotas and rigid numerical formulas. Since he saw the UC–Davis

Medical School admissions process as falling into the latter category, he ruled in Bakke's favor. His opinion also signaled that more precisely tailored programs—he cited a Harvard admissions pool with approval—should survive equal protection challenges if they individualized the consideration of each applicant.

For Justice Powell, academic freedom held the key to what he deemed the proper and constitutionally permissible consideration of race in the admissions process. He recalled that Justice Frankfurter, in the *Sweezy* case, had listed certain key ingredients of constitutionally protected academic freedom, among them "who may be admitted to study," along with "who may teach, what may be taught, [and] how it shall be taught" as "essential freedoms of a university . . . to determine in academic grounds."[14] In stressing the selection of prospective students, Justice Powell recognized the importance of faculty judgments in the type of admission process that he felt should pass muster. On that basis, expressly invoking academic freedom to protect the making of such judgments, Powell took sharp issue with the four of his colleagues who would categorically ban any use of race, whether inclusive or exclusive, in the admissions process.

When the Supreme Court revisited the issue of race-based admissions in 2003, sustaining one University of Michigan admissions program while striking down another, Justice Sandra Day O'Connor had take over Justice Powell's tie-breaking role. Her opinion, differentiating between permissibly individualized and impermissibly categorical race-based admissions policies, invoked academic freedom in a potentially helpful way, though the Court now relied far more heavily on the institutional quest for racial and ethnic diversity as the talisman. Specifically, Justice O'Connor declared that courts should "defer" to an "educational judgment" such as the one Michigan's law faculty had made in taking race into account in the admissions process. Such a judgment, she continued, "lies primarily within the expertise of a university. [This approach] is in keeping with our tradition of giving a degree of deference to a university's academic decisions, within constitutionally prescribed limits." Even more welcome to the academic community was Justice O'Connor's insistence that a reviewing court must presume that the institution acted in "good faith" until and unless there was "a showing to the contrary."[15] The significance of such language could easily be undervalued. Lawrence White, formerly chief legal counsel for the Pennsylvania Department of Education and Georgetown University, notes that the *Grutter* ruling "stands for a series of interrelated legal propositions. First, judicial review of colleges' academic decisions is limited in scope. Second, academic decisions are presumptively entitled to deference and are assumed to have been made in good faith. And, finally, it takes a heck of a lot of persuasive evidence to rebut the presumption and entice a court into reversing what faculty members and academic administrators have, in their wisdom, decided in the exercise of their professional judgment."[16]

Ironically, academic freedom figured almost more importantly in Justice Clarence Thomas's dissent than in Justice O'Connor's Solomonic majority opinion. For Justice Thomas, any reliance on academic freedom to justify race-based admissions was simply inappropriate and unwarranted. As he reviewed the history of academic freedom in the Supreme Court, two elements deserved greater prominence than recent judgments had recognized—one, that academic freedom protected only expressive activity (and thus did not apply to factoring race into the admissions process); the other, that most of the seminal cases just happened to involve university professors but really defined speech rights of public employees generally. It was crucial for Thomas that in all the cases cited in support of special solicitude for academic freedom "the Court did not relax any independent constitutional restrictions on public universities." In consequence of that view, declared Justice Thomas, "there is no basis for a right of public universities to do what would otherwise violate the Equal Protection Clause"—as he clearly posited that racial preferences would elsewhere. Since only Justice Antonin Scalia joined this opinion, a broader application of academic freedom, including University of Michigan admissions policies, seemed to command at least a bare majority of the justices. But the caution from Justice Thomas surely bears note.

Between these two admissions-policy cases, however, a quite different legal challenge to an unrelated University of Michigan policy raised the profile of academic freedom. A medical student named Scott Ewing had been dismissed from the MD program after failing the National Board exams. He brought suit in federal court, claiming that he should not have been dismissed outright for a single academic lapse. The appeals court ruled in his favor, but the Supreme Court unanimously reversed that decision. The Court's opinion emphasized the special—indeed exceptional—degree of deference that courts properly pay to academic judgments, even where the reviewing judges might well have resolved the matter differently. Thus "a genuinely academic decision" should not be set aside by a court "unless it is such a substantial departure from accepted academic norms as to demonstrate that the person or committee responsible did not actually exercise professional judgment."[17]

The basis for such impressive deference was in part the absence of any generally accepted standards that a court might apply to the review of such actions. Of equal concern to the *Ewing* Court was a deep-seated judicial "reluctance to trench on the prerogatives of . . . educational institutions and our responsibility to safeguard their academic freedom, 'a special concern of the First Amendment.'"[18] Thus, only under egregious circumstances reflecting an abdication of responsibility by those within the academy would a court be free to second-guess "a genuinely academic decision" such as the dismissal of a student on scholastic grounds.

It is worth noting that both the *Ewing* and *Bakke* decisions primarily protected the institutional freedom of a university to make certain types of "academic judgments" without judicial interference rather than individual claims of professorial freedom. Although professors at highly selective institutions privately hold quite varied views on the wisdom of affirmative action or race-based admissions, the faculty and the administration have seemed in such cases to be on the same page. Thus, a judgment sustaining the use of race in the admission process validates an apparent campus consensus, creating no need to differentiate between the interests of professors and presidents or provosts respective interest. Such judgments need not anticipate the far more daunting task that would face a court in the event of dissonance between faculty and institutional policy, much less of direct conflict between a professor asserting individual academic freedom and an institution asserting a contrary position within the scope of its academic freedom. We address those perplexing issues in a later chapter and note for the moment only that the resolution of such disputes is much easier when the faculty, administration, and governing board at least appear to be in accord on policies that invite external challenge. Because such concord is not always present, the deeper question, whose academic freedom? needs to be faced, and we do so in a later chapter.

Academic freedom has received rather oblique, though still valuable, recognition in other legal contexts. Disputes arise periodically over the constitutionality—under the First Amendment's establishment clause—of government support for church-related colleges and universities. This issue has been several times to the Supreme Court, with the general result that such institutions may benefit more substantially and directly from public subvention than may elementary and secondary parochial schools. Crucial to this distinction has been the high Court's view of vital differences between the general run of church-related precollegiate schools on the one hand and religiously affiliated postsecondary education on the other. The four church-affiliated institutions in the test case seemed to the Court poster children for such a distinction.

Not only did the religious colleges "subscribe to a well-established set of principles of academic freedom." In addition, "the schools were characterized by an atmosphere of academic freedom rather than religious indoctrination" and fully subscribed to the basic policies of the American Association of University Professors. Thus, in summary, "many church-related colleges and universities are characterized by a high degree of academic freedom and seek to evoke free and critical responses from their students."[19] On that basis, the Court has consistently sustained public programs to aid religiously affiliated postsecondary institutions that would not, at least until very recently, have passed muster at the elementary or secondary level. It is especially in this context that one can appreciate the degree of deference the Supreme Court accords to a demonstrated institutional commitment to academic freedom.

Two other examples of such judicial deference are worth noting. When the Supreme Court sustained regulations that restricted the abortion-related speech of staff members at federally funded health clinics, Chief Justice William Rehnquist, citing the Keyishian loyalty oath decision, took pains to reassure the academic community that it need not fear the implications of such a judgment: "We have recognized that the university is a traditional sphere of free expression so fundamental to the functioning of our society that the Government's ability to control speech within that sphere by means of conditions attached to the expenditure of Government funds is restricted by the vagueness and overbreadth doctrines of the First Amendment."[20] The context has critical importance far beyond the college campus; Justice Brennan applied for the first time to civil rights and civil liberties the doctrine of "unconstitutional conditions"—the precept that government may not use its power to withhold or qualify benefits as an indirect way of stifling expressive and other freedoms that could not be directly suppressed or denied.[21] The academic community was not slow to seize upon this welcome recognition of its special status in the abortion-clinic funding case. Within months of the Supreme Court's ruling, a federal district judge was asked to (and did) distinguish the abortion-funding case in striking down a prepublication clearance and review rule that federal agencies had sought to impose on scholars as a condition of their receiving federal research grants.[22]

A decade later, the Supreme Court reviewed a challenge to the widespread practice of state universities in mandating that all students pay an activities fee, which typically supports a broad array of student organizations. Because somewhat similar levies had been successfully challenged elsewhere on First Amendment grounds (notably in the context of compulsory labor-union dues) students who chafed at the politically sensitive use of their mandatory fee payments launched a comparable challenge at several campuses. In 2000, the high Court sustained the University of Wisconsin's mandatory fee program and, to the surprise of many observers, sharply distinguished the campus setting from the unionized workplace. Central to this unanimous and highly deferential ruling was the Court's sense of the university as a special enclave, within which even judgments on extracurricular matters (such as student activities funding) deserved substantial deference of a kind not necessarily warranted in any other, seemingly comparable setting.

Although the University of Wisconsin did not rely primarily on its long and widely recognized commitment to academic freedom, nor did the dominant opinion stress that legacy in defining the appropriate degree of deference, the opinion reflected a comparable solicitude: "The University may determine that its mission is well served if its students have the means to engage in dynamic discussions of philosophical, religious, scientific, social, and political subjects in their extracurricular campus life outside the lecture hall."[23] On that basis, a substantially higher level of deference was appropriate when the fee-collector was a university rather than a labor union or any other type of organization.

This impressive and diverse body of law that protects academic freedom did not evolve in isolation or in a constitutional vacuum. Court decisions that expressly protect academic freedom provide only part of a complex amalgam of protective legal principles. Indeed, the Supreme Court's recognition of the constitutional rights of university professors paralleled and benefited substantially from other expansions of Bill of Rights-based protections. The speech of public employees affords a striking example of such complementary protection. When a Massachusetts policeman named John J. McAuliffe was fired in 1890 for speaking at a political rally and sought reinstatement in the courts, Justice Oliver Wendell Holmes (then a state court judge) summarily rejected the officer's claims: "[He] may have a constitutional right to talk politics, but he has no constitutional right to be a policeman. There are few employments for hire in which the servant does not agree to suspend his constitutional right of free speech as well as of idleness, by the implied terms of his contract."[24] For Holmes and his Massachusetts Supreme Judicial Court colleagues, public employment was simply a privilege that the commonwealth could grant or deny as it wished and on which it was free to impose virtually any conditions.

Three-quarters of a century later, Illinois high school teacher Marvin Pickering was discharged after he wrote to the local newspaper a letter that was highly critical of the school board's budget policies and priorities. The letter contained several factual errors, which especially angered the board. When he sued to regain his job, he found the state courts little more sympathetic than Justice Holmes had been to Officer McAuliffe. "A teacher who displays disrespect toward the Board of Education," ruled the Illinois Supreme Court majority, "is not promoting the best interests of his school, and the Board . . . does not abuse its discretion in dismissing him."[25] Pickering took his case to the United States Supreme Court, where he found a far more receptive audience—in fact, a majority that was now ready, for the first time, to declare Justice Holmes's view of public-employee speech misguided and benighted.

Justice Brennan now declared a dramatically different view of those who toiled (and occasionally tangled) in the public sector. Henceforth, government workers, such as Pickering, would enjoy at least partial protection for any statements they made on any matter of "public concern," since public employment could no longer be treated as a mere privilege to be conditioned or denied at the agency's whim.[26] Thus, even if an offending or contentious statement contained erroneous material, as Pickering's letter concededly did, dismissal could follow only if such misstatements had been made with reckless disregard of the truth or deliberate falsification—the very standard the Court had recently applied to libel actions brought by public officials. There were important exceptions, to be sure; public-employee speech that seriously disrupted internal morale, undermined client confidence in the agency, took excessive time away from the job, or simply demonstrated incompetence were not categorically protected in the public workplace, even though such statements remained within a citizen's right of free speech.

This ruling in Pickering's favor marked a radical change in the status of public employees, who in most states had previously been no freer to speak than was the hapless Officer McAuliffe. Eventually such protection would be extended beyond employees to government contractors and other beneficiaries. Not surprisingly, this doctrine has been of special benefit to politically active state college and university professors in their roles as public employees. Few if any sectors of government employment have over the years been more outspoken, or more likely to evoke legislative or gubernatorial wrath, than state college and university professors. Thus the special protection afforded by the doctrine of academic freedom has been substantially augmented by the general standards of public-employee speech forged in the *Pickering* decision. Because state college and university professors are all public employees, their speech on matters of public concern is at least as well protected as the speech of nonacademic government workers.

Recognition of public-employee speech rights reflected a broader transition in the high Court's thinking from a time when most government benefits were viewed merely as privileges that could be withheld or conditioned with impunity to the current, dramatically more protective, view. Under the heading of "unconstitutional conditions" the Supreme Court has over the last half century heightened markedly the obligations that government owes to its beneficiaries. The process began in the late 1950s, when the justices ruled that a California war veteran could not be required to sign a loyalty oath in order to obtain a tax exemption available to all who had been honorably discharged from military service.[27]

Under the leadership of Justice Brennan, this principle was to be progressively applied in myriad situations, including the use of public property for various purposes, contracting with government, enrollment at state universities and receipt of scholarships, residing in public housing, eligibility for welfare and other social services, and, of course, most facets of public employment among a broad array of beneficial relationships. Gone from Supreme Court jurisprudence was the once paramount but now discredited distinction between "rights" that were legally vested or otherwise inviolable and less firmly protected "privileges" that could be conditioned or withdrawn with impunity. In general, as a direct result of Justice Brennan's jurisprudence and its impact on myriad legal claims and interests, government may seldom use the power of the purse, or conditioned benefits, to entice or induce citizen behavior that it could not directly coerce or compel.[28]

There remain a few obvious exceptions to such a comprehensive declaration; for example, there seems little doubt that the federal government may constitutionally offer scholarships or loan forgiveness to students who agree after graduation to practice medicine or teach in severely underserved communities, even though clearly such service could not be compelled or conscripted. But such exceptions are rare; in most situations it would be accurate to say that, because it may not impose unconstitutional conditions, government may not "buy" citizen behavior that it lacks the power to command or coerce. The dramatic shift brought about by the *Pickering* decision in the law that governs public-employee speech offers a classic illustration of this much broader principle.

However, change was in the wind as Justice Sandra Day O'Connor announced her retirement after many years as a strong protector of speech in the public sector. The Supreme Court's 2005 term, and the replacement of Justice O'Connor with Justice Samuel Alito, brought a dramatic dilution of the free speech rights of public employees. On May 30, a new majority of the Court ruled that when a public worker's statements are made "pursuant to his or her official duties," they fall outside *Pickering*'s protection, which is henceforth confined to statements made "as a citizen." The specific case concerned a Los Angeles assistant district attorney named Richard Ceballos, who had been highly critical of the way his office had obtained a crucial search warrant; his critical comments, declared the majority, might well relate to a "matter of public concern" but more important—and disabling—was the way they related to his assigned tasks as a prosecutor. The implications for academic freedom were hard to avoid. Justice David Souter, writing for himself and three colleagues in dissent, warned that the majority's view could gravely "imperil academic freedom in public colleges and universities, whose teachers necessarily speak and write 'pursuant to official duties.'" Even the majority recognized the problem, noting that "there is some argument that expression related to academic scholarship or classroom instruction implicates additional constitutional interests that are not fully accounted for by this Court's customary employee-speech jurisprudence." But the majority avoided this portent because the issue was not squarely presented to them; they had no need to decide whether their ruling on a prosecutor's speech "would apply in the same manner to a case involving speech related to scholarship or teaching."[29]

The implications of the *Ceballos* ruling for academic freedom are deeply troubling in two respects. For one, where it is clear that a state university professor speaks with regard to his or her assigned academic specialty, the scope of constitutional protection now varies inversely with the proximity of that subject to the topic of the contentious statement. A perverse and troubling irony results: The scholar who discusses a matter that is quite remote from his or her academic discipline still seems to enjoy First Amendment protection, whereas the professor who evokes controversy while addressing the field in which he or she is an expert apparently forfeits such protection because such statements fall within that scholar's "official duties."

The second concern is equally grave. The line between speech within one's "official duties" and speech "as a citizen" is so imprecise that it offers little useful guidance to the conscientious scholar. Much like the pernicious disclaimer-type loyalty oaths that were invalidated in the 1960s, the operative standard that could place a professor's job at risk fails to provide the degree of clarity or certainty that courts routinely require of legislators and regulators when speech may be affected. Finally, and most deeply troubling, the *Ceballos* Court fundamentally failed to appreciate the critical difference between a university and its faculty, on the one hand, and the professional staff of a prosecutor's office on the other. Assistant district attorneys are hired and paid to carry out very specific tasks, albeit as legally trained professionals. Imposing limits on what they can say in the performance of their assigned duties may create valid free speech concerns but could be justified by the government's need to have prosecutors acting and speaking in substantial concert. In stark contrast, the government hires university professors to advance knowledge and seek truth and to challenge and stimulate their students. Any notion that the government's needs and interests are remotely comparable in these two situations not only misses the point but also poses ominous concerns for academic freedom. It is of course too early to tell whether such assimilation will actually occur. All we know is that Justice Souter's grave warning about the potential impact on professorial speech went largely unheeded, on the bench and far beyond.

As the applicable law developed, judicial solicitude for public workers would serve to benefit and protect government workers in a quite different way, with special value for university teachers. Along with free speech, procedural due process began to emerge as a parallel safeguard for those who were threatened with loss of government benefits. In a series of cases, the high Court ruled that various types of public benefits, especially a government job, could not be summarily revoked without some form of hearing. Even an aggrieved welfare recipient was now constitutionally entitled to be heard before benefits could be terminated. The application of this new safeguard to the academic community brought two major Supreme Court rulings in 1972, both of which contributed measurably to academic freedom.[30]

As a result of these two rulings, one coming from Texas and the other from Wisconsin, even a nontenured university teacher may assert that his or her interest in continuing academic employment is protected either as an element of "liberty" or of "property" under the due process guarantees of the Fifth and Fourteenth Amendments. Thus, the argument runs, government may not arbitrarily or summarily terminate a professorial appointment without breaching one of the most basic and fundamental of human rights. Only through a rigorous process—"due process" in legal parlance—may an adverse judgment result in the termination of such employment, especially where the catalyst is unmistakably the targeted professor's publicly expressed and controversial views. Thus such a person gains the right to challenge an official adverse action (typically nonreappointment to a future term) before an impartial body within the university. Although the Court made clear that such a claim would not automatically bring about reinstatement, simply enjoying the opportunity to contest a negative judgment vastly enhanced the rights of nontenured teachers.

Protection of public-employee speech is but one of the beneficial legal developments that has paralleled the emergence of, and enhanced, academic freedom. The First Amendment expressly protects only freedom of speech and of the press, and the right of the people "peaceably to assemble, and to petition the Government for a redress of grievances." Today we naturally assume that "freedom of association" is safely ensconced among First Amendment expressive rights, as indeed it is. What we tend to overlook are the recency of such recognition and the degree to which its emergence reflects a creative judicial gloss on the text of the Bill of Rights. A quick reference to the text of the Bill of Rights readily reveals that "freedom of assembly" is mentioned in the First Amendment, while the far more important "freedom of association" is not. How the latter liberty came to join the former is worth recounting.

In 1958, the Supreme Court faced the question whether southern states could demand and obtain membership lists from NAACP officers; recent experience amply supported the concern that such lists in hostile hands could lead to loss of employment, harassment, and even worse for those whose names appeared on them. The constitutional basis for withholding such sensitive information was unclear; thirty years earlier the Court had allowed New York to obtain such membership lists from ten Ku Klux Klan officials. Despite the obvious difference in context, and the Court's solicitude for civil rights activists, nothing in the Bill of Rights seemed quite apposite.

The high Court responded by simply declaring (without invoking any recognized precedent) that the First Amendment protects a "freedom of association," despite the absence of any mention of such an interest anywhere in the Constitution.[31] No justice has ever questioned the appropriateness of such recognition. Two years later, the Court applied this new concept to the case of Daisy Bates, an Arkansas teacher who had been dismissed when she refused, as state law mandated, to reveal to her employer the entire list of organizations to which she belonged.[32] Because she belonged to organizations that her school board might not approve of, among them the NAACP, the risks of compliance were manifest. The Supreme Court relieved her of this dilemma, noting that some memberships might be of legitimate interest to a government agency but that an indiscriminate demand of the type to which Bates was subjected was excessive and violated her freedom of association.

This recent but now firmly settled expressive interest has since been applied in myriad settings where freedom to associate—and occasionally not to associate—has proved an invaluable supplement to the more familiar expressive rights. It has protected, for example, the interests of minor political parties, of public employees who belong to the "wrong" party, and eventually even of less favored groups such as the Ku Klux Klan. Organizations have by this means gained legal protection against unwelcome or compelled association—most recently through a declaration by the high Court that the Boy Scouts of America had an expressive interest in not being forced to accept an openly gay scoutmaster despite a state antidiscrimination law that specifically protected sexual orientation.[33]

Several other protective doctrines have roughly paralleled the emergence of academic freedom and have measurably buttressed its principles. During the McCarthy era, the gravest threat to the academic community came in the form of legislative investigations, mainly at the federal level but also in a number of states. The Senate subcommittee that McCarthy himself chaired summoned from many sectors people who were suspected of disloyalty or subversive activity, or who were simply viewed as convenient sources of damaging information about colleagues, friends, and neighbors. It was, however, the academic profession that suffered most, perhaps in part because scholarly witnesses were less sophisticated and experienced than were those called from entertainment, journalism, and elsewhere, or perhaps because the reluctance to target a vulnerable colleague was greater among academics. Suffice it to say that the process of legislative inquiry interrupted at the very least hundreds, indeed almost certainly thousands, of academic careers, and many were totally destroyed.

What was striking about these forays was the virtual absence of any constitutional safeguards for suspected citizens summoned to testify in public or to be interviewed in secret sessions. Much of the damage done to academic and government careers could have been alleviated by even rudimentary procedural protections or by insistence by the courts or by Congress on a modicum of fairness. Just as the McCarthy era and the senator's power were waning, the Supreme Court first imposed limited procedural constraints on the scope and manner of legislative probes. Yet it was not until 1963, long after McCarthyism had ceased to be an imminent threat, that major safeguards emerged. A Florida legislative committee summoned a prominent NAACP official and demanded that he bring with him and be prepared to disclose membership lists. Recognizing that a mere assertion of associational freedom would not outweigh the power of legislative inquiry, the justices now declared that only a "compelling interest" in the targeted information would justify holding in contempt a recalcitrant witness.[34] From the time of that ruling, it has been clear that the worst excesses of McCarthyism could not recur, unless the Supreme Court were to abandon the safeguards it created starting in the early 1960s.

One case from that period has special value, and it also admirably illustrates judicial creativity. A young man named Edward Yellin had been called as a witness before a House committee that was investigating suspected subversive activity on college campuses. After Yellin had refused to answer specific questions about his political activities as an undergraduate at the University of Michigan, he was cited for contempt of Congress. When the case reached the Supreme Court, Yellin's academic freedom argument was unlikely to succeed, because he had long since left the campus and taken a job in industry. But the extensive congressional probing of his student political ties was nonetheless of deep concern to the academic community.

Even without invoking academic freedom as such, the high Court ruled in Yellin's favor and thereby established an extremely important procedural safeguard.[35] Yellin had initially expressed his preference for a closed hearing, but that request was denied and he was interrogated in public. The committee had adopted (but apparently forgot or disregarded) a rule under which any subcommittee witness's request to be heard in executive session must be referred to the full body. Admitedly, this had not been done despite Yellin's timely request.

It was on this basis that the Supreme Court dismissed the contempt, noting that the committee's conceded failure to follow its own rules—even though not constitutionally obligated to offer a witness such an option—created a due process issue. In several other comparable cases, a public body or agency has been taken to task for breaching an obligation it had voluntarily imposed upon itself. The resulting principle confirms one of Justice Oliver Wendell Holmes's memorable maxims: "Government must turn square corners"—even when the angle of the corner is of the government's own making. The *Yellin* case thus strengthens the conviction that the excesses of McCarthyism could not easily recur.

By this point it should be apparent that legal protection for academic freedom has many components, extending well beyond the decisions that expressly invoke that concept. Freedom of association, public-employee speech, constraints on legislative inquiries, and the broader concept of unconstitutional conditions have all made major contributions to the protection of academic freedom and free inquiry. Thus when observers such as Senator Carl Levin, who are familiar with the applicable legal safeguards, declare that a recurrence of McCarthyism is highly improbable, they rely heavily on what has happened in the courts over the past half century. During the early and mid-1950s, not only was there virtually no law expressly protecting academic freedom; there was also virtually no legal protection for outspoken public employees or other government beneficiaries, for recalcitrant legislative witnesses, or for those who wished to join or remain as members of controversial organizations. These rights have gained constitutional protection only since the late 1950s, confirming the sense that the world of the early twenty-first century is indeed starkly different.

Several recent and notable court cases illustrate how congenially this branch of the law has continued to evolve over the past half century. Consider first the case of Professor Michael Levin, a philosophy teacher at the City College of New York (CCNY). He had been a member of the faculty, with tenure, for two decades, apparently without conflict or contention on campus or beyond. In the late 1980s he submitted to an obscure Australian journal a review in which he ventured that African Americans had been less successful than Caucasians in most academic fields not because of racial bias but simply because "the average black is significantly less intelligent than the average white."[36] It was on this basis that Levin sought to explain the undeniable underrepresentation of minorities in scholarly fields such as his own. At no time did Levin ever discuss these views on the CCNY campus, much less seek to impose them on any of his students. They appeared only in the Australian book review.

When these writings came to public attention in New York, the response was one of outrage and indignation, on campus and well beyond. The City College faculty senate adopted a condemnatory resolution. State and municipal officials, white as well as black, demanded Levin's head. City College's president, an acclaimed African American psychologist and seasoned academic administrator named Bernard Harleston, concluded that he could not avoid opening an official inquiry into Levin's book review and possibly other writings. He launched the process with an accompanying statement, noting with caution that "the process of removing a tenured professor is a complicated one [because] tenure is the life blood of the College." The statement concluded that Levin's "views are offensive to the basic values of human equality and decency and simply have no place here at City College."[37]

Before the planned inquiry ran its course, however, Levin filed suit in federal court, claiming that his academic freedom and free speech had been abridged by the administration's actions. The suit also cited an offer that the Arts and Sciences dean made to students who were already enrolled in Levin's introductory philosophy course; each student received a letter, noting that because Professor Levin had "expressed controversial views" the student might wish to leave the scheduled section and instead enroll in a "shadow" section created as an escape vehicle. Finally, Levin claimed in his lawsuit that the CCNY administration had failed adequately to protect and preserve order in his classes after the controversy erupted.

The federal judge who heard the case, sitting without a jury, resolved virtually all the contested issues in Levin's favor. Viewing the administration's response as an excess of "political correctness," the court specifically found that the targeted investigation into Levin's published words was "admittedly predicated solely upon his protected First Amendment expression of ideas." The gratuitous creation of the "shadow" sections also abridged Levin's rights because of the absence of any student complaint or request; the effect of the dean's letters to Levin's students—apart from depressing his enrollments—was to "officially [condemn] his ideas as controversial and dangerous to the welfare of his students and the educational process in the College at large." The judge also backed Levin on the security issue, concluding that the CCNY administration had failed to protect him and his classes adequately in "retaliation for [his] First Amendment expression of ideas."[38]

When the case reached the federal appeals court, it came before a panel that was no less sympathetic to Levin's pleas than the district judge had been. The higher court was, if anything, even more troubled by the creation of the shadow sections but reserved its sharpest critique for the implication of President Harleston's declaration that "these views simply have no place here at City College"—an implicit threat to seek his removal from the faculty, despite the absence of any action to that end and the administration's clear recognition of the sanctity of tenure. Although the trial judge had entered an injunction against the college and its administration, the appeals court felt a declaratory judgment would suffice, partly because President Harleston had announced his imminent retirement.[39]

If bad luck comes in multiples, it has seldom been so clearly the case as at CCNY in the mid-1990s. Across campus, the even more volatile case of Professor Leonard Jeffries was unfolding. The parallels to Levin's case were uncanny. Levin and Jeffries had both been graduate students at the same time at Columbia University, and they had both been tenured professors at CCNY for many years, though apparently they had never met. But Jeffries, unlike Levin, held an administrative post, as chair of the Black Studies Program. What brought Jeffries to public attention was a speech he gave at the Empire State Black Arts and Cultural Festival in Albany. The speech contained not very subtle jibes at prominent educators—calling historian Diane Ravitch "a sophisticated Texas Jew" and caricaturing her as "Miss Daisy" in addition to accusing fellow historian Arthur Schlesinger, Jr. (whom he erronously labeled as Jewish) of seeking to derail multiculturalism at City College. But it was a virulent attack on racial stereotyping in film that really drew the headlines. Jeffries depicted "a conspiracy, planned and plotted and programmed out of Hollywood by people called Greenberg and Weisberg and Trigliani. . . . Russian Jewry had a particular control over the movies . . . and their financial partners, the Mafia, put together a financial system of destruction of black people."[40]

Reaction to the speech was immediate and intense. New York Governor Mario Cuomo, then a serious presidential prospect, exploded when he heard of the speech, finding Jeffries rhetoric "so egregious that the City University ought to take action or explain why it doesn't."[41] New York's senior senator, Daniel Patrick Moynihan, keenly familiar with principles of academic freedom from his own career, urged that "Jeffries ought to resign [and] if he does not, the trustees should."[42] At least one legislator launched a petition to compel Jeffries' removal from the faculty, and even some African American leaders expressed dismay. There were also rallies of support for the embattled scholar, and though the sponsors of the conference at which the catalytic statements occurred distanced themselves from Jeffries' views, they insisted on his right to express them.

Meanwhile, President Harleston faced an acute dilemma. As an African American, who had a short time earlier taken Professor Levin to task for a very different sort of racist comment, he could hardly overlook or condone Professor Jeffries' outburst. Thus, while deploring statements on or off campus that "undermine another racial or ethnic group" he cautioned that "the right to free expression and, indeed, to academic freedom, is not and cannot be absolute." The faculty senate considered the situation but declined to recommend any action beyond "disavowing and rejecting" the content of Jeffries' speech. As a result of so passive a response, the administration was again left to its own resources. Providentially, it seemed, Jeffries' term as chair of Black Studies was about to expire and, though his colleagues had voted to extend his appointment, the administration shortened that extension to less than a year. Soon thereafter, the CUNY board appointed a new chair, a senior Africanist from Yale.

Perhaps inspired by Levin's success, Jeffries also took his claims to federal court. Going well beyond the injunction that Levin requested, Jeffries now sought as well as vindication and reinstatement, $25 million in damages from fifteen named university officials, all alleged to have conspired to his detriment. The case came before the same federal district judge who had a short time earlier ruled in Levin's favor, although this time with a jury as well. Jeffries' lawyers insisted that the Albany speech had been the sole basis for the change in administrative assignment, whereas the college's attorneys claimed that the demotion had been simply part of a routine review of the campus academic organization and that the close proximity in time of the two events was purely coincidental.

Not surprisingly, the jury was skeptical when the college maintained that those officials who guided the review had been told to disregard Jeffries' volatile rhetoric. After the jury found in Jeffries' favor on the initial claims, they assessed record personal damages—$80,000 against each of four trustees and $50,000 against the president. Finally, on the issue of Jeffries' administrative position, the judge ruled that only full reinstatement would adequately redress the wrong that had been done. Although the judge conceded that Jeffries had made "hateful, poisonous and reprehensible statements" and had behaved in a "thuggish" way, the college had deprived him of his constitutional rights. Moreover, in the judge's view, the CUNY lawyers had been "dishonest" and even "cowardly" in their efforts to uncouple Jeffries' reassignment from his rhetoric.[43]

In the end, however, this seemingly stunning victory turned out to be a curiously Pyrrhic one for Professor Jeffries. The Supreme Court had just modified the law of public-employee speech in a way that gave greater deference, in hindsight, to an agency's adverse judgment about an outspoken employee. Thus the lower courts concluded they had no choice but to dismiss Jeffries' claims and to leave him, in the end, a tenured professor without any administrative assignment and, of course, without the damages to which he (and both lower courts) had felt he was entitled.[44] The case thus ended with a whimper, despite having created much excitement along the way and having also sent a strongly cautionary message to administrators and governing boards that might be tempted to take outspoken professors to task for their extramural statements.

Race and politics loomed large in one other case that deeply troubled this same federal appeals court in New York during this period. Professor Ernest Dube, a black South African, had been teaching for several years at the State University of New York at Stony Brook. In the prospectus for his course titled "The Politics of Race," he announced that he proposed to compare apartheid in South Africa, Nazism in Germany, and Zionism in Israel. Reports emerged that in his classroom he had asserted on at least one occasion, "Zionism is as much racism as Nazism was racism"[45] and had invited the class to share his view as to the parallels between the two. When this report became public, intense community pressure came to bear on the Stony Brook administration, demanding some adverse action. Governor Cuomo was quoted in the press as condemning "the failure of the University community to denounce Dr. Dube."[46] Some Stony Brook alumni wrote to declare not only their indignation but also their intent to withhold further contributions if Dube remained on the faculty. A faculty senate committee carefully reviewed Dube's teachings and found them to be well within the bounds of academic freedom, if admittedly controversial.

When Professor Dube became eligible for tenure, an ad hoc faculty committee recommended favorable action by a nearly unanimous vote. The campus academic administration concluded, however, that his published scholarship was insufficient for tenure and, on that basis, rejected the recommendation. Dube then went to federal court, claiming that this adverse judgment reflected primarily and inescapably the controversy over his widely publicized views on the asserted parallels between Zionism and racism. The district judge rendered a rather mixed opinion, refusing to dismiss the suit because a jury might find that "but for the exercise of his First Amendment right of free speech Dr. Dube would have been granted tenure." The court of appeals reached essentially the same conclusion, declining to dismiss the case and sending it back for trial.[47]

To keep the case alive at this stage, it was enough that Dube had alleged facts and circumstances that, if proved, would validate his claim that the tenure denial constituted retaliation for his unorthodox and widely publicized views. There seemed to be ample evidence from which a jury could conclude that tenure had been denied "as a result of the controversy surrounding his teaching." The court noted the potential relevance of Supreme Court rulings on academic freedom, though more on the procedural issue of qualified immunity—whether Stony Brook and State University officials should have known that denial of tenure to an outspoken professor impinged on constitutional rights.

The case was eventually settled before it came to trial, foreclosing any appellate review of the merits. But the clear implication of both preliminary federal court rulings was unmistakable: A state university may not base an adverse judgment about a professor's eligibility for tenure on contentious statements made in or out of class, even when those statements evoke intense hostility or threaten reprisal against the institution from government, alumni, community, or others. Although the precise role of academic freedom in this case never emerged as clearly as in other litigation, the court's inclination toward conferring constitutional protection on such contentious speech was hard to miss. No comparable dispute seems to have reached the courts since that time, thus leaving the *Dube* case as an isolated but portentous precedent.

Not surprisingly, it is in the college classroom that the law of academic freedom has evolved most clearly. Two cases from the Vietnam era helped to advance that process and (though largely neglected in later times) clearly deserve mention here. In the early 1970s, the Los Angeles Police Department (LAPD) sent undercover agents into University of California–Los Angeles (UCLA) classrooms, enrolled and posing as regular students, to compile dossiers on certain professors and report in detail the content of classroom discussions. These officers also attended private meetings of certain student political organizations and placed their reports in official police files. When this practice came to light, several UCLA professors, led by historian Hayden White, brought suit in state court against the police chief, seeking to put an end to this insidious form of surveillance.

The trial court dismissed the complaint, concluding that routine police surveillance infringed no constitutional rights of faculty or students. Several recent decisions in other, nonacademic settings, including one at the U.S. Supreme Court level, had declined to enjoin even clandestine information gathering by law enforcement agencies. But the California Supreme Court saw this case very differently and insisted it should go back for trial.[48] Characterizing the LAPD's challenged practices as "unprecedented in our nation's history," the court perceived a grave threat to privacy, freedom of association, and very specifically to academic freedom. After reviewing the relevant U.S. Supreme Court cases, from *Sweezy* through the loyalty oath rulings of the previous decade, the California justices concluded that "the police investigatory conduct at issue unquestionably poses at least as debilitating a threat to academic freedom" as those which the nation's highest Court had invalidated. A key paragraph of the California Supreme Court opinion is well worth quoting: "The crucible of new thought is the university classroom; the campus is the sacred ground of free discussion. Once we expose the teacher or the student to possible future prosecution for the ideas he may express, we forfeit the security that nourishes change and advancement. The censorship of totalitarian regimes that so often condemns developments in art, science and politics is but a step removed from the inchoate surveillance of free discussion in the university; such intrusion stifles creativity and to a large extent shackles democracy."[49]

What seems most remarkable about the *White* decision, and the key passage that explained it, was the California Supreme Court's solicitude for the university classroom as a uniquely sensitive and vulnerable place. Although routine gathering and recording of information by law enforcement agencies can seldom be challenged in court, even where such activity may adversely affect political association and expression, police surveillance in the college classroom seemed to the California court uniquely damaging to the process of teaching, learning, and inquiry. Such practices in the college classroom thus came to be treated very differently from comparable surveillance in society at large. The issue seems never to have returned to the courts, despite some evidence of clandestine probes and data gathering in the campus setting. The *White* case thus affords unique, though vitally significant, recognition of one especially sensitive form of academic freedom.

Another case from the Vietnam era exemplified a different dimension of academic freedom in the college classroom. After the tragic shooting deaths of four students at Ohio's Kent State University in early May 1970, the Portage County district attorney convened a special grand jury to investigate events that led up to and through the campus turmoil that brought in the heavily armed National Guard. The grand jury quickly turned its animus toward those faculty members and students who were perceived as the catalysts for that turmoil, according to the widely publicized report (which, under Ohio law, should have remained secret). Several Kent State professors who had been targeted by name in the report and against whom an indictment had been returned sued the state's attorney general in federal court, claiming abridgment of their constitutional liberties. In a remarkable ruling, the district judge agreed with the plaintiffs and resolved virtually every issue in their favor.[50] The court even ordered the public destruction of the official copy of the offending report, a highly symbolic act that occurred early one morning in the parking lot of Ravenna's courthouse when the county clerk used her cigarette lighter to ignite the discredited document.

The Kent State ruling is quite remarkable for its explicit contribution to the law of academic freedom. During the hearing in federal court, several faculty members testified in detail about the impact upon their teaching of the grand jury report's publication. As the district judge noted in his opinion, "instructors have altered or dropped course materials for fear of classroom controversy," citing specific literary works now deemed too risky to discuss in Kent State classes. Although teachers routinely modify their course syllabuses for various reasons, "when a university professor is fearful that [a particular poem] may produce 'inflammatory discussion' in a poetry class, it is evident that the Report's riptide is washing away protected expression on the Kent campus." The link to academic freedom was now apparent and forcefully stated: "The Report is dulling classroom discussion and is upsetting the teaching atmosphere. . . . When thought is controlled, or appears to be controlled, when pedagogues and pupils shrink from free inquiry at a state university because of a report of a resident Grand Jury, then academic freedom of expression is impermissibly impaired. This will curb conditions essential to the fulfillment of the university's learning purposes."[51]

The Kent State plaintiffs might have prevailed even without such explicit recognition of external threats to their academic freedom; the publication of the grand jury report so clearly invaded the mandated secrecy of such proceedings that some relief would surely have been warranted. In a nonacademic setting, however, such a ruling would have been quite narrow and would probably have taken little, if any, account of the impact of such rogue action on expressive freedoms. What was distinctive about the Kent State opinion was the length to which a federal judge went to determine the precise nature of the threat to academic freedom, reciting in detail the steps that understandably fearful professors had taken to modify their selection of classroom material. It is in that sense that the Kent State decision—curiously never appealed to an appellate tribunal that probably would have been more sympathetic to the prosecutor—remains as a notable milestone in the evolution of legal protection for academic freedom.

Speech in the classroom has generated litigation of a very different sort, with less consistent results. Professors occasionally enliven their courses with salacious language, which they employ for myriad reasons—to emphasize certain passages or principles, to expose sheltered students to a broader literary landscape, or simply to attract and hold the attention of a languorous late-afternoon section. Such unconventional teaching material often evokes both praise and rebuke, from colleagues as well as students. It is thus hardly surprising that the courts have found such disputes much harder to resolve than cases of the type we have just reviewed.

Consider the case of Professor Dean Cohen, who had taught English courses at California's San Bernardino Community College for many years. Though most of his students found Cohen's classes to be challenging and engaging, the term "abrasive" appeared occasionally on his evaluations. His periodic injection of four-letter words into his classroom, usually from literary sources, eventually brought a charge of sexual harassment at the behest of several female students. A college hearing panel found Cohen guilty of harassment, required him to seek counseling at his own expense, and further decreed that he must "become sensitive to the particular needs and backgrounds of his students, and . . . modify his teaching strategy when it becomes apparent that his techniques create a climate which impedes the students' ability to learn."[52]

Cohen then sued the college in federal court, claiming an abridgement of his free speech. The district judge deferred almost totally to the college's laudable desire to reduce claimed harassment in the interest of creating a more welcome environment for an increasingly diverse student body. The federal appeals court, however, saw the case very differently and ruled in Cohen's favor on virtually every contested issue.[53] The appellate court's conclusion that Cohen had been badly treated by the college did not, however, compel its endorsement of his teaching style or his choice of classroom language. Indeed, the Ninth Circuit appeals court noted that there were no applicable standards, in the Supreme Court's jurisprudence or its own, defining "what scope of First Amendment protection is to be given a college professor's classroom speech" and found in this case no occasion to offer such a definition. It was enough that the terms of the sexual harassment policy were unconstitutionally vague in their application to Cohen.[54]

The court sharply faulted the college administration for the use of imprecise inhibitory language to "punish teaching methods that Cohen had used for many years." The opinion was highly critical of the absence of any official warning that the institution now disapproved "his longstanding teaching style . . . which . . . had apparently been considered pedagogically sound and within the bounds of teaching methodology permitted at the College."[55] Apparent sympathy for Cohen's "teaching methods" and "teaching style" may be found elsewhere in this brief opinion. Thus, while technically leaving open the scope of constitutional protection for the classroom use of vulgar and taboo words, this court strongly implied a readiness to support, against institutional sanctions, a consistent and pedagogically valid practice of enlivening discussion with salacious language.

Less fortunate, though enmeshed in a strikingly similar controversy, was Michigan community college professor John Bonnell. Like Cohen, Bonnell regularly enlivened his English classes with salacious language for reasons that reflected, at least in substantial part, sound pedagogy. Several students complained to the administration that the atmosphere in Bonnell's classes became "extremely offensive" as his choice of language grew bolder during the semester—sometimes using vulgar or taboo words in the passages being studied but at other times "add[ing] his own personal comments."[56] Thus the targeted language seemed more often gratuitous in Bonnell's classes than it had been in Cohen's. The dean took Bonnell to task, but when the professor's language showed no marked improvement, the dean suspended him for three days. During that period Bonnell's students boycotted the classes that were offered by a substitute and signed petitions of support. An internal hearing affirmed the suspension, leaving no further on campus recourse.

When Bonnell challenged his suspension in federal court, his experience proved to be just the reverse of Cohen's. A sympathetic district judge ruled in Bonnell's favor and ordered his reinstatement on free speech grounds.[57] This time, however, the Sixth Circuit appeals court, sitting in

Cincinnati, ruled against the suspended teacher, noting the increasingly challenging tension between professorial classroom speech and the unacceptability of sexual harassment, in or out of class.[58] Treating the issue initially as one of public-employee speech, and accepting that much of Bonnell's expression did address issues of "public concern," the appeals court was less sympathetic to the salacious language that triggered the complaint and led to suspension.

Central to this judgment was the court's perception that much of Bonnell's linguistic deviance not only violated a valid sexual harassment policy but was "not germane to the subject matter." Finally, because Bonnell had raised an academic freedom claim, the court addressed that issue as well, though without offering much guidance. Noting that "academic freedom is not absolute," the appeals court expressly cautioned that protection for professorial speech does not extend "to the point of compromising a student's right to learn in a hostile-free environment." A contrary holding, warned the court, would imply "that the First Amendment may be used as a shield by teachers who choose to use their unique and superior position to sexually harass students secure in the knowledge that whatever they say or do will be protected." That interest in the end "outweighs [Bonnell's] claimed free speech and academic freedom interests."

Attempting to reconcile the *Cohen* and *Bonnell* cases, coming as they did from two federal courts of appeals nearly two thousand miles apart, affords valuable insight into the current scope of legal protection for academic freedom. Both involved vulgar or taboo classroom speech that offended a few students while engaging and exciting most others. There were a few factual differences between the two cases. It appeared (at least to the Sixth Circuit) that Bonnell used salacious language mainly in personal asides, whereas Cohen (as the Ninth Circuit viewed his classes) more often drew his vulgar words and phrases from the literary passages he had chosen for classroom attention, admittedly in part because of their linguistic variety.

There were also potentially important differences in procedure; Bonnell's suspension had followed a carefully prescribed path in the faculty handbook and in the collective bargaining agreement, whereas Cohen's sanction—especially the "become more sensitive to your students" decree—had been fashioned essentially from whole cloth without precedent or template. The standards that underlay the two sanctions were also distinguishable; the California junior college invoked against Cohen handbook language that the reviewing court deemed unacceptably vague and imprecise, whereas the operative standard in Bonnell's case was far sharper and carefully crafted. Finally, it is quite possible that judicial sympathy for professorial classroom use of salacious language had diminished in the five years between the two rulings. Suffice it to say that there is little certainty on the degree to which academic freedom protects the use of vulgar and taboo language in the college classroom.

One last case may suggest how varied—indeed improbable—are the situations in which courts need to define the limits of professorial speech and academic freedom. Two history professors at the University of Minnesota–Duluth shared a passion for military history, though on a relatively small campus neither could teach an entire course on that subject. The student history club, an adjunct of the History Department, invited each faculty member to submit a photo that revealed an avocation or special interest. The two teachers in question, Professors Albert Burnham and Ronald Marchese, relished the opportunity to flaunt their shared cocurricular passions. Burnham thus submitted a photo that showed him brandishing a pistol, whereas Marchese's photo pictured him with his arm extended to display an ancient Roman sword. Accompanying text described more fully the significance of the weapon each historian had chosen.

Initially this novel exhibit was apparently welcomed, even lauded, by the campus community. But two female colleagues (a faculty member and an administrator) soon filed a formal complaint about the weapons that were shown in the hands of Professors Burnham and Marchese. The catalyst for their charge was a perceived link between the weapons and a recent spate of threats on and near the campus, especially targeting two senior female professors. Responding to the complaint, the chancellor ordered the two offending photographs to be removed from the exhibit, despite vehement objections from virtually the entire History Department. As the dispute energized the Duluth campus, Burnham and Marchese went to federal court seeking the restoration of the two photos and an award of damages for alleged violation of their civil rights.

The district judge refused to dismiss the case, as the chancellor had urged, and ruled that the historians had at least stated a viable legal claim. A panel of the appeals court for the Eighth Circuit initially reversed that decision, but when the full court decided it should hear the case, a clear majority agreed with the district judge. This was strikingly a matter of first impression, lacking any guidance or precedent from more familiar free speech and academic freedom litigation. As its central premise, the appeals court found that "the expressive behavior at issue here, i.e., the posting of the photographs within the history department display, qualifies as constitutionally protected speech." Specifically, Burnham and Marchese "were attempting . . . to convey and advocate their scholarly and professional interests in military history." The students who conceived the exhibit, moreover, "were attempting to show their creativeness and interest in the scope of the teaching mission of the history department." Later, the court added that the photos "expressed the plaintiffs' view that the study of history necessarily involves a study of military history, including the use of military weapons." A footnote even suggested that the opprobrium of those who removed the photos might have been directed against "history department curriculum or Burnham's and Marchese's teaching methodology," adding that the target of the campus critics was unmistakably "the professors' history-based message."[59]

From this point the court's ruling could fairly easily have been anticipated. What were undoubtedly sincere concerns on the chancellor's part about a campus climate made apprehensive by the recent threats did not remotely justify the intervention he pursued, given the clearly protected nature of the photographs and their public posting. Doubt remained now only about the remedy. The chancellor had argued that he could not be held liable for damages given the novelty of the issue; federal law confers a "qualified immunity" and relieves a public official of such personal liability if an adverse ruling on the merits could not reasonably have been foreseen in an unfamiliar situation. But the court had no such sympathy for the chancellor, mainly because he had failed to establish a credible link between the historians' photographs and the anxious campus climate that had occasioned his intervention. Two judges dissented on that latter point, believing that qualified immunity should apply.

The *Burnham* case remains the only one of its kind, within or beyond the academic community. The appeals court had no occasion specifically to invoke academic freedom, because the ruling in favor of the two historians rested squarely on general public-employee speech principles. Yet it seems unlikely that a court would have been quite so sympathetic to a comparable claim in a nonacademic government workplace—especially in the context of recent threats that had targeted two prominent female staff members. The repeated emphasis in the opinion upon "the plaintiffs' scholarly and professional interests in military history" in characterizing their public expression evidenced a special solicitude on the court's part. And even beyond the basic ruling in the historians' favor, the summary rejection of the chancellor's qualified immunity claim would have been even less likely in a nonacademic setting. Thus the *Burnham* case belongs squarely among academic freedom decisions despite the absence of explicit reliance on the protective principles we have reviewed here.

The *Burnham* decision also reflected one other theme that ran through several earlier cases, notably those involving City College of New York professors Levin and Jeffries—namely, judicial aversion to political correctness within the academic community. One might recall the pointed comment of the federal judge in Levin's case that the dispute before him highlighted precisely that concern—over "what has come to be denominated as 'political correctness' in speech and thought on the campuses of the nation's colleges and universities."[60] Despite the absence in the *Burnham* opinions of explicit mention of political correctness, its influence on the court seems unmistakable. Of course the university campus is hardly the only place where one might find measures aimed at enforcing notions of political correctness, but the academic community has understandably been the focus of such aversion.

The cases we have reviewed here are merely illustrative and hardly definitive or exhaustive. Many others could have been cited under each of the relevant headings or topics. What is critically important, and transcends any selection of precedents, is how profoundly the state of the applicable law has changed during the academic careers of those who began teaching in the late 1950s. A half century ago, not only was there no law protecting academic freedom; but also, in fact, there simply was no constitutional protection for such closely related interests as the speech of public employees, procedural rights of government beneficiaries, or freedom of association, to cite only the most obvious among late bloomers in the constitutional garden.

Strikingly, the state of the law began to change just as the McCarthy era drew to a close. The Supreme Court's *Sweezy* ruling, which first embraced academic freedom as a majority concept, preceded by a matter of months the Senate's formal rebuke of Wisconsin's now out-of-control junior senator. The decisions that struck down disclaimer-type loyalty oaths closely paralleled the erosion of political pressure in most states to impose such tests on loyal public servants. By the first decade of the twenty-first century, all that had changed remarkably—even though academic freedom clearly does not protect all activity and expression the professoriate might wish and, in the eyes of some skeptical judges, extends no further than the general speech rights of public employees. At least as far as most courts are concerned, today's college professors enjoy a range and depth of legal protection for their activities, their writings, and their teaching that was unimaginable a half century earlier. Yet in areas the courts have not yet entered, or where they have only begun to address novel challenges and threats, not all signs are quite so positive, as the ensuing chapters show.

4

Academic Freedom in Times of Crisis

As he was preparing to teach his freshman history class on the afternoon of September 11, 2001, University of New Mexico Professor Richard Berthold learned of the attacks on the World Trade Center and the Pentagon. He greeted his students with a jocular comment: "Anyone who can blow up the Pentagon gets my vote." Within hours, news of Berthold's remark had gone far beyond the campus in Albuquerque. Several state legislators demanded his immediate dismissal, although he had held tenure for many years. Many alumni and other New Mexicans expressed their indignation and called for immediate action. One graduate actually filed suit against the university, claiming that Berthold's remark violated an old state law that barred state employees from teaching or advocating "sabotage, force and violence, sedition, or treason." Berthold received several death threats and was chased across campus by a motorcyclist who had been angered by his remark. A few days later, Berthold apologized publicly and profusely; he conceded that he had been "a jerk" and that his intended classroom joke had been "stupid."

The response of the university administration was surprisingly moderate, given the immediate post–September 11 climate and the intensity of the public outrage. Instead of the dismissal that many off campus had demanded, the president launched a careful investigation. Three months later, the university announced that a report had been received and that some adverse action was clearly warranted given the "unique vulnerability" that students felt in the immediate aftermath of the terrorist attacks. Professor Berthold, the university's provost noted, had "failed to act responsibly" and therefore should incur some sanction. An official reprimand was placed in his file, he was removed from further teaching of freshman courses, and he would be subject both to a rigorous post-tenure review as well as special scrutiny in the observance of faculty standards of professional behavior. Berthold greeted the news with an apparent sense of relief, noting that the reprimand seemed to him "an appropriate response to the callousness and stupidity I demonstrated on September 11."[1] The longer-term sanctions never went into effect, because Berthold retired from the New Mexico faculty at the end of the academic year, at the time under suspicion of possible sexual harassment because of remarks he had made about a female colleague.[2]

Berthold's may have been the earliest test of faculty speech after the terrorist attacks, but it was by no means the only one. The very next day, University of Texas–Austin journalism professor Robert Jensen wrote an op-ed for the *Houston Chronicle* in which he called the terrorist attacks "reprehensible" but went on to aim his "anger" equally at "those who have held power in the United States and have engineered attacks on civilians." Demands for reprisal poured into the office of the university's president, Larry Faulkner. The president's response was to express in the next day's *Chronicle* his own "disgust" with Jensen's article, calling the author not only "misguided" but a "fountainhead of undiluted foolishness." Faulkner found "some comfort in the fact that practically no one here takes his outbursts seriously." However, no adverse personnel action was taken or apparently even seriously considered against Jensen. Indeed, Faulkner's condemnation evoked from some UT-Austin faculty and students a concern that the president had spoken too harshly, sending (as one professor put it) "a very clear message that if you stick your neck out, we will disown you."[3]

A week later, a California junior college was the site of a quite different incident. Kenneth Hearlson, an instructor without tenure, faced several Muslim students in his Orange Coast Community College English class and reportedly charged: "[Y]ou killed five thousand people" and "you drove two planes into the World Trade Center." He was also accused of calling his Muslim students "terrorists," "murderers," and "Nazis" during the same classroom discussion. When college officials received a report of this encounter, they placed Hearlson on leave but refused off-campus demands for his immediate dismissal. Instead, like the University of New Mexico, Orange Coast commissioned a thorough investigation by a local attorney well-versed in educational matters.

After several months of painstaking inquiry, the attorney submitted a report that contained curiously mixed conclusions. On one hand, she found, Hearlson had been less than sensitive in his handling of a volatile issue, especially toward his Muslim students. On the other hand, the specific charges turned out to be "unsubstantiated." Apparently issues of possible Islamic complicity had been discussed in a hypothetical setting but without the stark accusations that had initially been reported. Instead of accusing his students of "driving two planes into the World Trade Center," he actually said something more like "you must at times feel as though you drove two planes into the World Trade Center." The college placed in Hearlson's file a formal letter of reprimand—a sanction that he received far less comfortably than had Berthold. In view of the substantial exoneration in the attorney's report, Hearlson complained that even a reprimand was comparable to a judge telling a just-acquitted defendant, "I'm going to punish you, even though you're found innocent."[4]

From California, Texas, and New Mexico the focus shifted a week or two later to New York City, still reeling from the terrorist attacks. A faculty group at City College, a campus in the CUNY system, sponsored a teach-in at which they shared critical views on issues of U.S. foreign policy. One of the speakers specifically blamed what he termed "American colonialism" for the recent terrorist attacks. Response to reports of the teach-in, far beyond the campus and the city, was prompt and intense. The City University's chancellor took the faculty critics to task, publicly faulting those who had made "lame excuses" for the actions of the terrorists. The board of trustees scheduled a discussion of the teach-in at its next meeting, with one trustee labeling the speakers' conduct "seditious" and another declaring that the board should at the very least formally vote to censure the faculty participants. Such a motion actually appeared on the agenda.[5]

Just before the meeting occurred, the board received a cautionary letter from the vice-chairman, former Yale University president (and First Amendment expert) Benno Schmidt. He urged his colleagues to recognize the degree to which academic freedom was at stake, noting that "the freedom of thought to challenge and to speak one's mind [is] the matrix, the indispensable condition of any university worthy of the name."[6] Almost without a trace, the condemnatory resolution disappeared from the CUNY board's agenda. No personnel action was ever taken against the teach-in sponsors or participants. Schmidt's plea had apparently found its mark, and the trustees agreed that the matter had received all the attention it needed. Within less than a year, Schmidt assumed the chairmanship of the CUNY board.

The most visible faculty speech incident took place a year and a half later and only a few miles away. Nicholas De Genova, a Columbia University assistant professor of anthropology, took part in a campus teach-in during the initial phase of the Iraq War. Among many provocative comments, he said at one point that he wished for "a million Mogadishus"—a pointed reference to the tragic events in Somalia that were so vividly portrayed in the film *Blackhawk Down*. Though a quite junior faculty member, De Genova was already known for his outspoken views; the previous spring he had attracted much attention for a starkly anti-Israel statement at a campus rally. But the response to his teach-in comment far surpassed the public reaction in any of the earlier incidents. Within days, more than one hundred members of the U.S. Congress signed a resolution calling for De Genova's immediate dismissal. Representative J. D. Hayworth, one of the sponsors, insisted that the issue was not "whether De Genova has the right to make idiotic comments . . . but whether he has a right to a job teaching at Columbia University after making such comments."[7]

The pressure on Columbia's administration was now intense. President Lee Bollinger, like Schmidt a seasoned First Amendment scholar and a champion of academic freedom, now found himself facing a critical test of his principles. His response was therefore predictable. He expressed very publicly his personal disagreement—he was "shocked," he said, by De Genova's statement—explaining that "this one has crossed the line, and I really feel the need to say something." On several occasions during the spring, Bollinger reiterated his "strong disagreement" with De Genova's views, each time insisting, however, that "under the principle of academic freedom, it would be inappropriate to take disciplinary action."

Bollinger's stance, obviously unsatisfying to many critics of De Genova's views, also evoked some of the same concern that greeted Texas president Faulkner's similar response to the Jensen article. A small number of Columbia faculty, and a larger number of students, feared that despite Bollinger's firm defense of academic freedom, his almost gratuitous personal disparagement had undermined that freedom; as one skeptic put it, such a rebuke from the university's president could "intimidate any faculty from speaking with similar positions."[8]

Only three days after public reports of De Genova's remarks at the teach-in became public, the controversy became fodder for the Fox News show *The O'Reilly Factor.* President Bollinger was invited to appear but understandably declined, anticipating Bill O'Reilly's charge that he was "hiding under his desk." (In fact, he was announcing the appointment of a new provost at the very hour of the Fox taping,and was thus genuinely unavailable.) The direction of the program was wholly unexpected. After a few preliminary glancing blows at Columbia's response, O'Reilly assured his audience that "if I were Bollinger I wouldn't fire this guy . . . because you've got to tolerate this kind of speech." He added an alternative and (apparently for him preferable) sanction: "I'd shun him . . . I wouldn't talk to him. I wouldn't invite him to any faculty things"—the latter prospect unlikely to be seen across the academic community as a severe penalty.[9]

Lest O'Reilly's views on the De Genova case seem wholly out of character, it may be helpful to fast-forward to one other outspoken faculty case on which he later expressed strikingly similar views. The outspoken faculty member that time was University of Colorado ethnic studies professor (and program chairman) Ward Churchill. Shortly after the terrorist attacks, he wrote and posted on an obscure Internet website an essay that was highly critical of U.S. foreign policy. In the essay he declared that "the men who flew the missions against the WTC and Pentagon were not 'cowards.' . . . [They] manifested the courage of their convictions." He also referred in passing to some of those who were working in the World Trade Center on the day of the attack as "little Eichmanns," even suggesting that some of the victims may have deserved their fate on that day. This essay did not come to light until the late winter of 2005, on the eve of Churchill's scheduled lecture at Hamilton College. The reaction was immediate and predictably intense. Despite widespread demands to cancel the lecture, Hamilton's president initially took a firm stance in defense of free speech. But the climate soon became so ugly, replete with death threats and other forces that imperiled student safety at the upstate New York college, that Hamilton withdrew the invitation and canceled Churchill's appearance.

The focus quickly shifted west to Colorado, especially to the flagship campus at Boulder. Although he resigned at once his position as chairman of the Ethnic Studies Department, Churchill not only did not disavow his essay, but also he actually raised the stakes; in an interview after the essay came to light, he added: "One of the things I've suggested is that it may be that more 9/11s are necessary." Colorado Governor Bill Owens (who had earlier insisted that Churchill should resign from the faculty) now demanded that the outspoken professor be summarily dismissed, a demand that was strongly supported by other politicians. A special meeting of the university's board of regents was called for the end of the week.

Even before the board met, its two newest members, both Denver lawyers, held a press conference at which they insisted that "the law requires a process to fire a professor" and that the board itself would "face substantial legal liability" should it ignore or slight that safeguard.[10] Instead, the regents directed the Boulder campus administration to undertake a thorough investigation—not only of the catalytic essay but also of several other charges that had surfaced in the interim, including claims of plagiarism and misrepresentation of Native American heritage. Several weeks later, the first phase of the inquiry was complete. The campus administration declared that Churchill's "profoundly offensive, abusive and misguided" statements would not justify his dismissal as a tenured professor because they were protected both by academic freedom and by the First Amendment against reprisal by a state university. The Churchill case then continued on a tortuous course.

After the "little Eichmanns" issue had been resolved in the outspoken professor's favor, a Boulder campus faculty committee turned to charges of research malfeasance. That body concluded that Churchill had committed repeated and flagrant research misconduct in remarkably varied forms. The campus Privilege and Tenure Committee, however, recommended only a one-year suspension, a relatively mild sanction, which would not jeopardize Churchill's tenure. But the University System's President, former U.S. Senator Hank Brown, immediately urged the Regents instead to dismiss Churchill since his research transgressions "seriously impac[t] the University's academic reputation and the reputations of its faculty" and confirm that "Professor Churchill is not qualified to hold a tenured faculty position" at Colorado. Brown's letter to the Board specifically rejected a claim advanced by Churchill's lawyers that the research concerns would never have surfaced but for the post–September 11 controversy. Otherwise, insisted the president, "the university could not maintain the integrity of its scholarly enterprise."[11]

Fox News and *The O'Reilly Factor* would not likely have overlooked the Churchill controversy, and indeed they did not. The day after the Hamilton speech was canceled, Churchill himself agreed to appear on the program. O'Reilly began by recounting recent events, expressing his relief that Hamilton had barred Churchill from speaking there. But turning to the outspoken professor's faculty status, the show's host declared: "I don't think he should be fired. That would send the wrong message to the rest of the world. America's a strong enough country to put up with the likes of Professor Churchill. Punishing him further would just make him a martyr." The program continued with the comments of a couple of Hamilton students and eventually a dialogue with Churchill himself, who seemed surprisingly calm under intense pressure.[12]

There is, to be sure, no explicit mention of academic freedom in either of these quite remarkable statements from O'Reilly, though his conviction that outspoken professors need be tolerated in our society is unmistakable in both. Moreover, O'Reilly's statements about both De Genova and Churchill were quite willingly volunteered; in no sense was there any imperative for the expression of a view either way on the continued faculty status of either of these embattled professors. Beyond their voluntary quality, the tone of both statements was striking, given the political creed of the speaker. One might expect to hear or read such reassuring views from a broad range of media commentators, in both print and broadcast media, but would not have anticipated such views in the immediate aftermath of the terrorist attacks or the advent of the Iraq War. The potential import of such comments, and their relationship to the current condition of academic freedom in a time of crisis, need be assessed at length. Before undertaking that assessment, however, note must be taken of several situations in which outspoken faculty have not fared quite as well as those we have studied here—a reminder of the reality that some pressures in the post–September 11 era have simply been too strong for even conscientious administrators to resist.

After a hiatus of several years, during which there were virtually no volatile encounters involving outspoken professors, the summer of 2006 brought such issues once again to the fore. Three separate incidents involved university teachers who had grown increasingly skeptical of the "conventional wisdom" about the September 11 attacks, and were particularly critical of the findings of the national Commission appointed to investigate the terrorist attacks. At the University of Wisconsin-Madison, political scientist Kevin Barrett emerged not only as an outspoken Muslim but as an active member of a group called Scholars for 9/11 Truth, committed to a revision of the prevailing views on the 2001 hijackings. He had written that, as a Muslim, he found no value in discussions with non-Muslims about the events of September 11; "either we discuss the compelling evidence that 9/11 was an inside job, or there is precious little to talk about." When these statements reached the news media, there was suddenly much to talk about. Many Wisconsin lawmakers and even a liberal governor expressed outrage, adding their view that Barrett should no longer be permitted to teach at the UW. When it came to light that he was in fact scheduled to teach one undergraduate course in the fall, indignation turned to insistence on the critics' part. One legislator, the author of a letter which nearly sixty of his colleagues would soon sign, insisted that "this case isn't about academic freedom [but] is a case of protecting students from the academic garbage that Mr. Barrett spews."[13] Lest anyone miss his point, the apoplectic lawmaker added: "The taxpayers of Wisconsin and the tuition-paying families aren't interested in supporting the University of Wingnuts in Madison."[14]

The university's provost responded quickly, insisting that Barrett's views were his own and not those of the institution; he also promised a thorough review to ensure "that his course content is academically appropriate, or high quality, and that his personal views are not imposed on his students." Within a month, the review yielded conclusions basically favorable to Barrett's retention. Though he not only lacked tenure but even a regular professional appointment, university officials defended his continued presence in the classroom, having satisfied themselves that Barrett did not use the podium or his relations with student to proselytize on political issues.[15]

Barely had the furor over Kevin Barrett subsided than a strikingly similar case emerged at the University of New Hampshire. Psychology Professor William Woodward was, like Barrett, an outspoken revisionist on September 11; he publicly maintained that U.S. leaders had lied about the terrorist attacks and were effectively involved in a conspiracy in which the nation that seemed to be the principal victim was deeply complicit. Unlike Barrett, though Woodward had taught for 35 years at UNH and had long held tenure. Thus when state officials and legislators in Concord and in Washington demanded Woodward's dismissal, the university responded that no such reprisal would follow. There seemed not even to be a need for the sort of review that had been undertaken in Madison. A campus spokesperson made clear the institution's posture: "What we're saying is that we support and are committed to academic freedom. . . . We may not agree with Professor Woodward, but he is entitled to his opinion." Professor Woodward declared that he was "gratified" by the university's response, and made clear that he had always warned students in classes where contentious issues might arise that his views were "controversial," and that most people would in fact disagree with his position. This exchange seemed to satisfy most of the Granite State; at least no further demands for Woodward's dismissal or removal from the classroom appear to have followed.[16]

The third of these roughly contemporaneous cases had a far less happy outcome. Professor Steven Jones had taught physics at Brigham Young University for many years and was long since tenured. He was also a devout

Mormon and until recently a fervent supporter of President George W. Bush. But he had lately become active in (and eventually co-chairman of) a national organization, Scholars for 9/11 Truth, whose central premise was that the United States was officially complicit in the attacks on the World Trade Center and the Pentagon. In the fall of 2005 he posted on the group's website a paper arguing that the impact of the hijacked airplanes could not possibly have caused the damage that occurred on September 11, and that the collapse of the towers must have reflected a "controlled demolition."

When Professor Jones' views reached the news media, BYU officials announced just before the start of the 2006 fall semester that he was being placed immediately on leave while his work was reviewed. The physics department of which he was a senior member distanced itself from his published views, explaining that it was "not convinced that his analyses and hypotheses have been submitted to relevant scientific venues that would ensure rigorous technical peer review" – though in fact the paper in issue had actually been peer-reviewed by two physicists. The university's official explanation for suspending Professor Jones pending a review of his scholarship on the events of September 11 was similar – "our concern is that Dr. Jones's work has not been published in scientific venues." Professor Jones thus remained in limbo for several weeks, while others alternately defended and castigated him and his unorthodox theories, and debated the merits of the suspension. In late October, however, he rendered the controversy moot by announcing his imminent retirement from the BYU faculty. Along with this change in status, Jones reaffirmed his doubts about the accepted theories about the terrorist attacks of 2001 and especially the collapse of the Twin Towers.[17]

The experience of Professor Jones reminds us that not all the post–September 11 controversies have evoked ardent defenses of academic freedom. In fact there have been several other cases that belong on the darker side of the ledger. The most significant contrary experience has been that of Palestinian-born computer science professor Sami Al Arian, who taught at the University of South Florida (USF) for over two decades and held tenure for much of that period. Ironically, his troubles began with an appearance on *The O'Reilly Factor* very soon after the terrorist attacks. Identified as a USF professor on the program, he conceded that he had made strongly anti-Israel statements—once even declaring in Arabic "Death to Israel" and that he headed an organization that raised funds in the United States to support Palestinian causes. The morning after his Fox

News appearance, the president's office at South Florida was flooded with calls and e-mails from angry alumni and public officials, anxious parents and nervous neighbors, demanding immediate action against Al Arian. Citing such pressures, the university did place him on paid leave for the fall semester and barred him from setting foot on campus. This status soon became a suspension, as the administration continued to investigate the case.

As the next academic year began, the University of South Florida filed suit in federal court, seeking an unprecedented ruling that it could with impunity terminate Al Arian's faculty appointment. When that request came before an obviously irritated federal district judge, she dismissed it and noted that the issue belonged back on campus in the grievance procedure and not in her busy courtroom. Then, in February 2003, the other shoe dropped; Al Arian and several others were indicted for serious violations of federal law for having raised funds for and providing material support to terrorist organizations in the Middle East. Less than a week later, the USF administration announced it had dismissed Al Arian—still without a campus hearing—citing not only the indictment but other related charges the grand jury had not invoked. The grievance process understandably ground to a halt the moment the indictment was revealed and Al Arian was incarcerated awaiting trial. The criminal case eventually came to trial in the federal court, where the jury acquitted Al Arian of the most serious charges but deadlocked on several other charges. During a protracted period of uncertainty over whether the government would reopen the prosecution on the surviving issues, Al Arian agreed in the spring of 2006 to plead guilty to a lesser offense and to accept deportation—an agreement that essentially ended both the criminal case and his dispute with the University of South Florida. Obviously many important issues remain unanswered.[18]

One other case deserves mention on the negative side of the ledger. Professor Tariq Ramadan, a noted Islamic scholar and Swiss citizen, accepted in the spring of 2004 an endowed chair at the University of Notre Dame.[19] He would become the first Henry Luce Professor in the Joan Kroc Institute—not a place where, as the *Chicago Tribune* opined with some irony, one would expect to find a dangerous radical. Informal assurances of a work visa had been given both to the scholar and to the institution—hardly surprising because he had traveled and lectured extensively in the United States. Thus he sent his furniture to South Bend, Indiana, and enrolled his children in local schools. But on the eve of his departure from Geneva, Ramadan learned that, on orders from the U.S. Department Homeland Security, the State Department had revoked his visa. Despite persistent efforts by Notre Dame and the media to get an explanation for this extraordinary action, none was forthcoming beyond vague references to a statute that authorized delays or reviews with respect to people whose presence might pose risks to national security. Ramadan's grandfather had cofounded a group once termed "terrorist" and he had written and spoken in a vein highly critical of Israel and of U.S. policy toward the Middle East. That was, however, merely a speculative basis for an action that was not only unexplained but unprecedented as well, given the status of the foreign visitor and the assurances he had received from responsible U.S. officials.

Though many groups protested the visa revocation, no change occurred and Ramadan accepted an interim appointment as a visiting lecturer at Oxford, apparently welcome in the United Kingdom. In the spring of 2006, a group of interested organizations, including the American Association of University Professors (AAUP), filed suit to challenge the constitutionality of the statute under which Ramadan's visa had been withdrawn. The complaint in that case described in detail the impact upon various academic groups and audiences in the United States of Ramadan's inability to assume his position at Notre Dame or attend scholarly gatherings in this country.[20]

In the summer of 2006, a federal judge called upon the government to stop evading the issue and to respond—either to grant Ramadan a visa or explain why it would not do so. The ruling specifically rejected the government's apparent premise that foreign visitors may be barred from the U.S. because their political views were deemed unwelcome. The State Department then offered a new pretext for Ramadan's exclusion—that he had donated some 600 Euros to French and Swiss organizations that provide humanitarian aid to Palestinians and which had been targeted in the U.S. for providing "material support" to Hamas. Ramadan's supporters filed a new lawsuit, early in 2007, directly challenging the PATRIOT Act's "ideological exclusion" provision, which authorizes denial of entry to visitors with uncongenial views, and which had not yet been adjudicated in this or any other case.

The Al Arian and Ramadan cases suggest that not every post–September 11 case has been resolved consistent with academic freedom principles. Yet these are both unusual situations—Al Arian because of the serious criminal charges that lurked in the wings and eventually resulted in his deportation, and Ramadan because he was a noncitizen seeking entry to the United States and was caught in a highly uncertain legal limbo that has thwarted others over the years who have been similarly treated. In the other widely noted cases, of which Berthold, Jensen, Hearlson, De Genova, and Churchill are exemplary, the outcome has been far more favorable, indeed quite unexpectedly so. Not only does recent experience in this regard contrast sharply with that of earlier times; the treatment of the outspoken professor since September 11 also contrasts with the ways in which other challenges and threats to academic freedom have evolved. In short, the good news may be somewhat more limited in scope than a cursory review might suggest.

The starkest contrast is between experience after September 11 and the fate of many scholars and teachers whose political views and affiliations were suspect a half century earlier. During the McCarthy era, hundreds, probably thousands, of university professors were suspected of disloyalty, often on what later became clear was the flimsiest of evidence or no evidence at all. At least a hundred college and university professors—many of them fully tenured—were dismissed during that dark and dismal period. Ellen Schrecker, who has most extensively chronicled the horrors of the McCarthy era, recounts the often tenuous grounds (sometimes little more than unsubstantiated rumors) that led to the destruction of careers, the ruin of academic lives, and the widening of distrust within an already fearful climate.[21]

One especially graphic incident illustrates the extent of anxiety, apprehension, and mistrust during that era. Jonathan and David Lubell had excelled as undergraduates at Cornell University's School of Industrial and Labor Relations in the early 1950s. They applied for and were accepted to the Harvard Law School. Their first-year grades were so stellar that both would have been invited to join the editorial board of the *Harvard Law Review* had the faculty not intervened. Because the Lubell brothers had belonged in college to a suspected Communist-front organization, and because they had refused to testify as to their political affiliations, their scholarships were revoked and the Harvard Law faculty decreed that they could not be elected to the *Law Review*. The premise of that startling directive was the faculty's belief that the Lubells' undergraduate activities and their recalcitrance would preclude their admission to the New York Bar, to which they presumably would apply after graduation. (The Massachusetts Bar had already demanded that Harvard expel the Lubells after their refusal to testify, but Harvard rejected any such demands.) The student editors were sharply divided and agonized over the faculty's edict. Some students, like Norman Dorsen (who later served for fifteen years as president of the American Civil Liberties Union) and Derek Bok (who became dean of the Law School and then, for two decades, Harvard's president) argued that the editorial board should defy the faculty and elect the Lubells anyway on the basis of their academic achievement. In the end, that view lost out to a majority who felt the faculty judgment simply had to be implemented, however differently the students might have acted on their own.

The Lubells were thus denied the honor and experience they had clearly earned. Ironically, when the time came for their admission to the bar, anti-Communist hysteria had abated. The Harvard law faculty's fear proved groundless, and the brothers were eventually admitted to the New York Bar, in which they practiced with distinction for many years. Years later, David Lubell recalled that "the whole atmosphere in the law school was one of great fear and intimidation," within which one who refused to accede to government demands for sensitive information was seen as "doing a great disservice to the law school and to Harvard."[22]

The catalytic forces in those dark days were, of course, substantially different from those at work a half century later. Professors came under suspicion (much like the Lubell brothers) largely on the basis of political affiliations or associations, real or suspected. Few were the victims of McCarthyism whose troubles came solely (as in more recent times) from a single unorthodox outburst, or one aberrant letter to the editor of a newspaper, or an op-ed piece expressing unorthodox views. Suspicion generally derived from covert sources, of which the target of inquiry might not even have been aware and thus could hardly avert or combat. Yet many careers were ruined or severely derailed on just such clandestine sources.

There are other dramatic differences between the two periods. The early twenty-first century has mercifully seen no successor to Senator McCarthy and his minions. Among those in Congress and in state legislatures who might conceivably have assumed the mantle of the red-baiters of the 1950s, no single lawmaker or even group of lawmakers has emerged with any comparable clarity or visibility. Attacks upon outspoken or aberrant faculty come these days from widely varied sources, seldom anonymous but also hardly household names across the country. The attacks also come from varied and even opposite perspectives—for example, sometimes from those who support the Israeli cause and at other times from those of avowedly Palestinian sympathies. Thus the superficial analogies that surely can be drawn between the post–September 11 period and the McCarthy era turn out to be less substantial and less ominous than might at first appear.

Nonetheless, it would be quite unwise to dismiss the analogy between the 1950s and the 2000s. Clearly in many respect the jury is still out, and it probably will be for some time to come. Of special note in this regard is an exchange between two U.S. senators in the spring of 2003 on the day that half-century-old transcripts of secret interviews with prospective McCarthy subcommittee witnesses were made public. The subject of this recent release was a group of potential witnesses, some of them university professors, whom McCarthy and his staff ultimately decided not to interrogate in public—presumably because they would not have made useful fodder for the anti-Communist crusade on which the senator was well along. One of those who ultimately escaped public humiliation, but clearly feared it, took his own life before learning of his reprieve.

This release of these long-secret files from the McCarthy subcommittee evoked sharply contrasting reactions from two lawmakers of similarly liberal views. Michigan senator Carl Levin, who had recently chaired the successor subcommittee, spoke first. He offered his hopeful view that a recurrence of McCarthyism was virtually impossible. "There's a greater awareness," he explained, "of McCarthyism and what the tactics can be used by people who are trying to quiet dissenters." And, he added, "there's greater resistance against those who would try to still voices that they disagree with."

Next to speak was Levin's junior colleague, Wisconsin senator Russ Feingold, who offered a less sanguine view. Having recently cast the only Senate vote against the USA PATRIOT Act, Feingold knew whereof he spoke: "What I'm hearing from constituents," he cautioned, "what I'm hearing from Muslim Americans, Arab Americans, Southasian and others suggests a climate of fear toward our government that is unprecedented, at least in my memory."[23]

The jury is still out, of course, on which of these two liberal senators was closer to the mark at the time or in succeeding years. Both brought to the Senate highly relevant experience. Senator Levin especially knows whereof he speaks. During his undergraduate years in Ann Arbor, the University of Michigan carried out one of the most shameful purges of tenured faculty members who held unorthodox political views. Summarily dismissed in those dark days were three professors who had invited suspicion of disloyalty either because of their controversial (though hardly illegal) affiliations or simply because they refused publicly to accuse colleagues of belonging to suspected organizations. Starting in 1990, the University of Michigan has annually and quite publicly atoned for its actions by sponsoring a lecture to honor the three dismissed professors.[24]

Other institutions have also taken steps to revive or sustain the memories of those dark days and hope, in the process of recalling the 1950s, to discourage a recurrence. The University of Washington, Rutgers, and Harvard, among others, have in various ways acknowledged and atoned for the treatment in the 1950s of professors suspected of subversion. In all, at least a hundred university professors were dismissed on the basis of suspected political affiliations during that dismal period. Surprisingly, those eminent institutions that have at other periods been the staunchest defenders of academic freedom and tenure behaved during those dark days as badly as did their less prestigious peers, of whom somewhat less would normally be expected.

Despite the distance in time and substance that separates current conditions from those of the McCarthy era, it would be naïve to claim that a recurrence would be inconceivable. Even Senator Levin did not offer so hopeful a view of the current climate, although his assessment was somewhat more hopeful than that of his junior colleague from Wisconsin. Levin's precise words are helpful here as the predicate for his more sanguine perspective: "I think there's a greater awareness of McCarthyism and what tactics can be used by people who are trying to quiet dissenters. And there's greater resistance against those who would try to still voices that they disagree with."[25] Yet even Levin wisely did not say "never" or "it can't happen again." If only because of his undergraduate experience in the early 1950s and his close attention in later years to the treatment of dissenters, he is keenly aware that any such total confidence would be misplaced—and of course quite dangerous at a time of great international unease. Anyone who ventured so cheery a view of conditions in the early twenty-first century would rightly be viewed with much skepticism, given the continuity of serious challenges to national security and the demonstrable susceptibility of the nation to hysteria and myopia.

Even so, a recurrence of true McCarthyism seems highly unlikely. For one thing, the current political spectrum includes no claimant to the McCarthy mantle—no prominent public official, that is, who has publicly blamed university professors or government workers as a group for the nation's foreign or domestic challenges. Those few lawmakers and public officials who did urge the dismissal of outspoken professors after September 11 spoke with surprising restraint, and most dropped the issue soon after the initial public response failed to sustain whatever brief momentum the catalytic incident may have triggered. For whatever reason, firing professors who seem naïve or disloyal or both appears to be an idea whose time came and went long ago, and it has not returned despite a potentially catalytic climate.

Those few legislators and other government officials who called for faculty purges or the banning of controversial speakers in the period after the World Trade Center and Pentagon attacks focused solely on a single transgression, seldom generalizing from the catalytic incident much less suggesting anything like a conspiracy among professors opposed to the war in Iraq or other controversial policies of the Bush administration. Moreover, even the harshest critics of twenty-first-century outspoken professors soon retreated, finding limited public support for faculty-bashing even in a national climate that remained anxious and skeptical long after the initial attacks of September 11. Not only has no ideological successor to Senator McCarthy yet emerged, but there have been no visible counterparts to any of the other lawmakers who threatened academic freedom and faculty speech in the 1940s and 1950s.

Noting such differences is relatively simple; what is harder is identifying the causes for the contrast between the 1950s and the early twenty-first century. Senator Levin is once again helpful, if only because he retains vivid memories of the earlier period. "I think there's a greater awareness of McCarthyism and what tactics can be used by people who are trying to quiet dissenters. And there's greater resistance against those who would try to still voices that they disagree with." Actually there is much in the climate of the early twenty-first century to support Levin's rather confident assessment. The "greater resistance" he notes is in fact quite dramatic. When on the first anniversary of the terrorist attacks the American Association of University Professors announced the creation of a committee to assess the current tension between national security and academic freedom, the association noted that no comparable group existed a half century earlier. Although the AAUP had created special committees to assess the impact of both World Wars I and II on academic freedom, its response to McCarthyism could charitably be described as too little and too late. Indeed, the successor group in its 2003 report generously characterized AAUP's McCarthy era response as "tardy but categorical," though others have assessed the organization's defense of academic freedom in the 1950s less generously.[26] The association eventually did take on loyalty oaths and campus speaker bans, but its voice was neither as firm nor as loud as it might have been and certainly not as prompt in stepping up to decry the red-baiting and witch-hunting that ravaged the academy. AAUP's tardiness was especially notable in light of the earliest postwar threat, the summary dismissal in 1948 of three senior professors by the University of Washington—an action that occurred two full years before Senator McCarthy's official launch of his anti-Communist crusade.

However, the AAUP was not alone in what now seems its undue reticence during the 1950s. Other groups that stepped up early and boldly in the current era—the American Civil Liberties Union (ACLU), most notably—were hesitant to appreciate the gravity of the McCarthy-era menace to free speech and thought and to confront that threat directly and forcefully. In part the greater readiness of such organizations to step up early and forcefully may reflect lessons they have learned over the past half century. It is also true that in the early twenty-first century an outspoken champion of free speech and civil liberties incurs far less risk in speaking out boldly, or in taking to court one's grievance against government, than such a person would have faced in the 1950s, where a climate of fear surrounded and inhibited even the most courageous of civil libertarians. There are today, moreover, several well-funded watchdog organizations that simply did not exist a half century ago but now form a major part of a protective matrix; groups such as People for the American Way are relative latecomers but are major players in the current context and thus undoubtedly embolden the traditional protective voices that understandably welcome such allies. These groups are ready to take on, both in court and in legislative chambers, even nascent threats to civil liberties and free expression to a degree that was simply (if understandably) absent a half century earlier. Thus there does seem ample support for Senator Levin's sanguine view that we are today blessed with "greater resistance against" would-be censors or red-baiters than could have been imagined a half century ago.

There are several other ameliorative factors in the current climate. A half century ago, dissent that was viewed as subversive or even unsettling all came from the left end of the political spectrum. Today the picture is far more mixed. Recall, for example, the disparate nature of the two earliest post–September 11 professorial outbursts. Professor Berthold, the New Mexico historian, had joked to his freshman class in a positive light about "anyone who can bomb the Pentagon." A week later, Orange Coast College's English instructor Hearlson shocked his community college class by accusing his Muslim students of "killing five thousand people" by "[driving] planes into the World Trade Center." Presumably these two outspoken teachers, who in end both received relatively mild reprimands, came from very different political perspectives on Middle Eastern issues and U.S. foreign policy. Such contrasts, which persist across the post–September 11 tableau, illustrate a complexity that was totally absent in the McCarthy era. A half century ago, all the "bad guys" were readily and neatly identifiable on one end of the spectrum, whether or not they had actually been charged with being Communists or "fellow travelers." Even those among their adversaries (e.g., Whittaker Chambers) who would not otherwise have qualified as heroes to conservatives or right-leaning idealists were treated as such simply because of their place on the political scale.

The role of the mass media also seems to have tempered the current climate. In place of the Walter Winchells, Westbook Peglers, and others who fanned the flames of suspicion and intolerance in the 1950s, those who might be seen as their spiritual successors in the twenty-first century are curiously silent or even supportive of outspoken scholars. Rush Limbaugh, Neal Bortz, Sean Hannity, Alan Combs, and others of their persuasion have been strangely silent on national security issues and have seldom pilloried or scapegoated left-leaning scholars as their predecessors did with relish a half century ago. And then there is the truly startling case of Fox News Bill O'Reilly, from whom one might have anticipated a torrent of anti-faculty rhetoric. On at least two occasions, O'Reilly has displayed what seems a remarkable sensitivity to what sounds like academic freedom. First, with respect to Columbia's brash anthropology professor De Genova and, later, in addressing the case of outspoken Colorado ethnologist Churchill, O'Reilly's comments were remarkably restrained, almost sympathetic, in ways one could not have imagined from his ideological precursors of the 1950s. Imagine Winchell or Pegler insisting that "America's strong enough to put up with the likes of" a college professor who called inhabitants of the World Trade Center "little Eichmanns" and lauded the September 11 hijackers for having "manifested the courage of heir convictions." Or imagine Dorothy Kilgallen urging her audience just to "tolerate this kind of speech" from a university teacher who'd just called for "a million Mogadishus." Clearly in certain important respects, at least, conditions today differ dramatically from those of the 1950s. These differences are arresting, if not easily explained or even fully understood.

In a similar vein, it would be valuable to explain the dramatically different response of the academic community to the genuinely divisive rhetoric of the Bertholds and Hearlsons, the De Genovas and the Churchills. There may be other important factors at work, not fully appreciated in the post–September 11 environment. For one, the bitter lessons that the academic world learned during the McCarthy era are not easily forgotten, especially when there are organizations with vivid institutional memories committed to sustaining those lessons. Thus, Senator Levin perceptively noted in the current climate "a greater awareness of McCarthyism and what tactics can be used" against dissent—an awareness that spans the political spectrum. Surely some trustees and regents at Colorado, CUNY, New Mexico, Columbia, and elsewhere who have been pressed to dismiss or at least discipline outspoken professors but have firmly resisted such demands may simply have long memories; others, especially their younger colleagues who never experienced the McCarthy era, may well have been reminded by their elders of the perils of treading that path again. Suffice it to say that important lessons seem to have been taught to and learned by governing boards in ways that deter repetition to a far greater extent than most close observers would have expected.

There is at least one other distinguishing factor. Those governing boards that were under intense pressure and could well have acted badly—indeed might even have been expected to do so under political pressure and far greater media scrutiny than existed a half century ago—may have received the best possible advice from academic leaders who just happened to be in the right place at the right time. Indeed, one could hardly exaggerate the providential presence of three eminent First Amendment scholars at the pivotal moment. When the City University of New York came under intense pressure to discipline several faculty who stirred intense controversy at a campus teach-in, and CUNY's chancellor actually endorsed such reprisal, the strategic role as board vice chair (and later chair) of First Amendment scholar and former Yale president Schmidt clearly turned the tide. He powerfully lectured his colleagues on the nature of free speech and their obligation as trustees to nurture First Amendment values by allowing such intemperate statements from their faculties.

Across town, Columbia's president Bollinger happened also to be an eminent First Amendment scholar in the right place at the right time. He responded from precisely that perspective to the intemperate De Genova outburst about "a million Mogadishus." And far to the southwest, free speech and press expert Mark Yudof had just returned to Austin as head of the University of Texas System when he was confronted by law enforcement pressure to authorize detailed background checks for all new faculty—a proposal that he summarily dismissed by asking, "Do we really need to know whether every Chaucer scholar ever ran a red light?"[27] In all three instances, the presence at the head of the institution of an experienced and highly respected First Amendment scholar at the critical moment seemed to make a vital difference—and in each instance served to mitigate a ruling or altered a policy that would otherwise, almost certainly, have been far more restrictive or repressive.

It would be hard to imagine a more felicitous match of people and institutions. In each instance, leaders such as Bollinger, Schmidt, and Yudof not only made decisions that were importantly protective of academic freedom. They also used these challenges to enlighten their colleagues on the broader issues, including the centrality of academic freedom, as well to educate the larger public, media, and lawmakers on the feasibility of protecting free speech and inquiry on the university campus at times when raw politics might have seemed to dictate a draconian response but ended up being surprisingly tolerant of the protective course actually taken. These were, indeed, prime examples of the right people being in the right place at the right time.

It would not be quite fair to imply that no such leaders were in critical roles during the McCarthy era. Indiana University's longtime president, Herman Wells, was extraordinarily effective in protecting the Bloomington faculty from legislative reprisals—even at a time when his state sent staunch conservatives like Homer Capehart and William Jenner to the U.S. Senate and Harold Velde to the House of Representatives. Other eminent academic leaders of the time did the best they could under challenging conditions; University of Wisconsin president Fred Harrington, for example, deserves some credit for the fact that Senator McCarthy managed to find Communists almost everywhere else but somehow never claimed that any suspect subversives were teaching on the Madison campus. Yet even highly protective leaders of the 1950s were seldom able to speak out boldly, at least not at the major state universities; University of Chicago president Robert Maynard Hutchins surely did decry witch-hunting and red-baiting with a clear and cogent voice but was almost uniquely protected by a sympathetic and understanding board.

A couple of other factors also deserve mention in accounting for current conditions. Senator McCarthy has had no ideological heir or successor in the twenty-first century. Indeed, there is a special irony that today's junior senator from Wisconsin, Feingold, cast the lone Senate vote against the USA PATRIOT Act. Moreover, the political spectrum is far more complex today than it was a half century ago. McCarthy's enemies were all on the left and seemed to speak with a common voice. Today, the pattern is far more mixed. The outspoken faculty critics at the CUNY teach-in really represented neither side of the Middle East debate, but they were as caustic about U.S. policy on Latin America and Asia as on Israel and Palestine. And on those campuses where Middle Eastern controversy has been most intense in recent years, the pressure for better balance and the removal of bias from the curriculum has come as much from one side as from the other—from pro-Palestinians as well as from pro-Israelis. Where controversial speakers have been blocked or disrupted since September 11, neither side has a monopoly; a predominantly conservative audience at a Sacramento State University commencement in 2004 shouted down liberal publisher Janis Heaphy, and arch-conservative advocate Ann Coulter received just the same intolerable treatment from a left-leaning audience at the University of Connecticut a year and a half later. Palestinian spokesperson Hanan Ashrawi was denied a podium on at least one Colorado campus about the same time a downstate Illinois audience prevented *New York Times* reporter Chris Hedges from bringing a quite different message to a campus commencement. Although such disruptions have been remarkably few, it would be impossible to generalize about the political persuasion either of those who have been kept from speaking or of those audiences guilty of silencing them.[28] Thus we have come from a time a half century ago when campus discourse was unmistakably right versus left to a time when even a score card often fails to differentiate viewpoints, and surely neither side has anything approaching a monopoly. Thus the very ambiguity of the current campus climate may pose the starkest contrast to the dark days of the 1950s and may also account in part for what seems a far freer and more open level of debate in the twenty-first century.

Two other events strikingly evidence a post–September 11 climate that seems both calmer and more complex than that of the Cold War era. In the winter of 2004, a federal grand jury in Iowa issued subpoenas to Drake University, demanding detailed information about an antiwar conference held on the Drake campus several months earlier. The subpoenas also sought records from the sponsoring organization, the Drake chapter of the National Lawyers Guild. Among the targeted materials were lists of all persons who had attended the conference, even though it later came to light that federal agents had attended the gathering and apparently had already compiled such a roster. The subpoenas also demanded copies of the periodic Lawyers Guild chapter reports that Drake required of all registered student organizations. The apparent basis for these extensive demands was a belief that the conference had triggered a physical protest shortly thereafter at a nearby military base, during which several protestors had tried to scale the fence, though none gained entry and no damage resulted.

News of these demands quickly reached the national news media. The Lawyers Guild promptly filed a motion to quash the subpoenas. Drake University's administration took a firm and bold stance in support of academic freedom and autonomy and the student group's privacy. National organizations such as the ACLU, AAUP, and others quickly entered the fray, protesting what seemed initially to be the first evidence of a possibly ominous resurgence of McCarthyism. Critics also noted that some of the information sought by the grand jury was specifically protected and made private by the Buckley Amendment, enacted by Congress in the 1970s to bar the release by colleges and universities of any but the most generic information about any of its students.

A few days later, an obviously embarrassed (and startled) United States attorney withdrew his demands—although not before a federal judge had briefly imposed an unprecedented gag on the parties. The federal prosecutor, at whose suggestion the grand jury had issued its orders, explained that he had never meant to chill anyone's free speech or academic freedom, insisting that he had no desire to target "persons peacefully and lawfully engaged in rallies, which are conducted under the protection of the First Amendment." The government's concern, he added, went no further than trying to discover the catalyst for illegal activity that had occurred soon after the conference at the nearby military base. This explanation satisfied few observers, though the withdrawal of the subpoenas at least provided a moment of relief and some sense of contrition on the prosecutor's part.[29]

At almost exactly the same time, there was trouble of a different sort in Texas. Several U.S. Army intelligence agents aggressively questioned students and staff members at the University of Texas (UT) at Austin about a conference held there titled "Islam and the Law: The Question of Sexism." The central theme of the conference was the status and treatment of women in traditionally Islamic cultures. The agents visited the UT Law School, seeking information about three Muslim men who had attended the conference and had aroused the suspicions of government lawyers from a nearby military base. When the agents sought a roster of the participants but were unable to obtain it, they apparently left the Austin campus empty-handed.

After UT officials and others expressed deep concern about these inquiries, the Army's Intelligence and Security Command issued in late March a quite remarkable formal statement of apology. The release specifically acknowledged that the agents had clearly "exceeded their authority" in seeking such information. Any such inquiry of civilians on U.S. soil, said the statement, could be conducted only by the FBI and not by military agents. Although this concession left open for another day the broader and more troubling issue whether any federal agent may seek such information from a nonsuspect civilian, especially a participant at a recent academic conference, the Defense Department's prompt disclaimer was nonetheless striking, if only as evidence that someone in authority was listening to the remonstrance of the University of Texas and others concerned about this random foray.[30]

Once again, the optimist and the pessimist would draw contrasting inferences from such experiences. In the pessimist's view, such government action should never have occurred at all. The fact that it got even as far as it did in Des Moines or in Austin gave evidence of a distressing lack of sensitivity to civilian rights, especially in the academic community, that would not have existed before September 11. To the optimist, however, the signs were at least mildly encouraging. Not only did two federal officials rather promptly back down; but also, even more comforting, both felt obligated to disclaim quite publicly any inclination to attack or threaten academic freedom and free inquiry within the university community. Perhaps even more reassuring was clear evidence that—in sharp contrast to the diffidence of the McCarthy era—two major universities and a host of national organizations stepped up immediately and boldly to demand official recognition of the inappropriateness and potential harm of such intrusive demands for sensitive information. Of course we can never know how such demands would have been met during the Cold War period, because they were seldom made back in those dark days and never with the clarity and firmness of the winter 2004 remonstrances.

So far, one would almost certainly have to concede, so good. At its traditional core, academic freedom seemed to have fared surprisingly well in the several years that followed the terrorist attacks of September 2001. Yet the early years of the twenty-first century have brought very different challenges to free expression and free inquiry on the college and university campus. Thus the unlikelihood of a resurgence of McCarthyism is indisputably reassuring, but it is only part of the story. The differences between the two periods are dramatic in ways that go well beyond the response from the sources of traditional threats. On the one hand, the typical catalytic events of the post–September 11 period have been isolated outbursts from individual professors who can fairly readily be dismissed as oddballs, dissidents, or marginal players in a profession within which extreme statements are widely tolerated and even expected. Far from reflecting a monolithic view on American foreign policy, the outbursts we have noted here cross the political and ideological spectrum; recall, for example, that Berthold's "anyone who can blow up the Pentagon" or De Genova's "a million Mogadishus" represent one viewpoint, whereas Hearlson's charge that his California Muslim students "drove two planes into the World Trade Center" comes from the opposite side. Thus, in many ways, the most visible challenges to academic freedom in the early twenty-first century, while hardly trivial, have not yet approached the gravity of the deep fear and suspicion that fueled McCarthyism a half century earlier.

Despite these many positive signs, and a dramatically different climate from that of earlier times of crisis, there is one area in which the post–September 11 experience has been a far less happy one. Freedom in scientific research has become an almost predictable casualty of heightened concern over national security. And because much of the most sensitive research takes place in university laboratories, the implications for academic freedom are not obscure. The threats and challenges have arisen in several distinct areas. All but inevitable in the aftermath of the terrorist attacks, for example, were the heightened restrictions that Congress imposed on access to and use of "select agents," chiefly certain biohazardous materials; such constraints have been largely accepted by the academic community with resignation if not enthusiasm.

More troubling have been added burdens imposed on the laboratory use of already regulated materials and, most especially, tighter restrictions on who may be employed in research involving such materials. The newly intensified controls cause some problems because of what they expressly cover—for example, on certain projects, barring the employment of graduate students from certain countries and even U.S.-born researchers who have been convicted of a nontrivial drug offense—but quite as much because of areas in which vagueness and discretion deny adequate guidance to those who are potentially affected. As the AAUP's Special Committee on Academic Freedom and National Security in Time of Crisis noted after reviewing such measures, "the requirement for security checks and uncertainties about the grounds for the government's denying access to select agents has serious potential implications for academic freedom." After assessing the overall impact of these new post–September 11 restrictions, a Massachusetts Institute of Technology faculty committee—fearing that the lists of proscribed people and materials would continue to expand—ventured that the institute "may rightfully decide that on-campus research in areas governed by these regulations is no longer in its interest or in line with its principles."[31]

Placing limits on the publication of research findings has been an especially contentious area. Soon after the September 11 attacks, the Defense Department proposed that scientists whose research was federally supported would need to obtain prior government approval before they could publish the results or even discuss their research at scientific conferences. The nearly universal indignation that greeted such a concept ensured its rejection, and the Pentagon shortly withdrew the proposal. Yet an alternative approach has brought to university-based research almost comparable constraints. Historically, federally sponsored research has been either classified or unclassified—the former being heavily restricted in several dimensions whereas the latter is largely free of official constraint. Some major research centers, such as the University of Wisconsin, flatly forbid classified research, believing that the limits placed on such activity are inimical to academic freedom. Other major research institutions, such as the University of Virginia, may discourage but do not forbid classified research, indeed suggesting that a flat ban like Wisconsin's may impair the academic freedom of those scientists who wish to accept support that is only available on a classified basis.

Into the post–September 11 mix entered a new element—"sensitive but unclassified" research, which is not technically classified but at the same time is far less open and free than that which is fully unclassified. In fairness, the concept did have limited recognition before the terrorist attacks, but its use by federal agencies has become far more extensive in the twenty-first century than it had ever been in the past. A 2002 statement by the presidents of the three National Academies of Science recognized the need for "balance between security and openness" but insisted that such balance is not fostered by the "poorly defined categories of 'sensitive but unclassified' information that do not provide precise guidance on what information should be restricted from public access." The "inevitable effect" of such policies, the statement concluded, "is to stifle scientific creativity and to weaken national security."[32] Although some members of Congress, including the Republican chair of the House Committee on Science, have expressed much concern about the hybrid nature of the "sensitive but unclassified" category, its apparently burgeoning use has not been forbidden.

Especially troubling in the post–September 11 climate has been foreign scholars' reduced access to the United States. The deeply disturbing case of Professor Tariq Ramadan, the withdrawal of whose visa we noted earlier, was hardly unique. In the spring of 2003, a Cuban expert on U.S.-Cuban relations, who had earlier lectured at Harvard and Johns Hopkins, was inexplicably denied a visa by U.S. authorities when he sought to attend a Latin American studies conference in Dallas. Ultimately, barely half the Cuban delegation was allowed to attend that conference, despite informal assurances that visas would be granted in time for their planned trips. Although in certain respects the processing of visas for graduate students and visiting scholars from "suspect" nations has markedly improved since the major glitches of the immediate post–September 11 period, serious problems remain. Inexplicably, a former Nicaraguan health minister was denied the visa she needed to teach at Harvard, and a distinguished Bolivian historian was simply kept in limbo for nearly a year awaiting the papers he needed to assume his teaching post at the University of Nebraska. And the Cuban delegates seeking access to an academic conference in Puerto Rico in 2005 fared even worse than had their compatriots two years earlier; this time none of the fifty-five prospective delegates to the Latin American Studies Association conference received a visa, though once again informal assurance had suggested up to the eve of the conference that all would be able to attend.[33]

Perhaps most troubling among the access restrictions concerns the export of "munitions"—a term that has come to include a broad array of scientific materials such as encryption software (the subject of extensive and ultimately successful litigation on behalf of academic cryptographers, discussed more fully in Chapter 7.) For the most part, focus has been on the statutory requirement that anyone seeking to export suspect materials must obtain a license. But in the spring of 2005 the Commerce Department shocked the academic community by announcing that it planned to adopt a "deemed export" policy. This new approach would target people rather than materials; it would require universities to obtain a license before employing any foreign national from certain countries on a U.S. laboratory research project involving sensitive technologies.[34] Opposition to this proposal from the academic community was intense, and in January, 2006, Commerce announced it had scrapped the particular plan—though leaving in place such onerous prospects as requiring universities to obtain licenses for foreign scientists who work with equipment that is on the export-control list, even if the actual research was exempt from licensing. Then, in mid-May 2006, to the great relief of the scientific community, the Commerce Department launched a comprehensive study of the whole array of such issues.

Something should also be said about the USA PATRIOT Act, perhaps the most visible piece of post–September 11 legislation. Several provisions have caused the academic community special concern—notably the "Business Records" section that empowers federal agents to obtain information about persons suspected of terrorist activity without a court order or warrant—illustratively, borrower records from libraries and purchase records from bookstores. Since the person from whom such records are sought may disclose such a demand to no one else—most especially not the subject or target of the inquiry—it has been virtually impossible to gauge the extent of such clandestine surveillance.[35] Though Congress did, in reauthorizing the PATRIOT Act early in 2006, slightly mitigate the gag provision, the most troubling features of this section remain in force.

Finally among legislative incursions, while most threats have come from Congress, state lawmakers have not been completely silent. Most serious among such actions seems to have been the passage of Ohio General Assembly of a state Patriot Act, one provision of which requires every new employee to certify his or her loyalty through a certificate that bears a striking resemblance to the disclaimer-type oaths of the 1950s. The law clearly and unequivocally applies to all faculty members hired by Ohio's public universities and community colleges after July, 2006. Specifically, it asks such invasive and troubling questions as "have you ever solicited any individual for membership in an organization on the U.S. Department of State Terrorist Exclusion List?." The applicant must attest that he or she "has not used any position of prominence . . . to persuade others to support" such an organization, nor "committed an act that you knew, or should have known, 'affords material support or resources' to any such organization." The statute lists six questions to which acceptable answers are essential to employment; an unsatisfactory answer, or even a failure to answer, may trigger an inference that the applicant has in fact aided a terrorist organization.

Of the vital terms in the statute and its implementing regulations, only "material support or resources" is defined; such other critical language as "persuade," "solicited" and "position of prominence" are left entirely to the applicant's conjecture. Although the Terrorist Exclusion List may be found on the State Department webpage, it designates 59 organizations, some of which (e.g., the Ulster Defense Association, the Japanese Red Army and the People Against Gangsterism and Drugs) hardly evoke images of current terrorist activity. Thus a person who might be supremely confident of his or her noninvolvement in Middle East controversy could conceivably be implicated through past affiliation with a wholly different sort of group. Given these several elements, Ohio's certificate requirement seems to create for a prospective professor or instructor at any of the state's public campuses a dilemma strikingly similar to that which plagued many loyal but conscientious scholars in the loyalty-oath era. Moreover, the practical efficacy of such security measures is highly doubtful; a genuine terrorist would probably be least deterred by such a requirement, convinced that risking a perjury charge for falsely representing his loyalty would be the least of his problems.

Although the certificate requirement became effective in the summer of 2006, there appears to have been no legal challenge nor even a serious remonstrance by those whose acceptance of a faculty post in Ohio now entails such an elaborate commitment. Although the law does provide for the exemption of "categories of employment," the academic community has apparently not sought such a dispensation, although university faculty would appear to qualify most clearly for such relief, given the substantial impact of any such burden on academic freedom. Indeed, the rather passive response of the academic world, not only in Ohio but elsewhere, remains puzzling. Granting the very substantial differences between the climate of the McCarthy era and that of the post-September 11 period, such a contrast is nonetheless quite surprising.[36]

Early in 2007 it appeared that Ohio might not be entirely alone in this dubious regard. California Assemblyman Chuck DeVore introduced a measure (Assembly Bill 137) that would forbid the employment in any state job of a "knowing member or financial supporter of an extremist terror network," without precise definitions of the key provisions of the bill. This proposal would also have the more benign effect of ridding California's Code of many clearly obsolete provisions that barred Communists or subjected them to various disabilities. (Although most such laws had effectively been declared unconstitutional decades earlier, their nominal survival on the statute books evidenced a relatively lethargic legislative weeding process.)

During the winter of 2007, a federal district court upheld against constitutional challenge a Florida law that barred students, faculty members and researchers at the state's public colleges and universities from using state or federal funds – or even private foundation grants administered by these institutions – for travel to Cuba or four other "embargoed" nations, however legitimate might be the academic or research focus of the trip. Even teachers and students at Florida private colleges are forbidden to use state funds for such purposes. The law had been adopted the previous spring after a Florida International University professor and his wife were accused of spying for Cuba.

Amid these manifold causes for potential concern about the condition of scientific freedom after September 11, three basic cautions are crucial. First, conditions were bound to change substantially after the terrorist attacks. Anyone who expects academic life ever to return to the conditions of September 10 is hopelessly naïve. Even if no further terrorist activity occurs on U.S. soil, many of the changes that have occurred must be seen as permanent and accepted as such. It is indeed a new world, and a world in which the academic community needs to accept the reality of change.

Second, it is important to separate what is from what is not a product of the terrorist attacks. Much of what today we see as directly threatening to academic freedom has far deeper and unrelated roots. For example, the major act of Congress that criminalizes "aiding and abetting terrorism"—the basis for the charges against Professor Al Arian, among others—was adopted in 1996 and, though slightly enhanced in later years, was fully in place when the hijacked planes hit the World Trade Center and the Pentagon. The FBI's omnivorous data-screening system called Carnivore, was a creature of the Clinton Administration and the mid-1990s. The extensive regulation of the export not only of munitions but of such seemingly innocuous material as cryptographic software dates back to the late 1980s and early 1990s and was firmly supported by the Clinton Administration. The Foreign Intelligence Surveillance Act Court, a key to many of the powers enhanced in the PATRIOT Act, came into being in 1978, including the infamous gag provision applicable to certain of its actions. Thus, while there are more than enough new threats that can be blamed directly on the national response to September 11, there are many other risks that were in place long before planes were hijacked as lethal weapons.

Finally, it is important to avoid self-inflicted wounds that may make conditions seem even worse than they are. Thus an early analysis of the Business Records section of the PATRIOT Act by a major professional organization told its members that the gag provision precluded even an inquiry to the university attorney. While the law does forbid any "disclosure" of a demand for records, that language could not plausibly be read as preventing confidential communication with a lawyer.

In the fall of 2002, the administration at the University of California-San Diego (UCSD) inflicted a very different sort of unnecessary wound upon itself when it told a radical student group that, under federal anti-terrorist laws, it must shut down its website because the site contained a link to an organization in Colombia that was on the State Department's list of terrorist organizations. While that may have been a prudent step, UCSD's vice chancellor for Student Affairs soon acknowledged that such an electronic link could hardly constitute "aiding and abetting terrorism." The point is that there are more than enough real and grave new threats to academic freedom without hypothesizing or imagining others.[37]

5

The Rights of Academic Researchers

Professor Richard Snyder, a nationally recognized expert on highway safety, taught civil engineering at the University of Michigan. In 1980 he published a study entitled "On-Road Crash Experience of Utility Vehicles," a product of sustained laboratory research. Shortly thereafter, as a direct result of his published research, Snyder became embroiled in a lawsuit of the kind that few scientists would ever expect to encounter.

Several victims of serious crashes that involved Jeep CJ-5 vehicles brought suit against the manufacturer, claiming that the auto's propensity to roll over made it inherently unsafe in ways that should impose liability on the producer. When the Jeep Corporation's lawyers learned of Snyder's study, they inferred that some of the background data might enhance their defense in at least one of the pending lawsuits. Thus they sought a court order to compel Professor Snyder to produce "any and all research data, memoranda, drafts, correspondence, lab notes, reports, calculations, moving pictures, photographs, slides, statements and the like pertaining to the on-road crash experience of utility vehicles" targeted by the recently published study. This was a novel and, for the researcher and his university, deeply troubling demand.

Snyder's lawyer immediately filed objections to the subpoena, noting that the researcher was not a party to the suit but merely an innocent bystander; that such deep intrusion into his process of inquiry would be "extremely burdensome" and would "have a chilling effect on researchers, scientists and educators"; and that he could not be compelled to testify as an expert against his wish (and presumably without compensation). Finally, the remonstrance argued that Snyder's First Amendment rights protected him from such compulsory disclosure—specifically, that "he has an academic privilege to refuse to testify." The motion to quash the subpoena also invoked several technical procedural concerns.

The district judge was strikingly unimpressed, even though by curious irony he was the one member of the federal bench in Southeast Michigan who had for many years been a law professor in Ann Arbor and thus had been a colleague of Professor Snyder's across campus. Judge Joiner began by stressing the need for courts to gather all relevant information and the concomitant duty of citizens to provide such information when it might be pertinent. As for Snyder's claim of academic privilege, the judge was unaware of any such source of protection in statute or in case law, and thus he flatly rejected any such basis for a researcher's recalcitrance.

Lest there be any doubt, wrote the judge in refusing the requested protection, "this court is unwilling to create a new privilege that would shield academics from testifying." In addition, the court could not find any First Amendment support for Snyder's plea; such limited protection as several courts had recently granted to journalists involved compelled disclosure of confidential information or sources, but Snyder had never claimed that promises of secrecy would be breached by the demands he was resisting. Thus, wrote Judge Joiner, "the court is not persuaded that the possibility of being subpoenaed will sufficiently chill writers and researchers to warrant a special exemption from the duty to provide evidence."

Finally, Professor Snyder insisted that such voluminous demands—virtually his entire laboratory would have to have been surrendered if Jeep's request were granted—would be disruptive and burdensome. Even if he were compensated as an expert witness—an inducement Jeep seemed unlikely to offer—such burdens would still be substantial and onerous. At this point Judge Joiner recognized the potential inequity of such a unilateral bargain. In concluding his opinion, he ruled that Snyder "is entitled to a reasonable fee for testifying" and might even assess "a charge for a portion of the expenses of the original research." But the bottom line remained intact—any burdens of compliance that could not be recompensed raised no constitutional free speech or academic freedom concerns within the federal judicial process.[1]

The case that Professor Snyder made for protection, which his former colleague on the federal bench rejected, merits closer scrutiny. First, among the basic tenets of scientific research is the principle that the investigator holds the right to decide when, where, and how the results of laboratory or other studies will be made public. Although certain research grants and contracts may reserve to the sponsor a limited opportunity to review results before publication, the delay that such a step may impose is usually brief, and any power to limit or defer disclosure is limited to the source of support. Otherwise, it is the researcher's judgment that must prevail in a free and open inquiry process. Second, and equally important, the time and medium of pre- or post-publication disclosure of research data, raw materials, and the like must also be determined by the investigator, unconstrained by judgments or imperatives external to the scientific process. Third, the risks of demanding premature disclosure of research findings—before the process or inquiry has run its course—are especially grave. Although an analogy to "pulling up the carrot to make sure it's growing" may seem simplistic, the parallels are more than superficial; getting back on track a research program that has been prematurely disrupted or truncated by judicial intervention may be almost as challenging as replanting the carrot that has been taken from the ground to asses its progress. Fourth, the hazards of externally compelled disclosure are especially severe when a researcher has promised confidentiality to human subjects or to their employer—or even where an expectation of confidentiality is fairly implied even though never made explicit. Finally, the burdens occasioned by such demands may appear to be chiefly a practical concern but may jeopardize the integrity of the research process in far more basic ways, especially in the case of a small laboratory faced with a massive demand for research data. And if an active scholar must go to court in response to such a demand, many additional days may be taken away from the laboratory. Nontrivial tangible costs may also be incurred, even if the university or a scientific organization provides a legal defense. Thus it is important to bear in mind the nature of the case that a subpoenaed scientist or scholar may offer against such compulsion.

Happily, some academic researchers have fared better in court than did Professor Snyder. In fact that early case had one precursor with a more benign outcome. Long before Erin Brokovich had made her exposés into headline news and fodder for Hollywood, Harvard public health professor Marc Roberts conducted extensive interviews with employees of Pacific Gas & Electric Company (PG&E) while studying how public utilities reached environmental decisions. A construction company brought suit against PG&E for a simple breach of contract in federal court. The plaintiff's lawyers learned about Professor Roberts's study and surmised that gaining access to his data might support their claims about the very process that had led to the claimed breach. On an exactly contrary premise, PG&E lawyers now also sought to comb Roberts's interviews. Thus, as not infrequently happens, both sides were pressing with equal vigor and legal power for access to the study's database. The researcher strenuously resisted, counseled by the very attorney who several years earlier had succeeded in gaining partial protection for confidential sources of a Harvard political scientist who had done sensitive research on the Vietnam conflict.

This time, a federal court ruled in Roberts's favor, though on somewhat narrower grounds than the First Amendment protection he had claimed. The judge noted that the information both sides sought could have been obtained in ways that would have been far less intrusive to the research process. There were serious doubts whether the survey data contained much of what either side was seeking for litigation purposes. Moreover, Professor Roberts was clearly an innocent bystander who had no stake in the litigation and had simply been drawn into someone else's dispute. Finally, recalling that Roberts had promised confidentiality to his interview subjects, the judge took special note of "the importance of maintaining confidential channels of communication between academic researchers and their sources."[2]

In the quarter century or so since the Snyder and Roberts cases, there have been well over a dozen reported cases involving efforts to resist demands in court for scientific data. Researchers have prevailed more often than they have lost, although success has most often correlated closely with pledges of confidentiality to human subjects, of the type that Roberts was able to invoke but Snyder could not. Scholars have, with varying success, asserted by analogy the limited protection that courts have conferred on journalists. Though the Supreme Court in the early 1970s rejected any First Amendment right to withhold confidential sources or information,[3] judges have typically insisted that one who seeks to compel testimony from a reporter must demonstrate that the requested information is essential, that it could not be obtained by less intrusive means, and that the demand is not unduly burdensome. Journalists, of course, have an important added benefit that researchers do not—so-called shield laws that have been passed by roughly two-thirds of the states, which expressly protect confidential sources save under the most exigent circumstances.

Despite the lack of such statutory protection, scholars have achieved a few of what would even qualify as notable victories in their efforts to resist compelled disclosure. In the 1980s several such disputes focused on demands for highly sensitive survey research done by scientists at the Centers for Disease Control (CDC; notably on use of the Dalkon Shield, which became a major target of massive and costly litigation). In rejecting such corporate demands for research data, the federal appeals court that reviews all CDC litigation warned of the impact that a compelled breach of confidentiality might have on "scientific and social research supported by a population willing to submit to in-depth questioning." In one such case, an unusually sympathetic federal court rebuffed a corporate demand for sensitive research data even though confidentiality had not been expressly pledged to the subjects, noting that participants in such a study might reasonably have assumed privacy was protected even in the absence of such a commitment by the investigator.[4]

A spate of concurrent cases involved the tobacco industry and, particularly, demands for research data on smoking cessation. When the industry and the research community (supported by the American Cancer Society) squared off in a New York state court in the 1990s, the subpoena was quashed partly in deference to the scholars' asserted "interest in academic freedom." The court expressed special concern about demands that would interrupt ongoing laboratory studies: "While these medical investigations are still in progress, they should not be subjected to examination and criticism by people whose interests are arguably antithetical to the medical scientists. It would have the effect of denying to these doctors the opportunity of first publication of their studies. It could also have a chilling effect and discourage future scientific endeavors."[5]

Such favorable outcomes are, however, far from predictable. Soon after they lost this quest in the state courts, the major tobacco companies decided to try their fortunes in what they hoped would be a more receptive federal forum. Scientists at the Mount Sinai Medical School, with the strong backing of the school's dean and the American Cancer Society, strenuously resisted demands for smoking-related research sought by the major tobacco companies. When they refused to deliver the data, the researchers were held in contempt, and they promptly appealed to the higher federal court. The court of appeals took note of the New York state court ruling and others that had protected scientific research but felt in no way constrained by such precedents.

To the contrary, the federal judges dismissed each of the protective premises, rejecting the asserted (and recently recognized) researcher's privilege. As for the claimed disruptive effect of such intrusion, recognition of that objection would effectively thwart all such demands since "most gainfully employed discovery targets could contend that compliance would take time away from their regular work." Moreover, the tobacco companies had offered to reimburse the individual scientists and the medical school for "reasonable expenses of compliance." That the subpoenaed scientists were innocent bystanders to the litigation was also of no avail; "the publication of their findings and conclusion invites use by persons whom the findings favor and invites reliance by the finders of fact."[6]

So strikingly hostile a view of a researcher's claim understandably alarmed the scientific community. The American Council on Education's general counsel, Sheldon Elliot Steinbach, cautioned that "medical advances depend on researchers being able to test their most speculative ideas" and warned that such a ruling sent to university researchers a "message . . . that the documents they create in the course of their research may be open to scrutiny, not only by colleagues and peers for the purpose of furthering science, but in the courtroom in civil litigation."[7] The best that could be said for the federal court ruling in this tobacco study case was that the court did at least distinguish two different situations in which subpoenas had been quashed—cases where there was either a clear threat to promised confidentiality or direct disruption of ongoing research that would enable others to use or disclose research findings before the principal investigator had a chance to publish—or decide not to publish—those very findings. To the scholars at Mount Sinai and other academic laboratories, those distinctions afforded small comfort.

The most recent researcher victory in the tobacco wars never even got to court. Several tobacco companies sought extensive data from ongoing smoking-related studies conducted by scientists at Johns Hopkins University's Medical School. When the news reached the office of the university's legal office, it outraged soon-to-retire Vice President and General Counsel Estelle Fishbein, who had long been recognized as the dean of university attorneys. She immediately notified the industry's lawyers that they would receive the research data they demanded "over my dead body"—making clear that her final act as Hopkins's lead attorney would, if necessary, be one of personal intervention. The industry's lawyers, apparently stunned by so bold and novel a response, dropped their demand and withdrew the subpoenas.[8]

The most recent reported case in this area also had a research-protective outcome, though one would be naïve to suppose it the last word on the subject. In the late 1990s a Microsoft-targeted antitrust suit in Boston's federal court suddenly focused on the research of two management professors, one at Harvard Business School and the other at MIT's Sloan School of Management. Their recent studies had resulted in a forthcoming book entitled *Competing on Internet Time*—the core of which was the ongoing "browser wars," the very subject of the government's suit against the software giant. Microsoft believed that certain statements that Professors Cusumano and Yoffie had tape-recorded from Netscape employees and had summarized in the forthcoming book would enhance the company's defense. Thus they subpoenaed the professors' notes, tape recordings and transcripts of interviews, and their correspondence with interview subjects.

The authors resisted such demands, noting that as part of the study they had promised confidentiality to all their subjects and had signed a nondisclosure agreement with Netscape barring the release of any proprietary information without the company's consent. The district judge ruled in the scholars' favor, balancing First Amendment and other concerns about such compelled disclosure against what seemed to be modest interests that Microsoft had asserted in support of its demands. The case soon reached the court of appeals, also based in Boston, which surprisingly (given its proximity to much cutting-edge research) had no prior experience with an issue that had perplexed most of its sister federal circuits.

Professors Cusumano and Yoffie prevailed on appeal as they had in the trial court. Several factors convinced the First Circuit that Microsoft had overreached. For one, these particular scholars were "strangers to the antitrust litigation; insofar as the record reflects, they have no dog in that fight." Moreover, the researchers fell within a category of claimants whose need for protection warranted a court's attention. Although journalists had generally fared better than scholars and scientists in their quest for protection against compelled disclosure, comparable interests were at stake, especially at this early stage in the process of inquiry; "academicians engaged in pre-publication research should be accorded protection commensurate with" that afforded reporters.

After determining who might claim such protection, the court of appeals addressed its scope, asking, "What is protected?" The *Cusumano and Yoffie* case posed no need to define the outer boundaries of such solicitude; the clear promise of confidentiality to the Netscape subjects weighed heavily against disclosure and at the very least shifted a major burden to the party seeking to compel disclosure. Even granting that Microsoft might have substantial needs for information that the notes and tapes might reveal, less intrusive means—mainly direct discovery from the very people who had been Cusumano's and Yoffie's sources—would presumably yield comparable data.

Finally, the scholars' inquiry process and the need to protect that process tipped the scale decisively against enforcing the subpoenas. What they had done in interviewing Netscape employees was precisely the manner in which conscientious and systematic scholars gathered critical data. Promising confidentiality in a sensitive corporate context "gives chary corporate executives a sense of security that greatly facilitates the achievement of agreements to cooperate." Conversely, demanding disclosure in violation of such pledges "would hamstring not only [these scholars'] future research efforts but also those of other similarly situated scholars." Then, in a somewhat florid coda, the court summarized the core of the ruling: "This loss of theoretical insight into the business world is of concern in and of itself. Even more important, compelling the disclosure of such research materials would infrigidate the free flow of information to the public, thus denigrating a fundamental First Amendment value."[9]

Celebration of the *Cusumano and Yoffie* ruling would have been premature at the time, and it would still be unwise today, even though no subsequent ruling on this issue appears to present a less favorable view. Several possibly limiting factors invite caution. For one, the First Circuit court of appeals focused heavily on management research of corporate entities, leaving some doubt whether they would have been equally protective had the issue arisen at the Harvard Medical School or in one of MIT's engineering laboratories. A more basic cause of unease was the exceptionally appealing circumstances of the case—the unambiguous (and clearly vital) pledge of confidentiality, on which the court relied heavily in balancing the contending interests, and the timing of Microsoft's demand for data that were central to a yet unpublished research study. Vary any one of those factors, and the balancing process would become far more difficult. Or posit a case in which the party seeking disclosure had established a somewhat more compelling case—suppose, for example, that many of Cusumano's and Yoffie's key subjects had recently left Netscape, or were otherwise unavailable, making the scholar's notes and tapes the only extant source of information critical to Microsoft's defense.

The central point is quite simply this: Scholars sometimes lose and at other times succeed in their quest for protection against compelled disclosure. Even when researchers prevail, the best that can be said is that the equities balance in their favor in the particular case. They may leave the courtroom with their data bases intact but without broader assurance that they would fare equally well on another round before a different court or with less appealing circumstances. Moreover, one may hardly forget that even victorious scholars have typically incurred some tangible costs—notwithstanding legal representation by a university or scientific organization—not to mention the inevitably and sometimes profoundly disruptive effect of months, even years, of protracted and often contentious litigation.

The current situation seems intolerably insensitive to basic academic values. One would expect better protection from a nation that so values scientific research in a competitive world and a global economy. For one brief moment in the late 1990s there was a prospect of such protection. Anticipating his final year in the United States Senate, New York's Daniel Patrick Moynihan invited proposals for legislation that might bear his name and enhance his legacy. Several civil liberties groups pleaded for a researcher-scholar's protective measure. Because the initial impetus came from the Thomas Jefferson Center for the Protection of Free Expression, the bill would be called the Thomas Jefferson Researcher's Privilege, and it would accord scholars a type of safeguard roughly comparable to what state shield laws conferred on journalists. The American Association for the Advancement of Science was prepared to offer testimony in support of the bill, mainly in the form of horror stories about subpoenas that had crudely invaded and disrupted the process of inquiry. Despite initial interest by Senator Patrick Leahy, then chairman of the Senate Judiciary Committee, and a few others in Congress, the bill never even reached the hearing stage before Senator Moynihan's retirement. Had Jefferson still been about, one hopes he might have managed to evoke a greater sense of urgency for the subpoenaed scholar, but his successors were unable to do so, even in the calmer pre–September 11 environment.

Ironically, the Senate was by then headed in exactly the opposite direction. Alabama's conservative Republican senator, Richard Shelby, sponsored a bill that made all federally funded research subject to the Freedom of Information Act (FOIA), and Congress enacted it. Designed to make more broadly available the results of government-sponsored studies, the actual law, in the view of an angry University of Chicago scientist, offered "a meat-ax approach to access to data when it's actually a fine scalpel that's required." Nils Hasselmo, president of the Association of American Universities, agreed that "FOIA is a blunt instrument when it comes to striking the right balance." Despite some moderation through implementing regulations, the Shelby bill only served to intensify the scrutiny to which scientists—at least the vast number of them receiving federal support—were now potentially subject.[10]

The use of the Freedom of Information Act as the lever to enter the research process contained a special irony. Several years earlier, Professor

Paul Fisher of the Medical College of Georgia found himself subject to extensive FOIA-based demands from the tobacco industry for data from his smoking-related studies.[11] Specifically, he presented in a published article a key research finding—that more than half of children whom he had surveyed between the ages of three and eight recognized R. J. Reynolds's vaunted symbol Joe Camel and associated this benign figure with cigarettes. When the dispute over the FOI request got to court, the university's lawyers offered no defense; because the terms of Georgia's Open Records Act did not exclude such research data from a broad definition of "public documents," there seemed no possible ground on which to resist disclosure. Thus the university attorneys joined the industry lawyers in demanding Fisher's compliance, despite the company's statement that it would use the subject data (as Fisher later summarized the company's avowed goal) "to knock on the children's doors and ask them if they actually said what I claimed they said in my study." After finding himself defenseless against the FOIA claim, Fisher left academia and entered private medical practice, feeling it was no longer "reasonable to continue on as a faculty member."[12] Freedom of information had clearly and unequivocally triumphed over academic freedom.

Within the academic community, it is basic that scholars determine what subjects they will explore and what issues they will pursue through research. A resolution recently adopted by the University of California's Academic Senate stated the consensus best: "Restrictions on accepting research funding from particular sources on the basis of moral or political judgments about the fund source or the propriety of the research, or because of speculations about how the research results might be used, interfere with an individual faculty member's freedom to define and carry out a research program."[13] The university may regulate the process of scientific inquiry in myriad ways—not all of them welcomed by their research faculty—but the institution does not dictate what shall and shall not constitute acceptable subject matter or topics of inquiry. Thus when a challenge to that basic premise unsettled the University of Delaware in the late 1980s, the entire academic community watched with a mixture of interest and concern. The central question was whether the institution could ever reject a research grant for which a faculty member had applied and which had been offered by an external sponsor. Dr. Linda Gottfredson, an assistant professor of Educational Studies, had received three grants from the Pioneer Fund, and was in the process of seeking a fourth grant when questions arose about the particular funding source. An established foundation based in New York, the Pioneer Fund had originally been chartered to provide scholarships primarily to white students, and "to aid 'study into problems of human race betterment.' "[14] But more recently the fund had supported research and related scholarly activity on the correlation between race and intelligence. Several Pioneer-sponsored studies specifically suggested that those of darker skin color might be innately less intelligent than their lighter-skinned colleagues, classmates and neighbors.

When Professor Gottfredson's colleagues learned about her possible future Pioneer Fund grant, several of them questioned the propriety of a state university's acceptance of support for campus-based research from such an organization. The university's president, E. A. Trabant, asked the Faculty Senate's Committee on Research to explore the issue and advise him whether, in its view, acceptance of such funding would compromise the institution's commitment to maintain a multi-cultural and multi-racial environment. (University approval of every research grant was needed because the university is invariably the grantee, although the faculty researcher is of course the principal investigator; although the investigator is the "grantee" in substance, the institution is the "grantee" for legal and technical purposes, and must therefore sign off on each award.)

The committee attempted, with limited success, to determine the precise goals of the Pioneer Fund and of the specific research project. A foundation representative, who agreed to visit the campus in Newark, Delaware, and meet with the committee, left most of the committee members uncertain about the critical issues within their charge. Despite a recent change in the Pioneer Fund's charter, the Research Committee remained skeptical about the claimed softening of the foundation's historic focus on the race-intelligence nexus.

Lacking clear proof either way, the committee concluded that accepting such a research grant on Professor Gottfredson's behalf would indeed compromise the university's dedication to equal opportunity, as long as the Fund remained committed to the intent of its original charter and to a pattern of activities incompatible with the University's mission. Primarily on that basis (though some technical concerns also clouded the issue) the Research Committee urged President Trabant to take the unprecedented step of disallowing such a grant. He accepted that advice, adding his own view that "the University has a right to set its own priorities for the support of scholarly activity." The board of trustees promptly endorsed the president's action, thus blocking Gottfredson's application for further Pioneer support.

Professor Gottfredson then took the matter to the Faculty Welfare and Privileges Committee, where she insisted that if the Research Committee's distinction between faculty "rights" and "privileges" survived, then so vital a "privilege" as seeking support from external support for research and related scholarly activity would be at risk. She added her belief that she had been tarred by a kind of "guilt by association" reminiscent of the McCarthy era. Though the Research Committee insisted it had taken no pejorative view of Gottfredson's research, she now argued that the rejection of a grant about to be made inevitably imposed on the investigator a very serious stigma.

The issue was soon referred to an outside arbitrator in accord with the collective bargaining agreement between the university and its designated faculty representative. Such recourse posed an especially acute dilemma for the campus chapter of the American Association of University Professors (AAUP). Because AAUP was the chosen faculty bargaining agent at Delaware, it organizationally had little choice but to, support Gottfredson's plea for reconsideration—even though, ironically, the chapter's president had been a member of the Research Committee that had urged rejection of Pioneer Fund support.

Arbitrators optimally seek a middle ground on which to resolve such disputes. Here the arbitrator did just that, ruling in Gottfredson's favor but on very narrow procedural grounds. Although both the Research Committee and the president had insisted they lacked adequate information on which to base a fully informed judgment about the Pioneer Fund and its research agenda, they had done precisely that in disqualify this particular funding source. Moreover, they had failed to examine the broader scope of Gottfredson's research, including a number of publications that bore her name—much less the content of the specific proposal that would have sought the now contested Pioneer Fund support. The arbitrator's report concluded, "The committee could not have found the investigator's work incompatible with the university's mission unless it had examined the content of the work." Thus the rejection was ruled in violation of the faculty's collective bargaining agreement. Indeed, a central premise of Gottfredson's appeal was that the Committee had probed unduly (and drawn adverse inferences from) not only the Pioneer Fund's apparent agenda but also the content of a faculty member's previous and current proposed research program. Thus the arbitrator found that the committee could not have made the pejorative judgment it did make without having scrutinized the content of Gottfredson's research; the committee insisted it had confined its inquiry to the mission of the Pioneer Fund, and had not disparaged their colleague's scholarship, but the arbitrator rejected that claim and concluded that the committee had acted improperly.

Once having decided the case on a narrow ground, the arbitrator did offer additional thoughts on the heart of the matter, the inescapable and perplexing issue of academic freedom. The Research Committee, in fairness, had not totally slighted that issue, if only because the president's charge had specifically directed them to address it. But the committee members had avoided major engagement by differentiating between faculty "rights" (such as pursuing research) and "privileges" (including obtaining sponsored research support through the university.) Thus, they insisted, they were not questioning Gottfredson's choice of a research agenda but only the source from which she had sought funding. Such a distinction, quite properly, disturbed the arbitrator, who saw the committee's and the administration's rationale as driven in large part by a wish to avoid bad publicity for accepting support for "racist" research. "Academic freedom," wrote the arbitrator, "is a contractually conferred right, and public perceptions alone, no matter how volatile, cannot suffice to overcome that right." With more than a touch of irony, the arbitrator recalled that the Research Committee had declared in its report that "the university's commitment to racial and cultural diversity is an essential part of, and not a rival principle in conflict with, the university's commitment to academic freedom."[15]

The issue is far more difficult than the arbitrator's comments might suggest, even though the conclusion to which he came seems quite sound. For starters, universities impose myriad conditions on all members of their faculty who seek approval of research grants and contracts. There are a host of financial restrictions and report requirements. Federal (and often state) law compels adherence to sometimes onerous regulations protecting human subjects and laboratory animals and ensuring equal opportunity. Many universities flatly forbid accepting support for classified research, even though such a policy may disadvantage its scientists in highly competitive areas. Support from "shadow" or undisclosed sources may be rejected by a university that insists on publicly identifying all research sponsors. Corporate-sponsored research—a complex issue addressed later in this chapter—may be constrained in certain respects, such as refusing to accept what the university may consider to be excessive sponsor-protective delays prior to publication of research findings.

However high the university's indirect cost recovery (overhead) rate may have been set by negotiation with the appropriate federal agency, every investigator across the campus is bound to seek recovery at that rate, even if competing proposals from peer institutions benefit from substantially lower figures. Increasingly in clinical medical research areas, principal investigators may be required to undergo extensive compliance training programs, lest the entire institution be declared ineligible. And as the Supreme Court's 2006 decisions sustaining the Solomon Amendment against constitutional challenge reminded the academic community, a faculty's conscientious objection to Defense Department policy on homosexuality does not excuse any part of a university receive federal funds from treating military recruiters less favorably than other employers.[16]

Such an enumeration of conditions and restrictions on university research is illustrative, though hardly definitive. But there is a vital difference between all these impositions, burdensome though they may be, and the judgment made by the University of Delaware about Professor Gottfredson's research grant. None of the welter of conditions just reviewed constrains in any way the subject matter of a scholar's research agenda. How one uses human subjects and treats laboratory animals is hardly trivial to a complex research project, but it does not go to the heart of a professor's right to choose on what topic he or she will devote creative energy and from what sources he or she may seek support. Had the Pioneer Fund been disqualified because its officers were guilty of income tax evasion or other serious crimes, the situation would have been dramatically different. In the Delaware case, as far as the Research Committee and the president knew at the time they made the fateful decision, the only flaw in the sponsoring organization was its ideology—specifically its approach to the relationship between race and intelligence. That, said the arbitrator, is simply not an acceptable basis on which to judge the eligibility of a research project or its sponsorship. Academic freedom demands institutional neutrality on such matters, however much that course may seem to undermine a commitment to (for example) racial equality.

Several familiar imperatives support such a judgment. Intervening between a scholar and a sponsor on ideological grounds assumes that the institution knows best, and that it may constrain a professor's choice of research topics for reasons of its own. If such reasons reflect no more than concern about public image—fear that legislators and others may take a dim view of a university that processes grants for "racist" research—we would readily recognize the insufficiency of any such rationale. More troubling, however, is the reason that President Trabant offered for his rejection of the Gottfredson grant: that facilitating such research on campus would gravely undermine the university's equal-opportunity commitment. Such a concern is hardly trivial, but one must ask what other basic institutional values (if any) would similarly be allowed to trump a professor's academic freedom in the research area. If racist research is unacceptable one day, could sexist or homophobic or anti-Semitic or anti-Palestinian projects be equally suspect in the future? Such a list either becomes open-ended and indeterminate or simply may not be permitted to exist at all.

Finally, such a claimed institutional capacity to judge the validity of research by its apparent mission (or that of its sponsor) makes a prior assumption that the funded project will in fact establish or confirm the apparent desiderata. To the contrary, a basic reason for neutrality in the matter of academic research is the reality that a given study may not yield the results for which its sponsors (and even its investigator) may have hoped, but it will perforce refute the threshold hypotheses. To assume in advance that research with an uncongenial goal will always generate uncongenial results fundamentally misconceives the process of discovery. Thus the Delaware arbitrator turns out to have been correct even for reasons that transcended his limited assignment.

Almost simultaneously, the Pioneer Fund issue arose at another institution, although with a result somewhat closer to the Delaware arbitrator's view. Dr. Seymour Itzkoff, a longtime professor of education and child study at Smith College, like Dr. Gottfredson sought Pioneer Fund support for research that some colleagues feared could endorse a malign correlation between race and intelligence. When those colleagues initially conveyed their concerns to him, Itzkoff offered to forego the grant. But Smith's president, Mary Maples Dunn, initially urged him to reconsider and to accept a grant he had clearly earned. During a delay in the process, the academic dean concurred, and the president so informed the investigator, stressing the primacy of Smith's commitment to academic freedom, although noting that the Pioneer Fund's goals were intensely distasteful to the senior administrators.

There the matter might well have ended but for Itzkoff's wish to bring it before Smith's board of trustees. In his appeal to the board, he charged that the administration had been hypocritical in judging both his research agenda and the sponsoring organization's mission. Like Gottfredson, he added his fear that the way the matter had been handled had "negatively affected my work both within Smith College as well as professionally in the world at large." President Dunn now felt a need to clarify her position for the trustees, and she did so by apprising the board of the Pioneer Fund's dubious legacy, as well as its apparent current research agenda. Given such concerns, she posited that the College would not accept direct institutional support from so tainted a source. But serving as the conduit for support of faculty research was a wholly different matter and, in her view, should be treated quite differently: "At the heart of any great academic institution is the freedom to pursue one's scholarly interests and I believe that the college should not restrict that freedom by placing any limitations on funding sources other than [procedural requirements generally recognized and imposed on academic research]."[17] At this point Itzkoff might well have declared victory—but President Dunn's eloquent statement was not to be the final word. By this time Pioneer Fund executives had learned of the controversy and, after making the first payment, suspended all future support for Itzkoff's project and those of any other Smith faculty. The foundation's announcement contained no hint of circumstances that might make future Smith investigators eligible for Pioneer support. Itzkoff soon left Northampton, and his departure apparently ended the saga.[18]

Stepping back from the Delaware and Smith experiences, we should note that this uniquely difficult dilemma arises in a gray area of the research policy spectrum. University-based investigators must, as we have indicated, abide by a host of conditions and restrictions that would not apply to research conducted in one's garage or basement laboratory; the problem is that few sponsors would make grants for garage or basement studies and therefore routinely insist on official university involvement and supervision. At the other extreme, there may be times when the institution might plausibly refuse to process a professor's research request for reasons that could implicate content—for example, if it did not meet the condition of a widespread policy that requires at least one currently active full-time faculty member among the investigators. Or if a classicist submitted a proposal bound for the Organic Chemistry Division of the National Science Foundation, the sponsored programs or grant-and-contract office could reasonably avoid embarrassment and wasted time and energy by refusing to process such a mismatched and futile proposal.

We come ever closer to the Pioneer Fund issue, which is clearly the most difficult and sensitive of all. Had the foundation insisted that its grantees could only publish research findings that were consistent with its bias on race and intelligence, no academic freedom issue would have been raised by a refusal to accept such a grant. Or if the foundation had refused to accept and agree to observe whatever nondiscrimination policies Delaware or Smith imposed on grantors as well as grantees, rejection of a grant would have abridged no faculty member's basic rights. But as far as the record reveals—and this was part of the Delaware arbitrator's concern—no such concerns entered the equation; both grantor and grantees were apparently in full compliance with relevant university equal opportunity policies.

One flaw in the Delaware process was the absence of any explicit research policy that even remotely addressed the issue. Suppose after such an experience a university adopted a rule that expressly forbade its faculty from receiving support for "externally sponsored research the stated or manifest goal of which is directly to undermine or thwart the university's legal commitment to ensure equal opportunity." The very act of framing such a policy makes clear why, at least at a state university, it would not survive. Consider the potential reach of such language: A professor seeks outside support to study the efficacy of the institution's own affirmative action program—a goal that could be deemed violative of the supposed language. Or an educational psychologist proposes to study, with support from Ford or Rockefeller, precisely the issues that Professors Gottfredson and Itzkoff planned to explore. Could it be said that such research would now be acceptable because its sponsor's goals seem benign rather than malign? These and other quite plausible examples suggest not only that a valid policy cannot be written to serve the stated objective, but also that the objective itself is not lawfully attainable.

Yet before leaving this perplexing topic, we should consider an even more daunting and only slightly less plausible variant. Suppose a deeply disaffected alumnus wished to finance research that would cause the demise of an institution he feels not only gave him a miserable education but also has harmed society in myriad ways. And suppose he found a faculty member who, recently rejected for tenure, shared his disaffection and would like nothing better than to conduct such a study? Together they devise a scheme to study in detail the campus utility and communications systems, with an eye to planting explosives at key points that will cripple operations and effectively bring the institution to its knees. The professor prepares a research proposal that meets all the content-neutral criteria and sends it to the sponsored-programs office, where it is likely to receive more routine scrutiny.

Consistency with the principles we have examined here would seem to compel the routine processing of this bizarre proposal. Yet the case seems to differ profoundly from the Pioneer Fund situations. As a threshold matter, a proposal that describes activity not remotely qualifying as research might be suspect from the start. Most institutions would routinely refuse to process proposals that were designed to facilitate clearly unlawful activity—how to distribute cocaine or heroin without risking arrest, for example, or how to obtain and disseminate child pornography with impunity, or how to beat the system through illegal gambling. Barring such proposals should not threaten anyone's academic freedom.

The far more difficult issue, though, is whether a university could validly refuse to support or condone research the object of which is to destroy the institution. Posing such a basis for rejection does, of course, invite comparison to Delaware's insistence that its laboratories need not be made instruments for the subversion of its equal opportunity commitment. Yet there does seem to be a difference of more than simply degree. Undermining a deeply held value is one thing; destroying the institution seems quite another matter. Perhaps in the end there is still some role for common sense in this tortuous process, where examples can always be found to test even the firmest conviction.

Potential threats to academic freedom in research remain to be discussed from two quite different sources—government sponsorship and corporate subvention of university-based research. When it comes to government—especially the federal government—massive support of laboratory research is bound to invite various risks and tensions. Certain principles suggest when an academic freedom issue might arise and when it clearly would not. Clearly government is under no constitutional duty to provide funding for research at all, much less for study in any particular field or discipline. Indeed, government is virtually free to cancel or terminate a current program quite abruptly, even though such action may leave university scientists and their institutions in dire straits because of commitments they have made to research staff and others. Moreover, government is largely free to effect major shifts in focus and emphasis—as national needs change, or simply as political realities alter over time. Again, the scientist whose research agenda is suddenly out of favor after receiving substantial largesse may have a political remedy but almost certainly not a legal one. Thus if the federal government declines to fund stem-cell research in any form, researchers who would benefit from a more benign policy may not complain of any deprivation of their constitutional rights. As in most such situations, they may well have political recourse but no legal remedies. Though recipients of federal research support seldom appreciate the frailty and potential fickleness of the support structure, such vagaries are an inescapable part of an essentially discretionary (and politically sensitive) program of federal funding.

Such principles of government discretion underlay the Supreme Court's 1991 decision in *Rust v. Sullivan,* upholding federal restrictions on funding for family planning clinics, the effect of which was to bar all clinic staff from counseling abortion on the federally funded premises. Indeed, the challenged regulations went beyond such a prohibition and actually obligated clinic staff to offer alternatives to pregnant patients.[19] A divided Supreme Court sustained this draconian policy, noting that Congress was under no duty to appropriate funds for such clinics, and if it chose to fund only abortion-free clinics no provision of the Constitution forbade such a preference. This approach might somewhat irreverently be described as a "follow the money" theory; Congress only pays for what it wants and need not pay for what it does not want, even if the disfavored expenditures have expressive elements, as counseling abortion clearly did in this case.

Initially the academic community feared that any restrictions on federal funding for higher education might now be placed beyond legal challenge. Yet the majority opinion contained one potential and welcome safeguard; Chief Justice William Rehnquist expressly noted that earlier cases had consistently treated "the university [as] a traditional sphere of free expression" within which government regulation was substantially curtailed by First Amendment analysis. A better answer was soon to emerge from the lower courts. About the time the *Rust* decision came down, The National Institutes of Health (NIH) notified Stanford University of plans for a major grant to study an artificial heart device. The notice cautioned that the grant might contain a confidentiality of information clause, which would require researchers to obtain government approval before publishing or otherwise publicly discussing preliminary research results. On behalf of the principal investigator, Stanford formally objected to this restriction. When NIH refused to modify the provision, and eventually withdrew the grant, Stanford sued to challenge the provision on constitutional grounds.

Predictably, the government insisted the confidentiality clause was simply illustrative of the power Congress and the executive branch now had under the *Rust* decision. But federal district judge Harold Greene sharply disagreed, and he struck down the clause on constitutional grounds, finding it to constitute a prior restraint on scientific expression. Unlike the *Rust* ban, which applied only to clinic staff while serving at the federally funded facility, the confidentiality clause denied to the Stanford researchers "the option of speaking regarding artificial heart research on their own time, or in circumstances where their speech is paid for by Stanford University or some other private donor, or not paid for by anyone at all." Indeed, it appeared that the ban would continue in force even after the grant period had ended. Thus the confidentiality clause did far more than follow the money; it followed the person, regardless of the funding source.

Judge Greene also took note of Chief Justice Rehnquist's special deference to the university, observing that the speech being curbed by the confidentiality clause "is the very free expression that the *Rust* Court held to be so important for the functioning of American society" and that any restrictions upon it must meet rigorous constitutional standards. The language of the confidentiality clause clearly failed the test; the operative standards (e.g., "could create erroneous conclusions which might threaten public health or safety if acted upon") were for Judge Greene "impermissibly vague." Thus the restriction would have a "chilling effect" upon scholars at "a premier academic institution, engaged in significant scientific and medical research for the benefit of the American people . . . [and which] may not be compelled under the law to surrender its free speech rights and those of its scientific researchers." Lest anyone might have missed the message, Judge Greene stressed in a concluding paragraph his profound distaste for official edicts that "subject to government censorship the publications of institutions of higher learning and others engaged in legitimate research."[20]

During the decade and a half that followed, the distinction between bans of the *Rust* type and those of the *Stanford* type became clearer and gained explicit Supreme Court recognition. In several cases (at least one of which involved higher education, albeit unrelated to academic freedom) the justices distinguished between public funding designed to convey a government message through private speakers—the *Rust* situation—and those intended to "encourage diverse viewpoints among private speakers," the latter more closely approximating most federal research support.[21] Obviously not all research regulations fall neatly on one side or the other of that line, though the generally useful distinction guided both policy and litigation.

However clear it may be that the government is not constitutionally compelled to fund any university-based research—much less research in a particular field—the *Stanford* case cautions that the same may not be said of government policies that forbid or inhibit research. Returning to the explosive issue of stem-cell research, suppose Congress were to ban completely any and all such scientific inquiry, regardless of funding sources. Although that prospect may seem implausible, a ban on human cloning is much closer to reality. Indeed, President George W. Bush has endorsed government efforts to prevent scientists from undertaking "reckless experiments" and has tried to persuade the United Nations to adopt an international ban on all forms of cloning. Several states (Arkansas, California, Iowa, Massachusetts, Michigan, and New Jersey among them) actually have passed laws that forbid experimental human cloning, though none appears yet to have been tested on constitutional grounds. Should such a national ban be imposed on U.S. academic scientists, and should it be challenged in court (as it surely would be), the long-dormant issue of the status of laboratory research would have to be faced squarely.[22] Although there are sympathetic statements in various court opinions, as we have seen, no categorical ruling exists either way on this profoundly important question. (The federal appeals court for the Ninth Circuit did in 2000 invalidate Arizona's ban on certain forms of fetal tissue research, but the ruling reflected the vagueness of the statutory language rather than a substantive judgment denying such authority to state government.)[23]

Legal scholars and scientists differ on the degree to which they believe the First Amendment protects laboratory research by analogy to more familiar forms of speech and press. Dr. Leon Kass, chair of the President's Council on Bioethics, has discouraged any such analogy, at least as applied to the human cloning controversy, noting that "I don't want to encourage such thinking."[24] Yet those who study the law of free expression take a quite different view. Several recent law review articles, notably one by University of Texas law professor John Robertson, a preeminent expert on law and science, suggest a close analogy between scientists and reporters, though recognizing that journalists lack basic constitutional protection for news-gathering. Professor R. Alta Charo, an expert in bioethics and law at the University of Wisconsin, argues that the process of scientific inquiry should be treated as "expressive conduct" because science that "challenges or explores cultural or religious or political norms . . . is exactly the sort of thing that fits comfortably in the spirit of the First Amendment." As far back as 1977, when this issue first arose, a group of prominent First Amendment scholars argued that free expression should encompass laboratory research, even in the absence of any court ruling that so declared.[25] Even Walter Berns, a conservative political scientist who has recently been at the American Enterprise Institute, told a congressional committee that "the First Amendment protected this kind of research," however grave his misgivings about government sanction for human cloning experiments. Thus the issue of First Amendment protection for scientific research remains curiously in limbo, with no certainty even when the courts will be called upon to address it, much less how it is likely to be resolved.[26]

Several other forms of government regulation have posed major concerns for academic freedom in research. Consider, for example, the matter of editorial collaboration with foreign scholars—an activity quite essential in many scholarly fields. Yet until late 2004, federal regulations severely constrained that process. Publication of an article coauthored by a U.S. scholar and a colleague from any of five trade-embargoed nations (Iran, Iraq, North Korea, Sudan, and, until the embargo was lifted, Libya) was viewed as a suspect export of technology for which a license was required. Although Congress had several times made clear its wish that the export embargo aimed at munitions and the like should not constrain the editorial process, the Treasury's Office of Foreign Assets Control (OFAC) continued to treat scholarly communications and publications essentially the same as shipments of arms and drugs for licensing purposes. A group of academic publishers and editors filed suit challenging (both on statutory and constitutional grounds) the validity of this severely restrictive interpretation. While the suit was pending, the Treasury Department substantially modified the rules, declaring that export licenses would no longer be required for coauthoring or publishing works by scholars from the embargoed nations. Although not all the constraints vanished overnight, the climate had markedly improved in an area that had long been deeply troubling to scholars and editors, especially in the chemical and physical sciences. A major threat to academic freedom thus at least receded.

The academic community's challenge to another dimension of export controls proved similarly successful. Starting in the late 1980s the export of cryptography—chiefly in the form of encryption software—became a major concern of federal regulators. The international transfer of physical objects was not the only target; at one point government lawyers even insisted that a U.S. mathematician who studied cryptography needed a license to share a scholarly paper with colleagues from abroad. Although the latter claim was eventually retracted in the litigation that soon brought these issues into court, the federal judge who decided the principal case never let the government forget the lengths to which it had sought to extend its regulatory reach.

Two major lawsuits, one in California and the other in Ohio, resulted in striking down the encryption export ban on familiar constitutional grounds.[27] Both courts had first to determine that cryptography was a First Amendment protected form of expression and not simply a utilitarian language for computer guidance. Once having recognized that the target of the export ban was a kind of speech to which the constitution applied, the rest was easy. The Supreme Court, several decades earlier, had set forth clear standards to govern the licensing of motion pictures. Although the analogy was imperfect, it seemed close enough to persuade the two federal judges in San Francisco and Cleveland that the federal government could no more apply sloppy procedures to barring the export of cryptography than cities could with equal lack of process regulate the showing even of X-rated movies. Thus was the export ban invalidated on familiar First Amendment grounds in a pair of rulings that had substantial value not only to cryptographers but to a far broader segment of the academic community that had followed these developments.

The most recent governmental threats to academic freedom in research concern the contentious issue of global warming. Several experiences suggest an unprecedented degree of government interference. Goddard Institute for Space Studies director James Hansen told reporters that on several occasions NASA public affairs staff intervened between him and the news media, on one occasion rejecting an interview request by National Public Radio (NPR) because of its presumed liberal bias. On a later NPR segment, Hansen explained that although he was never precluded from publishing research results, his efforts to communicate and explain his findings about global warming had been stifled by agency officials. About the same time there were revelations that a White House official and former oil-industry lobbyist, Philip A. Cooney, had removed or revised descriptions of climate research by government scientists, dealing with greenhouse gases, even after the reports had been fully reviewed and approved by subject-matter experts. Cooney's editing of the climate studies was reported by the *New York Times* as designed to "play down links between such emissions and global warming."[28]

What may be the most egregious example of such interference involved U.S. Representative Joe Barton, a Texas Republican who chaired the House Energy and Commerce Committee. In the summer of 2005, Barton sent letters to three climate scientists (as well as the National Science Foundation Panel) questioning "the significance of methodological flaws and data errors" in their federally funded global warming study. In addition to demanding extensive data related to a fifteen-year research project, Barton's inquiry reflected not a review of scientific literature or documents but a single *Wall Street Journal* article. Barton's letter evoked not only the predictable remonstrance from the scientific community but also the indignant reaction of a Republican colleague, Representative Sherwood Boehlert, chair of the House Committee on Science. In a letter that minced few words, Boehlert conveyed his "strenuous objection to what I see as the misguided and illegitimate investigation you have launched concerning [the three investigators.]" The letter continued: "My primary concern about your investigation is that its purpose seems to be to intimidate scientists rather than to learn from them, and to substitute Congressional political review for scientific peer review." Barton, in his colleague's judgment, had raised "the specter of politicians opening investigations against any scientist who reaches a conclusion that makes the political elite uncomfortable." What was striking was that such condemnation came from a fellow conservative Republican—one whose views on the merits of the issue may not have differed markedly but whose firm commitment to protect scientists from political pressure stood in stark contrast to that of Barton.[29]

Although such forays and intrusions severely jeopardize the integrity of research in areas such as global warming and climate change, do they abridge academic freedom? For the most part, the scientists who have been targeted work in government laboratories and not on university campuses, making the academic freedom claim somewhat remote. The government as an employer does have certain authority that would not extend to the government as a sponsor or regulator; to delay publication of controversial findings is one thing if the study is specifically commissioned by an agency and conducted by its own staff wholly in its facilities, but it is quite another if that agency has contracted with a university and members of the faculty to conduct studies in campus laboratories. Moreover, there seem to be no cases in which adverse personnel judgments or official sanctions have resulted from such crude political interference. Finally, it is not clear that any of these politically prompted intrusions have ultimately denied to the public and the scientific community access to important and accurate information about such issues as global warming and climate change. This area deserves close and careful scrutiny, whether or not academic freedom has yet been abridged.

The final and in many ways most perplexing area of concern for academic freedom in research is that of corporate sponsorship. Technically, of course, no private company can, as a matter of law, abridge a professor's First Amendment freedoms because the Bill of Rights constrains only government. Moreover, to a greater degree than is the case with government-sponsored research (where a given federal program may effectively be the only funding source) academic scientists are entirely free to seek or refuse funding from a particular corporate source. It is also more often possible for the investigator, or the university on his or her behalf, to negotiate terms and conditions with corporate sponsors in ways that rigid and pervasive federal regulations may preclude when dealing with government subvention.

Yet the relationships between academic scientists and corporate research sponsors have become vastly more extensive, more complex, and more troubling to guardians of academic freedom in the past quarter century. Although industry still provides only about 7 percent of all sponsored university research, corporate grants represent the fastest growing sector, and because of matching grants, cost-sharing, and the like, the corporate sector directly influences something closer to a quarter of the total university research budget. Moreover, notes Jennifer Washburn in her recent book, *University, Inc.*, the collective corporate influence "is generally thought to be far greater than [the 7 percent figure] would suggest." The impact of corporate sponsorship has been disproportionately invasive in certain fields.[30]

Dr. Marcia Angell of the Harvard School of Public Health and former editor in chief of the *New England Journal of Medicine*, laments what she perceives as a steady decline in once vaunted scholarly independence resulting from the rapid rise in drug industry research sponsorship. "The boundaries between the academic medical colleges and the drug companies," she warns, "are becoming ever more porous." What was once a healthy arm's-length relationship seems to Angell to have "broken down" as the historic principle of university control of the research data and its analysis, including the timing and location of published results, has been progressively compromised as a result of rapidly escalating corporate subvention of campus research. The quantitative data may help to explain this pressure; in 2004 Stanford University's internationally renowned medical school received 9 percent of its total research budget from drug companies.

There has been significant change not only in the scope of the university-industry relationships but also in the structure of such arrangements. When the University of Southern California's engineering school agreed several years ago to create for ChevronTexaco what amounted to an on-campus research and development office, both the company and the school described the arrangement as "a new model," the scope of which was "more extensive than the traditional university research contract." Corporate staff would codirect the institute within the engineering school, would share in choosing research projects to be funded, and would work jointly with students and faculty.

The potentially corrosive effect of such a changing dynamic seems not yet to have been fully felt by the American academic community. There have been several worrisome forays—for example, as National Public Radio reported in the summer of 2005, a series of phone calls from a Merck official to the superior of a Stanford University medical researcher whose early studies on the cardiovascular implications of Vioxx use evoked corporate concern. Other university scientists working in the same area also received similar inquiries, along with suggestions that more drastic action might be warranted should the researchers not "stop making outrageous comments" about the suspect drug. University of California–San Francisco clinical pharmacology professor Lisa Bero, who had done extensive research on how drug company funding may influence academic science, remarked of the Vioxx exposés: "I didn't realize how powerful drug companies thought they were—for example, having enough influence over a [university medical] department to say, 'Change what your faculty member is saying.' You know, I haven't ever seen that documented before." On the same program, Dr. David Rothman of Columbia University's College of Physicians and Surgeons described the increasingly insidious relationship in this way: "No one can take a call from a drug company high official critical of an investigator and not realize that behind that call is the implicit reminder, implicit threat, 'If you can't control your folks, how do you expect us to continue to do business with you?' "[31]

There has been at least one later Merck-related incident. Late in 2005, cardiologist Eric Topol lost his position as chief academic officer of the medical college of the Cleveland Clinic very soon after he had testified adversely to Merck's position in a pending case brought by the family of a deceased Vioxx patient. Specifically, he charged in his testimony that Merck had acted irresponsibly and had committed scientific misconduct with respect to Vioxx and the analysis of possible risks in its use. The medical school administration insisted that the reason for the removal of Topol's administrative assignment was a general reorganization and that the proximity in time to his adverse testimony was purely coincidental. As with many such cases, a close causal connection between such a public comment and a change in status may be difficult if not impossible to establish.[32]

Lest blame be directed exclusively at the pharmaceutical industry, evidence of interference has begun to emerge from other corporate sectors. In the spring of 2006, for example, a faculty committee at Oregon State University filed a scathing report over administrative handling of a controversy surrounding a forestry graduate student's research. The student, Daniel Donato, had completed and sought to publish research that directly undermined the Bush administration's case for salvaging burned trees by logging. The paper also angered some in the timber industry—a special concern for the College of Forestry, which not only had close and long-standing ties to the industry but also received partial support from logging tax revenue. Indeed, several forestry professors had actually sought to block publication of the controversial piece in *Science* magazine. Although that attempt to derail the research process failed, it led the faculty committee to castigate the "inability of the [college's] leadership to recognize the academic freedom issues involved in their participation in the letter to *Science* calling for delay of the Donato paper." This incident was hardly the first of its kind; a quarter century ago the University of Oregon's Law School Clinic faced substantial lumber industry pressure to alter its policies in representing plaintiffs in environmental suits that had angered the industry.[33]

Perhaps the most celebrated recent controversy over corporate sponsored research played out during 2006-07 in the University of California. The Board of Regents seriously considered a policy that would ban UC faculty and researchers from accepting any support from tobacco companies. The resolution described the tobacco industry's use of sponsored research to invite "public deception" as a "rare and compelling circumstance" that warranted curbing research support. The response was predictably divided. The faculty senate at UC-San Francisco, the state's premiere academic health center, supported such a prohibition. The rationale for such a ban was increasingly apparent; a federal court ruling against nine tobacco companies noted that "friendly scientific witnesses" had been identified and "subsidized with grants from the Center for Tobacco Research . . . [while the companies] often hid the relationship between those witnesses and the industry." Especially suspect was the research of a UCLA scientist whose studies were financed by the tobacco industry, and was viewed by the company and its lawyers as "clearly litigation oriented." The American Cancer Society wrote to the Board of

Regents accusing this researcher of misrepresenting scientific evidence to deny the harmful effects of smoking and second-hand smoke. The ACS letter identified the UCLA scientist as "someone who is at one of the UC institutions and who was used by the tobacco industry through its funding."

Even within the Board, however, there were contrary views. Some Regents feared that a ban on tobacco-funded research would, as one Board member put it, "establish a dangerous precedent that threatens academic freedom" and could "convey a signal that we do not trust the judgment of our world-class academics, faculty and administrators at the University of California." Actually, both sides invoked academic freedom to support their respective positions. A strongly anti-tobacco funding scientist at UC-San Francisco, for example, argued that since the "purpose of the university—and the reason we have 'academic freedom'—is to protect the search for and dissemination of truth, continuing to accept tobacco industry funding is antithetical to the very purpose of the university."

The proposed Regents policy was carefully reviewed by a statewide University Committee on Academic Freedom. In mid April, that group unanimously opposed the suggested research ban, finding in it the potential for "a precedent that could adversely affect the faculty as a whole and undermine the function of the University to contribute to the advancement of knowledge." The putative tobacco funding ban also seemed sharply at variance with a recently revised academic freedom policy, the central premise of which was that "teaching and scholarship be assessed by reference to professional standards . . . [which] lie within the authority and expertise of the faculty as a body." Thus, "only the faculty have the competence and right to make judgments about the quality of research conducted at the University of California."

The academic freedom committee report also invoked a larger context within which UC faculty received substantial research support from industries which could conceivably be targeted in the future if tobacco funding could be proscribed. Noting that "the wine industry is closely connected to the University of California" and that at least twenty UC scientists received funding from the Mars Candy Company (which had recently funded a faculty chair in Developmental Nutrition), the committee cautioned that all such funding was potentially at risk if tobacco industry support proved unacceptable. The report closed with a rhetorical question: "Would the Regents entertain a prohibition on the acceptance of funds to conduct stem cell research because it is offensive to those opposed to the destruction of human embryos to obtain the cells?"

Not surprisingly, the May meeting of the statewide academic senate assembly overwhelmingly endorsed the faculty committee's conclusion. By a vote of 43-4 the system-wide faculty body urged the Regents to abandon the quest to restrict the flow of arguably tainted funds—despite the undoubted concerns about the potential hazards both to science and to the public welfare. Meanwhile, significant exceptions remained; the School of Public Health on the Berkeley campus, for example, had some time earlier resolved to forego tobacco funding for research, joining the Harvard Medical School and other prestigious academic units. The debate is likely to continue, and (as the UC academic freedom committee cautioned) may shift from today's tobacco focus to other industries, products and concerns. Surely such issues will not disappear from the academic landscape.

Nor are such concerns unique to the United States. Not surprisingly, similar debates have affected Canadian universities. Most notable and of greatest concern to Canadian scholars and scientists are the cases of two University of Toronto professors and researchers—Dr. Nancy Olivieri and Dr. David Healy—who had written and spoken critically about possible risks for patients from the use of drugs manufactured and distributed by major corporate sponsors of university-based research. Both scientists were removed from important academic positions, although in both cases the university insisted that the removals were unrelated to the whistle-blowing activities of the scientists or the manifest displeasure of the corporate sponsors. Adverse and damaging comments about both scientists were widely (though anonymously) circulated within and beyond the University of Toronto community.[34] Because Canadian protection for academic freedom and comparable faculty interests is radically different from that in the United States, based entirely on contract rather than constitutional law, analogies are difficult if not impossible to draw.

Given all the problems this relationship has recently created, should the academic community simply refuse to accept any corporate funding for campus-based research? Some eminent scholars have so argued for years; the University of Wisconsin's Nobel Laureate, biochemist Howard Temin, insisted that the academic community (including his own university) would be far better protected if it simply spurned such funding, whether or not particular grants could be termed "tainted." The uneasy response invokes several practical realities. Professor Temin, his colleagues gently reminded him, could afford to travel the high road in part because his seminal research was supported mainly by the American Cancer Society, thus freeing him of any need to seek corporate support—a luxury that many of his equally energetic colleagues in engineering, business and agriculture did not enjoy. Moreover, should universities opt out of such relationships, corporate-funded research would undoubtedly continue at comparable levels, but would now shift to company laboratories or separate research centers and institutes substantially divorced from the academic community. While such arrangements would surely ease the conscience of many in the university world, the cost of such realignment would be substantial—not only in drawing some highly productive scholars permanently away from the classroom to the corporate lab, but also in reducing opportunities for graduate student research on cutting-edge issues, and most deeply in creating two separate cultures of the kind that flourish in many other countries where the uniquely American research university model has never been adopted. Most research scientists at Germany's eminent Max Planck Institutes hardly ever see (much less advise or mentor) a student; only the director typically holds professorial rank at the nearby university and thus provides a narrow bridge between the campus and the laboratory. Thus the benefits of renouncing industrial research support may well outweigh any possible benefits, although that debate is likely to persist indefinitely.

Clearly corporate influence on the research agenda and process do pose serious threats to academic freedom that merit closer attention than either partner typically gives to them in creating or enhancing relationships. For one, complete disclosure should be a sine qua non, including all benefits that scholars and faculty members may derive from any facet of the relationship. Graduate students need be told substantially more about the university–industry nexus than is currently the case at most institutions. Second, the university should never hold any equity interest in a corporate venture in which its own faculty members are beneficially involved; the analogy to a coach or player who bets on his own sport may seem imperfect, but becomes more apposite on closer analysis. Third, the principles of academic freedom and due process should protect all participants in corporate-sponsored research as fully as they protect those who conduct studies on campus supported entirely by institutional funds. Finally, the extent of permissible ties with corporate ventures must be determined largely by the affected faculty, with the result that (as actually happened to two biochemists in different departments at the University of Wisconsin in the 1980s) one professor may be lauded by colleagues for entrepreneurial success, while another may be rebuked and even forced to leave the academy in order to maintain such a relationship. If such guidelines as these are scrupulously applied, not all problems posed by corporate-sponsored research will vanish or abate, but the climate should be more tolerable than it has been in recent years.

In all the diverse areas we have surveyed, the relationship between academic freedom and freedom in research has been and remains complex. In recent years the complexity has magnified, as pressures for compelled disclosure of research intensify on one hand while corporate demands for confidentiality increase on the other hand, as the volume of sponsored research continues to grow, and as conditions imposed upon both government and corporate sponsored research become more burdensome and intrusive, the need for clear recognition and declaration of the rights of researchers also intensifies. The process of achieving such protection sometimes looks easy, as when courts step in to quash subpoenas or strike down governmental constraints on research. In other areas the quest for protection remains elusive and uncertain. Meanwhile, academic research and academic freedom remain somewhat uneasy partners in a vital but largely shapeless structure.

6

Intersections of Academic and Artistic Freedom

In the spring of 1990, at the height of the "culture wars" over federal funding for controversial works of art, a group of legal scholars, university leaders, and arts advocates gathered for two days at the Wolf Trap Center in Northern Virginia. Their mission was to craft a strong endorsement for artistic freedom at a time of unprecedented national hostility toward, and deep anxiety within, the arts community. The document that emerged from these discussions, and was soon made public, boldly recognizes the link between artistic expression and academic endeavor. The Wolf Trap statement declares that those who create and perform works of art on the university campus are as fully protected as those who write and teach in more traditional media. In particular, insisted the conferees, "artistic expression in the classroom, the studio, and the workshop . . . merits the same assurance of academic freedom that is accorded to other scholarly and teaching activities." And because artistic presentations and performances by students and faculty "are integral to their teaching, learning and scholarship, these presentations merit no less protection."[1]

This declaration thus stressed vital links between academic freedom generally and the centrality of artistic expression within the academic community. Not only is it important to note that many creative and performing artists are essentially sheltered within the academic community, where they may pursue interests and talents for which there simply is no market beyond the campus confines; equally important is the reality that the boldest and most novel artistic expression usually occurs within academic confines—more likely on the university theater stage than on Broadway or in Hollywood, more often in the campus art gallery or museum than in Fifty-seventh Street galleries or Rodeo Drive boutiques. Thus the campus setting is the testing ground, and the protections of academic freedom are indispensable to the creative process of artists who are closest to the cutting edge.

The Wolf Trap statement was a brave and hopeful declaration, reflecting the firm convictions of its signers. Yet the prospects for its acceptance, even within the academic community, were quite another matter. The years that followed would bring nearly as many repudiations of the Wolf Trap principles as affirmations. By the end of the decade, the United States Supreme Court would, by nearly unanimous judgment, sustain the authority of the National Endowment for the Arts to "take into consideration," in making grants to artists and arts organizations, "general standards of decency," along with the more familiar canons of "artistic merit" and "artistic excellence."[2] In the broader community, artists' rights claims would continue to meet an uneven reception, as lower federal courts struggled with issues of artistic freedom. One federal judge in the mid-1990s actually ruled that New York City could treat sidewalk sellers of their own artistic creations no better than hot dog and souvenir vendors were treated, the court barely conceding that "there is some expressive content in works of fine art."[3]

Back in the academic setting, some forms of artistic expression have recently become particular targets of controversy and repression. The performance of controversial plays on college campuses has been a persistent object of intense criticism, from sources both external and internal. Indeed, in a bizarre coincidence, on the very same day in late February 2006, *The Washington Post* and *The New York Times* ran closely concordant stories that recounted the recent rise in such pressures, especially at church-related institutions.[4] The headline on the *Times* story captured the tension reflected in both accounts: "At Religious Universities, Disputes over Faith and Academic Freedom." Thus, the hopeful words of the Wolf Trap statement continued to describe an ideal relationship between artistic freedom and academic freedom, whereas actual campus experience remained far less hopeful for those who created, displayed, and performed controversial works of art.

Such troubling conditions on the college campus reflect a far broader uncertainty in legal and public policy circles about the status of artistic expression. A few years before the Wolf Trap conference, a legal scholar who had closely followed this subject described a curious state of ambivalence even among champions of free speech and inquiry: "Artistic expression has been assigned derivative and second class status in the views of many [F]irst [A]mendment thinkers, the Supreme Court, and other courts. . . . [F]rom a [F]irst [A]mendment perspective, the ideal kind of expression is political discourse, and all other kinds of expression, including artistic expression, are accorded lower degrees of [F]irst [A]mendment protection depending on their similarity to political expression."[5] Many factors apparently contributed to such second-class citizenship for the creative artist and the performer. For one, courts have never been comfortable in making artistic judgments or defining the scope of protection for the arts. Justice Oliver Wendell Holmes, over a century ago, refused to embroil the Supreme Court in deciding whether lithographed circus posters constituted "fine art" in a copyright case. "It would be a dangerous undertaking," he warned, "for persons trained only to the law to constitute themselves final judges of the worth of pictorial illustrations."[6] Holmes's scrupulous avoidance of such issues gained added significance in light of his own personal appreciation of the fine and performing arts. Yet his caution has been consistently heeded throughout the century that followed.

From time to time, to be sure, the Supreme Court has declared abstractly that artistic expression does enjoy First Amendment protection. Even creative works that could hardly be deemed "fine art" seem at times to merit such solicitude. Thus in the mid-1970s the high Court ruled that use of a municipal auditorium could not be denied to producers of the rock musical *Hair*, unless "we were to conclude that live drama is unprotected by the First Amendment—or subject to a totally different standard from that applied to other forms of expression."[7] Yet the basis for the judgment in *Hair*'s favor was much less the content of the musical and more a gravely deficient procedure for allocating access to the municipal theater's stage.

Several other factors may help to explain the persistent reluctance of courts to embrace the arts with the same enthusiasm through which they welcome other expressive media. The paradigm of protected speech has always been political messages, viewed as the paramount concern of the First Amendment's framers and, for some, the sole beneficiary of its protections. On several occasions, courts have explicitly disfavored nonpolitical speech in contrast to politics. The New York street-vendor case from the mid-1990s contains a classic example of this pejorative comparison: "Items bearing words that express political or religious views are much closer to the heartland of First Amendment protection of 'speech' than the apolitical paintings in these cases." Eventually the appeals court for the Second Circuit reversed this judgment, adopting a far more benign view of artistic expression, but the district judge's ruling had done much damage in the interim.[8] And only a few years earlier, that very same court of appeals had offered its grudging concession that "artwork, like other nonverbal forms of expression, may under some circumstances constitute speech for First Amendment purposes."[9] Nor were such disparaging views atypical, as becomes evident in a later canvass of some university arts cases.

Although courts seldom explain why they view artistic expression so skeptically, certain profound contrasts between art and other media may offer some insight. For one, it is basic to our constitutional jurisprudence that we in the United States protect unpopular, even hateful, speech in major part precisely because we demand counter-speech rather than repression. As Justice Louis Brandeis eloquently articulated in 1927, "If there be time to expose through discussion the falsehood and fallacies, to avert the evil by the processes of education, the remedy to be applied is more speech, not enforced silence."[10] That seems all well and good when the message is political. But when it comes to the arts—even the finest of fine arts—Justice Brandeis's classic formula simply doesn't fit. Works of art do not contain or declare "truth" or "falsehood" as do the vast majority of print messages. And in the rare case in which a painting or sculpture may imply something that seems false, refutation or counter-speech would seem irrelevant; there is no way in which the juxtaposition of a dissimilar work can "expose the falsehood or fallacies." "More speech" in an artistic setting may well serve various values but not the interest that Justice Brandeis stressed in his insistence on the refutative or remedial force of further discussion. Thus the core values reflected in First Amendment protection for most controversial speech apply imperfectly, if at all, to artistic media.

This mismatch or asymmetry is well illustrated by a recent case that deeply divided a university campus and produced a highly instructive federal court decision. As part of the 2003 annual sculpture exhibit at Washburn University, a public institution in Topeka, Kansas, a jury of art professionals chose one piece that outraged the Roman Catholic religious community the moment it was unveiled. Entitled "Holier than Thou," the statue depicted a Catholic bishop with a contorted facial expression and bearing a miter that some critics interpreted as a "stylized representation of a phallus." The artist, a Catholic by birth and religious training, recalled frightening childhood experiences in the confessional booth, though he insisted that he had no intent to demean or disparage his own faith. The response from much of Kansas's Catholic community was, however, immediate and intense. The appeals court, in a masterpiece of understatement, would later note: "One of the purposes of art is to engage us intellectually and emotionally.

This work apparently has fulfilled that function . . ." A group of offended Catholics, including a Washburn professor and a student, filed suit in federal court, claiming that the prominent placement of the statue on their campus deprived them of religious freedom and violated the First Amendment's establishment clause.

The district judge dismissed the lawsuit, ruling against the plaintiffs on their novel constitutional claim. In the summer of 2005, the Tenth Circuit appeals court affirmed that ruling and thus ended the litigation. The professor's and student's complaint cited no evidence of hostility on the university's part toward any particular faith or toward religion in general. Nor had the plaintiffs shown how the display of the statue amounted in any way to endorsement or sponsorship of a religious (or anti-religious) viewpoint. The inclusion of religious symbols in public art displays was hardly novel, as the U.S. Supreme Court had observed at least once by citing the myriad religious paintings in the National Gallery. The appeals court also recognized the role of artistic freedom on a state university campus, noting that although "Holier than Thou" had not been created for course credit, its extracurricular origins should not suggest "it was not part of Washburn's educational curriculum." The appeals court also noted with approval the administration's commitment "to extend the educational environment . . . beyond the classroom to encompass various stimuli including art, theater, music, debate, athletics and other activities."[11] Thus not only did the plaintiffs fail in their quest to have the offending statue removed from the Washburn campus; they also inadvertently helped to produce an appellate court ruling unusually sympathetic to artistic freedom as a component of academic freedom. As this chapter shows, such welcome judgments remain to this day as much the exception as the rule.

Mention of the "Holier than Thou" case serves a quite different purpose, to which we now turn. Suppose Washburn officials had heeded the complaints from the Catholic community and had wished quite publicly to assure the sculpture's detractors that no offense to their faith should be inferred—following Justice Brandeis command that "the remedy is more speech, not enforced silence." When the focus of campus or community hostility is artistic expression, however, refutation and rebuttal simply do not avail. Beyond the possibility that the artist might attach a disclaimer or explanatory note to the work disavowing any anti-Catholic animus, there seems no way in which an institution could correct a "fallacy" or "falsehood" generated by the visible public display of a controversial work of art. The placement alongside "Holier than Thou" of the sculptured head of a handsome bishop, adorned by a normal-size miter, would hardly appease critics; indeed, apart from creating much confusion, such juxtaposition would probably serve only to accentuate the offensive features of the offending work. Thus, quite simply, one dramatic difference between works of art and almost all other forms of expression is the absence of an opportunity for counter-speech to correct the record or allay falsehood. "More speech," uniquely in this context, is likely to make matters worse, not better.

Contrast the actual Washburn University case with a hypothetical though quite plausible one in which the sculptor, instead of creating a physical object that caused offense, wrote a letter to the editor that appeared in the campus newspaper, in which he verbally recalls a deep-seated childhood fear about the confessional, including a graphic verbal account of his recurrent dreams of menacing clergy with elongated headgear. Such a letter probably would offend many Catholic readers, even deeply, although the predictable reaction would have been far different from the immediate response to the unveiling of the "Holier than Thou" sculpture at the center of the campus. Readers upset or offended by the letter might, of course, submit their own responses in defense of Catholicism, perhaps faulting the author of the letter for distortion and overreaction or contrasting their own benign childhood experiences. They might also chastise the paper's editor for publishing such a one-sided and predictably offensive statement, thus legitimizing its thesis. Such letters would undoubtedly be printed, in the best traditions of college journalism, and readers would be left to draw their own conclusions. This is precisely how "more speech" works, bringing balance and reason to print messages, even though offering little if any guidance to artistic controversy.

The Washburn sculpture case and the variant just examined illustrate another vital contrast among different media of expression. Apart from the opportunity that any indignant reader of the campus newspaper would presumably have had to reply in the same medium, the impact of a similar message in two contrasting forms could hardly be more different. Even those Catholic readers who might have been deeply offended by such a letter would hardly have responded as did those who viewed the statue at the center of a busy public campus. The vivid and immediate impact of a graphic visual image, in two or three dimensions, is far deeper than that of words that may convey a comparable message. The potential effect of a letter upon its readers, moreover, is qualitatively very different from the impact of a visual image upon its viewers. There is simply no way in which a verbal account of lingering fears about Catholic clergy could remotely match the deeply visceral effect of a painting or sculpture. The visual imagery of the sculpture is profoundly different, not only in its immunity to verbal refutation but even more in its capacity to evoke intense outrage and indignation.

There is a closely related hazard, which we revisit later but which deserves mention here—that works of art, at least when displayed prominently in public spaces, may effectively compel the attention of a "captive audience" in ways that verbal expression hardly ever does. Although a potentially offended viewer may sometimes avert his or her eyes, at least if there has been advance warning of offensive imagery, there are times and places when offense may occur before avoidance is possible, or space limits may effectively preclude such a protective response. Indeed, so substantial is this concern about the preemptive effect of artistic displays that the Wolf Trap conferees took note and then expressly cautioned that "mere presentation in a public place does not create a 'captive audience.'"[12]

In all these important respects, then, artistic expression differs profoundly from other media. Its impact is invariably—sometimes dramatically—different, and its capacity to affect emotions is far deeper. A diminished level of First Amendment protection for the arts does seem to reflect these differences, whether appropriately or not. Although it may not be logical that works of art should enjoy a lower constitutional status because they have a greater capacity to arouse strong feelings, there seems little doubt that courts define the scope of such protection with such qualities clearly in mind.

Finally and perhaps most obvious among such catalytic distinctions is the fact that artistic expression is usually nonverbal or at least not primarily verbal. Historically, the First Amendment has been seen as a safeguard for verbal expression, whether through spoken or written words. Indeed, even today a few strict constructionists still refuse to speak of "freedom of expression" or to countenance constitutional solicitude for symbolic messages, even though the Supreme Court long ago declared that such nonverbal protest as wearing black armbands in protest of the Vietnam War was "closely akin to pure speech" and thus fully protected.[13] For the traditionalists, only words really deserve First Amendment protection because in their view it was words that the framers meant to safeguard—overlooking the importance to the framers' generation of such nonverbal acts of political protest as the Boston Tea Party.

Yet the absence of words, quite as much as the irrelevance of political messages, reinforces other factors in explaining the curiously lower level of protection that many courts have afforded the arts. It is not simply that the presence of words comforts traditionalists; equally significant is the absence from the realm of the arts of such limits upon verbal excess as the judicially approved sanctions for speech that creates a "clear and present danger," or libels a private person, or invades one's privacy. Ironically, the one such First Amendment limit that does apply to the arts—indeed, really applies *only* to the arts—is that of obscenity. Yet even here, art is demonstrably different. The Supreme Court's definition of obscenity declares that a work or publication may be banned only if it is found to lack serious redeeming value when judged as a whole. Among those values are not only "literary," "political," and "scientific" quality, but "artistic" value as well.[14] From that standard has emerged a simplistic but generally accurate journalistic formula: if it is art, then it cannot be obscene. One could not, with comparable confidence, exonerate any publication that contains literary or scientific or political material, at least until the work had been found not to lack "serious" value of the relevant type to rebut the charges of obscenity.

The case law that defines artistic freedom in the academic setting is surprisingly—some might add mercifully—spare. Such issues get to court with surprising infrequency, though it may well be that a rational artist, even one subject to censorship pressure, would feel well advised to avoid litigation at all costs. There have, however, been a handful of notable cases that warrant review here. The earliest case, in the 1960s, involved a then brash young artist named Chuck Close, who would decades later be celebrated for the boldness as well as the quality of his paintings. As an art instructor at the University of Massachusetts at Amherst, Close accepted an invitation to exhibit some of his works along a well-traveled corridor in the student union. The paintings contained some nude figures, a few with explicit and detailed genitalia.

The display soon evoked considerable comment on the campus, some of it quite hostile. The campus administration ordered the exhibit removed, calling its contents simply "inappropriate." Close promptly brought suit in federal court, claiming that his First Amendment rights had been abridged by the university's action. The district judge proved quite receptive to such a novel plea. The site seemed an appropriate forum for artistic display. The artist had complied fully with applicable campus rules in responding to the invitation to post the now controversial exhibit. Thus the court ruled that in labeling Close's artworks "inappropriate," the university had imposed an adverse view on protected artistic expression, without any applicable standards for making such a judgment, and thus owed it to Close to restore the exhibit promptly.[15]

The case did not end there, however. The university pressed on to an appeals court that was normally (and notably) sympathetic to free speech claims—for example, having recently overturned a Vietnam war protestor's conviction for draft-card burning, which the Supreme Court would later reinstate. But Close fared much less well in that court than did the antiwar protestors or draft resisters, and eventually he lost the very first modern case at the intersection of academic and artistic freedom. The appeals court seemed far more deferential to the administration's judgment on what was and what was not considered "appropriate" art on the campus.[16] The reviewing judges' skeptical view seems to have been influenced substantially by the venue of the exhibit—"a passageway regularly used by the public, including children," where such images might indeed be deemed "inappropriate."

This court was also deeply troubled by the potential impact of Close's paintings on passers-by: "Where there was, in effect, a captive audience, [the administration] had a right to afford protection against 'assault upon individual privacy' short of legal obscenity." At least one other factor seems to have fueled the appeals' court's skepticism. Whereas the district judge had found considerable merit in Close's work, the appeals court evinced only disdain for the removed paintings, expressing doubts whether such creations even merited any constitutional protection. The opinion began with a strikingly hostile comment: "There is no suggestion, unless in its cheap titles, that [Close's] art was seeking to express political or social thought. [Other cases, such as those enjoining campus speaker bans] involve a medium and subject matter entitled to greater protection than [Close's] art. We consider [Close's] constitutional interest minimal."[17] The import of such judicial disdain seemed clear: Words, almost any words, have a higher claim on First Amendment protection than does almost any work of art, most notably art that does not embody "political or social thought," which Close's works did not contain. Although the court stopped just short of holding that avant-garde paintings rank no higher than obscenity, the implication seemed headed in that direction.

The legal fortunes of academic artists thus began in a most unpromising fashion, and more hopeful prospects were not immediately apparent. Not long after Close's ignominious defeat, a parallel case emerged in California.

A graduate student in art at Cal State–Long Beach, one William Spater, submitted ten life-sized nude figures of plaster and wax as the core of his master's degree project. Some of those figures depicted sexual and erotic acts. The critical issue was that of public display, a standard requirement for degree completion. The dean, after viewing Spater's works, concluded that their public exhibition would be "inappropriate" because of the "frankly sexual subject matter." Spater, with the backing of the art faculty, protested this ruling, and the dean eventually relented, with the concurrence of the campus president. The scene quickly shifted to the state capitol in Sacramento, where a legislative hearing brought enough political pressure to bear on the Cal State University system that its chancellor reversed the Long Beach decision and canceled the exhibit.

Spater and several fellow art students then filed suit in a state court, presenting a novel claim of artistic and academic freedom. The trial judge had no sympathy for such a claim, viewing Spater's works as "about an inch away from an act of perversion." This judge dismissed all the claims, and the court of appeals affirmed because it concluded that Spater had effectively waived any constitutional claims he might once have had. There was, however, a revealing footnote in which the appellate court made at least passing mention of the First Amendment claim it had conveniently avoided—citing the recent Close ruling in Massachusetts but also noting precedents that would have supported the artist's claim against arbitrary denial of public gallery space for controversial exhibits.[18] It would, however, be some time before a more sympathetic case could reach the California courts, and different artistic media would be involved.

The next academic artist to take his claims to court fared slightly better, though the case hardly registers a triumph. Albert Piarowski was chairman of the art department at a downstate Illinois community college. He contributed several of his own recent works, specifically stained-glass panels, to the annual art faculty exhibit. The display site was a heavily traveled area, immediately adjacent to the central mall of the college's main building. The gallery in fact bordered the corridor through which students and visitors would pass en route to classes, offices, and meeting rooms on upper floors. Three of the panels immediately evoked concern, because their stained-glass images gave subtle hints of racially disparaging or demeaning stereotypes. One panel depicted (as the court would later describe it) an apparently African American woman "crouching in a posture of veneration before a robed white male whose most prominent feature is a grotesquely outsized phallus (erect penis) that the woman is embracing."

This and several other images in Piarowski's exhibit evoked extensive concern from students and staff, and especially from African American clergy in the community. There was special anxiety about the potential impact of these panels on campus visitors at a time when the college was aggressively seeking to increase its minority enrollment. Senior administrators told Piarowksi to relocate his stained-glass panels—suggesting a rather remote fourth-floor gallery near the art department office. When the artist refused to comply, the president ordered his works removed entirely.

Piarowksi then went to federal court, claiming that the college had violated his artistic and academic freedom. The district judge dismissed the suit in a brief and unreported opinion. But when it reached the Seventh Circuit court of appeals, it drew a panel chaired by Judge Richard Posner, who was already recognized as the most prolific scholar on the federal bench. The central issues in the case were largely matters of first impression, enabling Judge Posner to shape the field as he had done and would do in many other areas of the law. He began with the still surprisingly unsettled question of whether works of art deserved constitutional protection at all; that issue seemed to him to have been resolved in the artist's favor since the Supreme Court and other lower courts had held that the First Amendment embraces "purely artistic as well as political expression." Moreover, he cautioned that had the college "opened up the gallery to the public as a place for expression, it could not have regulated that expression in any way it pleased just because the gallery was its property or because the artist happened to be a member of the college's faculty."

Piarowski's claim, however, proved less persuasive to the appeals court than such welcome language might have implied. Several distinctive factors eventually undermined the artist's case. The display site was not really a generally open "public forum," the court ruled, but one that the college had opened only to the works of faculty and students. There was also the college's quite valid concern about its image because of the potential effect of the panels on the African American community. Thus, said Judge Posner, "if we hold that the college was forbidden to take the action that it took to protect its image, we limit the freedom of the academy to manage its affairs." Further, there was the ambiguous matter of the site—one where the wide visibility of potentially offending images justified a higher standard than might have governed a less sensitive venue. Moreover, the college had decreed only the relocation—not the removal—of the troubling images. Piarowski's refusal even to consider a potential path of relocation suggested to Judge Posner that he was "more interested in becoming a martyr to artistic freedom" than in resolving a practical problem for which he—as chair of the art department—after all bore substantial responsibility.

Although Judge Posner and his Seventh Circuit colleagues ultimately rejected Piarowski's claims, they also stressed that the law had progressed some distance since the Close case. Even though Piarowski's suit was ultimately unavailing, Judge Posner wanted the art and legal worlds to know that the Illinois artist at least received a far more sympathetic reception than had his Massachusetts predecessor. The difference in the approved remedy or consequence was striking—"the issue [in Close] was removal, not relocation." Had the Illinois college administration barred the exhibit entirely or compelled its removal, the artist "might have been discouraged from creating similar work in the future." The potentially chilling effect on Piarowski's liberty also seemed substantially diminished; "the abridgement of freedom of expression is less, when the college says to him, "you may exhibit your work on campus—just not in the alcove off the mall." Thus although Piarowski himself failed in his quest for complete vindication, the cause of artistic freedom in an academic setting surely improved along the way.[19]

Another difficult case, this time involving a student artist, soon reached the same tribunal and offered Judge Posner another vehicle for his views on artistic freedom. David Nelson, who was studying painting at the Chicago Art Institute, submitted to the annual display of original student work a singularly provocative painting. Entitled "Mirth and Girth" the work portrayed Chicago's late (and revered) Mayor Harold Washington, clad only in a white bra, G-string, garter belt, and stockings. This bizarre attire reflected an unconfirmed rumor that when the city's first African American mayor arrived in critical condition at the emergency room, he was wearing female undergarments beneath his business suit. Although the exhibit was not open to the general public, news of Nelson's painting soon became common knowledge across Chicago.

The Chicago City Council ordered that the work be removed at once and threatened to terminate city funding for the Art Institute if it remained on display. The school's president declined to intervene, asserting the school's and its students' artistic freedom. Three aldermen then decided to take matters into their own hands. They marched into the gallery where the student exhibit was on display, removed "Mirth and Girth" from the wall, and were about to carry it from the building when they were stopped by guards. By the time the controversial painting reached the president's office, it had suffered a foot-long gash. A city police officer was directed to take the painting into municipal custody, where it remained until it was returned to the artist the following day.

Nelson promptly filed suit in federal court against the three aldermen and other city officials, seeking damages for a claimed violation of his constitutional rights as an artist. The case languished in the courts for nearly five years, mainly over procedural disputes, until finally the court of appeals, speaking through Judge Posner, directed the trial judge to reach the merits of the matter. The aldermen insisted that, without preemptive action of the type they had taken, Nelson's provocative painting would have triggered riots, so profound was citizens' esteem for Chicago's first African American mayor and his legacy. Though Judge Posner doubted the imminence of such a response, he assumed the officials' fears were justified, and then used the occasion to address broader aspects of artistic freedom: "[Where an] artist's intentions are innocent, at least innocent of any desire to cause a riot, but his work so inflames the community as to cause a riot in which people are killed and injured . . . First Amendment rights are not subject to the heckler's veto. The rioters are the culpable parties, not the artist whose work unintentionally provoked them to violence. . . . [Cases involving punishable incitement do not mean] that police and other public officials can seek to protect the populace at the expense of the artist, by 'arresting' the offensive painting rather than the violent rioters."[20]

Judge Posner's treatment of this novel and bizarre case was illuminating, and comforting, for those who seek guidance in defining artistic freedom. The Nelson opinion contrasted the issue at hand with that of verbal incitement—the classic demagogue who, in Justice Holmes's famous maxim, "falsely shouts fire in a theater and thereby caus[es] a panic"[21] and who may be punished for pure speech. For the artist, even one who deliberately creates an intensely provocative work like "Mirth and Girth," Judge Posner seems to offer a very different standard—one that not only attributes benign motives to the artist but also recognizes the need for broader First Amendment latitude for the artist than for the political speaker. Thus, even if Chicagoans had in fact stormed the Art Institute to protest the display of Nelson's offending work and to demand its removal, no criminal sanctions could have been imposed on the artist, but they could have been imposed only on those who reacted in so violent and destructive manner to the painting. Such a result offers a strikingly different and far more sensitive view of artistic freedom than the one that courts had previously offered or, for that matter, than the one that Judge Posner himself offered (albeit in a different context) in the Piarowski case.

It now seems fitting to turn from the visual arts to the even more perplexing arena of the performing arts. Plays have been, if anything, even more contentious on the college campus than have paintings and sculptures. Suitably illustrative is the saga of Nassau Community College on Long Island and its perilous commitment to present Chris Durang's *Sister Mary Ignatius Explains It All for You*. The play had opened off Broadway in the late 1970s to wide critical acclaim. Its extended run on Broadway won for its author an Obie Award for best playwright of 1980. The centerpiece of the play is a Catholic nun who fatally shoots two of her former students. One of the victims is a gay man who has returned to his secondary school to complain that the nun's teaching had adversely affected his life in various ways. Understandably, some critics viewed the theme of the play as sacrilegious or blasphemous and expressed their sense of affront during its commercial run in Manhattan. When the skeptics learned that *Sister Mary Ignatius* was scheduled for ten performances at the community college in heavily Catholic Nassau County, the chorus of criticism intensified. Pickets surrounded the office of the county executive, demanding cancellation of the play, with the support of the diocesan weekly newspaper and even the local chapter of the American Jewish League.

Meanwhile, the hero of the matter was Nassau Community College's president, Sean Fanelli, who stood firm in his defense of the planned performance of Durang's work. As a devout Catholic, he acknowledged his appreciation of the intense hostility that many of his neighbors felt, though he noted that all but one of the cast members were also Catholic. He then explained his refusal to alter the college's course, in a letter to one of the protestors: "Were I to cancel this production, I believe I would do to you and others, and especially our students, a grave disservice. Such a cancellation would have a chilling effect upon academic freedom and freedom of speech as well. It would be tantamount to censorship and would greatly curtail the free exchange of knowledge and ideas so important to a college community."[22] Fanelli later warned a journalist, "If I were to begin censoring plays, I don't know where it would stop."[23]

When opening night arrived for Sister Mary Ignatius, the auditorium was sold out, although some members of the audience had to cross highly vocal picket lines, which were led by none other than Nassau County's district attorney. The play did go on, as Fanelli had insisted it would, thus striking a forceful blow for artistic freedom on the campus stage. And despite the toll that the incident took on the college's president and on public support for the institution, Fanelli continued to serve with courage and distinction—heading off two other very different threats—for a decade and a half, receiving accolades for his staunch defense of academic and artistic freedom from the American Association of University Professors (AAUP) and other groups.

Although such incidents of threatened censorship are mercifully rare, the intensity of those that do occur more than offset their infrequency. Not all of them have nearly as happy an outcome as that in Nassau County. There was, for example, Catholic University's much more recent decision to force off its campus a scheduled (and faculty approved) student production of Tony Kushner's acclaimed *Angels in America* because of its gay themes and sexually explicit scenes. Noting that the university "reserves the right to determine the appropriateness of public presentations to insure consistency with the university's mission," Catholic's administration ruled that a performance on the campus would violate such standards.[24]

Later, Catholic University was to be joined by Providence College in forcing off the campus planned productions of *The Vagina Monologues*. The University of Notre Dame had initially announced that it would not permit on-campus presentations of that production and other provocative dramas because (in the new president's view) that would imply institutional endorsement of values at odds with those of the Catholic church; Notre Dame's administration later reversed course, however, and declared that 'Monologues' might be performed on campus.[25] Of course private colleges and universities are for the most part beyond reach of the First Amendment and thus may impose such standards on their students and faculty with legal impunity. Only peer judgment, and possibly formal inquiry and rebuke by such organizations as the AAUP, constrain such actions within the independent sector of higher education.

However, when it comes to the public sector—state-supported colleges and universities—the First Amendment applies as fully to drama as to other expressive activity. Several notable cases illustrate the tension between the real world of public higher education and controversial or contentious theater. In the early 1990s the California courts considered a challenge to a ban imposed by the San Diego Community College District on a scheduled public performance of a play called *Split Second*. The stated basis for the ban was twofold. First, there was concern about an abundance of ethnically offensive epithets and other taboo and vulgar language in the script. Second, the administration was also troubled by a scene in which a black New York police officer is shown killing a white suspect but is later exonerated when he lies about the incident. Some critics attacked the play on religious grounds, whereas others based their opposition on the life-imitates-art parallel between the content of the play and a strikingly similar real-life case then pending in the San Diego criminal courts.

Without ever bothering to read the script, senior officials at the college responded to such pressures by canceling the play. A faculty member and one of the students involved in the production then brought suit in state court, alleging on the college's part a violation of their artistic freedom and free speech. The trial judge dismissed the suit out of hand, finding in it no viable constitutional claims. But the appeals court took a very different view and sent the case back for a full trial. The higher court allowed that the college's concern about adverse community reaction was justified, but it cautioned that such anxieties would not warrant suppressing a controversial play on a campus stage.

Several other arguments pressed by the college got rather short shrift from the court of appeals. The administration insisted that it canceled the play in part to dispel possible attribution to the institution of offensive or abhorrent views that were to be expressed on the stage. The California appeals court flatly rejected such a claim: "No one could reasonably argue that a school which presented a play by Shakespeare was thereby advocating the social and sexual mores of 17th century England which are implicit and often explicit in Shakespeare's works." The college had also offered in support of its ban a "captive audience" concern, which the court found equally untenable—if only because the administration had rebuffed the director's offer to arrange purely private performances of the play from which the general public would be barred.

Finally, the court noted that—far from advocating or even condoning any of the risqué language or the actions in the script—permitting the performance of such a play "simply recognizes this reality [of taboo language] and uses it to create the emotional tension necessary to develop the moral and philosophical issues which are central to the play." Thus the professor and the student actor won a signal victory, despite a vigorous dissent, in the California appeals court. The case represents a rare judicial visit to the campus stage –and one on which the curtain closed with some welcome recognition of artistic freedom.[26]

One other case merits close attention, albeit in a legally very different context. Once again Judge Posner was to write the coda and to reveal further his keen sensitivity for artistic expression. In the late summer of 2001, Indiana-Purdue University at Fort Wayne scheduled an on-campus production of Terrence McNally's *Corpus Christi*. The play depicts Jesus Christ as a homosexual who engages in sexual relations with some of his disciples. In a passage the court described as "not untypical," one of the disciples yells to Christ, dying on the cross, "Hey, faggot! If I was the son of God I wouldn't be hanging there with my dick between my legs. Save us all if you're really Him." Despite its critical acclaim, *Corpus Christi* was widely condemned as sacrilegious and blasphemous, and it frequently incurred efforts to ban its performance.

The Fort Wayne production was designed to satisfy a graduate student's thesis requirements and had full approval of the theater faculty. But when a group of conservative Hoosiers learned of this plan, they filed suit in federal court seeking to enjoin any such performances on public property. No fewer than twenty-one state legislators joined the citizen plaintiffs in the suit, thus raising substantially the profile of the case. The university had gone to some lengths to disclaim any endorsement of the play and its message, issuing an elaborate formal disclaimer even before the suit was filed.

The plaintiffs insisted, however, that use of state property for such a performance amounted to formal sponsorship of anti-religious views in violation of the First Amendment's required separation of church and state and also abridged their religious liberty under the free exercise clause. The district judge dismissed the suit, finding the campus theater an appropriate site for the exercise of a broad range of expressive interests. Because the play was about to open, an appeal was expedited to the same federal court in Chicago that had ruled on the stained-glass panels and the "Mirth and Girth" exhibit. Judge Posner was not impressed by any of the plaintiff's arguments. The claim that a public university may not "provide a venue for the expression of views antagonistic to conventional Christian beliefs" struck him as "absurd." He continued that such a notion

> would imply that teachers in state universities could not teach important works by Voltaire, Hobbes, Hume, Darwin, Mill, Marx, Nietzsche, Freud, Yates, Heiddeger, Sartre, Camus, John Dewey and countless other staples of Western culture. It is true that a public university that had a *policy* of promoting atheism, or Satanism, or secular humanism, or for that matter Unitarianism or Buddhism, would be

> violating the religion clauses of the Constitution. . . . But that is not charged . . . The student whose project it is to produce Corpus Christi . . . is of course not an employee of the university . . . and] was not told to put on this offensive play—it was his own idea; and there is no evidence that if the play attacked some other religion, the university authorities would have forbidden it.

Later in the opinion, Judge Posner warned that "the government's interest in providing a stimulating, well-rounded education would be crippled by attempting to accommodate every parent's hostility to books inconsistent with their religious beliefs." And, as the coda, he concluded: "The quality or lack thereof of Corpus Christi and other post-modernist provocations is a matter for the state university, not federal judges, to determine."[27]

Although this ruling fully and finally settled the particular dispute in the student's and the university's favor, one slightly sour note remained. As a dissenting court of appeals judge suggested, there was a latent tension between the *Corpus Christi* ruling and Judge Posner's deference to the relocation of a controversial art exhibit in the Piarowski case. To that proffered analogy, Judge Posner gave short shrift: "Piarowski was a case about a public college's own efforts to control an exhibition of offensive art on its premises; it was not about private citizens trying to prevent a public college from permitting the exhibition of offensive art, or in this case theater, as part of its curricular program."[28] This reply offered just a hint that if the ban had been internally imposed rather than being wholly the product of external political pressure, then the outcome would have been less clear to Judge Posner and quite possibly different. Such speculation invites consideration of the hardest case of all, one in which censorship occurs because the college administration accedes to community pressure by canceling a controversial play or forcing it off campus. That precise issue awaits further adjudication.

In addition to the few cases involving live performances, there is at least one important ruling about the showing of controversial films on campus. A film series at the University of Nebraska–Lincoln planned to present on a campus screen Jean Luc Godard's widely acclaimed but contentious *Hail Mary*. The film was deemed blasphemous in some quarters because of its contemporary and irreverent account of the birth of Jesus. Skeptics, including a prominent state senator, insisted the film not be shown. Acceding to such pressure, senior administrators overruled the film-series manager and canceled the planned screening. A group of would-be viewers then went to federal court, seeking a declaration that their rights had been abridged.

The district judge ruled in favor of the filmgoers and against the university, relying on the Supreme Court's recent curbing of subjective removal of controversial books from public libraries. The judge's ruling gave clear guidance to state college and university administrators on the handling of delicate and sensitive arts issues: "Even if the cause [for canceling the film] had been only the fact of controversy . . . cancellation would not have been justified, because actions taken by an arm of the state merely to avoid controversy from the expression of ideas is an insufficient basis for interfering with the right to receive information."[29] In some respects, this was a remarkably easy case, if only because of the blatantly political pressure and the ideological bias to which university officials so readily acceded. However, the court's recognition of a viewer's First Amendment right to insist that a controversial film not be barred from a state university campus was highly significant. Such a ruling served to advance artistic freedom well beyond the interests of those who had created and those who were to perform a live drama; when the material in issue is film, and none of the creators or even the distributor shows up to challenge the cancellation, the First Amendment interests are far less familiar. Their protection through such a judgment as that in the Nebraska film case adds a vital dimension to academic and artistic freedom.

One other campus motion picture case had a somewhat murkier, though still generally favorable, outcome. The regents of Oklahoma State University banned a scheduled campus screening of Martin Scorsese's *Last Temptation of Christ* because of scenes that some critics considered blasphemous. As in Nebraska, a group of would-be viewers went to federal court, seeking a reversal of the ban. Before ruling on the merits, the judge invited the regents to reconsider their action, which they proceeded to do, leaving implementation to the administration. The response was creative and apparently dispositive. Campus officials told the student group that sponsored the film to delete from ads for the film the customary phrase "brought to you by the students, faculty and staff of OSU." In its place the sponsors were to insert a disclaimer that "the showing of this film does not reflect an endorsement of its contents by the OSU Board of Regents or Oklahoma State University." The advertising copy was changed accordingly, and the film was presented, apparently without any disturbance in the normally tranquil community of Stillwater.[30]

The matter did not end there, however. The plaintiffs went back to federal court, seeking damages for what they claimed was, nonetheless, unlawful censorship. The trial judge dismissed this claim, ruling that the matter had now become moot—not only because the screening of *Last Temptation* had gone smoothly, but also because the regents had amended their policies on campus speech and especially artistic expression. The appeals court, however, proved to be slightly more sympathetic to the students' claim and sent the case back to the trial court, where the would-be viewers of the film might yet establish a constitutional claim: "If proven, a violation of First Amendment rights concerning freedom of expression entitles a plaintiff to at least nominal damages."[31] Thus, despite what seemed a Solomonic compromise and an apparently comfortable resolution, First Amendment concerns did not yield easily.

When challenging artistic materials are used in the college classroom, a very different tension comes into play at the intersection of artistic and academic freedom. The specific issue that arises occasionally, though dramatically, is how far students should be warned, and their professors should be obligated to warn, of controversial material in arts classes and presentations. Two major universities have struggled with the issue. In the mid-1990s, Vanderbilt University's dean of arts and sciences became aware of such student concerns after a classroom incident and directed one faculty member to warn his classes, at the start of each semester, of any sexually explicit material he intended to use in the course. Although this directive was ostensibly aimed at a single professor, it caused other Vanderbilt faculty to wonder whether they might now incur some risk by including suggestive—or even what seemed to them innocuous—material in their lectures. The American Association of University Professors considered the issue through its standing committee on academic freedom and tenure and offered a firm if gentle caution.

On the one hand, the AAUP recognized that Vanderbilt's action presumably reflected the association's long-standing conviction that "professors avoid any exploitation, harassment, or discriminatory treatment of students" and "should be careful not to introduce into their teaching controversial material which has no relation to the subject or to fail to present the subject matter of the course as announced to the students." Moreover, given the realities of the classroom and the student-teacher relationship, students must in some sense be seen as a captive audience. On the other hand, imposing a broad obligation on all faculty to warn at the start of the semester of any classroom content that any student might find offensive could gravely inhibit academic freedom. A word to the wise apparently sufficed and the Vanderbilt issue apparently did not recur.[32]

The situation for Iowa's public universities was, however, to prove somewhat more complex. In the early 1990s Iowa's board of regents and even the governor received complaints about the content of certain films that were shown in classes at two of the state's public universities. Three incidents were cited, two of them involving films with gay and lesbian content. The regents responded by inviting the state university faculties to develop policies that would adequately warn students of potentially offensive course content. Failing such self-regulation, the regents strongly hinted they were prepared to take more drastic action. Under that alternative, warnings would be required "when course materials include explicit representation of human sexual acts that could reasonably be expected to be offensive to some students." The implication was that an objecting student would be excused from the particular section and could freely drop the course if no alternative proved adequate.

Such a policy seemed to pose potentially serious problems not only for those who taught art and art history but also for members of medical faculties who used visual materials in teaching courses in such fields as anatomy, obstetrics and gynecology, and urology. Although the regents insisted that they had no intent to constrain such teaching, Iowa's public professors were not reassured. Nonetheless, the faculties at Iowa State and Northern Iowa did accede to the regent's directive and developed responsive policies. Only the University of Iowa demurred; its faculty had the firm backing of the president in insisting that, rather than crafting a new policy, professors should be able to invoke traditional principles of professional responsibility. The regents continued to press for something more specific. Eventually, with patience wearing thin on both sides, Iowa's president augmented the faculty's proposal by calling upon professors simply to afford their students "adequate indication of any unusual or unexpected class presentations or materials." That alternative now seemed to satisfy the regents as well.

The controversy did not end quite there, however. A group of still dissatisfied Iowans launched a Campaign for Academic Freedom, charging that the new policy was no better than the vacuum it purported to fill—and in fact might even make matters worse because it could be read as open-ended on the subject matter to which it applied. Citizen critics also noted that the new policy failed to define by whose views or standards potentially offensive material might be judged "unusual or unexpected."

The regents eventually concluded that the whole exercise had been misguided, or at least that it seemed to have created more problems than it solved. Any reference to "unusual or unexpected" was eventually removed, and Iowa's regulation (or more accurately nonregulation) of anticipatory course content returned to the default policy that continues to apply in other states.[33]

The Iowa episode served mainly to expose the inherent difficulty of crafting such language in so sensitive an area of academic life. Perhaps the only lesson of value derived from Iowa's painful experience was the unwisdom of seeking to alter or undermine the long-standing AAUP precepts that university professors may be told in the broadest sense to teach what they have been hired to teach, to keep out of the classroom wholly extraneous controversial material, and not to harass, exploit, or discriminate against their students. Crafting more precise cautionary language might be desirable, but it poses an elusive goal. The Iowa experience did provide a graphic reminder of the special concerns that properly arise when sexually explicit or sexually related material finds its way into the college classroom—especially when students have enrolled in a course where the prospect of being exposed to such material is neither an inherent risk nor one that has been specifically anticipated in the syllabus or elsewhere. Inherent in students' freedom to learn is the freedom to learn in a climate untainted by such hazards.

A new twist has recently been added to the process of protecting students from unwitting exposure to offensive material. Professor Dennis West, a specialist in film studies and Spanish at the University of Idaho, distributed to his film students on the opening day of fall 2006 classes, a "statement of understanding." Students were asked to acknowledge by their signature their appreciation of the potentially offensive content of films they would be viewing during the semester. West's premise was that "film is an extraordinarily powerful medium," likely to offend or even shock some sheltered or inexperienced undergraduates—a risk of which he had been increasingly reminded in recent years. Some of West's colleagues were concerned by the implications of such a procedure, although they recognized that film courses pose a special challenge that might warrant an unusual approach. Academic freedom experts elsewhere noted other concerns: Students might feel that by signing the statement they had been given a veto over course content, thus impinging upon the instructor's academic freedom—though West himself insisted he had not abdicated his role in selecting the films but was merely warning students of potentially abrasive material to which they might be exposed. Jonathan Knight, director of the AAUP's academic freedom office, voiced a rather different concern that students signing the statement might feel they had thereby waived their right to debate the academic value of controversial films. For him, the preferable approach would be simply to "describ[e] the content in the syllabus" in a way that provided the requisite advance notice and warning to wary students. Professor West at least deserves commendation for devising a novel approach to this daunting task.[34]

One final area in which major academic freedom concerns have arisen is that of government funding for the arts. Although the United States has lagged pitifully behind most other developed nations in the level of support for the creative and performing arts, the modest largesse that has come from government sources often carries burdensome conditions and restrictions. Such constraints have especially encumbered support from the National Endowment for the Arts (NEA). Because the Wolf Trap conferees convened at a time of intense controversy about arts funding, it was hardly surprising that the concluding statement contained this recommendation: "Public funding for artistic presentations and for academic institutions does not diminish (and indeed may heighten) the responsibility of the university community to ensure academic freedom and of the public to respect the integrity of academic institutions. Government imposition on artistic expression of a test of proprietary ideology or religion is an act of censorship, which impermissibly denies the academic freedom to explore, to teach and to learn."[35]

This bold declaration reflected the ideal, but surely not the reality, of arts funding in the early 1990s. Indeed, at the very time of the conference the nation was beset by "culture wars" in which controversial art was the principal target. The National Endowment for the Arts had been visibly harmed in public and in Congress by revelations that its funds had been used to create such contentious works as Andres Serrano's "Piss Christ," depicting a cross immersed in a bucket of the artist's own urine. There had also been extensive publicity about NEA support for a retrospective exhibit of photographs by the late Robert Mapplethorpe—controversial in several communities and ultimately the target of criminal prosecution in Cincinnati on both obscenity and child pornography charges.[36] Thus by the time the Wolf Trap conferees gathered, the gap between the ideal scope of artistic and academic freedom on the one hand and government policy on the other had dangerously diverged in ways that would soon bring the issue from the public arena into the courts. Several battles were to follow during the ensuing decade.

An increasingly indignant Congress had adopted in the late 1980s specific language proposed by Senator Jesse Helms of North Carolina, who was not generally seen as a friend or protector of the arts. This language barred the use of NEA funds for the creation of works that were "obscene," and it went much further. Artistic material "might be considered obscene" if, for example, it contained "depictions of sadomasochism, homoeroticism, the sexual exploitation of children, or individuals engaged in sex acts and which, when taken as a whole, do not have serious literary, artistic, political or scientific value." This statute delegated to the NEA difficult issues of interpretation, implementation, and enforcement. Grantees were soon required, as a condition of receiving any NEA support, to agree in writing that they would not use federal funds to create any works that violated any of the Helms Amendment criteria. The imposition of such a duty on artists who had survived the rigorous competition and had been found deserving of government largesse struck at the heart of artistic integrity and autonomy.

The language to which artists were compelled to subscribe bore little resemblance to what the Supreme Court had decreed in a host of decisions about sexually explicit material that reached back to the 1960s. Because a criminal sanction may, under the First Amendment, be imposed on one who sells or distributes a work that is legally obscene, government support could presumably be denied on the same grounds. But the Helms Amendment language went unimaginably further—reaching even "individuals [presumably adults] engaged in sex acts," a category that the Supreme Court had clearly placed on the nonobscene and First Amendment-protected side of the line. "Sadomasochism" and "homoeroticism" were less obviously unconstitutional criteria, though in the absence of any statutory definition were equally vague and imprecise. "Sexual exploitation of children" might imply a legislative design to reach child pornography—material that lay well beyond the boundaries of free speech—though without any of the concomitant definitions or safeguards that applied to criminal prosecution of pornographers. The Helms Amendment language thus went so far beyond what the First Amendment allowed government to constrain that one marvels that a majority (indeed 80 percent) of U.S. senators could ever have agreed to impose such conditions.

The NEA immediately recognized the constitutional problems and sought to cushion the blow on the arts community. A proviso was added to the certificate requirement, assuring prospective grantees that the Helms Amendment language would be construed as being consistent with the Supreme Court's obscenity standards, thus implying that elements such as sadomasochism and homoeroticism—not to mention depiction of normal adult sex acts—could not disqualify an otherwise eligible artist. The constitutional issue soon came before a federal judge in Southern California, when the Bella Lewitsky Dance Company and the Art Museum of Newport Beach (both longtime and widely respected NEA grantees) challenged the Helms Amendment and the certificate procedure on First Amendment grounds. The federal judge had little patience with the NEA's attempt to avoid the constitutional problems inherent in the intolerably overbroad and imprecise Helms language and thus invalidated the entire procedure.[37] Artists who depended on government support might well feel chilled by such imprecise provisions and might well forego public largesse simply to avoid the realm of uncertainty that the statute created.

In addition, the NEA's attempt at salvage did not succeed in its plausible goal of avoiding precisely that risk. Because it was an administrative agency and not a court, reasoned the judge, there was no way in which it could legally apply the "community standards" that were a vital ingredient of obscenity judgments. Nor could an artist be confident that a commitment to track Supreme Court standards issued by one NEA chairman would be binding on his or her successor. Finally, and most basically, the application of obscenity law to controversial artworks presupposed an array of procedural safeguards—vital ingredients of due process—that only a court could provide. Thus in the hope of making things better, and seeking to forestall a constitutional decree, the NEA had ironically made things worse. The Helms Amendment, in short, should have been declared dead on arrival. The decision of the Justice Department not to seek appellate review of the case conceded as much.

The district court's ruling was quite remarkable in several respects that merit closer scrutiny here. The denial of funding to an artist (or any other government beneficiary) does not automatically constitute censorship, even if the manifest basis for rejection is official displeasure over the content of that artist's work. Indeed, the most basic applicable principle is that government is under no constitutional duty to fund the arts at all, much less to fund any individual artist or arts organization. Just as the government need create no such program to support the arts, it is equally clear that any such program that has been created may be abandoned at will and for any reason (including official disapproval of the content of works that have been nurture by the program). Within any such program, government may confine support to a designated medium or subject, thereby disfavoring all others—even if such a preference reflects a particular political or other bias about the content or message. The range of options that government enjoys in choosing whether to create such a program to aid the arts—and how to shape and structure any program it does create—sharply differentiates legal challenges to the denial of discretionary funding from claims generated by penalties or sanctions. Yet as the *Bella Lewitsky* case made clear, government's largesse is not immune to legal review; there may be times and conditions that warrant judicial intervention—not to tell government that it must fund (or not fund) any particular artist but only that it may not dispense or withhold funds in certain ways.

Even before the *Bella Lewitsky* ruling, members of the creative community were busily engaged in advancing the cause of artistic freedom—notably in explaining to Congress why heavy-handed curbs on funding the arts could threaten academic freedom. Several prominent performing artists, led by Joseph Papp, refused to accept NEA funding during this period because of the taint they felt the Helms Amendment conditions imposed upon it. At least one major university publicly and visibly spurned such a grant as an act of protest. Early in 1990 the University of Iowa formally refused an NEA grant for the publication by its University Press of a collection of poetry.[38] The work in question was the twentieth annual issue of the Iowa Short Fiction Awards, the oldest series of short fiction published by any academic press in the United States. The director of the press was candid, indeed graphic, in stating the rationale for this unprecedented action: "It's not that I plan to publish obscene material. But the money stinks under these conditions. It reeks." The director of the Iowa Writers Workshop lauded this rejection as "courageous," noting that while "[Joseph] Papp can get the money elsewhere, [the Iowa Press] is not going to be able to do that." The university did, however, obtain the requisite support from private sources, indicating in that and other ways its support for the bold step that the Iowa Press had taken to protest the Helms Amendment's conditions.

Actually by the time of the *Bella Lewitsky* ruling, the offending statutory language had been replaced, a factor that undoubtedly strengthened the government's resolve not to appeal but to cut its losses at the district court level. Though the Senate vote to adopt the Helms Amendment had been overwhelming, eighty of the one hundred Senators now agreed, barely two years later, to repeal that very language. In its place came new and seemingly more benign language, in two parts. The first provision of the 1990 law charged the NEA's chairman to take into account in the grant-making process "general standards of decency and respect for the diverse beliefs and values of the American public."[39] Soon after this new language took effect, NEA officials sought to reassure artists that they did not deem the decency reference to be binding on their allocation process, though the precise import of that statement would remain unclear for much of the ensuing decade, eventually dividing the United States Supreme Court on that very issue.

The new restriction was soon challenged in federal court, this time by Karen Finley and three other controversial performance artists whose grants had been suspended (after virtually final approval) because of NEA concern that they were not sufficiently respectful of "standards of decency." Under close judicial scrutiny, the new language fared little better than the conditions it had replaced. Although the artist-grantee no longer had to sign a certificate or disclaimer, the risks posed by the substitute language were comparably chilling and potentially inhibiting to creativity. Judge A. Wallace Tashima, who would soon be elevated to the Ninth Circuit Court of Appeals, had no hesitation in declaring that those who seek government grants enjoy First Amendment freedoms comparable to those who are the target of civil or criminal sanctions, thus resolving for the purpose of this case a question that had clouded constitutional analysis of such issues.[40]

Going further, Judge Tashima drew a striking parallel between academic and artistic freedom, quoting at length from the statement of the Wolf Trap conference. By analogy to the safeguards that academic freedom assures to university professors, wrote Judge Tashima, "professional evaluations of artistic merit are permissible, but decisions based on the wholly subjective criterion of 'decency' are not. . . . The right of artists to challenge conventional wisdom and values is a cornerstone of artistic and academic freedom."

This judgment and the future course of the artists' challenge were pending at the time of the 1992 presidential election. Conventional wisdom suggested that the incoming Clinton administration would quickly drop the matter at the trial court level, leaving Judge Tashima's ruling as the final word. To the surprise of most observers, the new president and his legal team seemed, if anything, more aggressive in regard to issues of decency in the arts than had been their predecessors, who had abandoned the Helms Amendment litigation in the district court. Thus an appeal was promptly taken to the Ninth Circuit, where the case languished for an unprecedented four years. On the very day of the 1996 presidential election—a coincidence that could not have been unintended—the appeals court affirmed Judge Tashima's ruling that "standards of decency" could not constitutionally be imposed on the arts-granting process. The Ninth Circuit was no less troubled than the district court by the vagueness of the operative language, which "gives rise to the danger of arbitrary and discriminatory application" and warns that "funding may be refused because . . . the art or the artist is too controversial." Moreover, the challenged language was unmistakably viewpoint and content restrictive in ways the Supreme Court had found inconsistent with First Amendment freedoms in other settings. Finally, the appeals court was unpersuaded by the NEA's insistence that the decency language was merely advisory and nonbinding.[41]

A dissenting judge in the court of appeals saw the case very differently. For him, the challenged restrictions were well within the constitutional power of Congress, in part because the decency language must be read as hortatory or advisory and not as mandatory. His view turned out to be prophetic, since a nearly unanimous Supreme Court was about to see the case in precisely this posture. Justice Sandra Day O'Connor, writing for herself and six colleagues, upheld the restrictive language mainly on the ground that it was designed to be advisory; such statutory guidance to an agency head contrasted sharply with other situations where Congress clearly intended to "prohibit the funding of certain classes of speech."[42] Moreover, the justices could readily envision potentially valid applications of the decency language; indeed, the clear intent of Congress to stress diversity in the highly selective grant-making process actually seemed to the majority a laudable feature of the challenged provision.

Only two justices viewed the statutory language as binding or mandatory, and they drew diametrically different conclusions from their shared premise. Justice David Souter would have invalidated the decency language when defined as mandatory, agreeing with the two lower courts that imposing such conditions on the grant-making process abridged First Amendment freedoms. Justice Antonin Scalia, at the other extreme, was equally firm in upholding such language on the premise that, when it came to grants and subsidies, Congress could impose viewpoint criteria on highly competitive allocations. For him, "the nub of the difference . . . between 'abridging' speech and funding it [is] a fundamental divide, on this side of which the First Amendment is inapplicable."[43] When the dust settled, only two of the nine Supreme Court justices offered any guidance on the critical issue of the case—whether denial of funding properly equates to direct regulation—and they were so sharply split on the direct implications of their views for the case before them that they left the matter virtually unresolved. The *Finley* case thus deferred to another day and a different context the most basic issue shaping the constitutionality of arts-funding programs.

One other feature of the *Finley* case, which shaped the future course of arts funding, deserves mention. The majority stressed the need to permit, in so highly competitive an environment, government's use of certain inevitably imprecise criteria. Insisting that arts grants be awarded on a purely content-neutral basis such as first-come, first- served, might avoid constitutional concerns about subjectivity and lack of precision, but it would have created a wholly unworkable process inimical to the NEA's mission. Thus the Supreme Court condoned the selective criteria that had been in the statute since its enactment in 1965—"artistic merit" and "artistic excellence"—despite the inevitably subjective and imprecise language.

Such recognition of unavoidably subjective judgments now offered to the incoming NEA chairman, Ann-Imelda Radice, an inspired alternative. Indeed, Judge Tashima had noted in his opinion striking down the decency language that the whole problem could be avoided if a grant were denied at the final stage for lack of artistic excellence, even if unwelcome sexually explicit content were the obvious rationale for the rejection. Early in her term, Chairman Radice did in fact turn down two grants for university-based exhibits of works that had not only been enthusiastically endorsed by the NEA panels but also had been lauded by experts and critics.[44] The content of each exhibit was, however, somewhat controversial—more because it was avant-garde or cutting-edge art than because of sexually explicit imagery.

The two affected institutions, Massachusetts Institute of Technology (MIT) and Virginia Commonwealth University (VCU), protested vigorously, pointing out that one of the exhibits was at the very time of the NEA's rejection featured on the cover of a respected art journal. Arts lawyers and First Amendment experts conferred, and they concluded that a legal challenge would be pointless. Such action now seemed to be immune from legal challenge for the very reason that Judge Tashima had suggested and that Justice O'Connor recognized: if "artistic merit" and "artistic excellence" are constitutionally acceptable criteria, their wholly subjective—even disingenuous—application lies beyond the power of courts to gainsay. That conclusion followed even when all evidence supported the claim that what prompted the rejection was lack of decency rather than lack of excellence or merit. As long as NEA officials invoked no criteria other than excellence, they were home free, at least as far as the courts were concerned. Both VCU and MIT eventually secured private funding, and both exhibits opened more or less on schedule, despite the complete absence of anticipated NEA support.

Radice's seemingly cynical actions had immediate repercussions. MIT's art gallery director declared that she and her staff were "distressed to the point of outrage," so clear did it seem to them that the real (if carefully muted) reason for the rejection was concern over the exhibit's controversial content. When the news of Radice's actions became public, the NEA sculpture panel suspended its deliberations as an act of visible protest. Noting that reversals of panel recommendations had been extremely rare in the past, and that some explanation other than disagreement over artistic excellence had invariably accompanied any such rebuff, the panel's spokesperson explained that "we wanted to . . . protest the autocratic and unilateral actions of Ms. Radice. . . . The grants she reversed were, in the eyes of our panel—*all* the members of our panel—very mainstream, the kinds of projects most museums around the country are involved in."[45]

The whole issue was about to become moot for a wholly different reason. About this time the level of federal funding for the arts was substantially reduced—by roughly 40 percent in the mid-1990s. Concurrently, the structure of federal support for the arts was fundamentally altered. Congressional action virtually took the NEA out of the business of making grants to individual artists and small arts organizations—thus ensuring there would be no recurrence of the challenges that had been so contentious in the past.

The interdependence between artistic freedom and academic freedom is so central and durable that one might have expected the former to have fared better under the aegis of the latter. Much of the most challenging and controversial art is created (or performed) on the college and university campus. Many eminent composers, painters, sculptors, printmakers, and playwrights are also university teachers, who find a congenial home—a sort of safe haven—in the campus gallery, recital hall, and studio. It is, moreover, fine arts and theater professors who most often and most vigorously test the limits of taste and audience tolerance. Thus, one may take comfort from the relatively few occasions on which academic freedom in the arts seems to have been directly threatened by institutional policies and judgments.

Indeed, the record of the academic community in recognizing and protecting the artistic freedom of students as well as faculty is immensely reassuring, despite occasional lapses of the type noted in this chapter. Hostile pressures against the arts have come almost entirely from off campus—from Congress, state legislatures, local government, and the like. It is these forces that have tested the mettle of the academic community and its collective commitment to resist such challenges that threaten to subvert a vital component of academic freedom. The noble sentiments and eloquent words adopted at the Wolf Trap conference did indeed declare the ideal for the condition of both academic and artistic freedom in the university community. The reality is, as we have seen, somewhat less reassuring.

7

New Technologies

Academic Freedom in Cyberspace

As academic communications have evolved increasingly from print to digital format, major changes in the applicable standards might have been expected. E-mail messages between colleagues, and between professor and student, are surely different—and pose different challenges—from the typed or handwritten notes on which the university world has relied for well over a century. Some changes are obvious; information that appears on a teacher's or a student's webpage may evoke very different reactions from the same material in a more traditional form, even if the content is identical. It was unexpected that courts would confer a substantially lesser level of protection for academic freedom when the medium changed. Yet that is precisely what has happened in the digital age—to material posted on webpages, to individual electronic messages, and to the process of garnering vital research data from the Internet. This chapter both describes these altered standards and disputes the underlying premise that alteration of the medium warrants diluting the safeguards for academic communications.[1]

Early in the fall semester of 2004, the normally peaceful Indiana University–Bloomington campus was shaken by a novel controversy. Business school professor Eric Rasmusen had, like many of his faculty colleagues, created a personal webpage on the university's computer server. On that page he posted course assignments and other information for his business students. But Rasmusen went a bit further than other users of the system, expressing on the webpage his aversion to homosexuality and specifically declaring his opposition to the employment of gay men as school teachers. Because, in his view, "male homosexuals, at least, like boys and are generally promiscuous," hiring such men as teachers "puts the fox in the chicken coop."

Shortly after these statements appeared on Rasmusen's webpage, angry voices, both on and off the campus, demanded their removal. Rasmusen at first offered to delete the offending comments while university officials reviewed the controversy, for which there seemed to be no applicable policies or standards. But the very next day, after a university lawyer assured him that he had breached no rules, Rasmusen restored his homophobic statements.

While the matter was under review, campus chancellor Sharon Brehm addressed the Faculty Council, keenly aware that she could not avoid mention of the webpage issue, now topic A on the Bloomington campus. Directly facing Professor Rasmusen, who just happened to be an elected member of the council, Brehm declared that she found his posted statements to be "deeply offensive, hurtful, and very harmful stereotyping." She added her belief that such views were at variance with the university's "commitment to inclusion and respect for diversity." She insisted, however, that such public pronouncements by a member of her faculty were fully protected by the First Amendment and by principles of academic freedom, however offensive she and others might find the content. Given the uncertainty of the rules and policies that governed such a webpage fracas, she announced that an inquiry was being launched. That investigation would probe the applicability of whatever pertinent policies existed and would explore the possibility of shaping new rules that would more precisely govern faculty web postings.

Predictably, Chancellor Brehm's moderate response failed to satisfy either side of the dispute. The harshest critics of Rasmusen's statements expressed their deep disappointment that the administration had not more vigorously denounced such homophobic sentiments posted prominently on a university medium and had not insisted that they be banished from the server. Meanwhile, Rasmusen's supporters (not all of whom shared his views on homosexuality) charged that the chancellor had gravely chilled the climate for professorial expression. One faculty member, in fact, noted that although the U.S. military also holds anti-gay views, "the chancellor does not go out and denounce the Army."[2]

The novelty of the Rasmusen incident is matched by the paucity of guidance to be found in existing college and university policies. Expression of even the most blatantly homophobic views in a traditional medium—a letter to the local newspaper, an appearance on talk radio or television, for example—would without question be fully protected by core principles of academic freedom, however offensive those views might be to the campus community. Posting the same statements on a faculty webpage, however, may pose very different concerns.

Rasmusen's critics, in fact, identified factors that they believed altered the equation and warranted a different approach in cyberspace. For one, the offending statements could have been inadvertently accessed by students who were simply seeking information about his courses and assignments and had quite plausibly gone to the instructor's webpage as the logical (indeed perhaps the only) reliable source of such guidance. Although faculty webpages and blogs often contain extraneous material, through which a student might have to navigate in quest of curricular guidance, most such postings would not likely cause offense—let alone the depth of psychic harm potentially inflicted by Rasmusen's homophobia.

Moreover, because anyone (outsider as well as student) would normally reach the webpage through the Indiana University server, a plausible inference of institutional sponsorship might arise, despite the disclaimer that typically accompanies that section of the web. Finally, since the institution that maintains the server has total practical control over every bit or byte of the posted content—in sharp contrast to the situation in the general news media where contentious faculty views may appear—there is a more than plausible claim of official complicity when an academic administration simply acquiesces after such offensive content has been brought to its attention and removal is requested.

Rasmusen's posting was not the first time such issues had troubled a major university campus. The case of Northwestern University (NU) engineering professor Arthur Butz had been deeply divisive for decades, long before faculty webpages surfaced. In the mid-1970s, soon after he gained tenure, Butz wrote and published a book entitled *The Hoax of the Twentieth Century,* which denounced the Holocaust and declared that 6 million Jews in Western Europe had taken their own lives or had fallen victim to a strange illness. Calls for Butz's dismissal from the Northwestern faculty abounded, coming even from prominent university trustees, alumni, and a few of his colleagues.

Northwestern's administration nonetheless stood firm, insisting that as long as Butz continued to fulfill his responsibilities in teaching engineering and never intruded such views into his classroom or otherwise imposed them on students, academic freedom fully protected such aberrant rantings. To this day Butz has met all expectations in his teaching of engineering and has scrupulously keep Holocaust-denial out of the classroom and away from his students. Ironically, one of his graduate teaching assistants failed to respect this very line and was denied reappointment; he made available in class a list of readings for any students who might seek refutation of Holocaust-denial. So it was he, and not Butz, who brought the issue into the classroom, thus breaching the uneasy truce that has for decades kept this volatile issue in proportion.

This tenuous entente was gravely threatened, however, when Butz went online in the late 1990s. On his university webpage, he proclaimed himself the author of *The Hoax of the Twentieth Century* and briefly summarized the book's outlandish thesis. This electronic venue also contained links to other websites on which (or through which) an interested or curious web surfer could easily access a broader universe of rapidly burgeoning electronic hate material about the Holocaust and related issues.

Some of those who had uncomfortably tolerated Butz in book form now declared war on the website. The Simon Wiesenthal Center, a vigilant and durable watchdog of neo-Nazi activity, including Holocaust denial, now demanded that Northwestern adopt a different view of its outrageous professor's role in the new medium. Even if *Hoax of the Twentieth Century* were readily available in the university library and freely sold in its bookstore the institution could distance itself from any possible claim of complicity. Now, however, Mark Weitzman, director of the Wiesenthal Center's Task Force Against Hate, charged that since the webpage appeared under university auspices, "in effect [Butz is] using the university as a shield for hyping anti-Semitism and Holocaust denial."[3]

The Wiesenthal Center was hardly alone in arguing that the change in medium raised the stakes—that Butz online posed a far graver threat than Butz in print. A *Chicago Tribune* editorial comment, for example, argued that Northwestern was "metaphorically giving Butz free stationery with NU's letterhead on it." The critique continued: "In effect, it is also paying Butz to make his material denying the Holocaust available to millions of Internet users around the world." Despite such claimed distinctions, and pleas for a revision of policy, Northwestern remained firmly committed to its pre-Internet view of Butz and his academic freedom. University president Henry Bienen characterized Butz's views as "a contemptible insult to all who experienced the horrors of that time and their families." But he saw no occasion in Butz's case to vary Northwestern's firm policy on Internet use generally and the content of faculty webpages in particular: "The network is a free and open forum for the expression of ideas, including viewpoints that are strange, unorthodox or unpopular."[4]

According to university policy, only two conditions applied: posted views must not be represented as those of the university and the entire content must be expressly covered by a blanket disclaimer that reaffirms the distance between the institution and the individual. A report issued about that time by the Anti-Defamation League (ADL) titled "Extremist Use of the Internet" asked rhetorically whether stands such as the one Northwestern had taken with regard to Butz's webpage were any longer defensible or whether the new medium of the Internet did not call for new and more restrictive policies. "What is lost, and what is gained," asked ADL, "when an Arthur Butz is allowed to publish his false, ideologically driven assertions with what appears to be the imprimatur of a respected institution of higher learning?"[5]

Another major midwestern university was soon to be roiled by a similar controversy. Washington University (St. Louis) offers its faculty the nearly universal opportunity to post both curricular materials and personal views on university-hosted webpages. Physics professor Jonathan L. Katz relished the chance to share with visitors to his website not only recent and exciting breakthroughs in research on gamma-ray bursts (his academic specialty) but also links to the professor's recent writings on several contentious subjects. Many of the linked articles expressed vehement opposition to the war in Iraq and other Bush administration policies. But the one that started a campus uproar in the fall of 2005 offered access to an essay entitled "In Defense of Homophobia." In that piece Katz boldly announced his belief that homosexuality is a "moral judgment" and, like bestiality and incest, is condemned by the Bible.

With specific reference to the prevalence of AIDS in the gay community, Katz declared his conviction that "the human body was not designed to share hypodermic needles, it was not designed to be promiscuous, and it was not designed to engage in homosexual acts." After insisting that homophobes do not encourage violence against gay people but simply avoid them, Katz concluded: "I am a homophobe, and proud." Such views seem to have been confined to the web; Katz (like Butz) has been scrupulously careful to avoid mentioning such matters in his classes—a task undoubtedly made easier by his academic discipline. "It's not difficult," he explained, "to keep political issues outside of a physics class."

An op-ed in the student newspaper was among the earliest voices to demand an official response to Katz's webpage. The student editor first analyzed and rejected Katz's reasoning but then added that even more troubling to him was "that these essays . . . are hosted on University-owned Web space, funded by our tuition." The author of the op-ed, soon interviewed by the *St. Louis Post-Dispatch,* acknowledged the dilemma that any conscientious guardian of free expression faced in addressing Katz's postings. On one hand, there is "part of me that thinks this is hateful and should be removed. Should we let anybody we want on a University-based Webpage say 'I hate gays' or 'I hate Jews'?" On the other hand, the student journalist concluded that such hateful material "should be left up there on his Web site. . . . Do I want to say that just because I don't agree with his opinion that it should be removed?" Other students seemed less tolerant; the president of the Pride Alliance, for example, expressed fear that gay and lesbian students might feel uncomfortable taking any of Katz's courses or informally seeking guidance from him after his homophobic views became apparent.

Predictably, Washington University officials opted for the more benign view. Katz had been a tenured professor for many years and a distinguished research physicist for a quarter century. The administration insisted it did not—indeed effectively could not—monitor and regulate the content of faculty webpages. The only constraints the institution felt it could conceivably impose on professors who used its digital display were compliance with federal and state law, avoidance of copyright infringement, and not posting material that was defamatory or harassing or that occupied "inappropriate amounts of band width." An official statement added, with specific reference to the current controversy, that "as long as Professor Katz does not use his university-conferred authority in matters related to students . . . to reward those who share his views or punish those who do not, and does not otherwise participate in any discriminatory activity . . . he has a right to free speech to express his opinions under the Web policy of the university."[6]

To what extent do such early encounters suggest that academic freedom online may afford university teachers and scholars less protection than comparable principles have in the print era? There is little doubt that, whatever those risks, communication between faculty and students and among colleagues are already dramatically more digital, and they will increasingly occur in electronic form. Yet there is now emerging a wholly new basis for institutional concern about material that faculty members post on their university-based webpages. The potential risks that a present or prospective student may encounter blatant Holocaust denial or homophobia on a professor's webpage while seeking course information or a faculty profile have barely surfaced.

Those risks are at least quantitatively greater than the more familiar risks that students (and colleagues) may be offended by material posted on a professor's office door or bulletin board, if only because print material of this sort is usually physically separate from course assignments and the like and appears at a site where editorial or political views are predictable. When a professor does post offending material on a website rather than a physical bulletin board, its discovery may evoke harsh criticism both of the poster and of the institution. Thus far, however, the official positions that Indiana, Northwestern, and Washington universities have espoused seem quite consistent with principles of academic freedom fashioned in the days of print communication. These institutions have consistently said and done the right thing, insisting that the change in medium should not diminish the level of protection for the message.

Most colleges and universities have not yet been tested in this volatile area. Comprehensive state universities and private liberal arts colleges are far less likely than the three major Midwestern campuses we have observed to have policies on the books remotely addressing controversial or offensive webpage postings. Lacking such policies, they may well respond instinctively—and badly, at least in terms of academic freedom. Even now, there is a nagging sense that conditions in cyberspace are becoming so different that a new approach may be needed—or at least that challenges posed in cyberspace need a sharper analysis with the benefit of a better appreciation for the potential hazards of this profoundly new medium. In short, maybe we need a better answer to the *Chicago Tribune* writer's claim that Northwestern is effectively "paying for Butz, who earned tenure in 1974, to make his material denying the Holocaust available to millions of Internet users around the world."[7]

The universe of the Internet is profoundly different from the print world in several other respects that may affect academic freedom. A short and simple response to questions that reflect such differences—that safeguards for free speech and press have always adapted to new technologies and should as readily do so this time—may yield the right answer, but one that is hardly satisfactory for our purposes or to those who insist that web postings must be treated differently. Thus a review of several relevant and basic contrasts offers a useful point of departure.

Certain obvious differences between old and new media have no direct bearing on academic freedom, though they are worth noting. An electronic message may instantly reach readers across the country and indeed around the globe, in sharp contrast to any form of print communication. Although a digital message, once posted, can be infinitely altered over time—another significant difference—the initial message may never be retracted once it has been sent or posted. Indeed, the first posting may remain accessible on "mirror" sites despite all efforts to suppress, remove, and expunge it.

Moreover, it is common knowledge among those who study electronic communications that digital messages often evoke far greater anxiety (even fear) on the part of their recipients than does the same text in print. Such greater impact may reflect in part the uncertainty about (if not the anonymity of) the sender. It may also derive from the absence of any "affect" accompanying an e-mail or chat room posting—no tone of voice, no facial expression, no other familiar indicia by which a reader or listener might judge the seriousness (or jocularity) of the sender of a more traditional message. Lacking such familiar guidance, an already anxious recipient may well assume the worst.

Digital messages may also contain far more vivid and alarming visual images than are possible in equivalent print messages—witness, for example, the use by a militant anti-abortion group on its "Nuremberg Website" of blood-dripping fetuses and an invisible hand that crosses out the name of a physician targeted for imminent assassination. However, certain potentially unlawful uses of spoken and printed words have no counterpart on the Internet; "incitement" to violence, for example, requires face-to-face communication of a sort that simply cannot exist in cyberspace. "Fighting words" exist only when two contentious persons are facing one another at close enough range to evoke a physical attack.

Finally, electronic messages enter the home to a degree that even the more traditional broadcast media seldom do—and with a growing likelihood that a computer user will be inadvertently assaulted by an offensive and unwelcome message (classically, the startling imagery that greets a careless browser who enters whitehouse.com instead of the benign whitehouse.gov.). Such differences as these, and others with which we are becoming increasingly familiar, do set digital communication apart from print messages, though not in ways that bear directly on academic freedom. What now merits our closer attention are several distinctions that directly implicate such safeguards in ways that the academic community is only gradually coming to appreciate.

For starters, consider the extent to which traditional concepts of academic freedom in teaching presuppose a familiar distinction between what occurs in the classroom and elsewhere. The value of that spatial contrast is clear enough in the familiar physical learning site that has four walls, a floor, and a ceiling. Increasingly, however, the "classroom" may be a course webpage, a chat room or a newsgroup devoted to the subject matter of the course, an electronic bulletin board, links posted to course-pertinent materials, and other digital "places" that clearly have no familiar physical boundaries. Not only do students communicate with their professors and instructors regularly through e-mail (in fact, probably far more than in face-to-face office or after-class and hallway visits), but also much of the subject matter of regular in-person courses is exchanged through electronic channels. When it comes to increasingly popular online course offerings, moreover, the absence of any traditional physical classroom marks a dramatic break between a familiar physical setting and the novel virtual one in which teaching and learning occur with increasing frequency.

The other vital component of academic freedom—research—also deserves to be viewed very differently in cyberspace. As noted later in this chapter, a host of difficult and novel issues arise here. Although a university does to some degree control a scholar's recourse to print materials by its management of library collections, and certain materials may occasionally be off limits to some users, the potential for limitation or denial of access is vastly greater when the institution maintains and therefore controls the gateway to the Internet. A repressive administration may, for example, curtail student and even faculty access to certain categories of materials—either by barring such access directly or by refusing to subscribe to certain research sources or data banks that are not automatically available to every Internet user. Or, as one state (Virginia, which is discussed at length below) has done by legislation, government may bar the use of public computer equipment and networks to access certain categories of electronic or digital materials—thus ushering in a host of new challenges in the Internet era.

Publication, as the channel by which the results of research are shared and disseminated, also merits reexamination in the Internet era. The faculty webpage incidents just reviewed suggest ways in which institutional management of the server and computing network make possible a type of intervention that has no counterpart in the print era; if, for example, one's own university press refuses to publish a scholar's writings, myriad alternative outlets exist free of such constraints. As online publication becomes increasingly dominant in scholarly communication, such distinctions are ever more portentous for academic freedom.

One other very familiar distinction—between a faculty member's appearing to speak for or represent the institution on the one hand and, on the other, speaking only as an individual—also becomes blurred in cyberspace. In the print world, it is relatively simple for a professor to comply with the universal mandate that one does not purport to represent the institution unless he or she is authorized to do so. In the faculty weblog incidents, however, we recognized the greater ambiguity of online messages, and hence the far greater difficulty of drawing such a line, when a professor's statements are widely accessible through the university server. On that site, despite the ubiquitous disclaimer of institutional approval, a plausible inference of attribution seems far more likely.

After taking stock of these threshold distinctions, we turn to two major areas in which academic freedom faces risks in cyberspace that were nonexistent or at least relatively modest in the print world. The matter of privacy in communication offers a vivid illustration. When faculty members receive their messages in writing—typically through the mails or by phone—protecting a right to absolute privacy is relatively simple. The administration does not open sealed envelopes in or on their way to a professor's mailbox (and for material sent through the U.S. mails may not legally do so). Phone messages may be intercepted or monitored only under the most extreme conditions, carefully detailed in federal wiretapping laws. But when communication occurs by e-mail, instant messaging, and the like, and it increasingly does, the basic nature of privacy changes quite dramatically. Every university routinely (if randomly) backs up some portion of each day's electronic communications and thus quite inadvertently invades communication privacy in ways that have no counterpart whatever in the print environment. And quite apart from what the system operator or Information Technology Center may do, any person who receives any electronic message may immediately forward it to one (or many) others, without the approval or even the knowledge of the sender.[8]

The far greater flexibility of digital messages may have graphic implications for academic freedom. Consider, for example, the sobering experience of Professors Gary Stringer and Frank Glamser, longtime tenured teachers at the University of Southern Mississippi. They had been harshly and openly critical of the appointment of a new vice president for research and were especially disenchanted by what seemed to them manifestly inadequate credentials. They were also publicly disparaging of the president who appointed this senior administrator, for this and a host of other reasons. When Stringer and Glamser were brought up on dismissal charges for their anti-administration activity, some of the most potentially damaging (and hitherto secret) pieces of evidence against them became public for the first time. The general tenor of their attack had been well known across campus, but the specific content that was now revealed was far more acerbic.

During the dismissal hearing, the accused professors learned for the first time that, following their initial indictment of the administration, the president had directed a university lawyer to monitor closely their e-mail messages, with the aid of the information technology office (which of course had ready access to their communications). Such an extraordinary intrusion could be justified, the president insisted, because the faculty critics had publicly "disparaged" the new vice president and had done so "with reckless disregard for the truth." This claimed warrant for invading otherwise private e-mails also included allegations that the faculty critics had misused state property (in ways that were never specified) and had undermined confidence in the university administration—though arguably the latter action involved the public criticism far more than the hitherto confidential e-mails.

Faculty reaction at Southern Mississippi to revelations about the e-mail diversion was swift and predictably critical. The case was eventually settled; the outspoken professors were reinstated to their faculty positions, although as the result of a quite novel sanction, they were thereafter barred from teaching. They were also compelled as a condition of redemption to promise that they would "refrain from offering public criticism or commentary about the university's internal administrative operations." But the settlement failed to address the diversion of the disaffected professors' private e-mails, and it did not offer any assurance that the next faculty critic might not be similarly treated. Thus substantial anxiety persisted on a campus where a grave threat to academic freedom had gone unredressed.

The central premise of that anxiety was the long-standing and deeply held belief that what professors say to one another about how they regard the campus administration—regardless of the medium in which they exchange such views—remains absolutely confidential. A besieged president does not open sealed letters or intercept phone conversations or send spies into the faculty lounge during morning coffee—and should such invasive tactics ever be used and revealed, any administration that invoked them would be universally condemned. But in cyberspace, it is already apparent that things may be quite different. What seems most unsettling about the Stringer-Glamser case at Southern Mississippi was the relatively modest degree of concern, both on and off campus. Had the diverted messages been sent through traditional communication channels, condemnation of such interception would have been nearly universal.[9]

The case of Virginia Tech professor Martha McCaughey compounds the newfound fears about the sanctity of faculty communications. In the spring of 2002, she watched helplessly as campus police removed a university-issued computer from her faculty office. The hard drive was then scrutinized for messages, all without McCaughey's approval or assent. The administration justified that extraordinary action as part of an investigation of a recent rash of homophobic messages and slurs that had defaced campus facilities. Given her role as director of the university's Women's Studies Program, at least a tenuous basis existed for assuming Professor McCaughey could have received an incriminating message from one of those responsible for the defacement. An official spokesman explained that Virginia Tech had the right to search her files because the computer was university property and that the "owner" could reclaim or use such property as it saw fit. This extenuating statement added that, in accordance with an official policy of which most faculty members were unaware, "the university reserves the right to copy or examine files on university [computer] systems."[10]

Actually McCaughey's messages did contain one that was highly relevant to the defacement and that she had earlier forwarded to others. When she was initially notified that the campus police wished to access the original message, she offered to make it available, but campus computer security officials insisted that only the original would yield meaningful clues. Upon being served with the demand for her entire computer, Professor McCaughey balked, on the ground that her hard drive contained much other material, including some in which her copyright was professionally significant. She also pleaded that she was about to leave campus in order to visit a critically ill parent and simply could not sort through electronic files before departing.

It was on return from this visit that she found the police officers at her office preparing to confiscate the computer. After the computer was returned to her office some days later, McCaughey conducted surveillance of her own and found that files other than the declared target of the official inquiry had been accessed, including one bearing the seemingly suggestive caption "Sex Toy Parties McCaughey" (the contents of which, despite its tantalizing title, had already been published in a highly reputable scholarly journal). In recounting her experiences in an article published soon after she left Virginia Tech, McCaughey voiced concern about the ease with which adverse inferences might be drawn from a review of several digital files with wholly innocent origins: "I couldn't help being shocked that my academically legitimate files looked like obscenity."[11] Because McCaughey had already accepted a position at another university in a neighboring state, there is no way of knowing whether any reprisal (or for that matter redress) might ever have followed this unsettling experience.

There was another, possible explanation for the administration's sudden interest in one professor's computer. About the time of the seizure, Virginia Tech had offered its graduate deanship to a distinguished scholar from the Pacific Northwest who made no secret of her lesbian sexual orientation. The candidate seemed on the verge of accepting the offer when she received an anonymous e-mail warning that Blacksburg and Virginia Tech were less than hospitable to gay and lesbian faculty. When senior administrators learned of this glitch in a seemingly smooth process, they were understandably anxious to discover the source in order to refute the claim. Professor McCaughey might have been seen as a possible author of the message, or she might at least have received a copy; on either assumption, preemptive access to her computer might have solved the mystery. In fact, her hard drive contained no trace of such communication. Meanwhile, the graduate dean candidate accepted Virginia Tech's offer, on condition that a teaching position could be found for her longtime partner, also a promising scholar. The whole saga thus had a happy ending, leaving in limbo the authorship of the ominous e-mail message. Yet the experience provided graphic evidence both of the temptation that university administrators may occasionally feel to impound a faculty member's digital data—when such interception could not be imagined if the same material were in print form—and of the urgent need to define adequate safeguards for the privacy of electronic communications as a vital element of academic freedom.

One other incident deserves brief mention as we assess the state of electronic privacy for university professors. Irene Wechselberg, a librarian at the University of California–Irvine, had taken medical leave during a prolonged illness. The campus administration, citing an increasingly urgent need to maintain the flow of library business, authorized the diversion of Wechselberg's e-mail inbox to her supervisor. When the ailing librarian learned of this action, she declared to a reporter: "That's just an invasion of privacy." Eventually she brought suit against the university in state court, claiming a breach of her legal rights. Ironically, at that very time the University of California system administration was well along in crafting what would become one of the most protective institutional policies on potential e-mail diversion. Redirecting private messages would be permissible under the new policy, absent the employee's consent, only when such an extraordinary measure was authorized by a court-issued subpoena or in "critical operational circumstances"—and even then every effort must be made to obtain the user's approval or at least inform the user before the diversion occurs.[12]

The most recent disturbing encounter also occurred in California, this time in the state university system. Professor Stuart Hurlbert taught biology at San Diego State for over a third of a century, during which time he was no stranger to controversy. Soon after his retirement in the fall of 2006, he faced an administrative demand that he stop using his university e-mail account to organize rallies against illegal immigration and to correspond with the Minutemen (a group that espoused anti-immigration activities). The campus administration insisted its decree was unrelated to the content of Hurlbert's messages but reflected a state policy that university resources not be used for "nonwork activities." To Hurlbert, such a rationale was simply subterfuge; noting that his colleagues routinely used campus e-mail to solicit him and many others for myriad causes, he insisted that "it's routine to use e-mail; that's what makes the whole thing so silly." Whether or not Hurlbert could document his claims of selective or discriminatory enforcement of the "work-related only" policy, the critical distinction is that such an issue would never have arisen had the contentious messages been sent by mail or by telephone or distributed through other campus media. Once again, such an encounter underscores the vulnerability of electronic communications in ways that may directly and substantially affect academic freedom.[13]

Concerns of people such as the Mississippi, Virginia, and California professors and librarians are well founded. About the time of these incidents the *Chronicle of Higher Education* surveyed the increasingly complex situation under the ominous caption, "Your E-Mail Message to a Colleague Could Be Tomorrow's Headline." Two conclusions pervaded the article: one, that the current state of the law was alarmingly unprotective of faculty electronic messages; and two, that few professors who used e-mail extensively had any clear awareness of the vulnerability of their presumably private communications to intervention by prying eyes both on and off campus.

Even if a university embraces on its own a reasonably protective policy, such as that of the University of California, the state of general law turns out to be remarkably unhelpful to sensitive campus communications. For one thing, state university professors and staff members are all public employees, and as such their communications are often subject to access under freedom of information and public records laws. Thus the *Chronicle* article warned: "Journalists in search of wrongdoing (including some at the *Chronicle*) and litigants looking for damning evidence are catching on, and they're using state freedom-of-information laws to pry open the e-mail accounts of administrators as well as professors."[14] Such pressures cannot easily be resisted, at least in those states where state college and university professors are state employees.

One would expect, however, that a faculty member would normally enjoy far more substantial and reliable protection against invasive tactics practiced by his or her own institution. Juxtaposed against that hope, however, is the practical reality that the information technology center on every campus routinely and indiscriminately backs up some portion of every day's electronic correspondence simply as part of its management of the computer system, with no desire to snoop or peek into private communications. Yet the very fact that third parties have such indiscriminate and unregulated access to what may be highly personal and sensitive messages marks a dramatic difference among communications media.

Even if the campus administration may target a particular user's messages, as at the three institutions that generated the incidents reviewed here, expectations of privacy have turned out to be illusory. In 2003 the Federal Court of Appeals for the Third Circuit gravely undermined such expectations by ruling that an employer did not violate existing privacy law by searching a cache of electronic messages that a suspected employee had sent and that were thus stored on the company's server.[15] Although federal law does forbid actual interception of electronic communications, that ban turns out to apply only to unconsented access at the very moment of transmission, and specifically exempts the owner of an e-mail system from any legal claim that an employer's downloading of an employee's messages could constitute an unlawful seizure of stored digital content.

That ruling left open the question whether a university professor might be better treated in this regard than the general run of computer users. The answer was not long in coming, and it was surprisingly discouraging to academic freedom hopes and expectations. Another federal appeals court gave what seems to be the definitive (and surprisingly negative) answer. Although the subject matter was child pornography that a professor had downloaded—hardly the best context for a test case—the court's dismissal of the professor's privacy interest presumably applied no less broadly to the status of much more acceptable digital materia! Noting with approval that applicable computer-use policies "prevent . . . employees from reasonably expecting privacy in data downloaded from the Internet onto [u]niversity computers," the court cautioned the defendant professor that he "should have been aware that network administrators and others were free to view data downloaded from the Internet."[16]

A slightly more hopeful view of the privacy claim within an academic setting—this time at the behest of a student—came from a spring 2007 ruling by the federal court of appeals in California. A University of Wisconsin student named James Heckenkamp became the target of an electronic search when a San Diego company notified campus officials in Madison that someone on the UW network had hacked into the company's system. When the hacker was identified as Heckenkamp and criminally charged for his unlawful electronic entry, university and corporate officials discovered that he had apparently gained unauthorized access to portions of the university's network as well. Much of the basis for the criminal charges involved material that UW officials had obtained through a search warrant, but also through remote access to Heckenkamp's account. The student's lawyers argued that such evidence should be suppressed because it had been obtained in violation of his Fourth Amendment right of privacy. On that novel and crucial issue, the appeals court essentially split the difference. On one hand, the judges recognized that a student in a state university dormitory room had "a reasonable expectation of privacy" for his personal computer and its hard drive, and the information they contained. On the other hand—making this a pyrrhic victory for Heckenkamp—the court eventually ruled that UW officials nonetheless had acted lawfully in conducting the electronic search because "the university's interest in maintaining the security of its network provided a compelling government interest in determining the source of the unauthorized intrusion into sensitive files."

Given the dismal state of federal law, any viable protection for professors' e-mail privacy must therefore come from one or both of two other sources—institutional policy and state law. Both have been partly responsive, under growing and often intense pressure from privacy groups, state employee organizations, and academic organizations such as the American Association of University Professors (AAUP) Committee on Academic Freedom and Tenure, which has twice issued a comprehensive report on these very issues. The AAUP statement recounts the myriad risks and threats to academic freedom in digital communications, and it urges the adoption of institutional policies substantially more protective than the policies that have permitted some of the transgressions encountered in this chapter.

Among the surprisingly small group of institutional policies, that of the University of California (UC) system remains a model. Its central premise is that the university "respects the privacy of electronic communications in the same way that it respects the privacy of paper correspondence and telephone conversations." The UC policy goes on to insist that before access is granted or messages are diverted, the user's consent must be obtained unless either there is a legally unavoidable demand (a search warrant, subpoena, or freedom of information request) or there exist "critical operational circumstances."

Even under such exigency, however, the California policy requires that, where time does not permit seeking the user's consent, the university must at the earliest opportunity notify the affected person of the specific action that has been taken and of the reasons for taking it. Each campus is required to establish and publicize a process for "review and approval" of any access or diversion that was allegedly authorized under the stated exceptions.[17] Although several other universities have taken similar steps, none has been legally required, leaving faculty on many campuses subject to invasions of the kind that have occasioned the concern and anxiety noted here.

In an ideal world, urges the AAUP policy, institutions should involve their faculties in shaping such policies, and they should address several vital issues. Notably, the policy should spell out (even more clearly than does that of the University of California) the process by which "critical operational circumstances" are to be determined and by whom; provide for notice to the affected person and some minimal time lag even when responding to an inexorable demand like a Freedom of Information Act request or a subpoena; ensure that when diversion or access does occur, the contents of any affected messages may be used or disseminated no more broadly than is necessary—addressing Professor McCaughey's lament—or kept for any longer time than absolutely required; and address related issues such as "acceptable computer use policy," including the elusive question of when and for what reasons a faculty member may ever be barred from using the network or server.

Limited protection has also been provided by a few sympathetic state legislatures. Connecticut law, apparently the first to afford such protection, requires employers (both public and private) at least to notify their employees before gaining access to e-mail messages and other computer files, even though the employer typically owns the equipment and may broadly regulate its use. California has also adopted as state law a relatively protective standard, consistent with a generally benign treatment of employees, both public and private, in the Golden State. Other states have considered similar measures, although the issue has yet to emerge as a high political priority for state office seekers.

Meanwhile, the state of the law remains both underprotective and inconsistent or eclectic in its coverage, creating a climate in which university professors should recognize electronic privacy (or lack of it) as a major academic freedom concern. The courts have barely begun to address these issues and have understood them poorly when cases have been adjudicated. Colleges and universities seem anxious to avoid the need to establish policy in this still unfamiliar field. Invasions of electronic privacy and expression such as those reviewed here could be widely replicated, often without even the degree of knowledge that brought these events to public attention and concern. If, for example, a hostile or suspicious administration simply monitors e-mail messages but never announces that it has done so and makes no public use of what it learns from that process, a faculty member's most private communications might be subtly used for malign purposes—not only without recourse but even without knowledge of the sort that would counsel caution or a change of medium. Such is the currently unsettled state of the law and policy in an area of vital importance to academic discourse.

Access to information in digital form is the other major area in which academic freedom and the Internet have coexisted uncomfortably. Colleges and universities (especially those with conservative religious affiliations) have been known to restrict access to certain print materials, or limit the list of potential users, although (apart from conserving original copies of priceless manuscripts) such restrictions are virtually unknown at the major centers of scholarship.[18] Thus it was unsettling when the issue of access to "alt.sex" newsgroups first surfaced in the early 1990s, evoking a wholly uncharacteristic response from the academic community.[19] Stanford University was apparently the first to impose any limits on access to such sources through its computer system—although, in response to widely adverse comment, the ban was quickly lifted and the issue apparently never recurred in Palo Alto.

Less happy was the experience at Carnegie-Mellon University (CMU), which had ironically just earned acclaim as the nation's "first fully wired campus." Attention was initially drawn to salacious digital material by a widely publicized study of Internet content that had been prepared by a CMU undergraduate. Although the study was later substantially discredited because of what was at least grave exaggeration, its sensational claims persuaded the CMU administration in late 1994 to restrict computer user access to alt.sex newsgroups through the campus network (fittingly nicknamed "Andrew" in honor of both its patrons). In response to immediate protest on campus and far beyond, the administration modified the policy so as to grant unfettered access to text content but continuing to bar access to sexually explicit visual images within the newsgroups.[20]

A faculty-staff committee was appointed, charged with assessing the policy and its rationale. The group proposed an uneasy compromise, which was accepted: access would be restricted only where the purpose and content were presumptively unlawful, or where a newsgroup (regardless of its purpose) consistently flouted legal canons. When the Faculty Senate took up the issue, it proposed a far more creative solution: designate Andrew as a library, a step that, under Pennsylvania law, would exempt the system from potential criminal liability for containing or making available any material that could be deemed legally obscene.

Yet the CMU administration continued for some time to justify something short of completely open access on two premises: that local servers carrying such material "could make the university complicit in the provision of illegal materials to members of the CMU community" and that, as part of a global network, "university servers provide feeds to servers at other locations." Carnegie-Mellon students are nothing if not creative in matters of technology, and one student group outdid itself by launching what they called a "censorship page," which contained none of the suspect sexual content but rather hyperlinks by which users could access such material despite Andrew's inhosptiality.[21]

Although Carnegie-Mellon and other universities eventually relaxed or abolished such improbable restraints on Internet access, the initial experience left scars and lingering apprehension. At least one such restrictive access policy ended up in federal court. Former governor and senator David Boren had just become president of the University of Oklahoma (OU) when citizen complaints reached his office about the amount of salacious material that could be accessed through the university's server. Access to several categories, notably the most salacious of the alt.sex newsgroups, was simply denied through the university's network. That early action, reported the *Chronicle of Higher Education,* angered some of whom had initial reservations about the academic sensitivity of a person from so political a background.[22]

An assistant professor of journalism, Bill Loving, filed suit in federal court to challenge the policy on First Amendment grounds. Believing he could adequately represent himself, though he lacked legal training, Loving soon learned to his dismay that a federal civil rights plaintiff must show some legally cognizable injury in order to prevail. When the judge asked him in the preliminary court hearing whether he might not be able to use a private account and a home computer to obtain access his university station would not provide, Loving conceded that such was the case. His lawsuit was promptly dismissed by an irritated federal district judge.[23] The court of appeals summarily affirmed the dismissal of the case with comparable annoyance.[24]

The irony of Professor Loving's abortive lawsuit is that he might well (with a lawyer's guidance) have made a quite different and far more compelling argument in the one court test to date of restrictive university access policies. The potential availability of certain materials through alternative sources does not as a constitutional matter automatically blunt or thwart an otherwise valid constitutional claim of access. When the Supreme Court addressed a closely analogous issue in the context of public school library constraints, the principal argued that students who really wanted to read the books that had been removed from the school library had only to go to their local public library or bookstore. That alternative, wrote Justice William Brennan, is simply not responsive; the Court made clear that if a First Amendment right of access exists at all, the person who asserts such a claim also enjoys the prerogative of designating the time and location of its exercise and may not be forced to accept an alternative source that government may favor.[25]

Such recognition of a reader's right of access could imply—though need not—that every library is legally obligated to acquire all works any given reader might wish to find there. A viewpoint-based pattern of nonacquisition may be constitutionally vulnerable—one federal appeals court so held some years ago—but for the most part a patron's interest extends only to materials already in the library's collection. Yet such an interest would clearly have helped Professor Loving, since most of the materials he wished to access through the university's Internet connection were already effectively within its collections. That conclusion follows because when access to digital material is officially restricted or denied, the proper analogy is not to a library's refusal to acquire material not yet on the shelves but rather to the removal of materials already bought and cataloged.

Regrettably, Professor Loving never raised such a claim, and the federal judges in Oklahoma thus had no occasion to address it. Because the issue has arisen nowhere else, we have no sense of how it might fare elsewhere if it were properly presented. The precise issue soon became moot at Oklahoma; the university adopted a two-tiered system of computer access, under which faculty and certain authorized graduate students had unlimited access through the B network, and undergraduates and others had less extensive access through the A channel. Alt.sex[[au: ok?]] newsgroups became—and remain—available through the B network.

Sexually explicit material was to trigger the other major controversy—one that may pose the gravest threat to academic freedom of all those that have arisen in the Internet age. Conservative Virginia lawmakers crafted in early 1996 a bill that would prevent state employees from using state-owned or -leased computers to access sexually explicit material, at least without the approval of a "supervisor" in pursuit of a "bona fide agency-approved research project."[26] The General Assembly of Virginia, in enacting so sweeping a ban, apparently assumed that other states would soon follow suit, though none ever did so. A constitutional law professor warned the House committee that approved the bill that it could not impose such a ban any more than it could constitutionally "forbid a custodian in the capitol from bringing a personal copy of *Penthouse* or *Hustler* to read during a coffee break."[27] Yet the bill passed overwhelmingly, and the governor signed it into law. Virginia thus became the first and (after more than a decade) is still the only state to impose so draconian a restraint.

Because the law clearly applied to all professors at Virginia's fifteen state colleges and universities, they provided the potentially most promising plaintiffs for the inevitable federal court challenge. Eventually six public college teachers did come forward, incurring considerable risk because of the sweep of the law and its popularity. Each plaintiff asserted and described a valid research need to access material that might be deemed "sexually explicit," along with serious doubts about the feasibility of seeking or obtaining the requisite supervisory approval. These plaintiffs represented a range of disciplines and a variety of research interests—art, medicine, English, sociology, and, in the case of the lead plaintiff, political science.

Professor Melvin Urofsky, a long-tenured and highly esteemed teacher of government and public policy, declared that his own research and that of his students had been severely constrained by the broad sweep of the statute and its imprecise terms. The absence of any statutory definition of "sexually explicit material," most notably, left each professor to assess potential risk on his or her own; such vagueness would cause many prudent professors to steer well clear of the zone of potential danger. Only the University of Virginia was unrepresented among potential plaintiffs; Polley McClure, the vice president for information technology, essentially mooted their potential claims by granting blanket dispensation to each of the academic areas, deeming any professorial use of targeted material use to be a "bona fide agency-related research project."

When the matter reached federal court in Alexandria, the trial judge to whom the case was assigned could hardly have been more congenial to the faculty members' pleas. Judge Leonie Brinkema had spent a decade as a professional librarian before attending law school. She had recently invalidated on broad free speech grounds a Virginia county's mandate to filter all public access Internet terminals in the county libraries; she would later become much more renowned as the judge who presided at the trial of Zacarias Moussaoui, the putative twentieth September 11, 2001, hijacker.

Lawyers for the commonwealth now advanced in federal court two arguments in support of the law, justifying its application to professors along with all other public employees. First, they insisted, the state owned the computers in question and on that basis could set rules for their use as well as how state workers spent their time. Second, they claimed, the General Assembly had a valid interest in protecting the integrity of valuable and sensitive hardware from possibly damaging use or misuse.

Judge Brinkema made short shrift of both claims and resoundingly invalidated the law. In her view it was both over- and underinclusive at the same time, failing First Amendment tests at both ends of the spectrum. The ban was overbroad because it covered much material that surely posed no threat to any of the commonwealth's valid regulatory interests; nothing about sexually explicit material endangered the system or any of its components. The law seemed to her seriously underinclusive, as well; myriad other questionable uses of state-owned computers might equally divert time and attention from the business of the commonwealth but had been of no concern to the General Assembly. Nor could she perceive any logical basis for the blanket exemption of all law enforcement officers and not simply the officers whose vice assignments might merit such protection.

Finally, Judge Brinkema addressed the dispensation or waiver provision, which government lawyers claimed would adequately facilitate legitimate research needs. The key flaw that she found in that argument traced back to a 1965 Supreme Court case in which the justices had ruled that people who wished to continue receiving periodicals from Communist countries could not be forced to return a signed postcard expressing such a desire. Such a mandate would potentially impose an excessive price on the exercise of an undoubted First Amendment right to receive information that was entirely lawful, and it risked unduly chilling the free speech rights of many scholars and others. The fatal flaw that Judge Brinkema saw in the approval process was that it "placed unbridled discretion in the hands of state administrators"; the Supreme Court had struck down such delegation because [in Judge Brinkema's words] unfettered authority "can be expected to invite arbitrary enforcement and to chill the exercise of speech rights." "Indeed," she added, "the Act's requirement that approval decisions regarding sexually explicit materials be made public . . . suggests that this was in fact the purpose of the approval provision."[28]

That was exactly how Judge Brinkema viewed the exemption in the challenged law; for a scholar to be forced to appeal to a supervisor (whoever that might be in the academic hierarchy) and to detail his or her reasons for wishing to access sexually explicit material seemed to impose an unacceptable burden, made worse by the statutorily mandated public disclosure of any such requests that were granted. Moreover, she expressed serious doubts whether the restrictive language in the statute would even accomplish its apparent—and intellectually vital—purpose; there were many academically valid projects that a scientist or scholar might simply be unable to persuade a supervisor were demonstrably agency related.

Thus Judge Brinkema's ruling recognized far more than the frailties of an imprecise and casually crafted state statute. Central to her decision was a keen understanding of the basic academic freedom concerns that the six plaintiffs advanced—that professors are different from the general run of public employees, that their choice of research projects cannot be crudely constrained by state law, and that the very process of seeking official approval to pursue a chosen avenue of inquiry severely threatens academic freedom. That judgment was not, however, to prevail for long.

Actually the challenge facing the six professors in court was far graver than the newly victorious plaintiffs may have appreciated. The relish with which Judge Brinkema dispatched the Virginia statute may well have invited a false sense of confidence about the eventual outcome. In at least three respects, the preliminary ruling made this case seem considerably easier than it really was. For one, the statute had never been applied; no professor or other state employee could demonstrate any sanction applied or threatened for accessing sexually explicit material with state-owned computers. One of the plaintiffs had been admonished by a dean about some slightly risqué material he had posted on his webpage, but such activity was not covered by the statute and thus did not provide any evidence of its potential reach. Thus the challenge was purely speculative—genuine and sincere, beyond doubt, but conjectural in the absence of any actual application.

Second, what the plaintiffs were asserting was not a traditional right to speak, publish, or teach—these being familiarly protected forms of expression—but rather a right to access material that might contribute to the process of scholarship. There was, as noted earlier, a reputable basis in Supreme Court jurisprudence for a First Amendment claim of access to information, but that interest had never been fully developed and had not even been invoked in recent and possibly relevant rulings. Thus the plaintiffs had somehow to get from a right to speak to a right to receive information. For Judge Brinkema, with her decade of professional librarianship, making that leap was quite logical; for other judges who lacked her perspective and background, the analogy would be less obvious and more difficult.

A third sense in which the plaintiffs may have been unduly optimistic derived from the unavoidable impression of special pleading created by a lawsuit that had been brought solely by university professors, seeming (if only by implication) to demand uniquely favorable treatment for academics. Had nonprofessorial plaintiffs shared in the burden of taking this challenge to court, the possible stigma of seeking special treatment might have been diluted, although any possible claim of academic freedom would also have been diminished. The choice of plaintiffs thus represented a considered judgment, and one that may have altered the equation in the plaintiff's favor at least in the district court.

Although the challenged law of course applied to all Virginia state employees, in practice college professors were about the only ones who could mount a very appealing legal challenge; the claim that a custodian or prison guard or motor vehicle inspector needed to access sexually explicit material from the Internet during working hours would probably have given even Judge Brinkema more amusement than constitutional concern. Yet, at the same time, the risks of mounting such a distinctive case for professorial access were substantial. The dilemma facing those who planned the constitutional challenge was thus inescapably daunting: A nonfaculty -plaintiff test case would have been wholly ineffectual, yet a suit of the kind that was actually filed could be seen as yet another example of professors somehow placing themselves and their interests above the masses and seeking special favors. Judge Brinkema understood college professors and their research needs from her many years as a librarian; it was unlikely that most of her judicial colleagues would adopt nearly so benign a view of scholars and scholarship.

The case soon came before a far less sympathetic federal court of appeals, which sits in Richmond barely three blocks from the Capitol in which the statute had been enacted. On first hearing of the appeal, a panel of three judges reversed the district court ruling, disagreeing with Judge Brinkema at almost every turn and giving credence to the asserted state interests as well as the process by which the ban was implemented and could be dispensed. Had that been the end of the case, the Virginia academic community would have been dismayed, but life on the Old Dominion's campuses would have gone on. In fact, by this time the statute had been somewhat mitigated anyway; depictions must be "lascivious" before access to them could be barred, and they must constitute the "dominant theme" of the suspect material. Although the court case was still addressed to, and ruled only upon, the language of the original law, the practical constraints on Virginia public employees were already somewhat less onerous. Thus had the litigation ended with the panel ruling, adverse though it was, the worst potential would have been averted.

Another shoe, this one bearing spikes, was about to drop. The full court of appeals decided to hear the case—something that usually happens only when the panel that rendered the initial judgment expresses views out of line with the tribunal's majority. Here, however, it seemed obvious that the rehearing—en banc, as it is called—would simply reinforce the panel's conclusions and give their ruling far broader import. That is precisely what happened in the full appeals court. Simply sustaining such a law would have posed a serious threat to academic freedom, because comparably severe restrictions on the research of state university professors had seldom even been suggested, much less validated, by a prominent federal appeals court.

The prevailing opinion, expressing the views of seven of the twelve judges who ruled in the majority, was in fact devastating.[29] It not only equated the speech of state university professors to the expression of any other public worker but also went on to dilute substantially the scope of First Amendment protection for all government employees. Specifically, on-the-job speech deserved no special solicitude; public employees could speak freely outside the workplace but deserved no First Amendment protection in the performance of their assigned tasks.

The majority then turned to academic freedom, of which little remained intact when they concluded. For them, the answer to claims such as those of the professorial plaintiffs was simple: Academic freedom protects institutions not individuals. When disagreement or discord occurs, the institution—or the commonwealth if it is the source of the challenged policy—always prevails. This was a strikingly novel premise, for which the academic community was utterly unprepared—though in retrospect should have been anticipated. How the *Urofsky* majority reached such a startling conclusion deserves some elaboration.

After a lengthy review of the major cases that supported academic freedom claims, the court disavowed any constitutional basis for professorial activity or expression. Such claims were dismissed as a form of special pleading, leading to the outlandish notion that a professor might enjoy greater freedom than a capitol custodian. To the extent that case law might imply any special concern about teaching (which would be hard to overlook in the cited precedents), such apparent solicitude resulted from what this court now perceived as the accident that "teachers were the first public employees to be afforded the now universal protection against dismissal for the exercise of First Amendment rights." And to the degree that claims of academic freedom deserved any judicial deference at all, that was to protect the interests of the institution and not the individual; in the event of conflict between the two, the former would routinely prevail. Lest any doubt remain, "the [Supreme] Court has never recognized that professors possess a First Amendment right of academic freedom to determine for themselves the content of their courses and scholarship, despite opportunities to do so." So much for academic freedom; when everyone is on the same side, such claims might well prevail. But the moment there is discord, the institutional interest trumps and the individual loses.[30]

The concurring opinion of Chief Judge J. Harvie Wilkinson offered the only solace from the majority side of this ruling. He was the one judge on the panel who genuinely understood and appreciated the academic community and its quest for protection of free inquiry. Having clerked for Supreme Court Justice Lewis Powell, taught law at the University of Virginia and then served as a member of its governing board, Judge Wilkinson knew what professors did and why access to sometimes controversial sources and materials must be unfettered. Although he ended up agreeing with his conservative colleagues that the challenged law was valid—he found the asserted state interests to be substantial and their implementation acceptable—he departed dramatically from the majority view of academic freedom and higher education. The import of the prevailing opinion in this regard he found unseemly broad and deeply troubling: "By embracing the Commonwealth's view that all work-related speech by public employees is beyond public concern, the majority sanctions state legislative interference in public universities without limit."

Judge Wilkinson also perceived very differently the value of the relevant Supreme Court precedents—among which one of the principal rulings (the *Bakke* case on race-sensitive college admissions) had in fact been written by the justice for whom he had clerked a few years before the Court rendered it. Academic freedom was for him a special form of free expression; to which the Supreme Court had for wholly valid reasons given particular solicitude: "Democratic representatives may often choose to reject academic proposals, but rejection, not suppression, is the constitutionally tested course. . . . I offer no apology for believing, along with the Supreme Court, . . . in the significant contribution made to society by our colleges and universities." Moreover, as a special concern, the claimed "ownership" premise of the state's argument simply was not credible to Judge Wilkinson: "Virginia also owns the chairs on which plaintiffs sit and the desks at which they work . . . but the Commonwealth does not thereby 'own' their every thought and utterance."

Finally, Chief Judge Wilkinson was deeply troubled about the portent of his prevailing colleagues' view for the role of the Internet in academic research and scholarship. "As cyberspace expands," he observed, "webpages may provide more and faster access to information that will contribute to the understanding of social problems and ultimately to solutions for them. Insofar as state employees are concerned, the majority would allow the state to shut down this information resource at its whim. It is remarkable that Internet research with all its potential falls outside the majority's conception of public concern."[31]

This ruling by the full appeals court was not unanimous. Four judges dissented outright, though they were troubled far more by ways in which the prevailing opinion had diluted public-employee speech and less about the threat to academic freedom that centrally preoccupied Judge Wilkinson. For the four dissenters, Judge Brinkema had it right in the first place; the statute was both overinclusive and underinclusive, and its defense rested on asserted governmental interests that simply did not merit judicial deference. The United States Supreme Court was asked to review the case, but without explanation it declined to do so. Among factors that may have diminished the high Court's potential interest in the case was its uniqueness. Only Virginia had enacted such a law, and thus only the Fourth Circuit ever ruled on the validity of so severe a threat to academic freedom. Thus came to rest one of the most ominous chapters in the evolving history of academic freedom.

It may be worth asking, as a closing perspective on the issue of access, to what extent the *Urofsky* litigation has impaired the cause of academic freedom—and to what extent the resulting harm to faculty expression reflects the special nature of a new communication medium. There are at least two ominous conjectures that merit recognition. For one, the uniquely draconian restriction on accessing salacious material would not have been enacted in the first place without a growing sense that pornography and the like abounded on the Internet. Such a dim view of cyberspace was clearly the driving force behind enactment by the U.S. Congress, in the very same month as the General Assembly's action, of the Communications Decency Act and later of the Child Pornography Prevention Act, the Child Internet Protection Act, and several other measures aimed directly at Internet content.

Although some of these measures were eventually invalidated by a Supreme Court that was anxious to view this new medium in its best light, Internet content providers have not always prevailed in court, and the potential for further regulation persists. Quite simply, a law restricting the material that state employees could obtain and use would never even have been considered, much less adopted, had the perceived character of Internet content not been the catalyst for regulation. At least in that sense, academic freedom has suffered from the emergence of a new medium that in myriad other ways enhances scholarship.

The other blow to academic freedom came not from the legislature but from the courts. The uniquely hostile views expressed here by the prevailing opinion in the court of appeals went far beyond anything that needed to be said to sustain the challenged law—or for that matter was even pertinent to the central issue of a statute that limited the Internet access of all Virginia public workers alike. Yet the majority's judgment severely undermined basic principles of academic freedom as well as of public-employee speech. Although it is possible that so alarmingly negative a view was waiting in the wings, and it could conceivably have accompanied a rejection of faculty interests in a print-era case, there is surely some significance to their embodiment in the court's first Internet-access decision.

Earlier rulings from this unusually conservative appeals court had occasionally disappointed free speech and academic freedom advocates, though more because of the result than because of any sweeping disparagement of First Amendment claims. Indeed, in at least two contemporaneous public-employee speech cases, one of which actually involved an outspoken University of Maryland professor, this very court had seemed sympathetic to public workers' claims of free expression.[32] Thus the culprit does indeed seem (at least in part) to be the medium much more than the message or the messenger, giving added credence to the fear that academic freedom claims now face a new and daunting challenge in cyberspace.

Politics on the Internet has also created a host of new problems for the academic community. No less prestigious an institution than Princeton University was taken to task in the late 1990s by the American Civil Liberties Union (ACLU) for restricting students' use of the campus computer network to post partisan political messages. Negotiations between Princeton and the ACLU brought about a compromise under which student and faculty political postings were not barred so long the author avoided any inference of institutional sponsorship or endorsement.

The major challenge occurred, however, across the country at California State University–Northridge (CSUN), a rapidly growing comprehensive institution that serves the San Fernando Valley. Christopher Landers was a nontraditional undergraduate in his early thirties, deeply involved in Democratic politics. He had become especially active in supporting the state senate campaign of a friend, John Birke. On his university-based webpage, Landers posted a picture of the incumbent senator Cathie Wright, against whom Birke was running. The tableau opened as a standard head shot of the senator, but gradually morphed into a skull as audio commentary quoted statements that Wright had made in support of the tobacco industry (her acceptance of funds from which was a target of Birke's campaign). Senator Wright's staff soon learned of the evolving imagery and phoned the office of CSUN's president to demand its immediate removal—noting that California law flatly forbids any use of state property for partisan political purposes. The administration immediately complied, and the relevant section of Landers's webpage was down by the end of the day.

Landers was not deterred, however, and went immediately to California Superior Court, claiming that his freedom of speech had been abridged. A sympathetic superior court judge agreed, noting of the thirty-two-year-old plaintiff: "The kid was just engaging in politics, which he has every right to do." She added that such display of a student's political views seemed to her little different from affixing campaign stickers to a backpack worn to class or to the bumper of a car in the campus parking lot.

The university now faced an impossible dilemma. On the one hand, a state senator (who was almost certain to be reelected, as she soon was) had invoked state law to demand removal of the offending imagery. On the other hand, a state judge had ruled that the deletion of the webpage material was a clear violation of a student's free speech because it was clearly content-based and aimed at political expression. Such a novel challenge evoked creativity from the CSUN administration. First, it revised its computer access policy so as to limit student use of the network to "academic purposes and university business," a standard that would obviously exclude partisan political postings such as those that Landers had created and that had caused the problem.

Then the university's lawyers sought out a more seasoned superior court judge. The one before whom the case now emerged was David Horowitz, a senior colleague of the judge who had sided with Landers's free speech plea. Horowitz could hardly be seen as hostile to First Amendment interests; for years he had cochaired the American Bar Association's Conference Group of Lawyers and Media Representatives, the vehicle through which the organized national bar most vigorously pressed a series of free press and free speech initiatives, with Horowitz often as the spokesperson for the needs of the mass media. Horowitz now ruled that the university's revised policies were content neutral and could therefore be applied to Landers's webpage without abridging his freedom of speech.[33]

That judgment was never appealed and thus remains the final word in this intriguing episode. Senator Wright overwhelmingly won reelection and apparently sought no reprisal against the university. Yet troubling issues persist—notably whether by adopting a concededly content-neutral policy on acceptable use of the computing network a public university may effectively bar the use of an increasingly vital communications medium for political messages. For the moment, the academic community seems to have come to terms with this dilemma, typically by adopting policies similar to the one that got CSUN out of the acute bind in which Landers's politicking had placed it.

Student use of the Internet has posed several other daunting challenges for universities that respect free expression and, in the case of public institutions, are constrained by the First Amendment to protect it. Early in their freshman year, four male Cornell University students sent to a number of female fellow students a series of militantly sexist messages, including one that began, "Top 75 reasons why women (bitches) should not have freedom of speech."[34] The message contained some familiar, but nonetheless deeply offensive, gender-based jokes. There were also suggestions that women should be silenced to keep them from crying rape or saying no to requested sex, and they contained several references to forcing women to perform oral sex, while disparaging and mocking affirmative action, Oprah Winfrey, and feminists. When word of this posting became public, Internet users in Ithaca and well beyond the campus demanded some disciplinary action against the sexist freshmen; because their outrageous message had been signed, officials had no difficulty in identifying the offenders.

Cornell officials considered but eventually rejected imposing any formal sanction or penalty—not so much because of possible constitutional constraints but more because no existing student conduct policy seemed to cover such behavior. Instead, the administration devised a Solomonic solution, which appeared to satisfy almost everyone: the administration widely publicized the names of the offenders and the nature of their transgression, expecting (correctly) that public humiliation would be far more effective than any form of discipline. That assumption seems to have been sound; the four sexist freshmen were suitably chastened and apparently never heard from again.

A strikingly different incident occurred a year or two later at the University of California–Irvine, a campus with an unusually large Asian American enrollment. A Hispanic student sent individually addressed e-mail messages to some fifty-nine identifiably Asian students, citing their ethnicity with deep anger and hostility and threatening (among other menacing statements) to "kill every one of you personally." The e-mails came quickly to the attention of the United States attorney, who indicted the sender as the first person charged under a new federal law that for the first time specifically targeted Internet and electronic threats. A conviction soon resulted, and it was not appealed. The incarceration of the hateful message sender made moot any question about campus disciplinary action.[35]

One other incident brings us back to Virginia Tech, although on a matter quite different from the experience of Professor McCaughey. An undergraduate student managed to gain access to a supposedly secure chat room frequented by gay and lesbian students. Once in the chat room, the invader posted a virulently homophobic message, suggesting among other hateful statements that gay men "should be castrated and killed." Such an invasion of hitherto private electronic space not only frightened the regular users but also undermined the sense of security and comfort they had obtained from using this welcome and congenial site. After that experience, many of the gay and lesbian students feared they could no longer trust the site nor confidently confide their views to a group that might not be homogeneous.

Pressure was quickly brought to bear on the administration to discipline the homophobic invader, whose identity was readily ascertained by the administration. The problem was that no existing student conduct rules remotely covered such an offense. Had the invader physically barged into a closed meeting of a gay and lesbian group in the student union, existing policies would doubtless have prescribed a sanction. However, had the homophobic student simply posted his views on a campus kiosk or bulletin board or conveyed them in a letter to the daily campus newspaper, a state university would properly have treated such expression as protected by the First Amendment. The actual Virginia Tech case fell within an emerging but still imprecisely defined zone, somewhere between such familiar alternatives, with little guidance from print-era experience or policies. Virginia Tech eventually imposed minor discipline on the student for an unrelated charge, though neither the offender's identity nor the actual punishment was ever made public.[36]

A final and much later incident concludes this review. In the fall of 2005, the University of South Carolina was planning to build the first ever African American fraternity house in the long-established and traditionally white "Greek Village." Someone, perhaps but not necessarily a racist student, began posting offensively racist remarks about the plan on the university's computer system, strongly suggesting that the black fraternity was unwelcome in the Greek Village and that adverse consequences should be expected. The vice president for student affairs was not unprepared for a hostile reception but had not anticipated it would occur in digital form. When pressure came from several quarters for reprisal against those who had posted the hateful message, the administration concluded that such intervention would be unwise, even though the offenders could be identified. The vice president noted that "the Internet encourages people to do or say things they would not do in public," often in the false belief that such postings are anonymous. Yet the wiser course seemed to be to bring official pressure on the website operator and the heads of the white fraternities, as well as advance a university course aimed at teaching civility and tolerance. As at Cornell a decade earlier, formal sanctions were rejected in favor of an educational approach that seemed to be more consistent with the university's mission.[37]

The import of such experiences for academic freedom seems clear if not immediately obvious. First, if existing policies do not cover a transgression—however hateful and reprehensible the message may be—a public college or university has no business adapting to the situation a rule or regulation that simply does not fit, however intense may be pressure for some sanction or punishment and even though one who acted in a similar fashion through a print medium might well incur some penalty. Second, the crafting of new policies to address those transgressions or challenges that merit institutional reprisal or discipline is long overdue. When a university is actually in court or about to be taken to court—CSUN and Princeton on politics, or Oklahoma on alt.sex newsgroups, for example—the policy makers go into high gear. Lacking such an urgent catalyst, the process has been remarkably slow and cumbersome. Given the range and variety of well-publicized challenges such as those recounted here, one would expect to find today an abundance of responsive policies specifically aimed at digital discourse. Whether the catalyst is homophobic invasion of a secure chat room, or direct threats to Asian American students, or any of the myriad other potential challenges, any university that seeks to anticipate the next wave of creative student testing of its authority should have on its books some rule covering student activity and expression that does not merit constitutional protection.

Finally, institutions of higher learning must always indulge a strong presumption in favor of tolerating even the most offensive and troubling speech. Education is vastly preferable to regulation, quite as much in cyberspace as in more familiar physical space. Even where a conduct or disciplinary rule already on the books might seem to justify imposing a sanction, every effort should be made to educate rather than to regulate. That is, after all, what universities are charged to do and what they do best. Education is, in the end, the central justification for deference to academic freedom by those outside the university community. The point was forcefully stated by Justin Williams, the president of student government at the University of South Carolina, who happens to be African American and was thus troubled by the fraternity incident. In praising the administration's restraint after the racist postings about the black fraternity, Williams insisted that "just because a few people put some provocative things on the Internet, the university [should not] try to block sites or lock down their server. It's the university's job to educate, not legislate morality." Concluding the interview, Williams reflected: "This has been part of the university experience, a learning experience for students of all races."[38] All members of the academic community—especially those charged with nurturing new and unfamiliar communications media—would be well advised to take this young man's counsel to heart.

8

Whose Academic Freedom?

Professor Robert A. Brown had taught for nearly thirty years at California University of Pennsylvania and had held tenure for much of that period. In the fall of 1994, he gave an "F" to one of his graduate students in a practicum, who had attended only three of fifteen class sessions. The student appealed to the university's president, Angelo Armenti, who promptly ordered Professor Brown to change the failing grade to "incomplete." Brown refused this decree, insisting that grading was an inviolable faculty prerogative. Soon thereafter, he was suspended from teaching in his area of expertise and then became the subject of a critical review prepared for the board of trustees. Two years later the university formally terminated his teaching position. Brown filed suit in federal court, alleging several violations of his federally protected constitutional rights. When the district judge refused to dismiss the suit, ruling that Brown had stated a valid legal claim, the university appealed to what proved to be a far more sympathetic federal circuit court. The Third Circuit Court of Appeals reversed and directed the trial judge to dismiss the case.

The appeals court drew a sharp distinction between a professor's speech in the classroom and elsewhere, ruling that only extracurricular expression was now protected by academic freedom.[1] What happened in the classroom, in contrast, was the university's to control. That included the selection of curricular materials—a matter of which the same court had ruled adversely to a professor's claim several years earlier[2]—and now extended also to assessment of student performance. When it came to grading, the distinction seemed clear: "Because grading is pedagogic, the assignment of a grade is subsumed under the university's freedom to determine how a course is taught." This declaration was as novel as it was frightening—novel because a decade earlier a different federal appeals court had reached precisely the opposite conclusion in one of the few disputed grading cases,[3] and frightening because if appraising a student's performance was no longer a professorial prerogative, it was unclear whether academic freedom protected anything that happened in the classroom. Perhaps the most troubling feature of the Brown case was the way the court characterized the institutional interest to which it deferred— "the university's *freedom* to determine how a course is to be taught." The clear implication of such a statement is that any authority the university exercises in such a disputed area comes at the expense of the professor who would traditionally have acted. Thus, this court's declaration that the institution may compel a professor to change a student's grade clearly preempts a major exercise of academic freedom. Such a ruling also shifts a historically professorial task into administrative hands.

Perhaps those in the academic community who found the Brown decision alarming were simply naïve, or had been inattentive. The precise issue had seldom arisen in prior cases, where most institutional claims of academic freedom were either wholly consistent with, or actually advanced on behalf of, the interest of their faculties. The possibility that institutional and individual interests could diverge, or could even be diametrically opposed, never entered the equation. Yet close observers of the evolving doctrine of academic freedom might have detected ominous warning signs, anticipating the day when courts would have to adjudicate disagreements between institutions and their faculties who both claimed academic freedom protection under conditions where both could not possibly prevail. It would be useful to review the development of the legal context to understand better the basis for the Brown court's ruling and its implications.

Most court cases that recognize academic freedom claims entail little if any doubt whose rights are at stake. The interests of the university and of its faculty are typically so clearly concurrent that they are simply equated, even when the case implicates only the institution's rights or those of its professors. Thus, when the Supreme Court recognized an academic freedom rationale for the inclusive use of race in admitting students to highly competitive graduate programs, Justice Lewis Powell confidently invoked the freedom of a university "to determine for itself on academic grounds . . . who may be taught" among the constitutionally protected prerogatives of an institution of higher learning.[4] The central premise of that statement was an appreciation of the institution's role in safeguarding or protecting from a court's contrary judgment the highly sensitive academic process of shaping the criteria for admission and applying those criteria in the actual acceptance and rejection of applicants. Whether it was professors or their university who asserted that interest seemed almost irrelevant, and it surely had no impact on the outcome.

When the high Court revisited the issue of race-based admissions a quarter century later, the same convergence of interests shaped the outcome. Justice Sandra Day O'Connor, who had in the interim assumed Justice Powell's centrist role, sustained the University of Michigan Law School's inclusive use of race, invoking "the important purpose of public education and the expansive freedoms of speech and thought associated with the university environment." In the view of the majority for whom she spoke, the university had shown "a compelling interest in a diverse student body . . . [which is] at the heart of the law school's proper institutional mission."[5] This forceful declaration, notes Georgetown law professor and academic freedom expert Peter Byrne, "represents the most important victory to date for institutional academic freedom."[6] Moreover, it represents a classic situation in which the university speaks concurrently for its own interests and those of its faculty, and a sympathetic court recognizes both, without any suggestion of tension or adversity between those two sets of interests. Everyone, in short, is on the same page, making it unnecessary even to delineate the relevant claims.

In such cases, there is seldom any occasion to probe possible dissonance among relevant legal interests, much less to prioritize or rank them. The typical case presents a unified academic community, where the interests of the student, professor, and institution converge in opposition or resistance to some external threat. That comfortable consensus has, however, begun to fray in recent years. When the parties are not all on the same page, as they clearly were not in the grading dispute cases, courts face the unfamiliar and acutely uncomfortable task of choosing among competing or contending claims. Increasingly, judges have begun to have to assess priorities among such adverse interests, at times even adjudicating between opposing claims that assert equal levels of protection under the rubric of academic freedom. Yet if the parties take opposing positions in court, clearly one such claim must eventually trump the other. This chapter focuses on these types of situations and the implications of judicial resolution for the current status of academic freedom.

Long before the recent round of admissions cases, the Supreme Court had begun to hint that legally protected interests within the academic community could diverge in unusual situations. Since 1971, the Minnesota Public Employment Labor Relations Act authorized government workers to engage in collective bargaining with their employers. A specific provision obligated the relevant agency to "meet and confer" with union representatives on matters relevant to the agreement and its administration. When it came to community college faculty, who had been organized for some time in Minnesota, the law required the system's trustees to "meet and confer" with the faculty on educational policy matters. The statute also forbade any appearance before the board by instructors other than those representing the certified faculty union. Thus nonunion faculty members were effectively denied any chance to appear before or present their views to the board. That ban was challenged in a case that eventually reached the Supreme Court. Justice O'Connor wrote for the majority, upholding the Minnesota law and its application, noting along the way that excluded community college instructors were no worse off than they would have been had the "meet and confer" mandate never been enacted.

The high Court's analysis of academic freedom issues went well beyond what was needed to dispose of this relatively minor and technical dispute. After recognizing a "strong, if not universal or uniform, tradition of faculty participation in school governance," Justice O'Connor warned against excessive reliance on that tradition. "This Court," she cautioned, "has never recognized a constitutional right of faculty to participate in policymaking in academic institutions." Then, lest one miss the force of her warning, she added: "Even assuming that speech rights guaranteed by the First Amendment take on a special meaning in the academic setting . . . there is no constitutional right to participate in academic governance."[7]

That the same Justice O'Connor would nearly two decades later embrace with such enthusiasm the University of Michigan's academic freedom claim in the race-based admissions context suggests an important distinction: When the institution asserts an academic freedom claim on behalf of its faculty, and all parties are on the same page, resolution is relatively simple. But when the interests of faculty, on the one hand, and the administration or governing board, on the other, come into conflict, as they apparently did in the Minnesota community college case, such a conclusion may not follow. Interestingly, Justice Powell dissented in the Minnesota "meet and confer" case, arguing (along with Justices William Brennan and John Paul Stevens) that professorial academic freedom may not be confined to the classroom but should also encompass "freedom of faculty members to express their views to the administration concerning matters of academic governance."[8] Specifically, they insisted that the

Minnesota law posed a constitutionally unacceptable dilemma; it effectively compelled community college teachers to choose between their right to express to administrators their views on academic governance matters and the right to be free of compelled association with positions or views they might find abhorrent. Even these dissenters recognized, however, that when academic freedom claims collide rather than converge, the case becomes far more complex and harder to resolve than the simpler case of congruent interests.

The very next year, the Supreme Court recognized the emergence of such inevitable tensions in a different way. The case involved the reinstatement claim of a University of Michigan student named Scott Ewing, who challenged the medical school faculty's decision to bar him from taking the National Board examinations. The outcome of the case and the Court's degree of deference to faculty judgment on such matters are discussed in Chapter 3. Suffice it to say here that the Court gave almost total deference to faculty judgment on an assessment of academic progress, barely noting the potential force of the student's contrary claim. For the moment, what is notable about the Ewing case is the Court's recognition that "Academic Freedom thrives not only on the independent and uninhibited exchange of ideas among teachers and students, but also, and somewhat inconsistently, on autonomous decisionmaking by the academy itself."[9] This rather cryptic reference to the inherent tension between institutional and individual interests could not have been inadvertent, though it is far from clear just what purpose it was meant to serve. Catholic University professor and higher education law expert William Kaplin notes in a comment that the juxtaposition of such interests need not "entail a separation of the institution's interests from those of its faculty members, nor does it suggest that institutional interests must prevail over faculty interests if the two are in conflict."[10]

So sanguine a view of Ewing's "somewhat inconsistently" reference accurately reflects both the faculty-deferential outcome of the actual case and the apparent convergence of professorial and institutional interests as the dispute reached the high Court. Indeed, it is from this very opinion in Ewing that courts derive the most widely invoked standard of deference that guides and limits judicial scrutiny of academic judgments: "When judges are asked to review the substance of a genuinely academic decision, such as this one, they should show great respect for the faculty's professional judgment. Plainly, they may not override it unless it is such a substantial departure from accepted academic norms as to demonstrate that the person or committee responsible did not actually exercise professional judgment."[11] It would be hard to imagine a more sympathetic standard to guide and limit judicial intervention into academic matters; courts are required to accept the action of an institution of higher learning on any matter that might be challenged in court, unless there is clear evidence of complete abdication or of egregious misapplication or disregard of accepted academic norms.

In the same year as the Ewing case, Judge Richard Posner of the Chicago-based Court of Appeals for the Seventh Circuit drew upon his many years of teaching law to recognize, with characteristic sagacity, the now unavoidable tensions among conflicting academic interests. The case, appropriately enough, pitted a professor, the plaintiff, against a college, the defendant. The issue in dispute was whether a downstate Illinois community college had abridged an art professor's rights by relegating to a remote gallery area the professor's works, several of which struck campus visitors as potentially offensive or demeaning on racial grounds. The case was complicated by the fact that the aggrieved artist, Albert Piarowski, also chaired the college's art department and thus supervised campus display sites.

Judge Posner and his court resolved this dispute in favor of the college—partly because its apprehension of adverse or hostile community reaction was both reasonable and sincere and partly because relocation of a controversial exhibit seemed far less drastic a sanction than removal or prohibition. But Judge Posner recognized more explicitly than others had done that conflicts among contending academic freedom claims could no longer be avoided. Thus he noted the "equivocal" nature of this concept in such a dispute, the term being used both to "denote the freedom of the academy to pursue its ends without interference from government" and "the freedom of the individual teacher (or in some versions . . . the student) to pursue his ends without interference from the academy." The opinion then recognized a new challenge that other judges had either failed to appreciate or had avoided, as Judge Posner observed that "these two freedoms are in conflict . . . in this case."[12]

Yet there seemed neither the need to establish any priority among such contending interests, at least where the college had acted from so laudable a goal as to avoid offending the African American community and had gone an extra mile by providing alternative (albeit less desirable) display space for the suspect exhibit. We are properly grateful to Judge Posner for having posed the issue by recognizing the "equivocal" nature of a conflict between two sets of interests—one individual and the other institutional—where both could fairly be labeled "academic freedom." One of those interests must eventually prevail, and the other must yield, perforce, when such a dispute comes to court. That much we appreciate Judge Posner having told us—which is considerably more than most other courts have said on the subject, even when the tension has been palpable. What Judge Posner did not provide, and what we must now seek, is a path toward resolution of such inevitable and perplexing conflicts.

Cases like that of Piarowski arise from disputes between professors and their universities, to which we turn first, reserving until later the equally problematic tensions between students and institutions. Perhaps the simplest, most familiar starting point is the assignment of a teaching area or subject. What a teacher is hired and assigned to teach—whether junior college instructor or tenured senior university professor—is of course determined by the institution, typically through a department chair or professional school dean. Thus if a person who has been recruited and assigned to teach electrical engineering returns from a European vacation with a passionate desire to teach French history or Greek philosophy, such a wish might materialize through continuing or adult education but clearly not at the expense of regularly assigned engineering courses. Even the most ardent champion of academic freedom has not yet seriously argued for such a right of professorial self-determination.

It is not merely the general subject area that is the prerogative of the university's academic administration to assign. If an instructor teaches one or two sections in a multi-section introductory course, he or she may be expected to adhere to a common syllabus and to a timetable that not only ensures the uniform completion of the subject matter but also facilitates the occasional transfer of a student from one section to another. Indeed, there is ample consensus that, even in single-section courses, a college professor should stick fairly close to the script (usually a syllabus of the instructor's own design, though reflecting the stated goals and scope of the course). Thus in its most basic document, the "1940 Statement of Principles," the American Association of University Professors (AAUP) insists that although "teachers are entitled to freedom in the classroom in discussing their subject," it is equally clear that "they should be careful not to introduce into their teaching controversial matter which has no relation to their subject." A later clarification explains that the intent of the cautionary phrase was not to discourage controversy in the classroom, but rather to "underscore the need for teachers to avoid persistently intruding material which has no relation to their subject."[13]

Thus there seems little doubt that a college teacher is expected to instruct and guide students in the assigned subject—to offer the course for which he or she was recruited and is compensated. Such an obligation does not, however, mean that a professor may never stray from the syllabus or must eschew all controversy. Classically, those whose college classes met on the afternoon of September 11, 2001, or the next morning, could hardly have been faulted for departing from schedule and topic to share a sense of dismay and anxiety. Indeed, for a professor in any field to have insisted on business as usual amid such anguish and turmoil would seem evidence of extreme insensitivity at a moment of national tragedy.

Beyond such easy generalities, the analysis quickly becomes more difficult. Consider, for example, the case of Professor Phillip Bishop, whose religious convictions entered his teaching of physical education at the University of Alabama in ways that would land him and his academic superiors in protracted federal litigation. In most respects, Bishop fully met the expectations of a teacher of exercise physiology, his assigned specialty. But he would occasionally inject a comment or two that reflected his personal and deeply held religious values.

More than once he took a few minutes of class time to assure his students that he modeled his life after that of Jesus Christ. He then invited the class to "please let me know . . . if you observe something in my life inconsistent with Christianity." He also offered to students who were interested an optional, noncredit after-class study session titled "Evidences of God in Human Physiology"—reflecting a view occasionally expressed in class that the marvels of the human physique and its performance reveal a "creative force behind human physiology."

When the dean learned of these comments, he sent Professor Bishop a cautionary letter—on the one hand, reaffirming the university's commitment to academic freedom but, on the hand, also warning that injecting religious beliefs into the classroom and offering an optional course that advanced the "Christian Perspective" were "unwarranted at a public institution" and "should cease." The dean added his special concern that tolerating such comments from a professor in the Southeast could jeopardize the university's reputation, especially among colleagues around the country who "consider [Alabama] the Bible Belt."

Bishop initially asked that this cautionary communication be withdrawn. When the dean stood his ground and refused to rescind the letter or its warning, Bishop filed suit in federal court, claiming an abridgment of his free speech, religious liberty, and academic freedom. The trial judge ruled decisively in Bishop's favor, barring the university from deterring the targeted expression as long as students were assured of fair evaluation through a blind grading system. The judge noted that Bishop's comments had never disrupted or interfered with his otherwise exemplary teaching; in the court's view, faculty members are at liberty to divulge personal views in the classroom as long as they are not disruptive of classroom activities. The district judge added that the university could not reasonably claim it had to intervene to avoid an attribution of Bishop's views to the institution—an apparently disparaging reference to the "Bible Belt" remark.

When the case reached the court of appeals, about the only commonality with the trial court was a shared appreciation of the novelty of the conflict that lay at the heart of the dispute. The appellate judges saw the case very differently in almost all respects, and they enthusiastically sustained the administration's position. Because "a teacher's speech can be taken as directly and deliberately representative of the school," the university "necessarily has dominion over what is taught by its professors." Specifically, "the University's conclusions about course content must be allowed to hold sway over an individual professor's judgment." The appeals court also deferred to the university's conviction that it had a constitutional duty to make certain that religion was kept out of its classrooms, especially where there seemed any possible risk of professorial coercion of impressionable students. Such a risk did present itself in Bishop's classes, the court concluded.[14]

The *Bishop* case was in fact substantially more complex than either of the two courts appreciated. It offers a valuable vehicle for assessing curricular conflicts between an institution and individual professor. The mere presence of a professor and an administration in a federal courtroom, disputing their respective claims to shape the curriculum, was novel enough to merit close scrutiny. But there was more to complicate the equation in this particular case. Bishop never engaged in religious proselytizing in the classroom or, as far as the record discloses, even in extracurricular contact with his own students. Had he actively proselytized, administrative intervention would have been not only permissible but compelled to protect potentially vulnerable students. Furthermore, Bishop could not be faulted for persistently intruding into his classes "material unrelated to the subject;" on the contrary, he insisted that divine guidance was essential to understanding the mysteries and marvels of human physiology. Thus on the immediate issue before the court, the district judge's ruling in Bishop's favor seems far closer to accepted principles of free expression and inquiry.

The deeper issue of the *Bishop* case—how academic freedom should balance professorial speech against plausible institutional needs to protect students—was novel at the time and has barely been adjudicated since then. Presumably as a matter of academic "common law," a university professor may mention a personal religious affiliation, in or outside class, as long as such a reference implies no intent to influence students in matters of faith. Indeed, some teachers of religion insist that an instructor's failure to reveal a personal faith (or lack of it) unfairly keeps students in the dark about a matter central to the subject. Occasional attention to the nexus between religion and the subject matter of the course may also be permissible, in moderation—for example, Bishop's occasional mention of a possible role for divine guidance in explaining "the miracle of human physiology."

However, explicit proselytizing on behalf of or expression of hostility toward religious views and values seems wholly unacceptable. Even subtler expressions of belief could raise valid institutional concerns. Thus, persistent religious references, or even subtly attempting to influence or shape the religious views of students, might well cross this elusive line. Using university facilities or communications media for religious purposes may also be inappropriate—for example, the deeply religious professor who convenes faith-focused events in his or her faculty office or seminar room. Equally improper would be any professorial inquiry into a student's religious faith or affiliation or lack thereof. Even more clearly, any comment that demeans or disparages any religious faith—whether or not that faith is represented in the classroom at the time—seems a cause for institutional concern and, if repeated, may well warrant some sanction.

A state university's potential interest in curbing a faculty member's religious speech also deserves more attention than the *Bishop* courts gave it. The University of Alabama's claim that it had rebuked Bishop in order to avoid the obloquy and disdain of colleagues outside the Bible Belt offers at best a tenuous basis for curbing professorial speech. A basic premise of academic freedom is that concerns about the institution's image or reputation may not trump a professor's freedom of speech or inquiry—however superficially persuasive may be the claim that, by its inaction or seeming indifference, the university may appear to be condoning racism, or homophobia, or anti-Semitism, or other abhorrent views. An understandable desire to appear enlightened (or at least not benighted) within the academic community falls far short of what is required to suppress or constrain professorial expression. That part of the Alabama rationale was properly rejected by the district judge, and it never resurfaced in the appeals court.

However, protecting students from possible coercion, or even perceived professorial pressure, in matters of faith is an interest of the highest order. The relationship between professor and student is never one of equality (nor should it be); rather it is a situation in which the student is not only subordinate but also specifically at the instructor's mercy in matters of grading, graduate school and job recommendations, and the like. Thus the institution has not only authority but also responsibility to protect its students from exploitation, abuse, and harassment, even in subtle forms. That interest is fully recognized by policies of the AAUP and other faculty groups, even if the effect of such recognition may serve to elevate institutional authority at that moment over professorial expression.

Curiously, this institutional interest received the least attention from the federal courts in Alabama, though it should have been paramount. The risks of such pressure are undoubtedly far greater in the realm of religion than elsewhere; it would require much stronger evidence of alleged political pressure or inducement (or disparagement) to cross this line than would be needed with regard to religious views and beliefs. To that extent, then, the University of Alabama seems to have been on strong ground in believing that Bishop should at least be admonished.

There remains the question of how a properly concerned institution may intervene when it learns of such faculty transgressions. Here the truth seems to lie somewhere between the district court's complete vindication of Professor Bishop and the appeals court's equally firm validation of the university's sanctions. Surely the appeals court was unduly deferential to the administration in declaring that a university may issue such a decree as Alabama did because it "necessarily has dominion over what is taught by its professors."

Where the perceived transgression gives no warrant for dismissal or major sanction, a somewhat more restrained approach not only seems more appropriate, but it should also be adequate to meet institutional imperatives. Although informal admonition had apparently been tried without much success in Bishop's situation, the administration might have been expected to continue seeking less drastic solutions before issuing so stern a formal warning. Greater efforts might have been taken to protect students from possible coercion or untoward pressure without constraining so severely the professor's arguably protected speech. For that matter, a deeper inquiry might have established the degree to which Bishop's remarks had in fact unsettled students other than the few who formally complained. But given the appeals court's totally deferential standard, no such efforts were deemed necessary. Because the issues posed by the *Bishop* case seem not to have returned to the courts to date, this decision remains the last word on a most complex and troubling issue.[15]

In the testing of wills between an institution and individual professor, as we noted at the start of this chapter the matter of grading was bound to emerge as contentious. Most university teachers complete their entire careers without ever facing major conflict over a grade, save perhaps from the occasional dissatisfied student who claims that papers or exams or laboratory work have not been fairly appraised. In extreme circumstances, however, a dispute between a student and teacher may reach the administration, and if a dean takes the student's side, there is bound to be trouble. A dean or other senior administrator may, in extremis, decide to alter the grade in the student's favor, though doing so (especially in the electronic age) may turn out to be more difficult than nonacademics would suppose. Indeed, even if the instructor himself or herself wishes to change a grade (for no more substantive reason than to correct a technical error or oversight), the process for alteration is properly complex and difficult; for anyone other than the instructor (even the dean) to make such a change may be impossible.

Given such appropriate safeguards, the dean who supports the student's plea is more likely to direct the professor to make the change. When the person who entered the grade refuses to change it, the makings of a contentious court battle are readily apparent. Although such disputes have been litigated only a few times, the resulting judgments are among the most telling of academic-freedom-related dispositions. One such case involving an engineering professor named Natthu Parate, a native of India whose specialty was civil engineering, reached the federal courts in Tennessee in the late 1980s. During the fall semester of his first year of full-time teaching, in a course on groundwater and seepage, Parate gave a low grade to a student who had not only cheated on an exam but also had presented a falsified medical excuse. The student appealed to the dean, who directed Parate to change his grade and that of another student in the same course. Although Parate reluctantly acceded to this demand, he made clear the basis for resistance. Three years later, after repeated run-ins with the engineering administration, and threats about the future of his faculty appointment, Parate filed suit in federal court. The actions for which he had been chastised, claimed Parate, were constitutionally protected. Specifically, he argued that the decision whether or not to alter a grade went to the heart of a professor's academic freedom.

Although the trial judge dismissed the suit, the federal appeals court fully sustained Parate's claim, noting that a course grade is a form of "communication . . . virtually indistinguishable from the message communicated by a formal written evaluation" of the student's performance and is thus clearly protected under concepts of academic freedom. Specifically, ruled the higher court, "the freedom of the university professor to assign grades according to his own professional judgment is . . . central to the professor's teaching method." Resolving the dispute in the actual case, the court concluded that ordering a professor to alter a grade infringed upon "protected speech" and "would severely burden a protected activity." The court distinguished the situation in which the administration simply went in to alter the grade on its own; what crossed the line in Parate's case was compelling speech by a professor in a way that "precluded him from communicating his personal evaluation of" the student in question.[16] Such a ruling gave important primacy to the individual claim against the asserted institutional interest.

There matters remained for at least a decade. When the grading issue returned to court in the late 1990s, the climate had changed markedly. Two cases from Pennsylvania substantially reshaped the individual-institution dynamic. The first of the cases (both of which involved California University of Pennsylvania) dealt with Professor Dilawar Edwards's contested choice of teaching materials. For a course entitled "Educational Tests and Measurement" Edwards had chosen materials to which a few students objected, and which the department chair eventually vetoed. Edwards then went to court, claiming a violation of his freedom of expression. The case was tried before a jury, which found in favor of the administrators whom Edwards had sued. He then appealed, hoping for the same relief Parate had found in a higher court. His experience at the appellate level was to be starkly different.

In an opinion written by then judge (now Supreme Court justice) Samuel Alito, this court cited precedent to the effect that "a public university professor does not have a First Amendment right to decide what will be taught in the classroom," and then extended that authority from the undisputed realm of assigning courses to the far more sensitive matter of "choos[ing] curriculum materials in contravention of the University's dictates." Somewhat ironically, the court invoked several recent U.S. Supreme Court rulings, including those noted earlier that recognized academic freedom as an institutional interest broadly protected when threatened by external interference.[17] The Third Circuit appeals court also relied upon a very recent Supreme Court decision that had sustained a state university's authority to allocate mandatory student fees in ways that some fee-paying students found objectionable. Although that case in no way implicated the faculty-institution dynamic that was central to Professor Edwards's case, Judge Alito drew from it an adequate basis for judicial deference to institutional judgment to override, albeit in a very different setting, professorial discretion in the choice of teaching materials.

It was against the very same university that Professor Robert Brown reopened the very issue that seemed to have been settled in the teacher's favor by the *Parate* case. Brown, like Parate, had been ordered by the institution's president to change a failing grade to "incomplete," but he declined to do so. When he was suspended from all teaching for his intransigence, he brought suit in federal court, claiming deprivation of academic freedom and free speech. This court, however, was as strongly inclined to the institution's position as the *Parate* court had been to the professor's claim. Relying heavily on Judge Alito's recent opinion in the *Edwards* case, the appeals court now ruled in the university's favor and thereby created one of the broadest and most ominous precedents favoring institutional interests against those of the individual teacher.

The critical distinction in the *Brown* court's view of academic freedom was between speech that occurred inside the classroom and speech that occurred anywhere else. What happened in the classroom was the institution's to govern, with academic freedom protecting only extracurricular speech. Thus, said the court in rejecting Brown's plea, "because grading is pedagogic, the assignment of a grade is subsumed under the university's freedom to determine how a course is to be taught."[18] This declaration was as novel as it was frightening. This court drew a startling analogy between a university's right to insist that its faculty teach the assigned subject and the institution's authority to control the grading process—totally rejecting the *Parate* court's very different analogy between a professor's prerogative to shape course content and to evaluate student performance in that course.

Even more ominous was the way the *Brown* court characterized the institutional interest to which it deferred—"the university's freedom to determine how a course is to be taught." Without even recognizing the zero-sum equation that such a formulation implies—whatever the institution gains in this regard must come at the professor's expense—this court simply rejected Professor Brown's academic freedom claim by deferring completely to the asserted institutional dominion over everything that happens in the classroom. It was almost as though conflict between a teacher and an institution could not be tolerated, or at least not recognized.

The Third Circuit's reasoning could be summarized thus: if the university has inherent authority to assign courses in the first place (as all would concede), it may then exercise that authority not only to control the selection of course materials, as the *Edwards* court had ruled, but also ultimately to compel a professor to change a grade at the behest of an individual student, as the *Brown* judgment held. That such results reflect minimally, if at all, the Supreme Court's far more balanced view of institutional versus individual academic freedom hardly troubled the appeals court in the *Edwards* and *Brown* cases. And there is no indication (other than Justice Alito's earlier views) how the high Court would resolve such tensions; despite efforts to attract the attention of the justices, no such cases have been reviewed, leaving effectively final the widely varying (indeed irreconcilable) views of the lower federal courts.

The worst had yet to come. In the mid-1990s, the Virginia General Assembly enacted a ban on the use by state employees of state-owned or -leased computers to access sexually explicit material. The law did empower "agency heads" to grant exemptions for a "bona fide agency-approved research project." There was no doubt that the law was intended to apply to all professors at Virginia public colleges and universities. Though at least one institution, the University of Virginia, granted blanket exemptions to its faculty on the presumption that any proscribed computer use would entail bona fide research, scholars at the other campuses chafed under the law. Six of them, led by Virginia Commonwealth political scientist Melvin Urofsky, brought suit in federal court, the disposition of which is recounted more fully in Chapter 7. They claimed that the statutory ban made it risky if not illegal for them to access materials that might contain images that an officer might deem sexually explicit but would enhance valid research in art, medicine, anthropology, or a host of other academic disciplines. They also argued that compelling them to seek an exemption on bona fide research grounds before each computer search imposed an intolerable burden and risked stigmatizing the scholar (because all such exemptions were a matter of public record).

The district judge, who had been a professional librarian for a decade before attending law school, ruled in the professors' favor on virtually all issues and declared the law a clear violation of free speech and academic freedom.[19] The case then went to the Court of Appeals for the Fourth Circuit—one that had not weighed in on the grading issue or related academic matters. After a panel ruling that reversed the trial court's judgment and sustained the statute, the full appeals court heard the case. What was striking was not so much the outcome—upholding the Virginia law against important free speech claims—but rather the majority's insistence that academic freedom claims availed only the institution and not the individual professor, at least when their respective positions were not in accord. Chief Judge J. Harvie Wilkinson, who had been a law professor and later a member of the governing board at the University of Virginia, agreed with his colleagues that the law was valid, but he sharply disagreed with the approach his conservative colleagues took to the academic freedom issue.

What should concern us most about the Fourth Circuit's unprecedented ruling is the resolution of the unavoidable tension between the individual and the institution. Whatever remained of academic freedom after this court's deeply disparaging disposition of that basic issue clearly inured to the institution's benefit in the event of any conflict between a university and its professors: "to the extent that the Constitution recognizes any right of 'academic freedom' above and beyond the First Amendment rights to which every citizen is entitled, the right inheres in the University, not in individual professors."[20] Thus a professor might assert an academic freedom claim in a case where, like those involving academic sanctions or race-based admissions, everyone is on the same side. A judgment in the individual's favor might seem to recognize that person's individual interests. But such a view inexplicably now found no favor whatever with the Fourth Circuit, for whose majority academic freedom became an interest that might prevail if and to the extent a university board or administration asserted it, but it could never protect an individual at odds with the institution.

In the absence of any relevant recent Supreme Court rulings—the justices have been asked to review several of these cases but consistently have declined to do so—the lower courts have been left almost entirely on their own. The Sixth Circuit, which had ruled so strongly in Professor Parate's favor in the grading dispute, has adhered to its sympathetic view of individual claims. A Kentucky community college instructor was denied reappointment after he invited his class to suggest words that were often used by dominant groups to oppress marginalized groups—and the students not surprisingly mentioned epithets like "nigger" and "bitch." The court of appeals concluded that the college might be able to prove that non-speech concerns warranted the negative judgment.

As a matter of free speech and academic freedom, however, the appeals court made clear that termination of a faculty appointment could not be based upon the instructor's use of an admittedly controversial teaching style. Such a basis for negative judgment would improperly outweigh the teacher's pedagogically justified sanction of offensive language to enliven class discussion. Similar disputes between an individual and institution have not arisen often enough in other federal courts to permit generalization.[21]

One critical dimension of "whose academic freedom?" that remains largely unresolved is that of direct disputes between students and their professors. The grading cases provided a glimpse into such issues; technically the legal contest was between professor/grader and institution/grade changer, although the aggrieved and poorly graded student was almost certainly the real party in interest. Now, however, our focus shifts to several recent cases in which student and teacher directly faced one another in court, and the institution (although formally a party to the litigation) was really a bystander.

Christina Axson-Flynn, an aspiring actress, applied for admission to the University of Utah's Actor Training Program (ATP). The program had been remarkably successful in placing its graduates; for a Utahan seeking entrée to Broadway or Hollywood, this was really the only game in town—or at least by far the best game. Axson-Flynn was readily accepted and began her studies with high expectations. A problem soon emerged, however. Because she was a devout Mormon, Axson-Flynn found the recital of certain profane words and the playing of certain parts in assigned scripts at odds with her religious values and convictions. Specifically, she felt that public utterance of the words "God" and "Christ" in other than a reverential manner would be taking "the name of the Lord thy God in vain," and thus it would violate the Ten Commandments. She also insisted that recital from a script of the word "fuck" would debase her religious beliefs by vulgarizing what she believed, through her religion, to be a sacred act appropriate only within a marital relationship.

In her first semester, the faculty acceded to Axson-Flynn's wishes and offered her an alternative script that did not contain offensive language. On another occasion, she herself accommodated; when asked to play the part of an unmarried pregnant woman, she acquiesced but omitted several profane terms during the actual performance, and her instructor apparently did not object. Later in the semester Axson-Flynn and her teachers reached an apparent impasse. The faculty members present at her end-of-semester review declined to make any further accommodations and suggested she "talk to some other Mormon girls who . . . don't have a problem with this." Then they delivered an ultimatum: "You can choose to continue in the program if you modify your values. If you don't, you can leave."[22] Axson-Flynn seemed for a time ready—albeit reluctantly—to accept these conditions and enrolled for the spring semester.

Before the first month was out, however, she had retained a lawyer and filed suit in federal court, naming not only the University of Utah but also the individual Actor Training Program professors who had guided her and imposed upon her the conditions she now found unacceptable. Her suit claimed that she had been denied freedom of speech and religious liberty by a state university and its ATP faculty. The defendant professors, fully supported by the university and the state's attorney general, replied that their responsibility to prepare highly competent acting professionals necessarily entailed choosing assignments of the type they had imposed on Axson-Flynn.

Their response to the federal court lawsuit noted that this was not simply a theater course or even a drama major, where accommodation might have been possible; by contrast, professional training for a career on stage compelled exposure to material that might offend some students. Reciting abhorrent language or assuming an uncongenial dramatic role, they added, in no way attributed views to the performer comparable to, for example, a compelled pledge of allegiance or flag salute. Actors simply played parts or recited scripts, whether or not they shared the values or views of the character or condoned the character's language.

The district judge was impressed by such extenuating claims and ruled in the university's and the faculty's favor on all the issues. Citing the Supreme Court's *Ewing* standard, the judge recognized that the challenged assignments reflected reasonable pedagogical judgments that were entitled to a high level of deference. Compelling an actor in training to recite language or assume roles that might not be congenial to her religious values seemed to the federal judge indistinguishable from expecting a law student to defend an unwelcome or even abhorrent position in class discussion or in a moot court argument.

Thus the court first dismissed the religious-freedom claim, noting that the challenged assignments were binding on all ATP students, reflecting a facially neutral teaching structure, and imposed no discriminatory or selective burden on an objecting student. Later in the opinion, the district court reached a similar conclusion with regard to an asserted hybrid claim that sought to combine religious freedom protection with other constitutional interests. The Supreme Court's most recent and relevant 1990 ruling had so shaped Free Exercise jurisprudence that anything less than a singling out of religious values or motives for disadvantageous treatment would seldom avail even a deeply religious person contesting a neutral law or policy.[23]

Axson-Flynn's free speech claim also fared poorly. Though the challenged assignments did in the district judge's view entail "a degree of compulsion," the dispositive element was the absence of any imposed duty to "espouse an ideological position" against conscience. Thus the Supreme Court's compelled-speech precedents (for example, striking down a mandatory flag salute) simply did not apply here. Moreover, noting "the special academic setting in which this case arises," the district judge felt that substantial deference was warranted "to educators in their curriculum decisions." Such deference was "no less applicable in a clinical setting" than in the traditional classroom. Finally, there was a question whether the ATP professors were entitled to "qualified immunity" in the event they might be deemed to have abridged any of Axson-Flynn's interests. Here again the trial judge sided with the teachers and the university, noting the constitutionally novel and tenuous nature of the claims against them. So clear were the merits to her that she simply granted summary judgment and dismissed the suit.[24]

Because the trial judge simply rejected all of Axson-Flynn's claims, she found no need to define the extent of the professors' academic freedom interests. Academic freedom would have entered the legal equation only if some basis existed for awarding damages or other relief against the ATP faculty. When the case reached the court of appeals, however, that issue could no longer be avoided. The higher court recognized (from the *Ewing* case and elsewhere) the basic level of deference that judges should pay to academic decisions. But the Tenth Circuit Court of Appeals added an important corollary: such deference could be overcome by presenting clear evidence that the challenged university action was merely "pretextual," or that university policies had been applied unfairly or unevenly. The appeals court was troubled both by the "get over it" remark and by the "talk with other Mormon girls" suggestion from Axson-Flynn's faculty adviser, as well as by evidence that a Jewish fellow ATP student had been excused for a religious holiday. Despite obvious differences between accommodating for a single day of worship in the case of the Jewish student, and being asked in Axson-Flynn's case to alter the entire curriculum, the appeals court found sufficient doubt "whether [the faculty's] justification for the script-adherence requirement was truly pedagogical" to warrant sending the case back for trial on that very issue.[25]

In passing, the Tenth Circuit recognized that an academic freedom issue might now have to be addressed. Noting that the defendant professors relied on "the ill-defined right of 'academic freedom'" in their plea for judicial deference, the higher court declared itself quite unsympathetic; these judges simply did not "view it as constituting a separate right apart from the operation of the First Amendment within the university setting." Thus the very serious and substantial prospect of judicial intrusion into the curricular prerogatives of a university faculty simply was put aside. The *Axson-Flynn* case never went to trial. The university was now more than willing to settle and, in the process, to develop new policies on the issue of curricular mandates that might constrain a student's conscience. The resulting compromise would afford a future Christina Axson-Flynn an opportunity either to transfer without jeopardy to a different major or to seek an accommodation within the original program—hardly a complete resolution of the issue.[26]

Had the case gone further, recognition of serious and substantial academic freedom interests on both sides could hardly have been avoided. Although universities do have broad authority to assign basic course responsibility, within each course the instructor assigns reading and laboratory activities. A very different, though curiously analogous, case several years earlier anticipated the potential conflict. An Ohio State University veterinary student, Jennifer Kissinger, told her lab instructor that she could not, as a matter of religious belief, perform experiments on live animals. When she asked the dean and faculty for an alternative to the required course in veterinary surgery, her request was initially denied. After she filed suit in federal court, a substitute curriculum was developed; although she found parts of the alternative track unsatisfactory, the case was eventually settled. Meanwhile, however, the trial judge ruled in the university's favor, observing that "an educational institution has a strong interest in developing a standard curriculum for all students to follow, without numerous individual exceptions to fit individual beliefs which might compromise the quality of the education and the reputation of the institution." Students, concluded the district judge, "have no right to tell their teachers how they are to be taught."[27]

The *Axson-Flynn* case is even more difficult than the *Kissinger* case, as there was more intense pressure on both sides. On the student's side, there was surely a plausible claim of academic freedom. Although most of the focus in relevant policies is on faculty interests, several higher education organizations joined forces in the 1960s to draft (and then to revise in the 1980s) the "Statement on the Rights and Freedoms of Students." Among those rights is the "freedom to learn," an interest inseparable from the faculty's "freedom to teach." The statement specifically protects the freedom of "discussion, inquiry and expression" as an essential element of "minimal standards of academic freedom of students" that apply in the classroom, across the campus, "and in the larger community."[28] Obviously the drafters of such language saw it as a counterweight to external pressures—speaker bans, loyalty oaths, curbs on student organizations, and the like, all of which threatened the liberties of all members of the academic community, though with special impact on students.

What could not have been anticipated was the prospect that materialized in the *Axson-Flynn* case—that a curricular requirement clearly within a professor's academic freedom might effectively constrain a student's conscience-based freedom of "discussion, inquiry, and expression." Neither the trial court nor the court of appeals felt the need to reconcile those starkly contending interests, since each resolved the case on other grounds. Yet the prospect is unmistakable that such a poignant conflict may not be avoided when the next such dispute reaches court.

One twenty-first century case came even closer to forcing resolution of such a conflict. Christopher Brown, a graduate student in materials science at the University of California–Santa Barbara (UCSB), submitted a thesis to satisfy his master's degree requirements. The members of his committee approved the thesis and signed the degree-certification form. Brown then appended to the thesis a unique component—a page titled "Disacknowledgements," on which he proclaimed: "I would like to offer special Fuck You's to [various people, including a former governor, the University of California regents, the dean, graduate staff and the library director at UCSB, and others]." The graduate committee summoned Brown to a meeting at which its members made clear their profound displeasure at the addendum. They insisted that, in its embellished form, the thesis now failed to satisfy professional standards for publication in the discipline, even though the student had already completed the formal degree requirements. Brown's degree, the committee now announced, would be conferred only upon his withdrawal of the disacknowledgements section of the thesis. Although Brown eventually received his degree, the unauthorized addendum uniquely barred the addition of his thesis to the university library's collection of graduate dissertations.

Brown filed suit in federal court against the graduate dean, the library director, members of his graduate committee, and the campus chancellor. He claimed that the delay in granting his degree and particularly the exclusion of his thesis from the library abridged his First Amendment rights. The district court dismissed the suit in a brief unreported opinion. A three-judge panel of the Court of Appeals for the Ninth Circuit took the matter very seriously and rendered three distinct and widely divergent opinions. The net effect of their review was to affirm the trial judge's view that Brown had presented no valid constitutional claims. One judge reached that conclusion by giving great deference to the academic judgments of the graduate committee. A second judge concurred in the result, since in his view Brown's eleventh-hour addendum was "academically dishonest" and justified both the delay and the rejection. The third judge dissented, insisting that he found in the case a genuine free speech issue that federal courts could not so easily avoid. In his view, Brown should be given a chance to prove at trial that "the university was motivated by a desire to punish [him]. for making post-approval modifications to the thesis or by its disagreement with the views that he expressed in the disacknowledgements" and not, as UCSB officials claimed, by Brown's failure to follow the rules of the graduate program.[29]

The judge who wrote the prevailing opinion took a dim view of Brown's constitutional claims, given the student's contemptuous treatment of his academic mentors. Specifically, and surprisingly for a case involving a university graduate student, she considered his constitutional interests to be no stronger than those of a high school student whose free speech claims had been muted substantially by recent Supreme Court rulings. Indeed, this judge's reason for rejecting Brown's suit was more her skeptical view of the student's claims than a deferential view of the faculty's right to make academic judgments about the completion of degree requirements. If Brown's interests were not much greater than those of a Santa Barbara high school newspaper editor, then such a suit would fail almost without regard to the degree of deference that faculty judgments merit.

Judge Steven Reinhardt, the dissenter, saw the case very differently. For him, summary dismissal without a trial was inappropriate; Brown's lawsuit raised at least a plausible claim that the graduate dean and other university officials had rejected his thesis mainly because they found offensive the viewpoint expressed in his irreverent addendum. Such a claim, argued Judge Reinhardt, deserved at least its day in court. For him, reliance on high school student cases was "wholly inappropriate"—even for a college undergraduate, and especially for a graduate student at a research university. The core of the Supreme Court's dilution of high school free speech rights reflected both the age and immaturity of the students and the far greater degree of authority that secondary school administrators have always possessed.

In other contexts, cautioned the dissent, "because college and graduate school students are typically more mature and independent, they have been afforded greater First Amendment rights than their high school counterparts." Moreover, subsuming the university's several negative judgments about Brown's status and his thesis under the graduate school's "desire to further a legitimate pedagogical concern" tilted the balance excessively in favor of the academic administration and against an admittedly disrespectful and maverick student. Thus Judge Reinhardt would at least have given Brown a day in court as to "the university's motivation for imposing such extreme sanctions."[30]

An objective and dispassionate observer of academic freedom debates would conclude that the truth lies somewhere between these antithetical judicial views. On the one hand, Judge Reinhardt was clearly correct that Brown's claims should not have been rejected simply by analogy to expressive interests of high school students. He was also right that Brown had alleged in his lawsuit the imposition of viewpoint bias on the part of administrators and professors who were offended by "speech that was highly critical of university and other public officials." On the other hand, Judge Reinhardt virtually ignored the potential implications of allowing such a student claim to proceed to judgment in a federal court. Had his view prevailed, a host of problems would have ensued, some with grave implications for academic freedom. Among the defendants who were said to have constrained Brown's free speech were not only the dean and the chancellor but also the faculty members of his graduate committee. The potential for abridging their academic freedom by holding them liable for the apparently good-faith exercise of academic judgments about a graduate student's degree completion simply escaped notice by any of the judges.[31]

Had such a prospect been considered in Brown's case, the appropriate standard would have been the one declared by the Supreme Court two decades earlier in the *Ewing* case. The issue there was actually closely analogous to the one that Brown's suit raised—a state university faculty's decision to deny a graduate student the opportunity to complete a demanding degree program. The Supreme Court had been clear in rejecting Ewing's claim, noted above, that "judges . . . asked to review the substance of a genuinely academic decision . . . should show great respect for the faculty's professional judgment." Specifically, courts should not override such a judgment "unless it is such a substantial departure from accepted academic norms as to demonstrate that the person or committee responsible did not actually exercise professional judgment." That standard would seem to foreclose any judicial intervention into the academic judgments that excluded Brown's thesis from the UCSB library.[32]

There is, however, one nontrivial difference between the cases. Ewing's claim was indeed one of constitutional violation, albeit based on due process rather than free speech. Brown's First Amendment claim, by contrast, should not justify a dilution of the deference that courts properly pay to genuinely academic judgments. The *Ewing* decision did, however, leave open one intriguing possibility—as the Tenth Circuit Court of Appeals noted in reversing the *Axson-Flynn* judgment—that is, a faculty's claimed basis for an adverse academic judgment could turn out to be "a sham pretext for an impermissible ulterior motive."[33] Given that prospect, remote though it may seem in Brown's case, Judge Reinhardt may have been right to urge that the case be sent back to the district court—not necessarily for a full trial, but at least to give the student plaintiff a chance to show that his thesis had been barred from the library for motives no higher than protecting the image of California and university officials. Had Judge Reinhardt narrowed the issue in that way, he could hardly have been faulted for favoring a student's claim above faculty interests. His actual opinion, however, seemed surprisingly insensitive to the growing tension between professorial and student expressive interests.

A later case illustrates the tension in a rather different context. In 1961, a Princeton University graduate named Charles Robertson (heir to the A&P retail fortune) made a major gift to his alma mater for support of graduate study by students who were preparing for federal government careers, especially in the international arena. The fledgling Woodrow Wilson School was the primary beneficiary. In time, the initial gift of $60 million rose to more than $600 million. The number of Woodrow Wilson students actually headed for foreign-service careers, however, turned out to be fewer than either the donor or the university had anticipated. Thus the income from the rapidly growing endowment was allocated to a series of related purposes—renovating a building that Woodrow Wilson shared with other academic programs, supporting graduate students in cognate social science fields, encouraging joint and interdisciplinary graduate programs, and others. The governing body for the endowment was a committee of seven persons, three chosen by the Robertson family and four by Princeton, with the university's president chairing the committee in later years.

By the late 1990s the current generation of Robertsons became so disaffected by what they saw as Princeton's departure from the original intent of the gift that they brought suit in New Jersey state court. Their complaint sought not only a declaration that Princeton had departed unacceptably from the donor's wishes but also the return to the Robertson endowment of some $250 million that had allegedly been spent for unauthorized purposes. Princeton's defense included many claims—that the broad terms of the grant were properly read as permitting all the challenged expenditures, that the family trustees had been fully involved in the process over the years, and that nothing in New Jersey law prevented a private university from using designated funds for such related purposes.

There was, however, a special line of defense that directly involved academic freedom. The judgments and expenditures drawn in question by the Robertson family suit had all been made by the successive deans and faculties of the Woodrow Wilson School with approval by the provost and president. Although other persons might have reached different conclusions, Princeton insisted that such a possibility could not justify the intervention of a court to gainsay or overturn the challenged academic judgments and their consequences. Not surprisingly, the university's lawyers relied heavily on the *Ewing* case and its standard of deference—courts are not to overturn such judgments unless there has been so "substantial a departure from accepted academic norms as to demonstrate that the person or committee responsible did not actually exercise professional judgment."[34]

This language does seem to supply the proper template, even though it was developed for and has been mainly applied to student appeals. In the absence of any other standard, there is no reason to appraise differently a legal challenge to professorial and decanal judgments, whether the focus is on suspending a graduate student or spending income from an endowment. The potential implications of judicial intervention are similar, whatever the subject matter of the challenged judgment. Thus a New Jersey judge would need to be persuaded that the Woodrow Wilson deans and professors had, over the years, simply failed to exercise professional judgment before issuing even a declaratory judgment against the university, much less order funds to be returned to the endowment.

A rather different recent case poses comparably troubling issues. In late summer of 2005, a group of conservative Christian schools filed suit in federal court against the University of California (UC), challenging its student admission policies. The issue this time was not race or geography, as in past disputes, but rather religion. Specifically, the religious schools claimed that the UC admission standards reflected unconstitutional religious bias because they rejected certain textbooks that some Christian schools used in physics and biology courses. The university also refused to certify high school courses on creationism and intelligent design as meeting the entrance criteria. The UC admissions arbiters also found unacceptable the content of, and materials for, at least one secondary humanities course.[35]

A few weeks later, a second suit was filed against UC–Berkeley, claiming that its views on the origins of human life violated the religious freedom guarantees of the First Amendment and the state constitution. The specific target of the later suit was the posting and maintenance of a website, Understanding Evolution, designed to aid high school teachers, providing links to the views of many religious organizations that deem faith to be compatible with evolution. Support has been provided by the National Science Foundation, which was sued as a codefendant.[36]

The suit against the admissions policies directly implicated academic freedom interests. After all, it was the University of California (specifically the Davis campus) that in 1978 persuaded the Supreme Court of the centrality to academic freedom of judgments about "who may be admitted to study."[37] Although that ruling recognized mainly the academic freedom interests of the university as an institution, no major institution of higher learning would impose admissions criteria that did not reflect careful and conscientious faculty judgment—both in framing the standards and in their application. Thus the short (and sufficient) answer to the Christian schools' complaints should be that the admissions standards to which they object are fully protected by the doctrine of academic freedom.

There may, however, be a need for a longer and clearer answer. The Christian schools argued in court that their freedom to shape curriculum, hire faculty, admit and graduate students, and pursue many other educational tasks, is severely compromised by University of California admission standards that disadvantage their graduates in the highly competitive quest for college admission. Ironically, California has long been the state that regulates private schools—both secular and sectarian—least extensively. Whereas many other states impose detailed requirements on private school curricula—and several have been taken to court over the exercise of that very authority—California imposes little more than fire and safety standards. Curriculum, as far as authorities in Sacramento are concerned, is left to the schools. In these cases, however, the threat to private school autonomy is claimed to emanate from a different quarter, the UC System administration in Oakland.

The later challenge to the UC–Berkeley science webpage also implicates academic freedom in a novel and troubling way. The content of that Internet site is designed and updated entirely by a group of UC science professors. Their scholarly insistence that everything posted on that page is factually accurate and reflects sound scientific thought has been directly challenged by the lawsuit. Should a court accept the plaintiffs' claims, and were a federal judge to order alterations in or removal of the challenged website, such a decree would surely implicate the academic freedom of the site's creators, albeit in a novel fashion. Academic freedom encompasses the shaping of a scientific website's content quite as much as the content of a lecture, a scholarly paper, a course syllabus, or other more traditional forms of professorial expression. (These and other dimensions of academic freedom in electronic and digital communications are addressed specifically in Chapter 7.)

The time is long past when questions about "whose academic freedom" could be simply and neatly resolved. It is still the case that all the relevant expressive interests typically appear on the same side of a legal dispute, as recently as in the University of Michigan's defense of race-sensitive admission policies. There the minority (and most nonminority) students, faculty, and institution were on the same page, and the only question was whether their collective academic freedom claims justified the inclusive use of race in the selection process. Those who opposed such use of race posed substantial objections—and garnered the support of five justices in one case, four in the other. But in no sense could the countervailing argument be derived from or reflect academic freedom.

Increasingly, though, the relevant academic freedom interests are not in accord, and courts are being pressed for the first time to balance or weigh contending expressive claims from disparate sectors of the academic community. As this chapter suggests, conventional notions of academic freedom that were developed in times of accord and harmony are no longer universally applicable, or sometimes even helpful. They simply do not tell us whether Christina Axson-Flynn's desire for a curriculum that respects her faith should trump the faculty's choice of scripts and plays, or whether Christopher Brown may insist his thesis be filed in the library despite its disacknowledgements and the understandable outrage of his faculty mentors. Although it is impossible to anticipate the subject matter or even the general import of future disputes of this type, their emergence in the courts is so likely that refusal to adapt traditional academic freedom principles would seem to be heedless denial. We have entered a new ocean, where the waters are both turbulent and largely uncharted.

9

Bias, Balance, and Beyond

New Threats to Academic Freedom

Rating professors, their views, and their values has long been a favorite activity of college undergraduates. In the early weeks of 2006, however, such assessment assumed a bizarre new twist for students at the University of California–Los Angeles (UCLA). A conservative UCLA alumni group widely advertised its readiness to pay undergraduates for taping or transcribing lectures of professors who were perceived as overly liberal and to gather other evidence of ideological "imbalance" in the classroom. This plan was the inspiration of Andrew Jones, a recent UCLA graduate who in his student days had chaired the campus Republican organization. Before any current students had actually signed up for the project, Mr. Jones rescinded his bounty offer after university officials warned that taping lectures might well violate copyright law and subject the students to legal liability.[1]

The invitation to report and even spy on left-leaning professors remained, however, very much in force. The sponsoring organization—Bruin Alumni Association—had established a website proclaiming that the Southern California campus was overrun by "radical" professors, students, and administrators who "have made UCLA a major organizing center for opposition" to the Iraq War, the Bush administration, and other conservative interests. The webpage also indicted the university for offering the study of fields that are "irreparably anti-American and anti-capitalist" and for condoning an environment hostile to any student who does not "embrace political extremism."[2]

The withdrawal of Mr. Jones' offer to pay students as classroom monitors left unresolved several deeply troubling implications for academic freedom at UCLA and elsewhere. As the campus administration recognized, professors who were targeted in this way as "radicals"—and were so publicized on an Internet website—would almost certainly have no legal recourse. Only in the remote event they could sue for libel if a blatantly false and deeply damaging statement were posted, or could seek redress for misappropriation of their intellectual property, should any targeted professor even think seriously about going to court. Otherwise, the posting by a private group of even scurrilous comments about a faculty member's politics would seem beyond reach of the law and therefore an affront that simply must be tolerated.

Mr. Jones was hardly the first disaffected alumnus, parent or critic to launch such an initiative. By the time he made his short-lived offer to pay students as classroom spies, several websites were already up and running that contained highly critical comments about "imbalanced" professors. NoIndoctrination.org had been online for several years, posting detailed information about professors seen as overly liberal. Campus Watch (www.campus-watch.org) had for an even longer time posted reports of professors whose views on Middle East tensions were viewed as hostile to Israel or overly sympathetic to the Palestinian cause. Local campus groups had also established websites and weblogs that encouraged, and featured, candid discussion and critiques of "biased" teachers and their classroom comments, as well as indications of distortion in their published writings.

The emerging context, and the consequent threat to academic freedom, extends well beyond even these highly visible activities. Claims of political or ideological bias have caused substantial investigations to an unprecedented degree—most notably, though far from exclusively, in the now famous case of Columbia University's Department of Middle East and Asian Languages and Cultures.[3] On several occasions disaffected students have actually gone to court, seeking to compel a restoration of the "balance" they had found lacking in their college experience. Most notable among recent forays of this type was the legal suit filed in 2003 challenging a summer reading assignment for entering students at the University of North Carolina at Chapel Hill.[4] Also at Chapel Hill, a formal complaint was filed with a federal civil rights agency against an English professor on the basis of an after-class e-mail that one of his students read as disparaging to homophobic views.[5]

An even stranger and potentially more ominous challenge was a lawsuit brought against Temple University and two of its history professors by a former student who claimed that the completion of his master's thesis had been thwarted because of his political views. Specifically, Christian M. DeJohn (a National Guardsman with substantial military service) alleged in his federal court suit that the two professors had retaliated against him after he complained about receiving "anti-war" e-mail messages that had been circulated within the history department with apparent departmental imprimatur. The university and the professors responded that DeJohn had been at best a marginal student, and persuaded the district judge that the offending messages came not from a senior faculty member to whom they were erroneously attributed, but from a graduate student political club. In late April, 2007, the court dismissed the suit, ruling that no credible evidence of political bias or retaliation had been submitted.[6]

An even graver threat of this sort has come from legislation proposed in the United States Congress and no fewer than sixteen states, which would essentially mandate balance in university curricula and would occasionally offer avenues of recourse to aggrieved students.[7] Though none of these measures (subsumed under the title "Academic Bill of Rights," or ABOR) has yet made its way into law, the mere pendency of such proposals and their serious consideration by lawmakers invariably arouse anxiety and concern across the academic community. Such uneasiness is heightened by the same realization that swept the UCLA campus when Mr. Jones's offer became public—that university professors are essentially helpless against such hostile forces until and unless an adverse personnel action occurs. These new and ominous activities, and some possible responses to them, are the focus of this chapter.

These new threats differ dramatically from those that beset the academic community in earlier times, and some observers find them even more ominous than their more familiar antecedents. Ellen Schrecker, who literally wrote the book—*No Ivory Tower*—about the McCarthy-era devastation of academic freedom, recently argued that "today's assault on the academy is more serious" because "unlike that of the McCarthy era, it reaches directly into the classroom." With specific reference to the Academic Bill of Rights and similar initiatives, Schrecker added: "Such an intrusion not only endangers the faculty autonomy that traditionally protects academic freedom, but also threatens the integrity of American higher education."[8]

The central premise of virtually all these hostile initiatives is either that American college and university faculties have become unacceptably skewed to the left or liberal end of the political and ideological spectrum, or that they are severely biased one way or the other on such volatile issues as Middle Eastern politics. As a result, conservative faculty (or those in the minority on other matters) are said to feel isolated, unfairly treated at promotion and tenure time, and occasionally even persecuted. Similarly, students who lean to the political right are portrayed as feeling unwelcome on many campuses, and they are portrayed as potentially disadvantaged in grading as well as in less formal ways.

The data that support such charges are superficially impressive. A report published in the spring of 2005 by several reputable social scientists offered three conclusions that were seen as the first solid documentation of the "liberal bias" charges: First, the number of registered Democrats outnumbered registered Republicans (at least in the humanities and social sciences) by a ratio of seven to one. Second, this partisan imbalance has substantially worsened in the past decade or two, given lower ratios anecdotally available for earlier generations of academics. Third, there was growing and disturbing evidence of the effects of bias in professional opportunity and advancement; although publications and research support ranked first among desiderata for recognition and success, ideology ranked second and disadvantaged conservative scholars.[9] A later study reported that by party registration, Republicans were outnumbered by Democrats in a ratio of nine to one on the Berkeley and Stanford faculties. The news media embraced these reports with zeal; "Republicans Outnumbered in Academia," proclaimed a *New York Times* headline,[10] and the *Chronicle of Higher Education* headed its story "Conservative Professors Are Less Likely to Advance in Academe, Study Finds."[11]

There have been other indicia of such concern. *New York Times* columnist David Brooks devoted an entire column to his lament about "lonely conservatives" across the Ivy League, identifying for each institution a single holdout against the liberal tide: Harvey Mansfield at Harvard, Alan Kors at Penn, Donald Kagan at Yale, and others whose ideological isolation drew both Mr. Brooks's sympathy and his rebuke to elite institutions that in his view owed it to their students to be more ideologically diverse.[12] The summer of 2005 brought the publication of a new report on intellectual diversity by the American Council of Trustees and Alumni (ACTA), an organization founded by Lynne Cheney over a decade ago and deeply committed to articulating and disseminating conservative views within the academic world. Key points in this report included these: "Faculty imbalance, combined with the idea that the 'politically correct' point of view has a right to dominate classroom and campus discussions, has had fearful consequences for university life." Thus, "many of our campuses have become . . . islands of oppression in a sea of freedom. . . . The lack of intellectual diversity is depriving an entire generation of the kind of education they deserve." The ACTA report, not surprisingly, received wide attention, well beyond the conservative circles that were its primary audience.[13]

Finally, there have been anecdotal accounts of occasional classroom encounters that have left conservative students feeling isolated or unwelcome on mainstream campuses. One classic encounter received national attention. When Duke University history professor Gerald Wilson invited questions on the first day of his survey class, he was taken aback when a student asked him, "Do you have any prejudices?" Wilson quipped, "Yeah, Republicans." Most of the students laughed, but the senior history major who had posed the question—seeking, as it turned out, nothing more than stylistic guidance on writing papers—failed to find humor in this exchange. He brought the incident to the attention of Students for Academic Freedom, a national conservative watchdog group. Professor Wilson apologized to the student, explaining that he often joked about politics in his classes, but for that student (who soon dropped the course) the encounter left an indelible implication "that [Wilson's] politics would be a large part of the classroom experience."[14]

Infrequent though they are, reports of such incidents spread widely and abate slowly. Indeed, much of the pressure behind movements like those leading to the Academic Bill of Rights reflects just such alleged student concern. Sponsors of such legislation claim that they have received a host of complaints from such students, charging that their views were unwelcome on the campus and especially in the classroom, where liberal ideologies prevailed. These reports have been augmented by accounts of the travails of right-leaning professors—those "lonely conservatives" who were the focus of Brooks's harsh critique of faculty imbalance across the Ivy League.

Such charges have been rightly disputed on several grounds. For one, the data that sustain allegations of faculty imbalance usually reflect the most liberal segments of so-called liberal institutions—social science and humanities professors who teach at Ivy League universities and at highly selective liberal arts colleges. If the faculties in business, medicine, and engineering were added even at these otherwise liberal campuses, the resulting ratios might look very different. The charges also reflect rather small samples, whether or not they are technically representative. During one of the legislative hearings on the proposed Academic Bill of Rights, a Pennsylvania lawmaker who supports such measures asked the University of Pittsburgh's provost whether he was troubled by the fact that in recent electoral campaigns 119 members of his faculty contributed to Democrats, whereas only 33 had supported Republicans. The provost calmly replied that because Pitt's full-time faculty exceeded 4,000, one would need a far larger sample to draw any reliable conclusion about political bias or imbalance.[15]

More serious than the statistical superficiality of such charges are the implications on which they rest—that a professor who consistently votes for or even supports Democrats will somehow seek to indoctrinate students with a liberal or left-leaning viewpoint and that one who mainly supports Republicans will advance contrary views. Such assumptions are sharply at variance both with experience in the academic community and with the basic professional obligations of university scholars and teachers. Critics who claim that any imbalance in political affiliation creates a risk of classroom indoctrination have not only failed to document such a correlation with reliable data, but they also profoundly misunderstand the very nature of professional responsibility in the academy.

Strongly supporting the skeptics, a study released in the spring of 2006 cast serious doubt on claims that conservative students are victimized or placed at risk on supposedly liberal campuses. The study concluded after exhaustive analyses of relevant campus populations that students who identify as liberal and conservative fare about equally well in courses with politically charged content. After a longitudinal four-year analysis of the experience of roughly four thousand students who had declared their political orientation, the authors found that in the most volatile or sensitive of classes there was no perceptible correlation betw en performance and political persuasion. Indeed, the study seemed to co clude that conservative students on the whole achieved better grades in less sensitive courses in business, economics, and other apolitical subjects—although that was not the primary finding or the one that received media attention. Rather, the *Chronicle of Higher Education*'s headline "Study Casts Doubt on Claims That Conservative Students Face Discrimination in Classes" captured the theme.[16]

A later study, made public in the fall of 2006, confirmed such findings under the heading "Political Shocker: Faculty Moderates." In summary, this new study conducted by two University of Akron sociologists yielded two valuable conclusions: first, although "there are more liberals than conservatives on college faculties, . . . the proportions (while still significant) aren't as large as those found in some other reports" and second, "the most dramatic trend among the professoriate in recent years has been a shift toward the middle of the road"—the latter "particularly pronounced in some of the disciplines that enroll the greatest number of students."

Supporting these conclusions were a set of longitudinal data developed by the Carnegie Foundation for the Advancement of Teaching on the "political ideology of professors" in various disciplines over a decade. Typically, those who self-identified as "conservative" accounted for roughly the same percentage over time, as did the "moderately liberal," whereas those who considered themselves "middle of the road" increased several points. In certain key disciplines—allied health, biological sciences, business, computer science, and psychology—those reporting themselves to be "liberal" declined appreciably, whereas the "centrist" group gained at corresponding or even greater rates.[17]

The most recent appraisal of such claims appeared in the winter of 2007, in the form of a critical analysis sponsored by the American Federation of Teachers. Rather than engaging directly on the merits of the earlier, this critique focused instead on the methodology that had been employed in validating claims of faculty political and ideological bias. While conceding that such studies in the aggregate "suggest that college faculty are more likely to be Democrats than Republicans," little more could be claimed with a statistically significant level of confidence. Most common among the cited flaws in the earlier studies was a less than rigorous tendency to attribute to certain correlations a causal result—specifically, to infer or imply that "liberal dominance results in systematic exclusion of conservative ideas, limited promotion opportunities for conservative faculty, and expression of liberal perspectives that damage student learning." Thus, concluded education researcher and study author John Lee, "basic methodological flaws keep a critical reader from accepting the conclusions suggested by the authors."[18]

The inability to document the claimed correlation between faculty politics and bias is far more than anecdotal. Several striking revelations have seriously undermined the case advanced by such critics of academic imbalance. The movement for such measures as the Academic Bill of Rights is largely the creation of David Horowitz, a onetime radical student who, in the 1990s, became convinced that many universities and their faculties ill-served conservative students and colleagues and that some major reform was in order. During testimony before several legislative committees and in a flurry of campus speeches promoting his agenda, Horowitz cited two seemingly egregious examples of the intimidation and oppression of which he complained. One involved an unnamed Penn State professor who, as Horowitz recounted it, inappropriately showed his students the Michael Moore film *Fahrenheit 9/11* during a required class period. The other cited horror story involved a California professor (also unnamed) "who opposes abortion gave a student a low grade for supporting" a contrary view. When Horowitz was challenged during one of the Pennsylvania House Committee hearings to document these claims, he conceded that he lacked evidence to sustain or verify these charges. No individuals have yet been named in connection with either episode. Pennsylvania lawmakers expressed both perplexity and concern and warned Horowitz to use greater care in the future.[19]

Similarly elusive have been broader claims of student abuse or mistreatment on ideological grounds. When a conservative trustee of the State University of New York (SUNY) urged adoption of a measure that would force faculty recruitment to reflect greater ideological diversity, an extensive survey of SUNY's sixty-four campuses revealed that not a single student had filed a complaint alleging political bias anywhere in that vast system.[20] The principal witness before the Pennsylvania House Subcommittee's Philadelphia hearing was David Adamany, president of Temple University, one of the state's largest and most diverse public institutions. During his five years as president, Adamany and his administration had received no student complaints of mistreatment or ideological bias, despite a well-publicized procedure through which such concerns could be registered. Later in that hearing, a Temple professor who had been scheduled to testify about allegedly rampant political bias on his campus mysteriously failed to appear. The one and only student who did testify that day, and who lamented what he saw as a less than congenial campus climate, conceded that he had never filed a grievance through the readily accessible channel created for that purpose.[21]

Perhaps most damaging to those who have alleged unacceptable political bias on college faculties was the final report of the Pennsylvania House Subcommittee. The panel was created because one lawmaker convinced his colleagues that Pennsylvania students were inadequately protected from biased or imbalanced teaching on the state's public campuses. After extensive hearings, the subcommittee filed its report in the late fall of 2006. Not only did the final report conclude that evidence of the alleged bias had simply not been verified in any part of the commonwealth or any type of institution. In the end the subcommittee declined to endorse a statewide policy guaranteeing students' political rights, finding such a measure to be "unnecessary" because violations of those rights proved to be "rare." Although an earlier draft of the report included testimony by the inquiry's champion, Horowitz, and his allies, all such material disappeared in the final version, along with the proposal for a more explicit guarantee of student interests. An indignant Horowitz indicted the subcommittee for what he charged was "the breathtaking audacity of this theft of the report by the Democrats and the unions," adding his belief that a "cabal" of faculty leaders had persuaded "weak-spined Republicans" (who chaired the panel) to acquiesce in the "theft."[22] Meanwhile, the subcommittee's patron and sponsor, Rep. Gibson Armstrong, lost his reelection primary in a safely Republican district; though he blamed his defeat on having openly targeted campus political bias, the likelier explanation seemed to lie in unrelated local issues on which he was viewed as unresponsive.[23]

What was for a time the most widely celebrated claim of mistreatment of conservative faculty also turned out to contain more fiction than fact. Professor William Bradford joined the faculty of the Indiana University School of Law in Indianapolis in 2001—heralded as a decorated war veteran, an ardent patriot, and an Apache Indian. He claimed that two senior tenured colleagues had made life around law school acutely uncomfortable for him and that, during a third-year review, they had specifically faulted him as "uncollegial" on the basis of his manifest political views. He also claimed his two detractors had managed to block his path to tenure despite otherwise exemplary credentials. The case received widespread and generally sympathetic coverage, including a major article in the *Chronicle of Higher Education* and an appearance on the Fox News show *The O'Reilly Factor* during the summer of 2005. Then doubts began to emerge. Journalists probed Bradford's claims more deeply and soon discovered that he had never served on active duty, had received no military medals, and had essentially fabricated the charges that had brought him attention. Bradford quietly resigned from the law faculty, and the matter became moot.[24]

About the same time, a case of genuine faculty bias produced a very different outcome. Professor Robert Natelson had been teaching at the University of Montana Law School for many years, but his request to offer constitutional law had been consistently denied. Such rejection, he claimed, reflected bias against his conservative views, widely known since his unsuccessful Republican gubernatorial campaign. After two direct appeals, essentially bypassing the law school administration, the university's president responded to both internal and external pressure by appointing an outside committee to review the charge of political discrimination. The ensuing process would consume many months, a substantial commitment of Professor Natelson's personal resources and his political capital. Two outside experts—widely respected constitutional law teachers at University of Colorado and Arizona State—concluded that Natelson was indeed fully qualified to teach constitutional law and should not be denied that opportunity for ideological or other reasons. (The group's third member, a practicing lawyer, differed from that consensus, finding other flaws in the case.) Montana's dean and president promptly accepted the majority recommendation. Starting early in 2006, Natelson was at least able to teach constitutional law as he had fervently wished for many years.[25] That the Natelson case had as happy an outcome as the Bradford saga was dismal in its denouement suggests that the system is more than capable of addressing genuine claims of bias brought by conservative faculty—and that such bias does exist in rare instances—but that such claims need to be critically assessed and not simply accepted at face value.

From such recent experience, one might reliably draw several inferences: there is more than anecdotal evidence suggesting that liberals outnumber conservatives on many faculties, often by substantial margins. Professors on the political right may indeed feel less welcome in some departments than their left-leaning colleagues. In rare but deeply troubling instances, advancement within the academy is undoubtedly blocked or deterred by political considerations—not necessarily partisan, though surely ideological. To deny that such miscarriages of justice have occurred, or to dismiss them as trivial or bizarre, is as irresponsible as it is tempting for those on the more comfortably liberal side of the divide. Happily, organizations such as the American Council of Trustees and Alumni (ACTA) and the Foundation for Individual Rights in Education (FIRE) have been vigilant in protecting both liberals and conservatives in the academy from the excesses of political correctness and other ideological pressures.[26] The presence and energy of such groups give substantial confidence that even in an unbalanced academic world, the truly outrageous abuses of political dominance—by either side of the aisle—will be detected and exposed.

Students, meanwhile, may also find most campuses a bit more congenial to liberals than to conservatives in and outside the classroom. Some campuses are proudly or even defiantly skewed in their politics. At Antioch and Macalester, for example, at least three-quarters of the student body would self-identify as liberal, whereas at Hillsdale and Liberty the reverse would undoubtedly prevail. Yet students do have a wide range of choice, and they presumably exercise that choice with keen appreciation of the politically contrasting conditions that different campuses offer, along with widely variant academic programs.

Yet such data caution that claims of "bias," "imbalance," "ideological discrimination," and the like have been sharply exaggerated and presuppose an undocumented correlation between party affiliation or personal belief and pedagogy. Meanwhile, much mischief has already been wrought on the basis of such inferences and suppositions, however tenuous may be their foundation. It is now time to examine that response and its pernicious effects more closely.

A prime example of private pressure to redress perceived imbalance is NoIndoctrination.org. Its founder, Luann Wright, took up this cause after her son enrolled in English courses at the University of California–San Diego, the content of some of which she found disturbing. A former high school teacher, Wright especially objected to a syllabus that contained only race-related essays. One of those essays referred to men as "phallocrats," which was one among several terms that troubled the Wrights, both mother and son. From this experience emerged the new organization, most visible for its webpage.[27]

The website contains an invitation to students to post anonymous comments about classes taught by professors whom they find biased or imbalanced, and the professors are identified by name and by course. Students posting such critical comments are invited not only to describe the course and its content but also to rate the instructor's degree of perceived bias as "noticeable," "objectionable," or "extreme." The anonymity that is guaranteed to the person who posts such a critique reflects potential concern about reprisal or retaliation to which a student commentator might be subjected if he or she were identified before final grades had been submitted. Meanwhile, accused or targeted professors are invited to respond, and several have done so, with their extenuating comments accompanying the initial student critique.

NoIndoctrination.org proclaims itself "a nonprofit organization promoting open inquiry in academia." Although the sponsors claim to be neutral, virtually all the critical postings target courses and teachers deemed to be overly liberal or left-leaning. The webpage recites as part of its credo many pertinent policies on academic freedom, including pronouncements of the American Association of University Professors (AAUP)—policies to which the sponsors and the organization profess their own commitment.

There have been other intrusive and worrisome forms of surveillance. Campus Watch for several years specifically has targeted professors whose views on Middle East politics are seen as hostile to the Israeli cause or overly sympathetic to Palestinian interests. Still other sites reflect no special ideological agenda but simply invite disaffected students to vent their views about instructors whom they like or dislike. RateMyProfessors.com, for example, posts evaluations that usually reflect a small (and not necessarily representative) cross-section of usually disparaging student comments about professors in general.[28] Although promotion and tenure committees are unlikely to take such comments into account, students who seek guidance in choosing courses are somewhat less critical. Thus, when a particular professor is rated "hot" even by a handful of former students, or is lauded for being an unusually easy grader, enrollments may soar in response to a minimal and eclectic sampling of student views.

Such data-gathering channels may be intrusive, or annoying, and may occasionally steer students away from a particular course or professor, but wherein lies the threat to academic freedom? In the abstract, these faculty-bashing websites differ little from more traditional channels through which students have widely shared their views of courses and teachers—much as generations of Harvard undergraduates have done through the *Crimson Confidential Guide* and as decades of Berkeley students have done through the *Slate Supplement*. The premise of such media seems to be that the more such information is available, the sounder are choices that undergraduates make among a dizzying array of course offerings. Thus the new and focused websites could be seen as simply a logical extension into the digital age of time-honored and widely accepted rating systems.

Such oversight of the college classroom does, however, create an unavoidable risk of chilling the speech not only of professors who are viewed as "radical" and have been targeted on that basis but also of students whose views may arouse the interest of the monitoring groups. Even though promotion and tenure committees, or hiring committees at other universities, are most unlikely to give such assessments any credence in making personnel judgments, the same cannot be said of students, who are eager for any guidance in choosing courses, especially if it reflects peer judgments. Thus, enrollments may be adversely affected, and to the extent that a college teacher's stature reflects varying degree of popularity—quite apart from more immediate matters of self-esteem—the consequences may not be trivial, however unrepresentative and unscientific may be the samples that drive such posting. Thus, as an Associated Press overview of these new surveillance systems concluded: "To many professors, there's a new and deeply troubling aspect to this latest chapter in the debate over academic freedom: students trying to dictate what they don't want to be taught."[29]

The difficulty is, quite simply, identifying any avenue of legal protection or redress for professors who suddenly find themselves the target of such criticism. Several possibilities merit at least brief consideration. Most obvious would be to respond to errors or exaggerations in the website profile of one's courses or views. The value of simply correcting the record received support in the recent experience of a University of Washington sociology professor, who had been accused by an anonymous online critic of "thoroughly indoctrinating" his students in a course on social deviance. The suspect instructor was not only deeply embarrassed by such exposure but was especially troubled that the "student so completely misunderstood what I was teaching" on these topics. Even a minimal opportunity for rebuttal, of the sort that NoIndoctrination.org, for example, provides to its targeted faculty members, would be of some help in setting the record straight.[30]

There is also the remote possibility that such a posting would be so factually erroneous, and so potentially damaging to a professor's reputation, that it might invite a libel suit. Given the current state of the law of defamation, however, charges must be more than simply false and injurious to support a damage claim. Many university professors—especially those who are visible enough to invite such scrutiny—would likely be deemed "public figures" and would thus need to show "actual malice" (knowledge of falsehood or reckless disregard of the truth) before maintaining a successful libel suit.[31] When it comes to material posted on the Internet, there is an additional and serious barrier to such redress. Unlike print publishers (who are liable for everything they disseminate), those who provide Internet access or maintain a passive website may not, under a 1996 federal statute, be held liable for even outrageous and damaging statements posted by someone else.[32] Only the author of the offending statement can be held to account. Because most of the student critics on websites such as those examined here are anonymous, the only way a libeled professor could pursue legal redress would be by discovering the author's identity. But website proprietors typically refuse to disclose that information, believing that anonymity is vital not only to protect a student against reprisal from an aggrieved professor but also to sustain a steady flow of information and accusations for the website itself. Thus the theoretical possibility of a professorial libel suit turns out to be even more remote than a casual review of the seldom truly defamatory postings might suppose.

The removal of such familiar options brings us back to the one area that concerned UCLA officials enough to warn students about the hazards of accepting Jones's generous offer to monitor classes. The top of the announced-but-never-implemented Bruin Alumni pay scale was reserved for those enterprising students who could produce "full lecture notes, classroom materials, and tape-recordings of every class session."[33] Under existing copyright law, a professor's lectures are clearly protected against publication and distribution without the author's permission. However, it is equally clear that students enrolled in the course are free to take even verbatim notes for their own needs and are presumably just as free to share those notes with fellow students who missed the class for any of myriad reasons.

The rub comes here because the Bruin Alumni system falls somewhere between these two comfortable extremes. Citing the fact that any information of potential interest would be gathered by students who are clearly entitled to take classroom notes, and any posting of those notes would serve a pedagogical purpose (however unwelcome it might be to the author), Jones has insisted that UCLA lawyers had incorrectly chided potential student monitors, because the course materials and lecture notes would not be sold or published in their entirety.[34] Rather, the intent was to draw excerpts from the materials and to post only fragments or summaries. Such partial or limited use of someone else's intellectual property arguably falls within the scope of fair use, the doctrine that permits book reviewers or drama critics to excerpt small portions of protected material even for highly unflattering appraisals in the mass media. Thus it is far from clear that any UCLA professor may either bar an enrolled student from turning detailed lecture notes over to an outside organization or prevent that organization from posting on its website a stinging critique of the course that includes brief excerpts from the lectures—however unrepresentative those excerpts may be, and however unfair the implications of their use to appraise the instructor's views may be. In short, such intrusive tactics undoubtedly do pose a potentially severe threat to academic freedom, but one that lacks any meaningful prospect of legal remedy or recourse.

This rather bleak conclusion accords with the view adopted by the AAUP's Special Committee on Academic Freedom and National Security in Time of Crisis. In its report, filed two years to the day after the September 11, 2001, attacks, the committee lamented the recent proliferation of such classroom surveillance and professorial monitoring and the ominous implications for free expression on the nation's campuses. But the committee could envision no legal safeguard against such reprehensible practices. Nor would the group have wished to invoke such recourse even if it existed. "As private entities," the committee cautioned, such organizations as NoIndoctrination.org and Campus Watch "are protected by the First Amendment from state censorship so long as they stay within lawful bounds. They are sheltered by the same freedom of expression that we seek for ourselves, and they are equally subject to public rebuke." The report also addressed the plight of the individual professor who is unfairly targeted by such a website: Barring the remote possibility of a libel or copyright infringement suit, "the law demands . . . a certain toughening of the mental hide; such is the price of free speech."[35]

From this welter of possible options thus emerges little more than the AAUP Special Committee's suggestion of public rebuke as an avenue of recourse. Yet there has been no prospect of a "watchingcampuswatch.org" or "counternoindoctrination.org" yet visible on the web. Nor does it seem likely that, should such sites be launched, they would attract much attention within or beyond the academic community. Posting counterstatements or refutations that defend professors who have been unfairly tagged as "radicals" or as "Palestinian sympathizers" might make a record for the truth, but it would probably accomplish little else.

Early in the twenty-first century, pressure for balance in the college curriculum and on university faculties began to emerge from an ominous new source—state and federal legislation. For the first time in American history, the United States Congress and the legislatures of a third of the states gave serious consideration to bills that would in some form mandate political and ideological neutrality on the college campus. Such proposals reflected the tireless efforts of Horowitz, a onetime student radical who had become disenchanted with his former colleagues on the left and was convinced that higher education had not only become seriously imbalanced, but that many students were subject to unacceptable indoctrination in and outside the classroom.[36] The evidence supporting Horowitz's central premise was the very studies we reviewed earlier that suggested there might be political imbalance among college faculties, augmented by anecdotes that aggrieved students and parents had brought to his attention. But his critique went further and focused on individual professors who, in his view, had crossed the line to the detriment of higher education.

Early in 2006 Horowitz published an exposé of 101 university professors who exemplified the attributes he deplored. To prospective readers who might view college faculty as "harmless, antiquated hippies," Horowitz's publisher warned that, to the contrary, the targets of this book "spew violent anti-Americanism, preach anti-Semitism, and cheer the killing of American soldiers and civilians—all the while collecting tax dollars and tuition fees to indoctrinate our children."[37] Most targets of this new exposé took the book in stride, as they had been on Horowitz's radar in the past and were hardly surprised to find such a critique now between hard covers. But one object of such obloquy decided to fight back in court. Stanford University Middle East scholar Joel Benin filed suit against Horowitz and the publisher of a pamphlet he edited entitled "Campus Support for Terrorism." Professor Benin, a Jewish scholar who supports Palestinian rights and former president of the Middle East Studies Association, claimed that Horowitz's unauthorized use on the pamphlet's cover of his photograph (taken from his Stanford webpage) is a copyright violation.

In what appears to be the first counteroffensive in the Horowitz conflicts, Benin also took umbrage at the clear implication that he is a terrorist. Horowitz responded that he had not actually called Benin a terrorist but only an "apologist for terrorist groups"—a designation that he said he would be willing to defend in litigation.[38] What is novel about this exchange is that, for the very first time, it will be played out in a courtroom. Whether this novel case will yield any legal protection for targets of such criticism remains to be seen.

Long before writing the pamphlet that led to Professor Benin's lawsuit, Horowitz and his allies were pursuing a quite different course. They had drafted and promoted the Academic Bill of Rights, legislation specifically designed to mandate balance and combat bias in the college classroom. In slightly varying forms, the ABOR found its way into fifteen state legislatures between 2003 and 2006. Despite minor variations, these proposals shared several distinct elements. They often began by reciting universally embraced principles of academic freedom, drawn directly from policies of the American Association of University Professors—declaring, for example, that students are entitled not to be exploited or harassed in class and that faculty members are not to be selected on the basis of party or ideology. Students were to be graded solely on the basis of their "reasoned answers and appropriate knowledge of the subjects" and not "on the basis of their political or religious beliefs." Faculty members "will not use their courses or their position for the purpose of political, ideological, religious or anti-religious indoctrination." The selection of outside speakers and the allocation of funds to support their campus visits (as well as other student activities) "will observe the principles of academic freedom and promote intellectual pluralism." And to reinforce the commitment to an open campus, disruption of speakers or destruction of literature or "other effort to obstruct this exchange will not be tolerated." So far, so good, it would seem, even to the most ardent champion of academic freedom.[39]

The rub comes, however, in the form of several less benign mandates: First, the ABOR placed upon faculties a duty to make their students aware of viewpoints other than their own, recognizing that "academic disciplines should welcome a diversity of approaches to unsettled questions." Second, "curricula and reading lists in the humanities and social sciences should reflect the uncertainty and unsettled character of all human knowledge in these areas by providing students with dissenting sources and viewpoints where appropriate." Finally, institutions of higher learning (as well as academic professional societies) "should maintain a posture of organizational neutrality with respect to the substantive disagreements that divide researchers on questions within, or outside, their fields of inquiry."[40]

When such measures first surfaced on legislative dockets, the academic community reacted with predictable dismay. The Horowitz proposals seemed flawed in so many respects that a critic hardly knew where to begin. Even the seemingly innocuous provisions drew sharp rebuke from champions of academic freedom. Professor Joan Wallach Scott, a historian at the Institute for Advanced Study and former chair of AAUP's Committee on Academic Freedom and Tenure, testified before Pennsylvania's House Select Committee on Student Academic Freedom in the late fall of 2005.[41] After questioning the need for any remedial legislative action, Scott reported that she and her AAUP colleagues viewed ABOR as both a "misnomer as well as mistake," because it "ironically infringes academic freedom in the very act of purporting to protect it."

Specifically, charged Professor Scott, the proposed legislation "threatens to impose legislative oversight on the professional judgment of the faculty," an oversight that seemed not only unnecessary in light of self-regulatory commitment but also "dangerous [because] it recalls the kind of government intervention in the academy practiced by totalitarian governments . . . who seek to control thought rather than permit a free marketplace of ideas." Scott continued her critique, stressing that "by insisting that students have the same rights to academic freedom as their professors, [ABOR] deprives teachers of the authority necessary for teaching." Concluding her challenge to the proposed Academic Bill of Rights, Scott stressed what she sa·v as its central flaw: "by insisting that all courses and departments have 'balance' and 'diverse points of view' represented, [ABOR] would actually prevent colleges and universities from making the kinds of judgments that guarantee high quality teaching."[42]

The AAUP's detailed critique of the Academic Bill of Rights also focused closely on some of the more contentious of its specific language. For example, the claimed "right of 'access to a broad range of serious scholarly opinion'" could be read as inviting "diversity to be measured by political standards that diverge from the academic criteria of the scholarly profession. Measured in this way, diversity can easily become contradictory to academic ends." The ABOR's seemingly benign guarantee of fair grading of students could, for example, so constrain professorial assessment or appraisal of student performance that "faculty could not teach at all if they were utterly denied the ability to exercise this authority." Or, to take another superficially innocuous mandate—to keep controversial and unrelated matter out of the classroom—the ABOR "seeks to distinguish indoctrination from appropriate pedagogy by applying principles other than relevant scholarly standards, as interpreted and applied by the academic profession."[43]

This academic-freedom-based critique of the Horowitz/ABOR proposals reflects two deep and profound concerns. Most basically, such legislation would risk, or actually invite, a shifting of the locus of critical judgment about teaching and learning from university faculties and campus academic administrators to government agencies, and possibly even to the courts—and it would do so in far greater measure than has ever occurred in American higher education. The other concern is more practical: Much of the ABOR language—even phrases so seemingly benign and congenial with AAUP policies—harbors grave risks of interpretation and application (especially in unsympathetic nonacademic hands). Thus what might appear to many lawmakers a well-intentioned measure designed to enhance academic freedom turns out on closer scrutiny to pose many dangers that warrant its rejection. That debate is likely to continue for some years.

The Academic Bill of Rights has fared quite differently across the country. Comparable language that had been inserted in the House and Senate versions of the Congressional Higher Education Reauthorization Bill has remained on the table in both bodies. The Georgia legislature did pass a general resolution endorsing the spirit of the bill, although in a somewhat diluted form. Other states considered but eventually killed such measures before an actual up-or-down vote could be taken. That happened most notably in Ohio and Florida, where the public university presidents banded together to urge the defeat or suspension of such proposals.[44]

The Florida experience contained an additional and revealing twist. That state's version of the ABOR went further than that of most others, providing a statutory remedy for students aggrieved by political or ideological discrimination in the classroom. The proposal's sponsor, Rep. Dennis Baxley, having obtained the endorsement of a House committee, seemed prepared to play his trump—statements provided by a former police officer who, as a student at Florida State, complained of a professor who allegedly told his students, "Republicans don't get A's in my class." Baxley prefaced his presentation by assuring his colleagues that any among them who doubted the campus conditions he lamented were "either very naïve or you haven't talked to the students and faculty who live through subtle and sometimes not so subtle persecution every day."

Baxley had apparently not anticipated the response from Florida State's president T. K. Wetherell, who served earlier as speaker of Florida's lower house. The erstwhile speaker sharply faulted Baxley for lacking the courtesy to alert a former colleague to the pendency of such a charge. On the merits, Wetherell said he strongly doubted that such an incident ever occurred on his campus, noting that he had not "seen too many police officers around FSU who aren't willing to speak up." He then asked for names, dates, and other details. Baxley first apologized to his former legislative colleague, and then he quietly conceded he could not document the incident. Not long after that encounter, a private meeting held by Rep. Baxley with several leading Florida university presidents brought about the demise of the proposal.[45]

Horowitz, as it happened, also unwittingly contributed to the shelving of Florida's proposed ABOR. Testifying at an earlier committee hearing on the Baxley proposal, Horowitz claimed there were "scores of examples" across the country in which liberal professors had allegedly belittled or demeaned or insulted conservative students. A Miami Beach Democrat on the committee asked Horowitz for specific examples from Florida institutions. The best Horowitz could do was to note that the University of Florida had used student fees to bring Michael Moore to campus during the 2004 election. A university spokesman was ready with an immediate answer that seemed to refute the claim of bias or imbalance; the choice of speakers for the program in question had been made by the campus speaker bureau and, during the same period, had included New York Republican governor George Pataki and the former Bush White House press secretary Ari Fleischer. That process seemed closely concordant with the ABOR's mandate for a range of invited speakers who would promote intellectual pluralism.[46]

Colorado's legislative experience with the ABOR produced a slightly less happy outcome. The climate was more volatile than that of most other states where similar proposals were pending, given recent revelations of Professor Ward Churchill's post–September 11 rantings about "little Eichmanns" and the like. At a time when passage of the ABOR seemed a genuine possibility, the presidents of Colorado's public universities collaborated in the drafting of the Memorandum of Understanding. That document committed the presidents to "review [each institution's] student rights and campus grievance procedures to ensure that political diversity is explicitly recognized and protected." Implicit in that accord was a commitment to develop (if they did not already exist) and to publicize more widely official channels through which students might protest classroom harassment, intimidation, or indoctrination.[47]

Since the memorandum's adoption, there appears to have been but one relevant incident. A Native American political science professor at Denver's Metropolitan State College was the target of grievances filed by two students, Republican activists who claimed they had been victims of liberal classroom bias and ideological intimidation. Although Professor Oneida Meranto, a Navajo, vehemently denied the charges, and noted that one of the grievants attended but a single class session, she was subjected to a barrage of threatening e-mails and other messages and thus felt she could not safely cross the campus without an escort. Meanwhile, the student complaints were reviewed and eventually rejected, the college's president assuring Meranto that the institution "cannot and will not presume that your treatment of students reflects ideological bias or prejudice merely because you express your point of view." With an eye to the ABOR controversy—Horowitz has commented quite publicly on the case—the president added his concern that "'watchdogs' for 'political bias' who seek to remove professors holding a point of view will inhibit the rich dialogue that must take place in the classroom and destroy expressive freedom that is essential to the search for truth."[48]

It remains unclear how far the Meranto case may fairly be attributed to the pendency of the ABOR and the Memorandum of Understanding, since the student grievance procedures were already in place at Metro

State as at most other Colorado institutions. What is beyond doubt, however, as the Metro State president's statement suggested, is that widespread discussion of and publicity about such measures has created a climate in which students who feel aggrieved by uncongenial ideologies and unwelcome classroom experiences undoubtedly sense an empowerment that would not have been as apparent in earlier, pre-ABOR times.

Only two legislative bodies appear to have enacted any version of the Academic Bill of Rights. Missouri's lower house in the spring of 2007 adopted a bill that would require public colleges and universities to report regularly on specific steps they take to promote and protect "intellectual diversity." Specifically, the bill elaborated thus on the content of such an obligation: The mandated reports should address "intellectual diversity concerns in the institution's guidelines on teaching and program development and such concerns shall include but not be limited to the protection of religious freedom including the viewpoint that the Bible is inerrant."[49] This proposal evoked broad and deep concern not only from Missouri's campuses, but from far beyond the state and the academic community. In late spring, Missouri's state senate acceded to such appeals and declined to concur with the lower house, thus making the eleventh state in which proposed measures of this type failed to become law, despite garnering more than peripheral support.

The other near-miss occurred in South Dakota. That state's lower house did adopt an ABOR type proposal in the winter of 2006. Although somewhat milder than versions that had been introduced in other states, the South Dakota bill requires the state's public colleges and universities to file an annual report "detailing the steps [it] is taking to ensure intellectual diversity and the free exchange of ideas." This version of ABOR defines "intellectual diversity" as "the foundation of a learning environment that exposes students to a variety of political, ideological and other perspectives." The bill concludes with an enumeration of steps that institutions "may" (but need not) take in the course of their analysis—notably "includ[ing] intellectual diversity concerns in the institution's guidelines on teaching" and "includ[ing] intellectual diversity issues in student course evaluations." South Dakota colleges and universities might also choose to "create an institutional ombudsman on intellectual diversity."[50] Although passage of this bill was not preceded by lengthy hearings of the kind that have occurred in other states, the sponsors' citation of national studies of faculty political affiliations and alleged classroom bias left little doubt of a close kinship between South Dakota's reporting requirement and the more traditional or familiar ABOR mandates.

Now the ultimate and clearly most difficult academic freedom issue arises: Suppose South Dakota or some other state's governor actually signed into law some version of the Academic Bill of Rights. Would such a measure, once on the books, be vulnerable to a credible academic-freedom-based court challenge? The superficial response is that a law that simply declares a legislative preference or priority—especially when much of that declaration is consonant with established precepts of academic freedom—is immune from such a challenge. Surely if state lawmakers simply enacted the AAUP's 1940 statement or other policies protecting academic freedom and free expression, no legal recourse could be contemplated. By the same token, those portions of the ABOR that merely invoke or recite AAUP principles should be beyond challenge in the courts. Indeed, even those ABOR provisions that have been harshly criticized by academic freedom champions—the mandates for "plurality" and "diversity" and "reflecting the uncertainty and unsettled character" of the humanities and social sciences—may be disagreeable and unwelcome to most academics, but they seem to be little more than an expression of legislators' hopes that a broader range of views may find their way onto the nation's campuses. To that extent, the case for invulnerability has much to commend it.

The major proponent of a quite different view is Georgetown University law professor J. Peter Byrne, a longtime and close observer of academic freedom. His own writings reflect an objectivity on such matters that has made him a prime source for advocates on both sides of academic freedom debates. This time, however, he vigorously rejects the "merely declarative" view of the Academic Bill of Rights. "Enactment of ABOR," Byrne argues, would immediately "violate [constitutional academic freedom] on its face."[51] Professor Byrne reaches that conclusion for several reasons. He cites as a fundamental flaw of such legislation its indisputable premise that "faculties have [any] obligation to be viewpoint neutral regarding substantive disputes within their disciplines." Although neutrality may be constitutionally obligatory when it comes to institutional allocation of student activity fees, the same is hardly true for professors; "university faculties need not and, perhaps, should not be [neutral]."

Professor Byrne identifies several ways in which such bias-targeting measures seem to him clearly violative of free expression. First, he notes, "the ABR directly regulates two core university freedoms, determining on academic grounds who may teach and what may be taught." Second, he adds, "ABR represents a political effort to change the content of teaching and scholarship within existing fields," citing the Supreme Court's *Sweezy* decision for the view that such legislation "constitutes a 'governmental intervention in the intellectual life of the university.'" Third, Professor Byrne accurately observes that "courts have shown little patience with novel mechanisms to regulate speech on campuses," citing especially the eagerness with which federal judges have dispatched (on First Amendment grounds) every campus speech code that has been challenged in court. Finally, argues Professor Byrne, "ABR legislation seeks to displace faculty governance peer review by encouraging new regulatory bodies to oversee faculty functions."[52]

These are surely compelling claims, advanced by one who has perceptively analyzed such sensitive interests in academic freedom scholarship and litigation. Yet the conclusion to which this analysis leads, appealing though it is to professorial interests, may not be inexorable. In fact, there is much to support the contrary view—that pending ABOR measures cannot easily, if at all, be challenged in the courts. To the extent this latter view prevails, it imparts even greater impetus to defeating such measures before they become law, because once on the books they may be unassailable.

Any analysis of this perplexing issue must recognize that lawmakers often declare or express their views—even through formal legislation—in ways that remain beyond constitutional challenge. They commend citizens and organizations on myriad occasions. They designate particular days or weeks or months for the commemoration or celebration of an infinite array of causes. And legislatures frequently declare their views on a specific issue, assuming quite correctly that no citizen, however displeased by such a declaration, could ever persuade a court to enjoin or erase such action. Harder questions arise when legislative action goes beyond mere declaration of a view or belief. If a law contains no sanctions, and thus can not be directly enforced against a citizen, however inimical to individual liberties may be the underlying sentiment, it usually withstands legal challenge. Two notable exceptions should be set aside at this point—on the one hand, legislative endorsement or validation of religious views that violate the establishment clause's required separation of church and state and, on the other hand, legislative encouragement or validation of racial or gender or other forms of discrimination, where lawmakers may be viewed as part of a governmental threat to constitutionally guaranteed equality. Apart from these two special situations, however, legislators are for the most part free to declare their views in a noncoercive form, subject to recourse at the ballot box but not in the courtroom.

In the broader range of situations, mere legislative statement of a preference does not directly implicate constitutional rights to the degree necessary to sustain a legal challenge. If, let us suppose, a public college or university in an ABOR state fires, refuses to hire, or declines to promote an individual faculty member and invokes the relevant ABOR provision in doing so, that action may surely be challenged in court. Few principles are more central to academic freedom than the unacceptability of political or ideological reasons for personnel judgments; as one court of appeals made unmistakably clear in the 1980s, "an official of a state university may not restrict speech or association, even by subtle or indirect coercion or refusal to hire, simply because the official finds the views expressed by any group to be abhorrent."[53] Thus the victim of such bias surely would prevail in court.

The basis for the legal challenge, however, would be the institution's adverse action. Relevant provisions of the ABOR would bear at most a remote relationship to that action. Surely the university's president or chancellor could hardly avoid liability for such an unconstitutional judgment by claiming that "the ABOR made me do it." Even where the basis for an adverse action probably would not have triggered official reprisal or constraint until ABOR language suggested it—for example, charging a professor with "intruding unrelated controversial material into the classroom"—it is that action itself that would be legally vulnerable, not the abstract ABOR language that may have suggested such action. Hence the dilemma that seems to place the ABOR beyond legal challenge: An adverse personnel action, curricular revision, restriction of library or other materials, or other sanction that abridges academic freedom is legally vulnerable (or not) on its own merits, almost without regard to the catalytic or inspirational role the legislative language may have played.

It might now be useful to revisit Professor Byrne's core rationale for the strikingly different conclusion to which he arrives. He argues, quite cogently, that "ABR directly regulates two core university freedoms," specifically deciding on academic grounds "who shall teach and what shall be taught." If a university chooses to adjust its hiring or curricular judgments to please lawmakers by conforming more closely to ABOR precepts, it is far from clear that any "regulating" has occurred, at least at the state level. Much the same can be said of Professor Byrne's second critique—that "ABR represents a political effort to change the content of teaching and scholarship." So it would seem to be, but it falls far short of "governmental intervention in the intellectual life of the university," which is Professor Byrne's talisman. And while he rightly notes the disdain that federal judges have shown for "novel mechanisms to regulate speech on campuses," the cases in which restrictive speech codes (most notably) have been struck down on First Amendment grounds all contained evidence of specific sanctions or penalties that were not only on the books but the enforcement of which had actually been threatened.[54]

Take away the sanctions and federal judges might still have "little patience" with such measures, but they would be hard pressed to find sufficient evidence of demonstrated injury, which must exist as the predicate for a constitutional judgment. The last of Professor Byrne's cited concerns is subtler—that ABOR "seeks to displace faculty governance peer review by encouraging new regulatory bodies to oversee faculty functions." Mounting a constitutional challenge on that basis would be correspondingly harder, if not impossible. Courts have been far less sensitive to governmentally mandated shifts in governance than to restriction of individual or even collective expression in cruder forms. Thus it is far from clear that ABOR would be unconstitutional even if it did directly, of its own force, displace existing governance systems. When the most that can be said is that such legislation "seeks to displace" or "encourages 'institutional displacement of traditional governance,'" a conclusive First Amendment or academic freedom claim that would prevail in court remains at a distance.[55]

Finally, there is an even subtler theory that Professor Byrne did not press, though it is quite consistent with his views. Could it be said that ABOR—even the serious consideration of such proposals, let alone their adoption—so chills the climate for free speech and academic freedom in a given state that the mere pendency of such measures could be challenged even without any sanctions or potential for direct application? As noted in Chapter 3, courts have occasionally responded favorably to such claims—notably, in barring undercover police officers from spying on UCLA classes, professors, and students and in mandating destruction of the rogue Ohio grand jury report whose publication so frightened Kent State University faculty members that they eschewed controversy in their classes.

It is barely possible that a useful analogy could be drawn between such experiences and the enactment of an ABOR, especially if the predictable institutional conformity actually did take place. The theory on which such a claim might rest would be slightly different from those Professor Byrne describes. Indeed, the premise of such a challenge to the ABOR would be that the threat of penalties or sanctions—which concededly do not exist in any version of this legislation—simply are not essential to advancing a free speech claim on a professor's behalf. Not only is actual enforcement not vital under such a theory of potential recourse, but also even a prospect of direct enforcement by government seems not to be essential to the raising of such a claim.

As Professor Byrne sees it, the legally actionable threat in an ABOR state would reflect simply the changed climate that resulted from formal governmental endorsement of views and values so alien to free inquiry and expression. That changed climate, without more, resulting simply from such a legislative declaration, would pose an actionable threat to academic freedom. Should it be shown, in addition, that substantial numbers of recruited faculty have declined offers to join institutions in that state, so much the better. Suffice it to say that such a challenge would be far from easy or obvious. At this stage, however, it seems to offer the only likely basis for a successful constitutional indictment of ABOR and its progeny.

Finally, suppose a university administration or governing board were to become aware that a perilous imbalance exists in an academic department or professional school and, without the benefit of Horowitz's prompting, decides on its own to seek better balance. It would be naïve to deny that such conditions do exist even on the most distinguished of university campuses. And even the most ardent champion of faculty autonomy could not claim in good conscience that a quest for better balance is inherently inimical to academic freedom; indeed there is a powerful argument that broader tolerance for diverse viewpoints serves the interests of academic freedom. A widely shared commitment to offer to students a broad array of viewpoints, and to ensure that scholarly inquiry is pursued from many diverse perspectives, would certainly seem to warrant occasional attention to imbalance within schools and departments. The critical issue is far less whether any steps may be taken to redress apparent imbalance than who should initiate those steps and what specific steps might be consistent with academic freedom.

At the outset, it is perfectly clear what an institution may not do, however serious the current imbalance and however laudable its desire to improve the situation. To base a faculty hiring or promotion decision on ideology or political affiliation is of course impermissible, both in terms of policy and (for public universities) constitutional law. In the late 1970s the University of Maryland was charged with refusing to appoint Marxist

Bertel Ollman to a department chair because of his widely expressed political views. The administration insisted that its rejection of Ollman had nothing to do with his ideology, but that it reflected instead a negative assessment of his qualifications and experience. The federal courts, to which Ollman took his constitutional claim, eventually sided with the university and dismissed the suit. While accepting the administration's claim that nonideological considerations led to Ollman's rejection, the federal judge recognized the clear constitutional template that must govern such a case: "No more direct assault on academic freedom can be imagined than for school authorities to refuse to hire a teacher because of his or her political, philosophical or ideological beliefs."[56]

The appeals court affirmed, adding its equally clear conviction that ideology may play no role in academic personnel judgments.[57] The higher court also took favorable note of a recent case decided by an Arkansas federal judge, who had overturned the denial of renewal to a "professor with leftist political opinions" after finding that "the university was swayed by public controversy over the professor's employment."[58] Thus any such consideration of ideology in the faculty personnel process offers the clearest example of what universities may not do to redress perceived imbalance.

The same may not be said, however, about official statements of condemnation. If a president, chancellor, provost, or dean becomes concerned about the seeming bias of an academic unit, no principle of academic freedom precludes public expression of such concern. Much as university officials have felt free to express their disapproval of faculty outbursts in the post–September 11 era, their ability to speak out with regard to the condition of an entire school or department should not be seen as an attack on the academic freedom of members of that unit—unless, of course, the official statement contains an implied threat resembling City College of New York president Bernard Harleston's ill-fated declaration that "there is no place at City College for racism, anti-Semitism, [or] ethnic snobbism."[59] Merely expressing official disapproval, perhaps accompanied by a declared hope for greater balance in the future, does not by itself cross the line. Such a public indictment of an academic unit's collective ideology is likely to evoke much faculty anxiety and even indignation—but such concerns are political, not constitutional.

There must be other and better ways in which a university that seeks to redress an obvious and counterproductive ideological imbalance might address the problem. Perhaps the most obvious response would be to launch a formal investigation. Despite occasional claims that an official probe may threaten academic freedom, the process of inquiry is central to scholarship. It is what the academic community does best, and this community should most especially not resist bringing such a process to bear upon its own most troubling tensions. So it was that when Columbia University was beset by student complaints of bias and mistreatment in the Department of Middle East Languages and Culture, the chief academic officer appointed a prestigious faculty panel to conduct an intensive investigation. Several months later, after exhaustive inquiry including interviews with all relevant students and professors, the panel issued a report in late March 2005. Central to the committee's analysis was a rejection of charges of anti-Semitism within the troubled department. Although the panel did note one instance in which a faculty member had "exceeded commonly accepted bounds" in his dealings with an Israeli student, the broader charges of bias that had triggered the inquiry were not substantiated. That consensus predictably drew criticism from both sides—from pro-Israeli groups charging that the inquiry had failed to fault certain statements they found troubling in and outside class and from pro-Palestinians critical of the negative assessment of one faculty member's presumptively protected expression. Columbia's president, Lee Bollinger, promptly endorsed the report and accepted its conclusions, which included recommendations to pay closer attention to student grievance procedures, the advisory system, and to establish "a common, central university site to which students, faculty and administrators could turn to express concerns, though not necessarily grievances, about the quality of their experience at Columbia."[60]

Another very different incident reinforces the great potential value of careful investigation. About a week after the September 11 attacks, Orange Coast Community College instructor Kenneth Hearlson was charged by several of his students with pointing to Muslims in his classroom and shouting at them, "You drove two planes into the World Trade Center; you killed five thousand people." He was also reported to have called his Muslim students "terrorists," "murderers," and "Nazis." Resisting demands for immediate dismissal, the college administration commissioned a local attorney to undertake an exhaustive inquiry into the incident, while Hearlson was placed on leave for the balance of the semester. By December the investigation was complete.

The attorney concluded that, on the basis of all the evidence she had reviewed, Hearlson never made the inflammatory statements that were attributed to him. Rather, on the day in question, he had led a heated discussion of the hijacking and the attacks, during which provocative and troubling questions were raised. Hearlson, in short, was indeed less than fully sensitive to his Muslim students—and on that basis the college did issue a formal letter of reprimand, while reinstating him in his teaching position.[61] The Hearlson inquiry offers a classic example of the potential value to academic freedom of intensive inquiry, even under conditions where those who are the subject or target of such inquiry might well prefer a lower profile.

Beyond investigation, several other options may avail the university that wishes to achieve greater balance in constitutionally acceptable ways. There should be little doubt that a university administration may approve faculty hiring in areas of critical need without abridging anyone's academic freedom. If an economics department has just lost (or never had) a critical mass of quantitative economists, or a psychology department is seriously understaffed in the area of clinical specialties, few would doubt that the administration may target such needs or deficiencies in future faculty hiring. Ideology and politics play no role in such a judgment about core academic and scholarly qualifications. Thus a dean or provost may simply refuse to authorize faculty recruitment until and unless the unit that does the hiring has first filled critical gaps and addressed essential curricular needs.

When balance enters the equation, the analysis becomes more difficult, though similar principles should apply. Consider the field of Middle Eastern studies, and imagine a department that has no expert on Israel, or on the Palestinian state. It seems beyond doubt that such a department could be limited to recruiting a scholar who would remedy that deficiency. But suppose among the existing cadre of experts on Israel, there is no Zionist. And suppose there is intense student, alumni, and community pressure to add an avowed Zionist. In that situation, the solution should depend on the way in which the issue of a Zionist perspective enters the equation.

The critical difference should be between seeking a scholar whose expertise includes Zionism (whatever may be his or her personal views on that volatile issue) and seeking someone who has publicly expressed a Zionist viewpoint (which may or may not be consistent with that person's academic expertise). Both quests might be seen as directed toward balance. But they are fundamentally different in terms that are vital to academic freedom. A focus on expertise is entirely appropriate, even though it may indirectly serve the viewpoint goal—that is, one whose academic competence includes Zionism may well turn out to be an advocate for that viewpoint. But there is no guarantee of such concordance, as there would be when advocacy or viewpoint as such becomes the desideratum. This distinction is critical, if subtle. One may seek to achieve balance in the former sense, emphasizing expertise, but not focus on viewpoint or advocacy as the goal.

Appraisal of potential academic leadership offers another promising avenue of redress for the severely imbalanced unit. Surely an appropriate step in addressing an imbalanced unit would be to seek as dean or department chair a person with demonstrated skill in building consensus and, most especially, in bringing about balance in discussions of contentious issues. The institution might even view favorably a candidate's past success in achieving, through academically acceptable means, the very type of balance that is seen as seriously lacking. Conversely, it would abridge no one's academic freedom to pass over an otherwise qualified candidate whose record evidenced an absence of such skills or, even worse, a propensity for condoning division and discord. To seek to achieve or maintain balance by entrusting leadership to a person with a proven ability to build harmony and trust seems wholly appropriate.

There remains a far more difficult question—whether an incumbent dean or department chair may be removed for having consistently failed to redress a manifestly imbalanced condition within the unit for which he or she was responsible. Obviously the dean's or chair's own views, ideology, or affiliation may not be made the occasion for such intervention, though a thorough assessment of unsuccessful efforts to improve balance through faculty recruitment and retention would be a very different matter. Removing one who had tried and failed at achieving better balance seems a drastic solution, but it is not necessarily beyond consideration.

In future evaluations of a dean's or chair's administrative performance, it should also be permissible to take into account (and tangibly reward) efforts to achieve balance and success in meeting those goals—again, so long as the means used to do so are acceptable. Because institutions regularly assess and recognize success in achieving racial, gender, and ethnic diversity in faculty recruitment and retention, adding balance of this type to the equation seems not to distort the process. Care need be taken both in the way such a criterion is stated and in the way in which its achievement is measured through annual and longer-term assessments—but these are details of a type that should not deter the process.

Suppose, however, that such means simply fail to achieve the desired balance. Indeed, conditions may even deteriorate, as the outnumbered or minority members of a skewed department may become discouraged and depart, leaving only those whose dominant role created the initial problem. The administration might then be tempted simply to abolish the department and start over. That would involve the termination of tenured faculty positions, a process that might initially seem inconceivable. Surprisingly, however, AAUP policy does permit so drastic a step under carefully constrained conditions. Tenured faculty positions may be terminated as part of the "bona fide formal discontinuance of a program or department of instruction."[62]

Understandably, several stringent conditions apply. The judgment must be based "essentially upon educational considerations," as determined by a faculty body. The driving force may not include "cyclical or temporary variations in enrollment," but must reflect "long-range judgments that the educational mission of the institution as a whole will be enhanced by the discontinuance."[63] The AAUP policy also contains elaborate provisions to protect individual members of a discontinued department, including efforts to provide alternative employment at the institution or elsewhere. The question whether acute imbalance might warrant discontinuance of a distressed department seems never to have been tested. Such drastic actions are extremely rare. The occasion may be the de facto dismantling of a department, as with the Department of Demography at the University of California–Berkeley, which was officially eliminated—little more than deleting a nonfunctional budget heading—after the last faculty member assigned to that department had resigned and the only other readily accepted reassignment to a cognate field in which he held a joint appointment.

Discontinuance may also result from a merger of two institutions that results in severe and unproductive redundancy; for example, when the combining of Cleveland's Case Institute and Western Reserve University left two redundant departments of architecture; the undergraduate unit was discontinued with AAUP approval, and as many as possible of its faculty (though not all) were transferred to the surviving graduate program. At the least, where imbalance is the catalyst for proposed discontinuance, an especially rigorous faculty review of such an administrative initiative is clearly in order. The possibility seems at least worth discussing, in extremis, though with appropriate cautions and safeguards.

If the imbalanced department may not be discontinued, could an institution with substantial resources simply create an entirely new unit to cover the same subject matter—though with a far better balance among its founding faculty? Specifically, could the faculty of the now superseded department claim that such competition abridged their academic freedom? The cost of such a drastic solution readily explains the absence of any case studies by which to assess its impact. Yet a university enjoys sufficient authority over the basic structure of its curriculum that a judgment to create an arguably parallel unit would be hard to resist even if the effect of such action might be to drain away many of the students who would normally have enrolled in courses taught by the imbalanced unit's faculty. Creating interdepartmental competition, especially in order to enhance students' options and choices, is not inherently unacceptable, though it does invite close scrutiny and (even apart from the forbidding cost of such action) may be suspect as a remedy for perceived imbalance.

Several other measures with curricular implications seem more congenial to academic values. A concerned administration could, for example, create and fund a few new faculty positions that crossed departmental lines, specifically targeting the better balanced side of an unbalanced academic unit. At an even lower level of commitment, the administration might create a few campus-wide visiting faculty positions, with an eye to recruiting scholars whose expertise would offset the leaning of the imbalanced unit. Although some existing academic unit would need to prove a home for such visitors, as well as for the interdisciplinary appointees, there should be willing sponsors ready to take advantage of such an opportunity.

Thus, to return to the Middle East studies scenario, if the core department simply refused to hire anyone with expertise on Zionism, presumably an extra-departmental home for such a person could be found in some other fields such as history, political science, or religious studies. Surely no academic unit owns a discipline so completely that it not only may refuse to meet a manifest curricular need within its own ranks, but may also block remedial action by a sister department. The institution's commitment to offer a range and variety of subjects and courses surely transcends the turf claims of a recalcitrant department, regardless of balance or bias.

There may well be other avenues by which a university could seek to redress curricular imbalance that it perceives and wishes to change. The approaches suggested here are more illustrative than definitive. The central concern is that whatever is done in this sensitive area must reflect the academic judgment of the institution and its faculty, not the dictates of a state legislature or other governmental body, or pressure from a private organization of alumni or others. Any other approach would severely and substantially imperil academic freedom.

10

Academic Freedom in Perspective

Three basic questions remain to be addressed: First, does academic freedom really matter? Second, how secure is academic freedom? And third, how might academic freedom be made more secure? Although definitive answers are unlikely, these issues deserve attention in any such study as this one.

Does Academic Freedom Really Matter?

Two personal experiences, exactly a decade apart, may shed some light on the importance of academic freedom. In the winter of 1996, several Virginia legislators were determined to do what they could to restrict the spread of salacious material on the Internet. They introduced a bill that would forbid all state employees (save for those in law enforcement) from using state-owned computers to access sexually explicit material. Only formal approval by an agency head would sanction such activity—and even then only when it is related to a "bona fide agency-approved research project."[1] Substantial criminal penalties would accompany any proven violation.

Such a measure obviously posed ominous implications for libraries and universities and those who studied potentially suspect materials. Not only might art historians now be at risk for accessing and downloading images that could be deemed sexually explicit, but also many clinical faculty and researchers at the state's medical schools who used the Internet to obtain and share depictions that might also run afoul of such a prohibition were potentially at risk. Thus the conceivable reach of this novel measure raised alarm across much of Virginia's scholarly community.

When a hearing on the bill was scheduled in the Courts of Justice Committee of the General Assembly's House of Delegates, the academic and library communities fully appreciated the need to state forcefully the case against the proposal in academic freedom and free speech terms. Although deeply concerned, librarians (few of whom held tenure) could not risk such an appearance. When it seemed that a constitutional scholar should play that role, I readily accepted the invitation and testified a few days later. At the close of my testimony before a surprisingly hostile committee, I offered this analogy: "As I read the First Amendment, you can no more do what you propose here than you could bar a custodian in this [General Assembly] building from reading a personal copy of *Penthouse* or *Hustler* during his coffee break."[2] Several committee members angrily disparaged any such analogy; they insisted that the commonwealth's role with respect to the Internet was profoundly different, because access to digital material in state facilities involved the use of government property, and because the primacy of the commonwealth's official business must be favored. The bill unanimously passed the committee and the full House, became law, and soon ended up in federal court (in the lawsuit recounted in greater detail in Chapter 7).

Had an ordinary state employee, such as a professional librarian or a junior faculty member in one of the affected disciplines, presented such provocative and unwelcome testimony, he or she would almost surely have found his or her job in jeopardy upon return from Richmond. The situation was very different, however, for a tenured university professor, who is free to convey unwelcome and even unorthodox views to a legislative committee—indeed, who incurs by reason of his secure academic position and the expertise it reflects a duty to speak out on matters of public importance. Yet even senior professors are occasionally reminded of their vulnerability. During a legislative hearing soon after the incident reported here, Professor Rodney Smolla sharply criticized a proposal to restore moments of silence to Virginia's public school classrooms. Just after he left the committee room, he was beset by the bill's sponsor (who was also an architect of the Internet-access law), now flush with anger. "Your institution will pay for this," the indignant lawmaker warned, with obvious reference to the publicly supported College of William and Mary at which Smolla had taught for many years. Professor Smolla smiled, and calmly replied, "You're welcome to try, but you should know I've just moved to the University of Richmond." Recognizing this new venue to be not only a private university but also one closely tied to the Baptist Church, the lawmaker at once appreciated the futility of his threat. That seems to have been the end of the matter; not long after, Smolla became the Richmond law faculty's dean.

The other incident occurred almost precisely ten years later in Philadelphia. Pennsylvania's Republican-controlled lower house had created the Select Committee on Student Academic Freedom to inquire into allegations of bias or imbalance on the commonwealth's public campuses and specifically to assess claims advanced by one lawmaker that conservative students had been targets of discrimination and unfair grading at the hands of liberal professors. The committee held a series of hearings across the state in the summer and fall of 2005, turning up little evidence to support the claims of political bias or unfairness. The penultimate hearing was held in Philadelphia early in January. By this time the Democrats (including several who represented major academic communities such as Penn State and University of Pittsburgh) were not only disenchanted by the whole inquiry but also downright angry. At the January hearing several minority members went so far as to denounce the committee as "a waste of time."[3] Clearly the gracious role for a witness who welcomed their firm opposition to the anti-academic initiative would have been acquiescence, if not outright concurrence. Yet there was a need for someone to demur on the "waste of time" issue since the very act of holding such hearings had provided a welcome opportunity to present a contrary case on behalf of Pennsylvania's public universities and their faculties. Thus, at some risk of alienating our most supportive friends and allies on the committee, I ventured the view that the inquiry and the hearings had been far from a waste of time, but they had in fact been of much value in exposing the truth about bias and balance in the academy. Whereas fifteen other states had tiptoed around the issue, providing no opportunity for testimony from the academic community as well as from its critics, the Keystone State had uniquely created such a forum, for which some were deeply grateful. I suspect this encounter earned me few new "friends in Pennsylvania," to paraphrase the license plate message.

Thus the answer to the question "Does academic freedom matter?" depends initially on the respondent's experience. Most college and university professors will never encounter a serious threat to their independence or free expression. They may even resent the expectation that they join or support organizations that defend such freedoms when the risks seem so remote to their own careers and fields. Yet for the small fraction of academics who do encounter such pressures, there seems little doubt that academic freedom makes a major difference. Although by no means all of the thousand or so inquiries the national American Association of University Professors (AAUP) receives each year reflect academic freedom violations, a surprising number of the concerns that beleaguered or embattled professors report do implicate their free expression or inquiry in significant ways. The subject matter can be as varied as the focus of the two University of Utah physicists who evoked disdain and ridicule from the established scientific community when they championed cold fusion research, or of those who express views on racial issues as unsettling as those of Lani Guinier, or treat teen sex as unconventionally as Joycelyn Elders, or review European history as elliptically as Christina Jeffrey (or for that matter Arthur Butz). A bit closer to the mainstream, academic freedom certainly matters to the growing number of reputable scholars who have come increasingly to question the wisdom of U.S. foreign policy in the Middle East (and especially in Iraq), just as academic freedom safeguarded many academics whose outspoken opposition to the Vietnam War in the 1960s would surely have put them at grave risk without such protection.

Thus any sound answer to the question, does academic freedom make a difference? will vary vastly with the audience and the context. In an ideal world—"if men were angels"—such protection would be unnecessary because legislatures, boards, administrators, and senior colleagues would always recognize the need for independent thought and inquiry on a university campus, and they would impose no threats or intrusions. Yet the real world in which we live and teach is sufficiently different from such an ideal environment that basic safeguards are vital.

How Secure Is Academic Freedom?

The early years of the twenty-first century could be described, quoting Charles Dickens, as "the best of times" and "the worst of times"[4] for academic freedom. On one hand, outspoken scholars fared so much better than one would have expected in the aftermath of the September 11, 2001, attacks that one would at first be tempted to conclude that academic freedom is not only completely secure, but it is highly resilient as well. Remember that Professor Richard Berthold incurred only a reprimand for telling his freshman history class that "anyone who bombs the Pentagon gets my vote,"[5] and that Nicholas DeGenova got essentially a pass when he called for "a million Mogadishus,"[6] and that Ward Churchill wrote with impunity of the September 11 hijackers as men of conviction while demeaning their victims as "little Eichmanns,"[7] and that Arthur Butz remained a professor in good standing after he lauded Iran's president for Holocaust-denial; the moderate and deliberative institutional response to such incidents and others in the post–9/11 period suggests that academic freedom is indeed in excellent health.[8]

When in doubt about support beyond the academic world, one might well draw comfort from Fox News host Bill O'Reilly's thrice-repeated affirmation of academic freedom's value and importance, most recently when he insisted that "a university is a place where all views, even abhorrent views, are tolerated for the sake of freedom of expression."[9] There has been no resurgence of McCarthyism not only because there is no McCarthy a half century later—it would be hard to imagine a greater contrast than today's junior senator from Wisconsin, Russ Feingold the only one to vote against the USA PATRIOT Act—but for myriad other reasons, including dramatic changes in the law that protects free expression and inquiry, especially on the college campus.

So far, so good, one would have to observe. What's to worry about, then? Much of this book has documented the emergence of a host of ominous new forces and pressures that cloud and complicate the happy picture one would have if an overview covered nothing more than faculty personnel matters. Both federal and state courts have seemed surprisingly receptive to a new and deeply disturbing view of academic interests—whether the issue is who controls a professor's choice of teaching materials and assignment of grades, whether a professor can resist compelled disclosure of research in progress, who makes the final decisions in allocating endowment funds for the support of academic programs, or what happens when a student objects to an uncongenial course assignment.

Changes in the medium of expression have also produced dramatic changes—most notably in failing to accord to digital and electronic messages and information many of the protections that faculty have taken for granted through a century of paper and telephonic communications. Resource materials garnered through Internet searches have in several situations received far less protection than would routinely be accorded, anywhere in the academic world, to the same materials in print form. And when the medium is artistic, one that is hardly novel but becomes increasingly venturesome and therefore controversial, academic freedom has recently encountered a wave of challenges and limits, including conditions on grants to avant-garde artists, innovative theater and musical or film presentations, and other settings.

Then there are a host of new qualifications and exceptions to traditional safeguards for academic research—not only permitting a private litigant, for purely commercial gain, to compel the premature disclosure (and inevitable disruption) of research in process, or declining to protect vital and confidential relationships, but also through condoning direct government distortion of research on such sensitive subject matter as global warming and of the use of certain biohazardous and other security-sensitive materials.

The gravest of new threats to the integrity and independence of research may come, however, not from government but rather from entirely private sources. Some observers, in fact, perceive the threat to academic freedom from corporate-sponsored (and to some degree corporate-controlled) research as more serious than the worst that even an insensitive government may impose. When universities agree to draconian prepublication or internal review constraints, their faculties whose laboratory work depends on corporate sponsorship have little choice but to acquiesce, however uncongenial those restrictions may be to the process of scientific inquiry. Although institutions may guard against such intrusions or reduce the risks of compromise, the allure of corporate support—often extending well beyond specific research programs—seems too often to have "bought" not only the time and creativity of scientists, but also to have distorted the conscience of the academic community in vital areas. Thus the threat to academic freedom in research is by no means limited to government policies and restrictions, but it comes also and in worrisome measure from private research sponsors.

Finally, and to some observers most ominous of all, is an array of new threats to academic freedom from totally private sources. The conservative University of California–Los Angeles (UCLA) alumni group's recent offer to pay students to monitor the classes of "liberal" professors and tape lectures for posting on the organization's website may be the most alarming of such threats, but it is by no means the only troubling example. Such threats are potentially more ominous than traditional attacks on academic freedom for several reasons. For one, as historian Ellen Schrecker notes, "it reaches directly into the classroom"—a focus that causes her to find "today's assault on the academy . . . even more serious than [that of] the McCarthy era,"[10] about which she happens to be the consummate expert.

Moreover, such attacks by private groups are typically immune to any legal recourse; professors who are vilified on the burgeoning array of websites and blogs, such as NoIndoctrination.org and Campus Watch, clearly may not assert any First Amendment claims on their behalf against their students and others who are simply engaging in free speech of their own.

Nor (save in the most extreme circumstances) may an embattled professor whose views are distorted on such a webpage sue for libel; typically such a person would need to prove actual malice to get a defamation claim beyond the threshold in court, and that would be a daunting task in such cases.

Even the claim of copyright infringement (which caused the UCLA alumni group to withdraw its offer of remuneration for classroom spies) seems questionable in the context of students gathering information from and about courses in which they are properly enrolled. Thus what may be the most ominous feature of these new threats to academic freedom is their very immunity from any viable form of legal recourse. Those who find such tactics reprehensible may, and occasionally do, speak out and are welcome to launch and post replies on countervailing information sources, but that seems to be about the limit of possible retaliation. The academic community should register its abhorrence for such destructive tactics, wherever on the political or ideological spectrum they originate, but such a response leaves falsely charged or vilified professors essentially without any recourse against the newest threat to academic freedom.

To conclude our sense of how secure academic freedom is in the first decade of the new millennium: In conventional terms, not only is a resurgence of McCarthyism improbable for myriad reasons, but quite clearly the very forces that so gravely undermined academic freedom during the Cold War era simply have no counterpart in these times. That is manifestly good news, but clearly it is not the only news. A host of new forces and pressures now cast long shadows in very different directions. Celebration of the happy tidings would therefore be quite premature.

How Might Academic Freedom Be Made More Secure?

To the extent that current conditions reveal vulnerability in academic freedom, it is fair to ask what actions might provide better protection in the future. Several quite specific antidotes merit closer attention:

First, the academic community should be substantially more aggressive in seeking legal protection for vital interests of free inquiry and scholarship. Seldom have the organizations that effectively represent universities and their needs actually gone on the offensive; for the most part these groups have been more than fully occupied—and quite vigorously—in fending off threatened intrusions and restrictions, leaving precious little time or political capital for countermeasures. One example to the contrary may suggest a potential that has been less than fully tapped. Near the end of his long and distinguished career in Congress, Senator Daniel Patrick Moynihan invited suggestions for legislative measures that would enhance civil liberties. At the urging of the Thomas Jefferson Center for the Protection of Free Expression, he sponsored a bill that would create in the federal courts a researcher's privilege comparable to the legal shield that most states afford to journalists with respect to confidential sources. Other prominent senators, such as Vermont's Patrick Leahy, were prepared to lend their support to such a measure. The American Association for the Advancement of Science compiled a wealth of impressive testimony from scientists who had been victims of the sorts of incursions and forays described in Chapter 5 and who would have been only too happy to enlighten Senate committees about the risks to the research process of the currently unfettered discovery process. Sadly, Moynihan's term in the Senate ended before such hearings could be held, and the putative researcher's privilege law simply became part of the legacy of a lawmaker who had often championed the needs of higher education and was prepared to do so once more.

Another notable example of such rare initiative was the proposed Freedom to Read Protection Act, which would substantially have mitigated the most intrusive features of the USA PATRIOT Act's Business Records section, under which federal law-enforcement officers could demand such sensitive materials as library borrower and book-purchaser records without formal legal process and on mere suspicion of terrorist involvement. Publishers, librarians, and various free speech, free press, and scholarly organizations came together to draft and seek what proved to be surprisingly extensive congressional support for his measure. The bill came within one vote of passage, and in the eventual reauthorization of the entire PATRIOT Act its spirit was substantially incorporated in a much-improved Business Records Act—so much better, in fact, that the ACLU withdrew a pending court challenge to the previous language because its basic concerns had been so nearly redressed. What is striking about these two experiences is how infrequent have been such proactive requests to enhance the legal safeguards for academic freedom.

Second, the academic community needs to resist more vigorously potentially grave threats that arise in the courts, even though only a single institution may be directly affected. Although the American Council on Education and the National Association of College and University Attorneys keep a close watch on relevant litigation and fully inform the academic community of potentially threatening developments, the actual making of common cause in the courts is less frequent than one might wish, and it sometimes depends on the kindness of relative strangers. Thus when the onerous federal regulations on the export of encryption technology were being challenged in three lawsuits in the mid-1990s, a coordinated assertion of basic academic freedom interests occurred in only one case, and only because of the singular efforts of a San Francisco cyber-lawyer. In the other case that brought a ruling favorable to free inquiry and scholarly exchange, a courageous Cleveland law professor stood virtually alone save for one friend-of-the-court brief filed by the AAUP and the Thomas Jefferson Center.

One striking recent example to the contrary illustrates the potential of making common cause in major test cases. When the Supreme Court agreed to revisit the issue of race-sensitive admission policies at the University of Michigan, amicus curiae briefs were sought from and filed by a host of sympathetic organizations, drawn not only from beyond Ann Arbor but also well beyond the academic community. Especially persuasive to Justice Sandra Day O'Connor's favorable majority view of the law school's affirmative action program were compelling briefs filed by corporate CEOs and senior retired military officers, both groups lauding the role that affirmative action and race-based inclusive policies had played in their respective sectors of national life.

Yet the making of common cause seems the rare exception and surely not the rule. When New York University is effectively forced to settle with Kinko's over its method of compiling course materials, or Princeton is sued for allegedly departing from a donor's intent in the use of endowment funds for support of the Woodrow Wilson School, or Hampton University is sued for allegedly failing to silence libelous statements by one member of its faculty against another, much of the rest of the academic community is informed, and may be uneasy about the implications of such litigation, but does not readily come forward to support the manifestly common interests in ways that will apprise the courts of such shared concern.

Third, accrediting associations should focus more sharply and critically on academic freedom violations. Being accredited is a virtual necessity for an institution of higher learning—whether in terms of the eligibility of its students for federal financial aid or admission of its graduates to selective professional and other programs. One would suppose that an institution that had deprived its faculty of academic freedom might forfeit or at least jeopardize its accredited status. A few specialized accrediting groups—notably the Association of Theological Schools and the Association of American Law Schools—have imposed restrictions on previously accredited programs or have deferred admission of new programs in response to serious academic freedom violations. However, the major regional organizations (which accredit entire institutions rather than simply component programs) have been less aggressive in policing academic freedom conditions, even though their policies typically make mention of free inquiry and expression as general expectations. Closer attention to such issues within the accrediting community could substantially enhance academic freedom.

Fourth, academic administrators should be readier to initiate sanctions, including dismissal, against faculty members who abuse the special privileges and responsibilities of the professoriate. Despite the pervasive (and pernicious) belief that a tenured professor can never be dismissed, there are perhaps as many as fifty such dismissals in any given academic year, and sometimes there are substantially more than that. Typically those cases focus on such inexcusable faculty behavior as plagiarism, serious violations of criminal law, or blatant sexual harassment. But for various reasons, such adverse actions are seldom publicized, enabling the myth of professorial impunity to persist. Moreover, the AAUP (as the primary guardian of academic freedom) appears to have de-emphasized its highly visible concern for faculty responsibility and ethical behavior. The Association's long permanent Committee B, once second only to the group that protected academic freedom and tenure (Committee A) atrophied over the years and no longer exists on the association's roster. Although the AAUP does maintain a concern for professional ethics—a statement was recently adopted and issued that recommends limits on professors' assignment to students of their own textbooks from which the author derives royalties—such issues do seem to receive lesser attention than was once the case. A revival of the erstwhile level of faculty commitment to professional ethics and responsibility might be a salutary step in the enhancement of acceptance of academic freedom.

Fifth, the academic left should be far readier than it has been of late to make common cause with colleagues on the other end of the spectrum who share academic freedom concerns. Those who classify themselves as "liberal" often tend to disparage even the potentially sympathetic views of colleagues who describe their political beliefs and affiliations as "conservative." Such attenuation seems both unnecessary and counterproductive.

One example may suggest what the academic left often misses. During the deliberations of the AAUP's Special Committee on Academic Freedom and National Security in Time of Crisis, arguably the most valuable contributions were those of the resident conservative, a Georgia historian whose views on the Bush administration, U.S. foreign policy, and other contentious issues differed sharply from the liberal consensus. The simple presence of his name among the signatories at once signaled to conservative colleagues an unusual degree of balance within the committee, thus commanding a far broader and more receptive audience than would otherwise have been the case.

Within the group, he would constantly remind others that life could and would never be the same after September 11—that those who anticipated a return to normalcy were hopelessly naïve—and wisely insisted that the committee's final report open with just such recognition. Later, in fact, several fellow committee members who accepted this message refused to join an amicus brief in a national-security challenge case that refused to recognize this reality and posited a legal environment essentially unaffected by the terrorist attacks. Finally, the committee's most conservative member provided a constant reality check in the assessment of specific conclusions and recommendations, for which other members were appreciative even though such leavening would not likely have occurred without his intervention. The lessons of this experience suggest that the occasions on which, for example, the AAUP and the conservative National Association of Scholars could make common cause on issues of no less importance to the right and the left have been underestimated and the potential of collaboration undervalued.

Sixth, the promise for academic freedom of interests that are shared across the academic community also needs higher visibility. Again borrowing from the experience of the AAUP Special Committee on Academic Freedom and National Security in Time of Crisis, an early draft of the recommendations urged that faculties should establish and maintain closer ties than they had before September 11 with several campus offices—not only those of the dean of students and director of international exchanges, but also "the campus police and the university legal or general counsel."[11] Had such a proposal been offered during the Vietnam era, not only would the specific language have been removed, but the Committee's chair would as surely have been discredited. Conditions by 2003 were quite different; not only did this recommendation survive verbatim into the final report, but remarkably not one member of the academic community who has read the report—and occasionally offered critical comments on some of its other sections—ever demurred to the suggestion that closer ties with and greater trust in the university attorney and campus police might be advisable.

The potential involvement of governing boards also offers a fruitful and largely untapped avenue. The "Statement on Board Accountability," recently issued by the Association of Governing Boards, lists prominently among the "transcendent values" of American higher education (to which trustees and regents are accountable) the specific values of "academic freedom and due process."[12] Apart from the practical reality that any governing board would risk both legal liability and collegial condemnation for abridging protected faculty interests, most boards take considerable pride in the degree to which the institution they guide and govern respects such fundamental values. Moreover, because trustees tend to be drawn largely from business and professional fields, they are ideally situated to explain academic values (including academic freedom) to their sometimes skeptical colleagues and neighbors. Many a corporate executive has been deterred from openly disparaging tenure as unique to university professors when reminded by a knowledgeable colleague that the business world has its own forms of job security, quite apart from paying its executives salaries that surpass professorial incomes by several fold. The problem is that surprisingly little use has been made by the academic community of this invaluable resource—the amicus briefs from corporate CEOs in the Michigan affirmative action litigation providing a rare but welcome example to the contrary.

Seventh, the need for better understanding of academic freedom—starting with those who benefit from and depend most upon it—represents a critical and vital imperative. By analogy to the ancient maxim of the "fish who is the last to discover water," most university professors understandably take academic freedom and tenure largely for granted. Even when one or several members of a particular faculty are threatened with reprisal because they advocate unpopular views or broadcast unwelcome research results, most other members of that faculty tend to look the other way, confident that they will not be seen as troublemakers or malcontents—and usually they are quite correct. Indeed, life may even be easier for the rest of the faculty members if one or two or three of their colleagues have been weeded out and tranquility returns to campus. Few others are likely to adopt a "there but for the grace of God" view of the fate of the expendable or sacrificial mavericks. If lessons are learned, and if others within that same academic community are inclined to be a bit less venturesome after such an episode, little or no loss to the individual campus or to the academic community as a whole will be perceived.

Yet the central lesson one should derive from such experience reflects James Madison's wise caution that "it is proper to take alarm at the first experiment on our liberties."[13] What happened to one, or to a few, could happen to others, even to those who consider their views wholly conventional and their positions thus totally secure. What such predictable and pervasive complacency forfeits is the opportunity for the education not only of the immediately affected faculty but even more of the larger community. Those beyond the campus need to appreciate why the silencing or dismissal of a single faculty crackpot or nutcase potentially affects the entire community—in terms of the quality of education their children and grandchildren will receive, or the quality of scholarship provided to government, business, and the professions, or the capacity of the academic community to advance knowledge and pursue the eternal quest for truth. That, after all, is what academic freedom is all about, and that is why it matters to those who are not professors as much as to those who are. The sooner citizens at large appreciate that equation, the better they will be prepared for an uncertain future, as will be the academic community.

Notes

1. Discovering Academic Freedom

1. Jodi S. Cohen, "NU Professor Backs Denial of Holocaust by Iran Chief; Jewish leaders fear support could add credibility to view," *Chicago Tribune*, February 4, 2006, p. 5.
2. Elizabeth Campbell, "Students, Faculty Oppose Butz with Petitions," *Daily Northwestern*, February 17, 2006, http://media.www.dailynorthwestern.com/media/storage/paper853/news/2006/02/17/Campus/Students.Faculty.Oppose.Butz.With.Petitions-1921007.shtml (accessed June 8, 2007).
3. Allen Taflove, Uri Wilensky, Larry Birnbaum, "Faculty Reject Holocaust Denial," *Chicago Tribune*, February 17, 2006, p. 22.
4. Jodi S. Cohen, "NU Rips Holocaust Denial; President Calls Prof an Embarrassment but Plans No Penalty," *Chicago Tribune*, February 7, 2006, p. 1.
5. Fox News Transcript 020702cb.256: *The O'Reilly Factor*, February 7, 2006.
6. Quoted in Deborah E. Lipstadt, "The Threats from Holocaust Denials," *Chronicle of Higher Education*, July 28, 1993, http://chronicle.com/che-data/articles.dir/articles-39.dir/issue-47.dir/47b00101.htm (accessed June 8, 2007).
7. Mary Burgan, "Academic Freedom in a World of Moral Crisis," *Chronicle of Higher Education*, September 6, 2002, http://chronicle.com/weekly/v49/i02/02b02001.htm (accessed June 8, 2007).
8. Lee C. Bollinger, "The Value and Responsibilities of Academic Freedom," *Chronicle of Higher Education*, April 8, 2005, http://chronicle.com/weekly/v51/i31/31b02001.htm (accessed June 8, 2007).
9. Steve Chapman, "Antidote to Error is Debate: Truth Emerges When Crazy Theories Are Refuted, Not Silenced," *Chicago Tribune*, July 30, 2006, p. 15.
10. Deborah E. Lipstadt, "Threats from Holocaust Denials," *Chronicle of Higher Education*, July 28, 1993, http://chronicle.com/che-data/articles.dir/articles-39.dir/issue-47.dir/47b00101.htm (accessed June 8, 2007).
11. Jassett Chatham, "Butz's Denial of Holocaust Irritates Northwestern U," *Daily Northwestern*, February 7, 2006, http://media.www.dailynorthwestern

.com/media/storage/paper853/news/2006/02/07/Campus/Butzs.Denial.Of.Holocaust.Irritates.Nu-1920811.shtml (accessed June 8, 2007).

12. Campbell, "Students, Faculty Oppose Butz with Petitions."
13. American Association of University Professors, "Recommended Institutional Regulations on Academic Freedom and Tenure," *Policy Documents and Reports* (Washington, DC: AAUP, 2001) or online at www.aaup.org/AAUP/pubsres/policydocs/RIR.htm?PF=1 (accessed June 20, 2007).
14. Denise K. Magner, "Northwestern U. Fires Adjunct Who Taught about Holocaust," *Chronicle of Higher Education,* January 17, 1997, http://chronicle.com/che-data/articles.dir/art-43.dir/issue-19.dir/19a01602.htm (accessed on June 8, 2007).
15. American Association of University Professors, "The 1940 Statement of Principles on Academic Freedom and Tenure," *Policy Documents and Reports* (Washington, DC: AAUP, 2001) or online at www.aaup.org/AAUP/pubsres/policydocs/1940statement.htm (accessed June 20, 2007).
16. Matthew W. Finkin, "'A Higher Order of Liberty in the Workplace': Academic Freedom and Tenure in the Vortex of Employment Practices and Law," *Law and Contemporary Problems,* 53 (1990): 367.
17. Ibid.
18. James O. Freedman, *Idealism and Liberal Education* (Ann Arbor: The University of Michigan Press, 1996).
19. J. Peter Byrne, "Academic Freedom: A Special Concern of the First Amendment," *Yale Law Journal* 99 (November 1989): 339.
20. Ibid.
21. Leonard Levy, *Thomas Jefferson and Civil Liberties: The Darker Side* (Chicago, IL: Ivan R. Dee, Inc., 1989).
22. Byrne, "Academic Freedom," 271.
23. Donald A. Downs, *Restoring Free Speech and Liberty on Campus* (Oakland CA: The Independent Institute, and Cambridge, UK: Cambridge University Press, 2005).
24. Walter P. Metzger, "The 1940 Statement of Principles on Academic Freedom and Tenure," in *Freedom and Tenure in the Academy,* ed. William W. Van Alstyne (Durham, NC: Duke University Press, 1993).

2. Protecting Academic Freedom

1. "Honor Society Rejects Membership Bid," *Chronicle of Higher Education,* June 3, 1992, http://chronicle.com/che-data/articles.dir/articles-38.dir/issue-39.dir/39a00402.htm (accessed June 8, 2007).
2. Anita Kumar, "USF Faces Censure Vote Today," *St. Petersburg Times,* June 14, 2003, p. 1B.
3. Walter P. Metzger, "The 1940 Statement of Principles on Academic Freedom and Tenure," in *Freedom and Tenure in the Academy,* ed. William W. Van Alstyne (Durham, NC, and London: Duke University Press, 1993), p. 13.

4. Ibid., p. 14.
5. Ibid., p. 16.
6. Ibid., p. 15.
7. American Association of University Professors, "The 1940 Statement of Principles on Academic Freedom and Tenure," in *Policy Documents and Reports,* 9th ed. (Washington, DC: AAUP, 2001), www.aaup.org/AAUP/pubsres/policydocs/1940statement.htm (accessed June 20, 2007).
8. John Sedgwick, "Profs and Losses," *Boston Magazine,* March 2002, www.bostonmagazine.com/articles/profs_and_losses/ (accessed June 7, 2007); Richard P. Chait, *The Questions of Tenure* (Cambridge: Harvard University Press, 2002), p. 183.
9. Ellen Schrecker, *No Ivory Tower* (New York: Oxford University Press, 1986).
10. A successor AAUP Committee (constituted to address threats after the terrorist attacks of September 11, 2001) would tactfully describe the association's response during the McCarthy era as "tardy but categorical," noting that specific transgressions were investigated, with censure resulting in many cases, though a comprehensive report did not appear until 1956, when the once fearsome threat was waning.
11. Geoffrey R. Stone, *Perilous Times* (New York: W. W. Norton and Co., 2004), pp. 423–425.
12. Peter S. Canellos, "For Ex-Clinton Picks, Cold Comfort," *Boston Globe,* Oct. 27, 1996, p. A1.
13. Evelyn Nieves, "Whatever Happened to . . . Joycelyn Elders?" *Washington Post,* March 22, 2006, p. A19.
14. Ben Pershing, "Hastert Taps Scholar," *Roll Call,* May 2, 2005.
15. American Association of University Professors, "Sexual Harassment: Suggested Policy and Procedures for Handling Complaints," in *Policy Documents and Reports,* 9th ed. (Washington, DC: AAUP, 2001), p. 209, or online at www.aaup.org/AAUP/pubsres/policydocs/sexharass.htm (accessed June 27, 2007).
16. American Association of University Professors, "Recommended Institutional Regulations on Academic Freedom and Tenure," in *Policy Documents and Reports,* 9th ed. (Washington, DC: AAUP, 2001), Section 5(a), p. 25, or online at www.aaup.org/AAUP/pubsres/policydocs/RIR.htm (accessed June 27, 2007).
17. See Robert M. O'Neil, "Limits of Freedom: The Ward Churchill Case," *Change Magazine* (Sept.–Oct. 2006): 34–41, www.carnegiefoundation.org/chang/sub.asp?key=97&subkey=2016 (accessed June 27, 2007).
18. Chris Moon, "KU Prof Resigns Top Post," *Topeka Capital-Journal,* Dec. 8, 2005, Section A, p. A1.
19. "Report on Conclusion of Preliminary Review in the Matter of Professor Ward Churchill," *University of Colorado at Boulder News Center,* March 29, 2005, Univesity of Colorado at Boulder, www.colorado.edu/news/reports/churchill/report.html (accessed June 6, 2007).
20. *Jeffries v. Harleston,* 21 F.3d 1238 (2d Cir. 1994).

21. AAUP, "The 1940 Statement of Principles on Academic Freedom and Tenure," p. 6.
22. See generally Michael W. McConnell, "Academic Freedom in Religious Colleges and Universities," in *Freedom and Tenure in the Academy,* ed. William W. Van Alstyne (Durham, NC, and London: Duke University Press, 1993), pp. 303–324.
23. "Academic Freedom and Tenure: Nyack College," 80 *Academe,* 5 Sept.–Oct. 1994, pp. 73–79.
24. "Academic Freedom and Tenure: Brigham Young University," 83 *Academe,* 5 Sept.–Oct. 1997, pp. 52–71. See also Courtney Leatherman, "Faculty Group Censures Three Universities over Academic-Freedom and Tenure Issues," *Chronicle of Higher Education,* June 26, 1998, http://chronicle.com/che-data/articles.dir/art-44.dir/issue-42.dir/42a01401.htm (accessed June 27, 2007).
25. Alan Charles Kors and Harvey A. Silverglate, *The Shadow University: The Betrayal of Liberty on America's Campuses* (New York: Free Press, 1998).
26. Robert M. O'Neil, *Free Speech in the College Community* (Bloomington: Indiana University Press, 1997).
27. Gary Pavela, "Only Speech Codes Should Be Censored," *Chronicle of Higher Education,* December 1, 2006, www.chronicle.com/weekly/v53/i15/15b01401.htm (accessed May 16, 2007).
28. Donald A. Downs, *Restoring Free Speech and Liberty on Campus* (Cambridge, UK: Cambridge University Press, 2005).
29. Scott Smallwood, "Censure, Be Gone," *Chronicle of Higher Education,* July 11, 2003. http://chronicle.com/weekly/v49/i44/44a01101.htm (accessed June 8, 2007).
30. See generally Ralph S. Brown and Jordan E. Kurland, "Academic Tenure and Academic Freedom," in *Freedom and Tenure in the Academy,* ed. William W. Van Alstyne (Durham, NC, and London: Duke University Press, 1993), pp. 325–356.
31. *NLRB v. Yeshiva University,* 444 U.S. 672 (1980).
32. "Academic Freedom and Tenure: The Polytechnic Institute of New York," *AAUP Bulletin* 5 (Winter 1974): 416–420; "Academic Freedom and Tenure: Temple University," 71 *Academe,* 3 May–June 1985, pp. 16–27.
33. *Tilton v. Richardson,* 403 U.S. 672 (1971).
34. *Minnesota Higher Education Facilities Authority v. Hawk,* 305 Minn. 97 (Minn. 1975).
35. *Krotkoff v. Goucher College,* 585 F.2d 675 (4th Cir. 1978).
36. *Adamian v. Jacobsen,* 523 F.2d 929 (9th Cir. 1975).

3. The Constitution and the Courts

1. For an overview of academic freedom and legal issues posed by the Ward Churchill case, see Robert M. O'Neil, "Limits of Freedom: The Ward

Churchill Case," *Change* (Sept.–Oct. 2006): 34–41, www.carnegiefoundation.org/change/sub.asp?key=97&subkey=2016 (accessed June 27, 2007).

2. For two thorough and comprehensive accounts of the evolution and current scope of the law that protects academic freedom, see William A. Kaplin and Barbara A. Lee, *The Law of Higher Education,* 4th ed. (San Francisco: Jossey-Bass, 2006), pp. 607–722, and William W. Van Alstyne, "Academic Freedom and the First Amendment in the Supreme Court of the United States," in *Freedom and Tenure in the Academy,* ed. William W. Van Alstyne (Durham, NC: Duke University Press, 1993), pp. 79–154.
3. *Scopes v. State,* 154 Tenn. 105, 289 S. W. 363 (1927).
4. *State v. Epperson,* 242 Ark. 922, 416 S. W.2d 322 (1967), reversed, 393 U.S. 97 (1968).
5. *Berea College v. Kentucky,* 211 U.S. 45 (1908).
6. *Adler v. Board of Education,* 342 U.S. 485 (1952).
7. *Wiemann v. Updegraff,* 344 U.S. 183 (1952).
8. *Sweezy v. New Hampshire,* 354 U.S. 234 (1957).
9. Ibid.
10. *Keyishian v. Board of Regents,* 385 U.S. 589 (1967).
11. *United States v. Associated Press,* 52 F. Supp. 362 (1943).
12. Van Alstyne, "Academic Freedom and the First Amendment," p. 114.
13. *Bakke v. Board of Regents,* 438 U.S. 265 (1978).
14. Ibid.
15. *Grutter v. Bollinger,* 539 U.S. 306 (2003).
16. Lawrence White, "Judicial Threats to Academe's 'Four Freedoms,'" *Chronicle of Higher Education,* Dec. 1, 2006, http://chronicle.com/weekly/v53/i15/15b00601.htm (accessed on June 7, 2007).
17. *Regents of the University of Michigan v. Ewing,* 474 U.S. 214 (1985).
18. Ibid.
19. *Tilton v. Richardson,* 403 U.S. 672 (1971).
20. *Rust v. Sullivan,* 500 U.S. 173 (1991).
21. *Speiser v. Randall,* 357 U.S. 513 (1958).
22. *Trustees of Leland Stanford University v. Sullivan,* 773 F. Supp. 472 (D.D.C. 1991).
23. *Board of Regents v. Southworth,* 527 U.S. 217 (2000).
24. *McAuliffe v. Mayor and Board of Aldermen,* 155 Mass. 216, 29 N.E. 517 (1893).
25. *Pickering v. Board of Education,* 225 N.E. 2d 1 (1967).
26. *Pickering v. Board of Education,* 391 U.S. 563 (1968).
27. *Speiser v. Randall,* 358 U.S. 860 (1958).
28. See Robert M. O'Neil, *The Price of Dependency* (New York: Dutton, 1968).
29. *Garcetti v. Ceballos,* 126 S. Ct. 1951 (2006).
30. *Perry v. Sindermann,* 408 U.S. 593 (1972); *Board of Regents v. Roth,* 408 U.S. 564 (1972).
31. *NAACP v. Alabama,* 357 U.S. 449 (1958).

32. *Bates v. Little Rock,* 361 U.S. 516 (1960).
33. *Boy Scouts of America v. Dale,* 530 U.S. 640 (2000).
34. *Gibson v. Florida Legislative Investigating Committee,* 372 U.S. 539 (1963).
35. *Yellin v. United States,* 374 U.S. 109 (1963).
36. Michael Levin, "The Trouble with American Education," *Quadrant* (Jan. 1988): 19–23.
37. *Levin v. Harleston,* 966 F.2d 85 (2d Cir. 1992).
38. *Levin v. Harleston,* 770 F. Supp. 895 (S.D.N.Y. 1992).
39. *Levin v. Harleston,* 966 F.2d 85 (2d Cir. 1992).
40. Lance Morrow and Thomas McCarroll, "Controversies: The Provocative Professor," *Time Magazine*, August 26, 1991, p. 19.
41. Ibid.
42. Denise K. Magner, "Politicians Press Officials at the City College of New York to Punish Black-Studies Chairman for Remarks on Jews," *Chronicle of Higher Education*, September 4, 1991, http://chronicle.com/che-data/articles.dir/articles-38.dir/issue-02.dir/02a01901.htm (accessed June 7, 2007).
43. *Jeffries v. Harleston,* 820 F. Supp. 741, 828 F. Supp. 1066 (S.D.N.Y. 1993).
44. *Jeffries v. Harleston,* 21 F.3d 1238 (2d Cir. 1994).
45. *Dube v. State University of New York,* 900 F.2d 587 (2d Cir. 1990).
46. Ibid.
47. Ibid.
48. *White v. Davis,* 533 P.2d 222 (Cal. 1975).
49. Ibid.
50. *Hammond v. Brown,* 323 F. Supp. 326 (N.D. Ohio 1971). The district court ruling was reversed by the Court of Appeals for the Sixth Circuit chiefly on the issue of remedies rather than the substance of the trial judge's ruling; 450 F.2d 480 (6th Cir. 1971).
51. Ibid.
52. *Cohen v. San Bernardino Valley College,* 92 F.3d 968 (9th Cir. 1996).
53. Ibid.
54. Ibid.
55. Ibid.
56. *Bonnell v. Lorenzo,* 241 F.3d 800 (6th Cir. 2001).
57. *Bonnell v. Lorenzo,* 81 F. Supp. 2d 777 (E.D. Mich. 1999).
58. *Bonnell v. Lorenzo,* 241 F.3d 800 (6th Cir. 2001).
59. *Burnham v. Ianni,* 119 F.3d 668 (8th Cir. 1997).
60. *Levin v. Harleston,* 770 F. Supp. 895 (S.D.N.Y. 1992).

4. Academic Freedom in Times of Crisis

1. Robin Wilson and Scott Smallwood, "One Professor Cleared, Another Disciplined over September 11 Remarks," *Chronicle of Higher Education,* January 11, 2002, http://chronicle.com/weekly/v48/i18/18a01202.htm (accessed June 8, 2007).

2. Robin Wilson and Elizabeth Farrell, "At UT-Austin, a New Center for American Music; Outspoken Professor Quits at U. of New Mexico," *Chronicle of Higher Education,* January 3, 2003, http://chronicle.com/weekly/v49/i17/17a00701.htm (accessed June 8, 2007).
3. Robin Wilson and Ana Marie Cox, "Terrorist Attacks Put Academic Freedom to the Test," *Chronicle of Higher Education,* October 5, 2001, http://chronicle.com/weekly/v48/i06/06a01201.htm (accessed June 8, 2007).
4. Robin Wilson and Scott Smallwood, "One Professor Cleared, Another Disciplined over September 11 Remarks," *Chronicle of Higher Education,* January 11, 2002, http://chronicle.com/weekly/v48/i18/18a01202.htm (accessed June 8, 2007).
5. Robin Wilson, "CUNY Leaders Question Faculty Comments on Terror Attacks," *Chronicle of Higher Education,* October 19, 2001, http://chronicle.com/weekly/v48/i08/08a01101.htm (accessed June 8, 2007).
6. John P. Nidiry, "CUNY Trustees: Let Free Speech Flourish," *Newsday,* October 19, 2001, Viewpoints, A50.
7. Megan Greenwell, "Bollinger: No Plan to Reprimand De Genova: Bollinger Issued a Statement in Response to a Letter from U.S. Congress," *Columbia Daily Spectator,* April 10, 2003, http://media.www.columbiaspectator.com/media/storage/paper865/news/2003/04/10/News/Bollinger.No.Plan.To.Reprimand.De.Genova-2036801.shtml (accessed June 8, 2007).
8. Margaret Hunt Gram, "De Genova Teach-In Comments Spark Fury," *Columbia Daily Spectator,* March 31, 2003, http://media.www.columbiaspectator.com/media/storage/paper865/news/2003/03/31/News/De.Genova.TeachIn.Comments.Spark.Fury-2036920.shtml (accessed June 8, 2007).
9. Interview with Professor Robert O'Neil, *The O'Reilly Factor,* Fox News Transcript 033103cb.256, March 31, 2003.
10. John C. Ensslin, "CU Regents Won't Rush to Action in Controversy," *Rocky Mountain News,* February 3, 2005, www.rockymountainnews.com/drmn/news/article/0,1299,DRMN_3_4754496,00.html (access June 8, 2007).
11. Letter, President Hank Brown to Patricia Hayes, Chair, Board of Regents of the University of Colorado, May 25, 2007.
12. *The O'Reilly Factor,* Fox News Transcript 020101cf.256, February 1, 2005.
13. John Gravois, "Wis. Provost Will Review Teaching of Instructor With Controversial 9/11 Views, *Chronicle of Higher Education*, July 14, 2006, http://chronicle.com/weekly/v52/i45/45a01002.htm (accessed June 8, 2007).
14. Dee J. Hall, "Barrett to Talk on 9/11 Belief," *Wisconsin State Journal,* September 27, 2006, B1.
15. Gravois, "Wis. Provost Will Review Teaching of Instructor With Controversial 9/11 Views."
16. Scott Jaschik, "Another Scholar Under Fire for 9/11 Views," *Inside Higher Ed*, August 29, 2006, www.insidehighered.com/news/2006/08/29/woodward (accessed June 8, 2007).

17. Scott Jaschik, "9/11 Skeptic Will Leave Post at Bringham Young," *Inside Higher Ed*, October 23, 2006, www.insidehighered.com/news/2006/10/23/brigham (accessed June 8, 2007).
18. For a thorough analysis of the academic freedom implications of the Al Arian case, see "Academic Freedom and Tenure: The University of South Florida," 89 *Academe,* 3 May–June 2003, pp. 59–73.
19. For a comprehensive account of the Ramadan case, see Deborah Sontag, "Mystery of the Islamic Scholar Who Was Barred by the U.S.," *New York Times,* October 6, 2004, Section A, Column 3, p. 1.
20. Julia Preston, "Hearing for Muslim Barred by U.S.," *New York Times,* April 14, 2006, Section A, Column 6, p. 16.
21. Ellen Schrecker, *No Ivory Tower* (New York: Oxford University Press, 1986).
22. Kay Lazar, "Harvard Red Scare Revisited," *Boston Herald,* December 10, 2000, p. 26.
23. David Welna, "Closed-door McCarthy Transcripts Released," National Public Radio *Morning Edition,* May 6, 2003, www.npr.org/templates/story/story.php?storyId=1253219 (accessed June 8, 2007).
24. The first ten lectures are reprinted in Peggie J. Holingsworth, ed., *Unfettered Expression* (Ann Arbor: University of Michigan Press, 2000).
25. Welna, "Closed-door McCarthy Transcripts Released."
26. The relevant background and antecedents are discussed in the recent report, "Academic Freedom and National Security in a Time of Crisis: A Report of the AAUP's Special Committee," 89 *Academe,* 6 Nov.–Dec. 2003, pp. 36–38, www.aaup.org/NR/rdonlyres/5D2D9A5A-1935-4DF4-B402-57525CAF8CDD/0/Post911.pdf (accessed June 8, 2007).
27. Sharon Jayson, "UT System Revises Employee Policy: Each University Will Set Standards for Checking Backgrounds of Most Job Seekers," *Austin American-Statesman,* November 27, 2002, p. B6.
28. These and other incidents are discussed in "Academic Freedom and National Security in a Time of Crisis," pp. 55–56.
29. Sharon Walsh, "The Drake Affair," *Chronicle of Higher Education,* March 5, 2004, http://chronicle.com/weekly/v50/i26/26a00801.htm (accessed June 8, 2007).
30. Michael Arnone, "Army Says Intelligence Agents Went Overboard Questioning Academics in Texas," *Chronicle of Higher Education,* March 26, 2004, http://chronicle.com/weekly/v50/i29/29a01301.htm (accessed June 8, 2007).
31. "Academic Freedom and National Security in a Time of Crisis," pp. 42–48.
32. The National Academies, "Statement on Science and Security in an Age of Terrorism," October 18, 2002, www8.nationalacademies.org/onpinews/newsitem.aspx?RecordID=s10182002b (accessed June 8, 2007); for the background paper report, see Background Paper on Science and Security in an Age of Terrorism, October 18, 2002, www8.nationalacademies.org/

onpinews/newsitem.aspx?RecordID=s10182002, (accessed June 8, 2007). See generally American Civil Liberties Union, *Science under Siege,* June 2005.

33. See Jane Lampman, "Uncle Sam Doesn't Want You," *Christian Science Monitor,* May 11, 2006, p. 14.
34. Center for Strategic and International Studies, "Security Controls on the Access of Foreign Scientists and Engineers to the United States: A White Paper of the Commission on Scientific Communication and National Security" (Washington, DC: U.S. Government Printing Office: 2005).
35. See "Academic Freedom and National Security in a Time of Crisis," pp. 38–42.
36. See Robert M. O'Neil, "Questioning Ohio's Loyalty Requirement," *Chronicle of Higher Education,* December 1, 2006, http://chronicle.com/weekly/v53/i15/15b02401.htm (accessed June 8, 2007).
37. "Universities Have Applied the USA PATRIOT Act to Website Hyperlinks," Internet Business Law Services, Internet Law-Legal-Cyberterrorism, May 1, 2005, www.ibls.com/members/docview.aspx?doc=796 (accessed May 30, 2007).

5. The Rights of Academic Researchers

1. *Wright v. Jeep Corp.,* 547 F. Supp. 871 (E.D. Mich. 1982).
2. *Richards of Rockford, Inc. v. Pacific Gas & Electric Company,* 71 F.R.D. 388 (N.D. Cal. 1976).
3. *Branzburg v. Hayes,* 408 U.S. 665 (1972).
4. *Farnsworth v. Procter & Gamble Co.,* 758 F.2d 1545 (11th Cir. 1985).
5. *In re R. J. Reynolds Tobacco Co.,* 136 Misc.2d 282, 518 N.Y.S.2d 729 (Sup. Ct. 1987).
6. *In re American Tobacco Co.,* 880 F.2d 1520 (2d Cir. 1989).
7. Sheldon E. Steinbach, "How Frivolous Litigation Threatens Good Science," *Chronicle of Higher Education,* December 4, 1998, http://chronicle.com/weekly/v45/i15/15a05601.htm (accessed June 12, 2007).
8. Greg Winter, "Tobacco Industry in Fight to Get Universities' Data," *New York Times,* January 20, 2002, Section 1, p. 18.
9. *Cusumano v. Microsoft Corporation,* 162 F.3d 708 (1st Cir. 1998).
10. John Schwartz, "Research Law Fight: Right to Know, or to Squelch?" *Washington Post,* April 5, 1999, Section A, p. A7.
11. Liane Hansen, "Researchers Accuse Tobacco Industry of Intimidation," National Public Radio, *Weekend Edition,* February 27, 1994, Transcript 1060–5.
12. John Schwartz, "Research Law Fight: Right to Know, or to Squelch?" *Washington Post,* April 5, 1999, Section A, p. A7.
13. Quoted in Scott Jaschik, "Does Tobacco Money Taint Research?" *Inside Higher Ed,* September 21, 2006, www.insidehighered.com/news/2006/09/21/tobacco (accessed June 12, 2007).

14. Karen Grassmuck, "Grants From a Fund Accused of Racism Roil U. of Delaware," *Chronicle of Higher Education*, January 17, 1990, http://chronicle.com/che-data/articles.dir/articles-36.dir/issue-18.dir/18a03101.htm (accessed June 12, 2007).
15. Charlotte Allen, "Gray Matter, Black-and-White Controversy," *The Washington Times,* INSIGHT, January 13, 1992, Cover Story, p. 4.
16. *Rumsfeld v. Forum for Academic & Institutional Rights,* 547 U.S. 47 (2006).
17. Robert M. O'Neil, *Free Speech in the College Community* (Bloomington: Indiana University Press, 1997).
18. See generally, J. Philippe Rushton, "The Pioneer Fund and the Scientific Study of Human Differences," *Albany Law Review* 66 (2002) 207, pp. 209–262.
19. *Rust v. Sullivan,* 500 U.S. 173 (1991).
20. *Trustees of Leland Stanford University v. Sullivan,* 773 F. Supp. 472 (D.D.C. 1991).
21. *Rosenberger v. Rector & Visitors of University of Virginia,* 515 U.S. 819 (1995).
22. Brian Alexander, "Free to Clone" *The New York Times Magazine,* September 26, 2004, Section 6, Column 1, p. 26.
23. *Forbes v. Napolitano,* 236 F.3d 1009 (9th Cir. 2000).
24. Alexander, "Free to Clone," p. 26.
25. Ibid.
26. Ibid.
27. *Bernstein v. United States Department of State,* 945 F. Supp. 1279 (N.D. Cal. 1997); *Junger v. Daley,* 209 F.3d 481 (6th Cir. 2000).
28. Andrew C. Revkin, "Bush Aide Edited Climate Report," *New York Times,* June 8, 2005, Section A, Column 2, p. 1.
29. Andrew C. Revkin, "Two GOP Lawmakers Spar Over Climate Study," *New York Times,* July 18, 2005, Section A; Column 4, p. 14.
30. See generally, Jennifer Washburn, *University, Inc.: The Corporate Corruption of Higher Education* (New York: Basic Books, 2005).
31. Snigdha Prakash, "Merck's Efforts to Suppress Safety Concerns about Vioxx, Parts One and Two" National Public Radio, *All Things Considered,* 8:00 PM EST, June 9, 2005.
32. Alex Berenson, "Doctor Links Merck Trial to His Demotion," *New York Times,* December 10, 2005, Section C; Column 2, p. 3.
33. Michael Milstein, "Report Faults OSU Forestry Dean, Urges Reforms," *The Oregonian,* May 19, 2006, p. A9.
34. Karen Birchard, "Corporate Sponsorship, Lack of Freedom Said to Imperil Medical Studies in Canada," *Chronicle of Higher Education*, December 3, 2004, http://chronicle.com/weekly/v51/i15/15a04101.htm (accessed June 12, 2007); A Shafer, "Biomedical Conflicts of Interest: A Defence of the Sequestration Thesis—Learning from the Cases of Nancy Olivieri and David Healy," *Journal of Medical Ethics* 30 (2004): 8–24.

6. Intersections of Academic and Artistic Freedom

1. The statement is reprinted in American Association of University Professors, *Policy Documents & Reports*, 9th ed. (Baltimore, MD: Johns Hopkins University Press, 2001), pp. 35–36.
2. *National Endowment for the Arts v. Finley*, 524 U.S. 569 (1998).
3. *Bery v. City of New York*, 906 F. Supp. 163 (S.D.N.Y. 1995), reversed, 97 F.3d 689 (2d Cir. 1996).
4. Neela Banerjee; Gretchen Ruethling contributed reporting from South Bend, Ind., "At Religious Universities, Disputes over Faith and Academic Freedom," *New York Times*, February 18, 2006, Section A, Column 1, p. 12; Tom Coyne, "Catholic Colleges Struggle to Balance Religious Values, Academic Freedom; 'Vagina Monologues,' Gay Film Festival Stir Debate," *Washington Post*, February 18, 2006, p. B9.
5. Sheldon H. Nahmod, "Artistic Expression and Aesthetic Theory: The Beautiful, The Sublime and The First Amendment," *Wisconsin Law Review* 221 (March–April, 1987): 222.
6. *Bleistein v. Donaldson Lithographing Co.*, 188 U.S. 239 (1903).
7. *Southeastern Promotions, Ltd. v. Conrad et al.*, 420 U.S. 546 (1975).
8. *Bery v. City of New York*, 97 F.3d 689 (2d Cir. 1996).
9. *Serra v. U.S. General Services Administration*, 847 F.2d 1045 (2d Cir. 1988).
10. *Whitney v. California*, 274 U.S. 357 (1927).
11. *O'Connor v. Washburn University*, 416 F.3d 1216 (10th Cir. 2005).
12. American Association of University Professors, *Policy Documents & Reports* (Washington, DC: American Association of University Professors, 2001), p. 36.
13. *Tinker v. Des Moines Independent Community School District*, 393 U.S. 503 (1969).
14. *Miller v. California*, 413 U.S. 15 (1973).
15. *Close v. Lederle*, 303 F. Supp. 1109 (D. Mass. 1969).
16. *Close v. Lederle*, 424 F.2d 988 (1st Cir. 1970).
17. Ibid.
18. *Appelgate v. Dumke*, 25 Cal. App. 3d 304, 101 Cal. Rptr. 645 (1972).
19. *Piarowski v. Illinois Community College District* 515, 759 F.2d 625 (7th Cir. 1985).
20. *Nelson v. Streeter*, 16 F.3d 145 (7th Cir. 1994).
21. *Schenk v. United States*, 249 U.S. 47 (1919).
22. Sean A. Fanelli, "Drawing Lines at Nassau Community College," 76 *Academe*, July–Aug., 1990, pp. 24–26; Nat Hentoff, "Curtains for Sister Mary Ignatius?" *Washington Post*, July 19, 1985, p. A25.
23. "Protests Greet College's Plan to Present Satire about Nun," *New York Times*, July 14, 1985, Section 1; Part 1, p. 25, Column 1.
24. "Catholic U. Upset Over Production of Play With Gay Theme," *Chronicle of Higher Education*, October 4, 1996, http://chronicle.com/che-data/articles.dir/art-43.dir/issue-06.dir/06a03802.htm (accessed June 13, 2007).

25. Banerjee, "At Religious Universities, Disputes Over Faith and Academic Freedom," p. 12; Neela Banerjee; Jennifer Ochstein contributed reporting from South Bend, Ind., "Notre Dame's President Allows 'Monologues' and Gay Films," *New York Times,* April 6, 2006, Section A, Column 1, p. 19.
26. *DiBona v. Matthews,* 220 Cal. App. 3d 1329 (Cal. App. 1990).
27. *Linnemieier v. Board of Trustees of Purdue University,* 260 F.3d 757 (7th Cir. 2001).
28. Ibid.
29. *Brown v. Board of Regents,* 640 F. Supp. 674 (D. Neb. 1986).
30. *Cummins v. Campbell,* 44 F.3d 847 (10th Cir. 1994).
31. *Committee for First Amendment v. Campbell,* 962 F.2d 1517 (10th Cir. 1992).
32. See generally, Joy Price, "Art Prof Escapes Discipline; Vanderbilt Says He Must Warn Classes," *Washington Times,* March 21, 1993, Part A, p. A5.
33. Chuck Haga, "Film for 'U' Class on Gay History Spurs New Debate," *Minneapolis Star Tribune,* December 19, 1993, 1B.
34. Elizabeth Redden, "Yes, Please Offend Me (But Thanks for Checking)," *Inside Higher Ed,* Nov. 28, 2006, www.insidehighered.com/news/2006/11/28/idaho (accessed June 14, 2007).
35. American Association of University Professors, *Policy Documents & Reports,* p. 36.
36. *Cincinnati v. Contemporary Arts Center,* 57 Ohio Misc.2d 15 (Ohio Mun. Ct. 1990).
37. *Bella Lewitsky Dance Foundation v. Frohnmayer,* 754 F. Supp. 774 (C.D. Cal. 1991).
38. Judith Weinraub, "Iowa Press Turns Down NEA Grant," *Washington Post,* June 2, 1990, p. C9.
39. *National Endowment for the Arts v. Finley,* 524 U.S. 569 (1998).
40. *Finley v. National Endowment for Arts,* 795 F. Supp. 1457 (C. D. Cal. 1991).
41. *Finley v. National Endowment for the Arts,* 100 F.3d 671 (9th Cir. 1996).
42. *National Endowment for the Arts v. Finley,* 524 U.S. 569 (1998).
43. Ibid.
44. Diane Haithman, "Head of NEA Overturns Two Grants," *Los Angeles Times,* May 13, 1992, Part F, p. 1.
45. Diane Haithman, "NEA Peer Panel Suspends Work; Arts: The 'Demoralized' Body Protests the Decision by Endowment's Acting Chairman to Overturn Grants for Exhibitions That Include Graphic Sexual Imagery," *Los Angeles Times,* May 16, 1992, Part F, p. 1.

7. New Technologies

1. For a thorough canvass of these emerging issues, together with a number of recommended institutional policies, see Committee on Academic Freedom and Tenure of the American Association of University Professors, "Statement on Academic Freedom and Electronic Communications," November 2004,

www.aaup.org/NR/rdonlyres/21F345EE-4623-4B0B-A50F-69E4100D1D70/0/AcademicFreedomandElectronicCommunications.pdf (accessed June 14, 2007). This version reflected a substantial revision of an earlier statement issued in 1997.

2. For a review of and comment on the Indiana University weblog controversy, see Robert M. O'Neil, "Controversial Weblogs and Academic Freedom," *Chronicle of Higher Education,* January 16, 2004, http://chronicle.com/weekly/v50/i19/19b01601.htm (accessed June 14, 2007).
3. See David L. Wilson, "Northwestern U. Urged to Bar Webpage Denying Holocaust," *Chronicle of Higher Education,* May 24, 1996, http://chronicle.com/che-data/articles.dir/art-42.dir/issue-37.dir/37a02103.htm (accessed June 14, 2007).
4. See Pamela Cytrynbaum, "Web Site Entangles NU in Free-Speech Debate," *Chicago Tribune,* December 29, 1996, p. 1.
5. Anti-Defamation League, "Text of ADL Report on Extremist Use of Internet," *US Newswire,* October 21, 1997, pp. 8–9.
6. Kavita Kumar, "Debate Swirls Where Free Speech and Homophobia Merge: Washington University," *St. Louis Post-Dispatch,* October 2, 2005, p. B4.
7. Pamela Cytrynbaum, "Web Site Entangles NU in Free-Speech Debate," *Chicago Tribune,* December 29, 1996, p. 1.
8. See Robert M. O'Neil, "Who Owns Professors' E-Mail Messages?" *Chronicle of Higher Education,* June 25, 2004, http://chronicle.com/weekly/v50/i42/42b00901.htm (accessed June 14, 2007).
9. See Scott Smallwood, "2 Professors at U. of Southern Mississippi Settle for Pay Without Jobs," *Chronicle of Higher Education,* May 14, 2004, http://chronicle.com/weekly/v50/i36/36a01402.htm (accessed June 14, 2007).
10. See Jeffrey R. Young, "Virginia Tech Police Seize a Professor's Computer in Vandalism Case," *Chronicle of Higher Education,* April 26, 2002, http://chronicle.com/weekly/v48/i33/33a03701.htm (accessed June 14, 2007).
11. For Professor McCaughey's own view, see Martha McCaughey, "Windows without Curtains: Computer Privacy and Academic Freedom," 89 *Academe* 5, Sept.–Oct. 2003: www.aaup.org/publications/Academe/2003/03so/03somcca.htm (accessed June 15, 2007).
12. See Martin Miller, "Should E-Mail Be Private? UC, Employees Tangle Over Rights Of University To Access Computers Of Staff On Leave," *Los Angeles Times,* Nov. 12, 1995, Part A, p. 3.
13. Lisa Pertrillo, "SDSU Asks for Stop to E-mails; Professor to Defy Request and Contact Minutemen," *San Diego Union-Tribune,* Oct. 13, 2006, p. B-1.
14. Andrea L. Foster, "Your E-Mail Message to a Colleague Could Be Tomorrow's Headline," *Chronicle of Higher Education,* June 21, 2002, http://chronicle.com/weekly/v48/i41/41a03101.htm (accessed June 15, 2007).
15. *Fraser v. Nationwide Mutual Insurance Co.,* 352 F.3d 107 (3d Cir. 2003).
16. *United States v. Angevine,* 281 F.3d 1130 (10th Cir. 2002).
17. University of California, Office of the President "Electronic Communications Policy," (Issued: November 17, 2000, Revised: August 18, 2005), www.ucop

.edu/ucophome/coordrev/policy/PP081805ECP.pdf (accessed June 15, 2007).

18. See Thomas J. DeLoughry, "Colleges Worry About Schools Getting Obscene Material," *Chronicle of Higher Education*, January 27, 1993, http://chronicle.com/che-data/articles.dir/articles-39.dir/issue-21.dir/21a02902.htm (accessed June 15, 2007).
19. See Thomas J. DeLoughry, "'Newsgroups' and Sex," *Chronicle of Higher Education*, November 16, 1994, http://chronicle.com/che-data/articles.dir/articles-41.dir/issue-12.dir/12a02201.htm (accessed June 15, 2007).
20. See Robert M. O'Neil, "Free Speech on the Electronic Frontier," *Chronicle of Higher Education*, November 3, 1995, http://chronicle.com/che-data/articles.dir/art-42.dir/issue-10.dir/10a06801.htm (accessed June 15, 2007).
21. Ibid.
22. Patrick Healy, "Ex-Senator David Boren Is Powerful President of U. of Oklahoma," *Chronicle of Higher Education*, November 22, 1996, http://chronicle.com/che-data/articles.dir/art-43.dir/issue-13.dir/13a03201.htm (accessed June 15, 2007).
23. *Loving v. Boren*, 956 F. Supp. 953 (W.D. Okla. 1997).
24. *Loving v. Boren*, 133 F.3d 771 (10th Cir. 1998).
25. *Board of Education v. Pico*, 457 U.S. 853 (1982).
26. *Urofsky v. Allen*, 995 F. Supp. 634 (E.D. Va. 1998).
27. Brian McNeill, "ACLU, profs try to reverse state law banning computer access to explicit material," *The Collegiate Times*, November 5, 1999.
28. *Urofsky v. Allen*, 995 F. Supp. 634 (E.D. Va. 1998).
29. *Urofsky v. Gilmore*, 216 F.3d 401 (4th Cir. 2000).
30. See Jeffrey Brainard, "Appeals Court Upholds Virginia Law on Sexually Explicit Material Online," *Chronicle of Higher Education*, July 7, 2000, http://chronicle.com/weekly/v46/i44/44a03702.htm (accessed June 15, 2007).
31. *Urofsky v. Gilmore*, 216 F.3d 401 (4th Cir. 2000).
32. *Kariotis v. Glendening*, 2000 U.S. App. LEXIS (4th Cir. 2000).
33. Jeffrey Selingo, "Cal. Judge Upholds Northridge Policy on Material on Line," *Chronicle of Higher Education*, October. 3, 1997, http://chronicle.com/che-data/articles.dir/art-44.dir/issue-06.dir/06a03002.htm (June 15, 2007).
34. Thomas J. DeLoughry, "Colleges Criticized for Response to Offensive On-Line Speech," December 1, 1995, http://chronicle.com/che-data/articles.dir/art-42.dir/issue-14.dir/14a03201.htm (accessed June 15, 2007).
35. Sarah Lubman, "University of California student gets prison sentence for Internet hate crime," *San Jose Mercury News*, May 4, 1998.
36. These incidents are briefly described in Thomas L. DeLoughry, "Colleges Criticized for Response to Offensive On-Line Speech," *Chronicle of Higher Education*, December 1, 1995, http://chronicle.com/che-data/articles.dir/art-42.dir/issue-14.dir/14a03201.htm (accessed June 15, 2007).

37. James T. Hammond, "USC Won't Block Web Sites," *The State,* November 12, 2005.
38. Ibid.

8. Whose Academic Freedom?

1. *Brown v. Armenti,* 247 F.3d 69 (3rd Cir. 2001).
2. *Parate v. Isibor,* 868 F.2d 821 (6th Cir. 1989).
3. *Brown v. Armenti,* 247 F.3d 69 (3rd Cir. 2001)
4. *Regents of the University of California v. Bakke,* 438 U.S. 265 (1978).
5. *Grutter v. Bollinger,* 539 U.S.306 (2003).
6. J. Peter Byrne, "The Threat to Constitutional Academic Freedom," *Journal of College and University Law* 31 (2004): 79.
7. *Minnesota State Board for Community Colleges v. Knight,* 465 U.S. 271 (1984).
8. Ibid.
9. *Regents of the University of Michigan v. Ewing,* 474 U.S. 214 (1985).
10. William A. Kaplin and Barbara A. Lee, *The Law of Higher Education,* 4th ed., vol. 1 (San Francisco: Jossey-Bass Publishers, 2006), p. 262.
11. *Regents of the University of Michigan v. Ewing,* 474 U.S. 214 (1985).
12. *Piarowski v. Illinois Community College District 515,* 759 F.2d 625 (7th Cir. 1985).
13. American Association of University Professors, "1940 Statement of Principles on Academic Freedom and Tenure," in *Policy Documents and Reports,* 9th ed. (Washington, DC: AAUP, 2001), p. 3, or online at www.aaup.org/AAUP/pubsres/policydocs/1940statement.htm (accessed June 18, 2007).
14. *Bishop v. Aronov,* 732 F. Supp. 1562 (N.D. Ala. 1990), reversed, 926 F.2d 1066 (11th Cir. 1991).
15. Ibid.
16. *Parate v. Isibor,* 868 F.2d 821 (6th Cir. 1989).
17. *Edwards v. California University of Pennsylvania,* 156 F.3d 488 (3rd Cir. 1998).
18. *Brown v. Armenti,* 247 F.3d 69 (3rd Cir. 2001).
19. *Urofsky v. Allen,* 995 F. Supp. 634 (E.D. Va. 1998).
20. *Urofsky v. Gilmore,* 216 F.3d 401 (4th Cir. 2000).
21. *Hardy v. Jefferson Community College,* 260 F.3d 671 (6th Cir. 2001).
22. Ibid.
23. *Employment Division, Department of Human Resources of Oregon v. Smith,* 494 U.S.872 (1990).
24. *Axson-Flynn v. Johnson,* 151 F. Supp. 2d 1326 (D. Utah 2001).
25. *Axson-Flynn v. Johnson,* 356 F.3d 1277 (10th Cir., 2004).
26. Ibid.
27. *Kissinger v. Board of Trustees,* 786 F. Supp. 1308 (S.D. Ohio, 1992), affirmed, 5 F.3d 177 (6th Cir.,1993).
28. American Association of University Professors, "Joint Statement on Rights and Freedoms of Students," *Policy Documents and Reports,* 9th ed. (Wash-

ington, DC: American Association of University Professors, 2001), p. 261, or online at www.aaup.org/AAUP/pubsres/policydocs/stud-rights.htm (accessed June 19, 2007).

29. *Brown v. Li,* 308 F.3d 939 (9th Cir. 2002).
30. Ibid.
31. Ibid.
32. *Regents of the University of Michigan v. Ewing,* 474 U.S. 214 (1985).
33. *Axson-Flynn v. Johnson,* 356 F.3d 1277 (10th Cir., 2004).
34. *Regents of the University of Michigan v. Ewing,* 474 U.S. 214 (1985).
35. Jessica Zisko, "Fighting in Court for Faith in Class; Lawsuit: A Murrieta Christian High School Wants a Judge to Look at UC's Rejection of Courses," *Press-Enterprise,* December 8, 2005, Sec A, p. A01.
36. "Intelligent Design Opponents Invoke US Constitution," *Guardian Unlimited,* October 18, 2005.
37. *Regents of the University of California v. Bakke,* 438 U.S. 265 (1978).

9. Bias, Balance, and Beyond

1. Cindy Chang, "Conservative Alumnus Pulls Offer to Buy Lecture Tapes," *New York Times,* January 24, 2006, Section A, p. 14.
2. Piper Fogg, "No Bounty for Reports of 'Bias' at UCLA," *Chronicle of Higher Education,* February 3, 2006, http://chronicle.com/weekly/v52/i22/22a01203.htm (accessed June 20, 2007).
3. Jennifer Jacobson, "Columbia U. Issues New Grievance Procedures Amid Criticism of How It Handled Student Complaints," *Chronicle of Higher Education,* April 22, 2005, http://chronicle.com/daily/2005/04/2005041203n.htm (accessed June 20, 2007).
4. "Conservative Students Sue Over Academic Freedom," *Associated Press Dispatch,* December 20, 2004, www.courttv.com/news/2004/1220/students_ap.html (accessed June 20, 2007).
5. George Archibald, "Discrimination Against White Male Found," *Washington Times,* September 24, 2004, p. A01.
6. *DeJohn v. Temple University,* 2006 U.S. Dist. LEXIS 64911.
7. G. Jeffrey MacDonald, "Whither Academic Freedom," *USA Today,* May 18, 2005, p. 9D.
8. Ellen Schrecker, "Worse Than McCarthy," *Chronicle of Higher Education,* February 10, 2006, http://chronicle.com/weekly/v52/i23/23b02001.htm (accessed June 20, 2007).
9. Stanley Rothman, S. Robert Lichter, and Neil Nevitte, "Politics and Professional Advancement Among College Faculty," *The Forum* 3, no. 1 (2005) or online at www.cmpa.com/documents/05.03.29.Forum.Survey.pdf (accessed June 20, 2007).
10. John Tierney, "Republicans Outnumbered in Academia, Studies Find," *New York Times,* November 18, 2004, Section A, Col. 1, p. 23.

11. Piper Fogg, "Study Finds Conservatives Are Less Likely to Advance in Academe," *Chronicle of Higher Education,* April 8, 2005, http://chronicle.com/weekly/v51/i31/31a01201.htm (accessed June 20, 2007).
12. David Brooks, "Lonely Campus Voices," *New York Times,* September 27, 2003, Sec. A, Col. 6, p. 15.
13. American Council of Trustees and Alumni, "Higher Ed Failing on Intellectual Diversity," *Inside Academe* X, no. 4 (Fall–Winter 2005): 3.
14. Sara Hebel, "Patrolling Professors' Politics," *Chronicle of Higher Education,* February 13, 2004, http://chronicle.com/weekly/v50/i23/23a01801.htm (accessed June 21, 2007).
15. Bill Toland, "Pitt Provost: Political Bias Not a Problem," *Pittsburgh Post-Gazette,* November 11, 2005, p. B5.
16. Jennifer Jacobson, "Study Casts Doubt on Claims that Conservative Students Face Discrimination in Classes," *Chronicle of Higher Education,* March 30, 2006, http://chronicle.com/daily/2006/03/2006033005n.htm (accessed June 21, 2007).
17. Scott Jaschik, "Political Shocker: Faculty Moderates," *Inside Higher Ed,* September 19, 2006, www.insidehighered.com/news/2006/09/19/politics (accessed June 21, 2007).
18. John Lee, "Faculty Bias: Science or Propaganda?" American Federation of Teachers Report on behalf of Free Exchange on Campus, January 22, 2007, www.aft.org/pubs-reports/higher_ed/FacultyBiasStudies.pdf (accessed June 21, 2007).
19. Jennifer Jacobson, "Tilting at Academe: In Pennsylvania, a Republican Lawmaker Pushes Forward with Hearings about Political Bias at Colleges. Democrats Call Them a Waste of Time and Money," *Chronicle of Higher Education,* March 24, 2006, http://chronicle.com/weekly/v52/i29/29a02501.htm (accessed June 21, 2007).
20. Jennifer Jacobson, "Pa. House Committee Hears More Testimony on Liberal Views of State's Professors," *Chronicle of Higher Education,* January 11, 2006, http://chronicle.com/daily/2006/01/2006011105n.htm (accessed June 21, 2007).
21. Jennifer Jacobson, "Conservative Activist Admits Lack of Evidence for Some Allegations of Faculty Bias," *Chronicle of Higher Education,* January 20, 2006, http://chronicle.com/weekly/v52/i20/20a03301.htm (accessed June 20, 2007).
22. Scott Jaschik, "From Bad to Worse for David Horowitz," *Inside Higher Ed,* November 22, 2006, www.insidehighered.com/news/2006/11/22/tabor (accessed June 21, 2007).
23. Jennifer Jacobson, "Pa. Lawmaker Says Investigation of Professors' Bias Cost Him His Seat," http://chronicle.com/weekly/v52/i42/42a02302.htm (accessed June 21, 2007).
24. Ruth Holladay, "Truth Comes Out about Professor's Background," *Indianapolis Star,* December 4, 2005, p. 1B.

25. Jennifer Jacobson, "U. of Montana Accepts Panel's Ruling and Appoints Conservative Professor to Teach Constitutional Law," *Chronicle of Higher Education,* July 19, 2005, http://chronicle.com/daily/2005/07/2005071904n.htm (accessed June 21, 2007).
26. See Alan Charles Kors and Harvey A. Silverglate, *The Shadow University: The Betrayal of Liberty on America's Campuses* (New York: HarperPerennial, 1998); Donald A. Downs, *Restoring Free Speech and Liberty on Campus* (Oakland, CA: The Independent Institute, and Cambridge, UK: Cambridge University Press, 2005).
27. Thomas Bartlett, "Website Lists Professors Who 'Indoctrinate' Students," *Chronicle of Higher Education,* December 13, 2002, http://chronicle.com/weekly/v49/i16/16a01102.htm (accessed June 21, 2007).
28. Terry Caesar, "RateMyProfessors—or His Shoes Are Dirty," *Inside Higher Ed,* July 28, 2006, www.insidehighered.com/views/2006/07/28/caesar (accessed June 21, 2007).
29. Justin Pope, "New Campus Clash: Conservatives Call for Diversity," *Newark Star-Ledger,* December 26, 2004, p. 33.
30. Thomas Bartlett, "Website Lists Professors Who 'Indoctrinate' Students," *Chronicle of Higher Education,* December 13, 2002, http://chronicle.com/weekly/v49/i16/16a01102.htm (accessed June 21, 2007).
31. *New York Times v. Sullivan,* 376 U.S. 254 (1964).
32. 47 U.S.C.S. §230 (2006).
33. Fogg, "No Bounty for Reports of 'Bias' at UCLA."
34. Ibid.
35. American Association of University Professors, "Academic Freedom and National Security in a Times of Crisis", October 2003, www.aaup.org/AAUP/About/committees/committee+repts/crisistime.htm (accessed June 20, 2007).
36. Jennifer Jacobson, "What Makes David Run? David Horowitz Demands Attention for the Idea that Conservatives Deserve a Place in Academe," *Chronicle of Higher Education,* May 6, 2005, http://chronicle.com/weekly/v51/i35/35a00801.htm (accessed June 21, 2007).
37. Ibid.
38. John Gravois, "Professor Sues David Horowitz over Use of His Photo," *Chronicle of Higher Education,* May 26, 2006, http://chronicle.com/weekly/v52/i38/38a01301.htm (accessed June 21, 2007).
39. David Horowitz, "Academic Bill of Rights," http://studentsforacademicfreedom.org/abor.html (accessed June 26, 2007).
40. Ibid.
41. Joan Wallach Scott, "Testimony by Professor Joan Wallach Scott before the Pennsylvania General Assembly's House Select Committee on Student Academic Freedom," November 9, 2005, www.aaup.org/AAUP/GR/state/Academic+Bill+of+Rights-State+Level/Scotttestimony.htm (accessed June 27, 2007).
42. Ibid.

43. American Association of University Professors, "Academic Bill of Rights Legislation: Summary and Comments," www.aaup.org/AAUP/GR/ABOR/legislationsummary.htm (accessed June 27, 2007).
44. American Association of University Professors, "Resources on the Academic Bill of Rights," www.aaup.org/AAUP/GR/ABOR/Resources/default.htm (accessed June 27, 2007).
45. Kimberly Miller, "Lawmaker's Plan To Muzzle Professors Hits Snag in Senate," *Palm Beach Post,* April 22, 2005, A Section; p. 5A.
46. David Karp, "Lawmaker Aims to Squelch Political Bias in College Classes," *St. Petersburg Times,* April 6, 2005, p. 1B
47. Sarah Hebel, "Patrolling Professors' Politics," *Chronicle of Higher Education,* February 13, 2004, http://chronicle.com/weekly/v50/i23/23a01801.htm (accessed June 27, 2007).
48. Jennifer Jacobson, "A Liberal Professor Fights a Label," *Chronicle of Higher Education,* November 26, 2004, http://chronicle.com/weekly/v51/i14/14a00801.htm (accessed June 27, 2007).
49. House Bill No. 213, 94th General Assembly (MO, 2007), www.house.mo.gov/bills071/biltxt/perf/HB0213P.HTM (accessed June 27, 2007).
50. H. R. Res. 1222 Leg. 81st Sess. (S.D. 2006), www.legis.state.sd.us/sessions/2006/bills/HB1222p.htm (accessed June 27, 2007).
51. J. Peter Byrne, "Constitutional Academic Freedom after Grutter: Getting Real about the 'Four Freedoms' of a University," 77 *Colorado Law Review* (Fall, 2006): 929, 943–944.
52. Robert M. O'Neil, "Horowitz, Churchill, Columbia—What Next For Academic Freedom? Bias, 'Balance,' and Beyond: New Threats to Academic Freedom," 77 *Colorado Law Review* (Fall 2006): 985, 1006.
53. *Ollman v. Toll,* 518 F. Supp. 1196 (D. Md. 1981).
54. O'Neil, "Horowitz, Churchill, Columbia," 895, 1006.
55. Ibid., 895, 1008.
56. *Ollman v. Toll,* 518 F. Supp. 1196 (D. Md. 1981).
57. *Ollman v. Toll,* 704 F.2d 139 (4th Cir. 1983).
58. O'Neil," Horowitz, Churchill, Columbia," 985, 1010.
59. Patricia Cohen, "Neglect Proves to Be No Excuse," *Newsday,* May 12, 1993, p. 4.
60. Jacobson, "Columbia U. Issues New Grievance Procedures Amid Criticism of How It Handled Student Complaints," http://chronicle.com/daily/2005/04/2005041203n.htm (accessed June 20, 2007).
61. Robin Wilson and Scott Smallwood, "One Professor Cleared, Another Disciplined over September 11 Remarks," *Chronicle of Higher Education,* January 11, 2002, http://chronicle.com/weekly/v48/i18/18a01202.htm (accessed June 27, 2007).
62. American Association of University Professors, "Recommended Institutional Regulations on Academic Freedom and Tenure," *Policy Documents and Reports,* 9th ed. (Washington, DC: AAUP, 2001) Section 4(d), pp. 24–25, or

www.aaup.org/AAUP/pubsres/policydocs/RIR.htm?PF=1 (accessed June 27, 2007).

63. Ibid.

10. Academic Freedom in Perspective

1. *Urofsky v. Allen*, 995 F. Supp. 634 (E.D. Va. 1998).
2. Brian McNeill, "ACLU, Profs Try To Reverse State Law Banning Computer Access To Explicit Material," *The Collegiate Times*, November 5, 1999.
3. Jennifer Jacobson, "Conservative Activist Admits Lack of Evidence for Some Allegations of Faculty Bias," January 20, 2006, http://chronicle.com/weekly/v52/i20/20a03301.htm (accessed June 20, 2007).
4. Charles Dickens, *A Tale of Two Cities*, 1859, http://etext.lib.virginia.edu/etcbin/toccer-new2?id=DicTale.sgm&images=images/modeng&data=/texts/english/modeng/parsed&tag=public&part=1&division=div1 (accessed June 20, 2007).
5. Robin Wilson and Scott Smallwood, "One Professor Cleared, Another Disciplined over September 11 Remarks," *Chronicle of Higher Education*, January 11, 2002, http://chronicle.com/weekly/v48/i18/18a01202.htm, (accessed June 8, 2007).
6. Megan Greenwell, "Bollinger: No Plan to Reprimand De Genova: Bollinger issued a statement in response to a letter from U.S. Congress," *Columbia Daily Spectator*, April 10, 2003, http://media.www.columbiaspectator.com/media/storage/paper865/news/2003/04/10/News/Bollinger.No.Plan.To.Reprimand.De.Genova-2036801.shtml (accessed June 8, 2007).
7. John C. Ensslin, "CU Regents Won't Rush to Action in Controversy," *Rocky Mountain News*, February 3, 2005, www.rockymountainnews.com/drmn/news/article/0,1299,DRMN_3_4754496,00.html (accessed June 8, 2007).
8. Jodi S. Cohen, "NU Professor Backs Denial of Holocaust by Iran Chief; Jewish Leaders Fear Support Could Add Credibility to View," *Chicago Tribune*, February 4, 2006, Zone C, p. 5.
9. Fox News Transcript 020702cb.256: *The O'Reilly Factor*, February 7, 2006.
10. Ellen Schrecker, *No Ivory Tower* (New York: Oxford University Press, 1986).
11. American Association of University Professors, "Academic Freedom and National Security in a Times of Crisis," October 2003, www.aaup.org/AAUP/About/committees/committee+repts/crisistime.htm (accessed June 20, 2007).
12. Association of Governing Boards of Universities and Colleges, "AGB Statement on Board Accountability," January 17, 2007, www.agb.org/user-assets/Documents/AGB_BoardAcct_NEWweb.pdf (accessed June 20, 2007).
13. James Madison, "Memorial and Remonstrance Against Religious Assessments," 1785, Section 3, http://religiousfreedom.lib.virginia.edu/sacred/madison_m&r_1785.html (accessed June 20, 2007).

Index